A CAUTIOUS NEW APPROACH

CHINA'S GROWING TRILATERAL AID COOPERATION

A CAUTIOUS NEW APPROACH

CHINA'S GROWING TRILATERAL AID COOPERATION

DENGHUA ZHANG

Australian
National
University

PRESS

PACIFIC AFFAIRS SERIES

ANU PRESS

Published by ANU Press
The Australian National University
Acton ACT 2601, Australia
Email: anupress@anu.edu.au

Available to download for free at press.anu.edu.au

ISBN (print): 9781760463472
ISBN (online): 9781760463489

WorldCat (print): 1145171193
WorldCat (online): 1145170978

DOI: 10.22459/CNA.2020

Cover design and layout by ANU Press

Contents

Acknowledgements

The idea for this research emerged when I was working as a Chinese diplomat in the Pacific region between 2006 and 2011. I was puzzled by the lack of development in the island countries despite their endowment of fishery resources and a large inflow of foreign assistance. I also witnessed the rapid growth of Chinese aid to the region and the inadequate engagement between China and traditional donors. These observations prompted me to seriously consider whether and how different types of donors could cooperate to deliver aid and support the development in recipient countries. This led to my PhD research on China's trilateral aid cooperation in the Asia-Pacific region, which in turn has strengthened my interest in the region and in the disciplines of international relations and development studies. This book is based on my PhD thesis, which was approved by The Australian National University (ANU) in 2017.

I wish to acknowledge the valuable assistance that I have received during my preparation of this book manuscript and PhD study, without which this mission could not have been completed. It has been a process of exploration, commitment and self-discipline, as well as one of love, pain and joy.

I am grateful to Dr Stewart Firth for his kind support while I was converting my PhD thesis into this book. I am also deeply indebted to Associate Professor Sinclair Dinnen, Dr Graeme Smith and Dr Stewart Firth for their great support of my PhD study. Their motivation, patience and immense knowledge of China and the Asia-Pacific region have guided my research. I would also like to thank the rest of my panel: Professor Katherine Morton and Professor Michael Leach. Professor Katherine Morton offered her valuable comments regarding my whole thesis. As a top expert on Timor-Leste, Professor Leach offered his comments for

Chapter 6 regarding the China–US trilateral aid cooperation in Timor-Leste. Professor Morton and Leach's comments have made my analysis more rigid.

I would also like to express my sincere thanks to Associate Professor Nicole Haley and the Department of Pacific Affairs (DPA, formerly known as the State, Society and Governance in Melanesia Program) for offering me the PhD scholarship. My PhD research is supported by an Australian research training program scholarship. The DPA has been my home and I am indebted to the support from my colleagues there. Special thanks go to Ambassador and former Australian Agency for International Development (AusAID) Deputy Director-General James Batley, who provided kind advice for Chapter 5 and on the China–Australia trilateral aid cooperation, as well as to former AusAID senior official Steve Hogg, who provided valuable advice regarding my research program. Many thanks also go to other friends and colleagues at ANU, whose assistance during my PhD study and field work trips I have greatly valued. I am also grateful to all those who had kindly participated in my interviews during the field work stage of my research—in Australia, Cambodia, China, New Zealand, Papua New Guinea, Samoa and Timor-Leste—as well as to friends and interviewees from the United Nations Development Programme. Special thanks go to Dr Carolyn Brewer, a reputable editor at ANU, for editing my PhD thesis and to Capstone Editing for copyediting my book manuscript. I must also thank ANU Press and the DPA for providing publication subsidies for this book.

My love and thanks go to every member of my family in China and Australia. I am particularly grateful for the full support from my wife, Dr Zihan Yin. Her understanding, support and love have empowered me along my PhD and academic journey. I greatly benefited from her experience in completing her own PhD at Victoria University of Wellington in 2014 and in her academic research.

Finally, thanks to ANU! As its motto states, '*Naturam primum cognoscere rerum*'—'Above all to find out the way things are'. I hope this spirit of exploration will always guide me in the journey ahead.

Abbreviations

ADB	Asian Development Bank
AIBO	Academy for International Business Officials
AIIB	Asian Infrastructure Investment Bank
ANU	The Australian National University
ASEAN	Association of Southeast Asian Nations
AusAID	Australian Agency for International Development
BRI	Belt and Road Initiative
BRICS	Brazil, Russia, India, China and South Africa
CAITEC	China Academy of International Trade and Economic Cooperation
CASS	China Academy of Social Sciences
CATAS	China Academy of Tropical Agricultural Sciences
CDC	Council for the Development of Cambodia
CICETE	China International Center for Economic and Technical Exchanges
CICIR	China Institutes of Contemporary International Relations
CIDCA	China International Development Cooperation Agency
CPC	Communist Party of China
CPHL	central public health laboratory
DAC	Development Assistance Committee
DFA	Department of Foreign Aid (China)
DFAT	Department of Foreign Affairs and Trade (Australia)
DFID	Department for International Development (UK)

DITEA	Department of International Trade and Economic Affairs (China)
DNPM	Department of National Planning and Monitoring (PNG)
DPA	Department of Pacific Affairs (ANU)
FAO	Food and Agriculture Organization
FOCAC	Forum on China–Africa Cooperation
GDP	gross domestic product
HHISP	Health and HIV implementation services provider
IMR	Institute of Medical Research (PNG)
IPRCC	International Poverty Reduction Centre in China
LNG	liquefied natural gas
MAF	Ministry of Agriculture and Fisheries (Timor-Leste)
MAFF	Ministry of Agriculture, Forestry and Fisheries (Cambodia)
MCA	Ministry of Civil Affairs (China)
MDG	millennium development goal
MFA	Ministry of Foreign Affairs
MOFCOM	Ministry of Commerce (China)
MoF	Ministry of Finance
MOST	Ministry of Science and Technology (China)
MOU	memorandum of understanding
NGO	non-governmental organisations
NHFPC	National Health and Family Planning Commission (China)
NIPD	National Institute of Parasitic Diseases (China)
ODA	official development assistance
OECD	Organisation for Economic Co-operation and Development
PNG	Papua New Guinea
PRC	People's Republic of China
SASAC	State-owned Assets Supervision and Administration Commission

SDG	sustainable development goal
S&ED	strategic & economic dialogue
SOE	state-owned enterprise
SEZ	special economic zone
UK	United Kingdom
UN	United Nations
UNDP	United Nations Development Programme
UNIDO	United Nations Industrial Development Organization
UNTL	National University of East Timor
US	United States
USAID	United States Agency for International Development
WHO	World Health Organization
WTO	World Trade Organization

Glossary of Chinese Terms

The transcription of Chinese characters into the Roman alphabet follows the Pinyin system:

guikou danwei	Point of contact
hexin liyi	Core interests
hongyi rongli	Uphold justice and pursue shared interests
jiang zhengzhi	Talk politics
jianshe hexie shijie	Build a harmonious world
qinghao	Sweet wormwood (*Artemisia annua*)
shishi qiushi, liangli erxing	Be practical and act within one's capacity
taoguang yanghui	Hide the capacity and keep a low profile
xiaokang shehui	A moderately prosperous society
yijing cuzheng	Use economics to promote politics
yili xiangjian, yili weixian	Take a right approach to justice and interests by prioritising justice over interests
you ji you qu	To take while giving
yousuo zuowei	Make greater achievements
zhanlue jiyuqi	Period of strategic opportunities
zhengjing jiehe	Combine politics and economics
zhengque yiliguan	Right concepts of justice and interests
zhengzhi	Politics
zhengzhi gua shuai	Politics takes command
zili gengsheng	Self-reliance
zouchuqu zhanlue	Go global strategy

List of Figures

List of Tables

1

Introduction

China's cooperation with the Pacific island countries, or Chinese aid to these countries, belongs to the South-South cooperation in essence. It is the mutual assistance between developing nations, and differs totally from the western aid, the so-called Official Development Assistance, or the relations between western donors and the recipient countries.

— Cui Tiankai, 31 August 2012
(as cited in Liu & Huang, 2012)

The two sides [China and the US] reaffirmed their shared objectives in ending poverty and advancing global development through enhanced collaboration and communication under the principle that cooperation is raised, agreed, and led by recipient countries. China and the United States intend to expand their collaboration with international institutions to tackle key global development challenges. The two sides intend to continue expanding their discussion on development matters in future development-related meetings, such as, the nexus between development assistance cooperation and combating climate change.

— Governments of China and the US, 8 June 2016
(as cited in Xinhua, 2016)

The first statement above is extracted from an interview with China's incumbent ambassador to the United States (US), former Vice Foreign Minister Cui Tiankai, at the 24th Post Pacific Islands Forum Dialogue in Auckland in August 2012 (Liu & Huang, 2012). The second statement is taken from the outcome list of the eighth China–US Strategic and Economic Dialogue held in Beijing in June 2016 (Xinhua, 2016). A comparison of these two quotations, both representing China's official discourse, reveals a puzzling message. While insisting that there are substantial differences between Chinese foreign aid and Western aid, China is now committed to conducting development cooperation with the US. Notable questions follow immediately: Why is China willing to work with the US on aid delivery when the rivalry between the two is becoming more visible (e.g. in Asia and the Pacific)? What are China's attitudes towards cooperation with other traditional donor states and United Nations (UN) agencies? Is cooperation becoming a common phenomenon between China and traditional donors in the development realm? Some may argue that China has adopted reform and opening-up policies since the 1970s and that its relationship with Western nations has already been greatly improved. However, this argument is too general. It can neither explain why China conducts cooperation with Western nations in some areas rather than others, nor why China and Western nations will cooperate in the area of aid delivery while mutual mistrust lingers. These questions outlay the research theme of this book: Chinese foreign aid, especially trilateral aid cooperation.

China's growing strength is the backdrop of its expanding foreign aid scheme. China has presently become a recurring topic in the media, in academic research and even in daily life in the West. The world's most populous developing nation is striving to reclaim the glory that it seemingly lost fewer than 200 years ago. According to some estimates, China was the world's largest economy until the middle of the nineteenth century, boasting an economy that was nearly 30 per cent larger than that of Western Europe and its Western offshoots combined in 1820 (Maddison, 2006, p. 119).

Currently benefiting from its impressive economic growth in the previous four decades, China's re-emergence as a world power is increasingly felt in the international arena. In 2010, China overtook Japan as the second-largest economy. Initiatives such as the Asian Monetary Fund, the Chiang Mai Initiative/ASEAN+3 Macroeconomic Research Office and the Asian Infrastructure Investment Bank (AIIB) are often used as illustrative examples of the dynamic power shifts that have occurred from Japan to China in regional financial influence (Hamanaka, 2016, p. 4). The International Monetary Fund has estimated that China's gross domestic product (GDP) rate has surpassed that of the US in 2014, based on purchasing power parity; it has also predicted that if current trajectories continue, then the GDP rate will be 20 per cent higher than that of the US by 2020 (Carter, 2014).

In terms of overseas financing, the China Development Bank and China Export–Import Bank outstripped the World Bank by pledging $110 billion[1] worth of loans from 2009 to 2010, while the World Bank signed loans that totalled $100.3 billion from mid-2008 to mid-2010 (Dyer et al., 2011). The Brazilian, Russian, Indian, Chinese and South African (BRICS) New Development Bank (with a pool of $100 billion) was launched by China and the other four BRICS member states in Shanghai in July 2015—a move that some analysts perceived as a deliberate challenge to the World Bank. The China-sponsored AIIB was established in December 2015 in the face of opposition from the US and Japan. The Belt and Road Initiative (BRI) is another of China's ambitious projects, as well as a signature project of President Xi Jinping. At the first BRI forum held in Beijing in May 2017, Xi announced that the China Development Bank and the China Export–Import Bank would establish new lending facilities that were worth RMB 250 billion ($38.6 billion)[2] and RMB 130 billion ($20 billion) respectively to support BRI projects.

A heated debate is underway among Western observers regarding China's influence as a rising power on the global power structure and governance. Joshua Cooper Ramo (2004) summarised China's development experience and coined the term 'Beijing consensus'[3] as an alternative model of development to challenge the 'Washington consensus'. Maximilian Terhalle (2011) argued that the Copenhagen climate change conference in 2009 was a turning point in global governance—with emerging powers, including China, refusing to accept the demands of traditional powers and aspiring to reshape the international order. The rise of the G20 as a premium forum for international economic cooperation relative to other groups like the G8 and the Organisation for Economic Co-operation and Development (OECD) marks 'a historical shift in the balance of economic power' (Lowy Institute, 2011, p. 9). Francois Godemont, director of the Asia and China Programme at the European Council on Foreign Relations, argued that 'China's governance model at home is fundamentally at odds with the liberal international order' (Godement, 2017, p. 1). Professor Evelyn Goh from The Australian

---

1   Unless otherwise specified, $ refers to the US dollar in this book.
2   US$1 was equivalent to RMB 6.478 on 31 December 2015. This exchange rate is used consistently in the book.
3   It is worth noting that although the concept of 'Beijing consensus' has not had much influence in China and is not taken seriously, it has had an influence beyond China—both among traditional donors and among recipient states. Scholars such as Scott Kennedy argued that the 'Beijing consensus' is a misguided and inaccurate summary of China's actual reform experience (Kennedy, 2010).

National University (ANU) argued that China's rising influence in Asian countries is mixed and that this has often generated unintended consequences (Goh, 2016).

Some analysts have adopted a softer position, arguing that China and other rising powers (e.g. India and Brazil) are unlikely to cause revolutionary changes to the international order and that they are instead aiming to maximise gains via bargaining and balancing strategies (Hart & Jones, 2010; Kahler, 2013; Wang & Rosenau, 2009). In a similar vein, Gregory Chin and Ramesh Thakur have argued that China is pursuing a third road by selectively abiding by some international norms while pushing for changes to others; the authors further contended that China must shoulder greater international obligations that are consistent with its growing capacity (Chin & Thakur, 2010). John Ikenberry and Darren Lim have suggested that the China-initiated AIIB is similar to the Asian Development Bank (ADB) and World Bank in both its formal design and initial operations, and that it will thus more likely strengthen the rules, practices and norms within the current global order (Ikenberry & Lim, 2017, p. 16).

Relevance of Chinese Aid

Foreign aid is an integral part of China's growing strength. As a rising power, China is also an emerging donor[4] who exerts a growing influence on the international aid regime.[5] The impressive growth of Chinese foreign aid has become one of the most prominent developments in the international aid realm in the last decade, triggering debates regarding whether China will join or undermine traditional aid architecture.

Foreign aid is also an important component of donors' foreign policies, and China's emergence as a donor has significant—though presently unclear—implications in the arena of foreign policy. Chinese aid thus becomes an issue of enormous significance. The international community, especially Western nations and China's neighbours, are watching closely to observe whether China will follow a peaceful or increasingly assertive

---

4   Some analysts take issue with expressions like 'rising power' or 'emerging donor' though they are widely used by journals of international relations and development studies.

5   For example, China is providing large sums of foreign aid in the implementation of new initiatives such as AIIB and BRI, which both aim to boost China's influence in the realm of development cooperation.

foreign policy. After all, as China is poised to become a 'superpower' in global affairs, the direction of China's foreign policy will inevitably affect the interests of other countries. This issue is particularly significant, as China's foreign policy is seemingly becoming more assertive under the leadership of the Xi Jinping administration.

An evident example of this is the number of escalating territorial disputes between China and neighbouring Southeast Asian nations in the South China Sea, such as Vietnam and the Philippines—though relations with the Philippines improved after President Duterte took office in June 2016. China's relationship with Japan has also deteriorated, and China has established an 'air defence identification zone' in the East China Sea. Debates are centred on whether China is shifting the focus of its foreign policy from 'hiding the capacity and keeping a low profile' (*taoguang yanghui*) to 'making greater achievements' (*yousuo zuowei*),[6] and whether it is adopting a more assertive approach (He & Feng, 2012; Sørensen, 2015; Wang, 2011b; Yahuda, 2013; Zhu, 2008, 2010a). If such assertions and perceptions are true, why has China chosen to cooperate in some areas rather than others?

Against this broad backdrop, my book has settled on China's foreign aid as the main research topic. It aims to present original and in-depth research on Chinese trilateral aid cooperation—a new phenomenon of growing importance, but one with an extremely limited corpus of research literature. This will improve our understanding of China's foreign aid and its foreign policy in a broader sense.

This introductory chapter begins with a broad conceptualisation of China's foreign aid, including its prominent features, the concerns that traditional donors and analysts raise and the theoretical significance of the research on aid. It then examines the differences of aid principles and practice between China and traditional donors and introduces the topic of China's trilateral aid cooperation as the subject of my research inquiry. The third section of this chapter explains the original contributions that this research has made, followed by a brief introduction to my findings. The final section outlines the book structure.

---

6   This strategy was proposed by Deng Xiaoping in April 1992. To him, China could not afford to act as the leader of developing countries because China was weak. China needed to keep a low profile and develop into a more powerful country. Then, China could carry a heavier weight in global affairs.

Chinese Foreign Aid

Before commencing our examination of Chinese foreign aid, a brief definition of foreign aid is needed. Foreign aid can be defined in several ways, according to those who are 'receiving it' or 'giving it' (Riddell, 2007, p. 17). Official development assistance (ODA) is the most widely used measurement of aid. It is defined by the Development Assistance Committee (DAC)[7] of the OECD as the flow of resources from official agencies with the main purpose of economic development and promoting welfare in developing countries. To count as ODA, the flow of resources must have a grant element of no less than 25 per cent (Führer, 1994, p. 25).

Chinese foreign aid appears to substantially differ from the ODA that traditional donors provide. China does not categorise its aid according to the OECD ODA standards—on the contrary, it has explicitly distanced itself from traditional donors ever since it began providing foreign aid in 1950. China's first white paper on foreign aid (released in April 2011) stated clearly that 'Chinese foreign aid belongs to South–South cooperation and the mutual assistance between developing countries' (State Council, 2011d, p. 22). This point has been maintained as a basic principle for Chinese aid and has been a tool for China to dislodge the pressure and criticisms expressed by traditional donors regarding issues of aid transparency and cooperation. For example, as quoted at the beginning of the chapter, China's then deputy foreign minister and present ambassador to the US, Cui Tiankai, argued that Chinese aid to the Pacific Island countries is south–south cooperation, which differs totally in its nature from north–south cooperation (Liu & Huang, 2012); this was echoed by Tiankai's colleague Ambassador Wang Min at the high-level committee of UN south–south cooperation closing segment in September 2015 (Wang, 2015).

There are differences in the aid calculations between China and traditional donors. For example, military aid and the construction of sports facilities are included in Chinese aid, but they are excluded in traditional donor

---

7   The DAC is a forum of selected OECD member states that discusses aid and development issues, and it represents the majority of traditional donors.

aid; the costs of newly arrived refugees[8] in host countries are defined as ODA by traditional donors, yet they are not included in China's aid budget[9] (Bräutigam, 2011, p. 756; Grimm et al., 2011, 7). The calculation of Chinese concessional loans also merits attention. Although Deborah Bräutigam and other scholars such as Zhou Hong from the China Academy of Social Sciences argue that China calculates only the interest rate gap between its concessional loans and commercial loans as aid while the ODA covers the total loan value (Bräutigam, 2011, p. 756; Zhou, 2008, p. 40), a senior Chinese aid official clarified that China has begun calculating the total face value of concessional loans in its foreign aid since 2009 (Interview, Beijing, 4 August 2015). This concurs with the findings of Sven Grimm and another three scholars, who argued that the full amounts of Chinese concessional loans are included in the aid figures announced by China (Grimm et al., 2011, p. 7). Bearing this point in mind facilitates our understanding of the Chinese aid outlay.

The amount, scope and growth rate of Chinese foreign aid has been impressive in the last decade. According to China's first white paper on foreign aid, China's cumulative overseas assistance reached $39.5 billion (RMB 256.29 billion) from 1950 to 2009, covering 161 countries and over 30 regional and international organisations (State Council, 2011d, p. 22). In particular, the annual increase averaged 29.4 per cent from 2004 to 2009 (State Council, 2011d, p. 22). China's second white paper on foreign aid records a continued momentum of growth from 2010 to 2012, totalling $13.79 billion (RMB 89.34 billion) (State Council, 2014, p. 22). The figure for Chinese concessional loans in the first two white papers refers to the whole face value of the loans. Even when calculated by the grants, the interest-free loans and the interest gap of the concessional loans, Chinese foreign aid has more than doubled from $727 million

---

8   China is currently not a main recipient of refugees, though it has hosted refugees throughout history—including approximately 265,000 refugees from Vietnam in the 1970s; more than 20,000 refugees from India and Sri Lanka in 1980s, before they were transferred to the US and EU nations; refugees from Iraq after the 2003 Iraq war; and refugees from Myanmar during the civil war in Kokang Blocks in 2009. In June 2016, China joined the International Organization for Migration; an increased engagement could be observed between China and this organisation regarding migration, including refugee issues, in the future (Ifeng, 2015; Ye, 2016).

9   Deborah Bräutigam and Sven Grimm mentioned that China's aid budget does not include scholarship for foreign students to study in China. However, based on the author's interviews with China's Ministry of Commerce aid officials, the scholarship is included in China's aid budget. While most of these scholarships are under the portfolio of China's Ministry of Education, The Ministry of Commerce is managing some scholarships, such as those arranged through the newly established Institute of South–South Cooperation and Development.

(RMB 4.71 billion) in 2001 to \$2.22 billion (RMB 14.41 billion) in 2010 (Mao, 2011, p. 1). It should be noted that the statistics from China's white papers on foreign aid may not be completely accurate. One reason for this is due to China's large population living in poverty—it is understandable that the Chinese government would understate its foreign aid volume and reduce domestic discontent. Another important reason is that more than 30 ministerial-level agencies are involved in China's aid management, which makes it difficult for them to share aid data and produce an accurate figure on Chinese aid spending.

Based on official data, China was the 10th-largest donor worldwide from 2010 to 2012, as illustrated in Figure 1. A recent report from the research institute of the Japan International Cooperation Agency in 2016 noted that Chinese foreign aid reached \$4.9 billion in 2014 alone and that China's rank among donors jumped from 16th in 2001 to ninth since 2013 (Kitano, 2016, p. 29). As a useful comparison based on OECD's latest data, China provided \$3.4 billion of foreign aid in 2014, while other donors such as the US, Australia, India and Brazil provided \$30.98 billion, \$3.49 billion, \$1.39 billion and \$316 million, respectively (OECD, 2017).

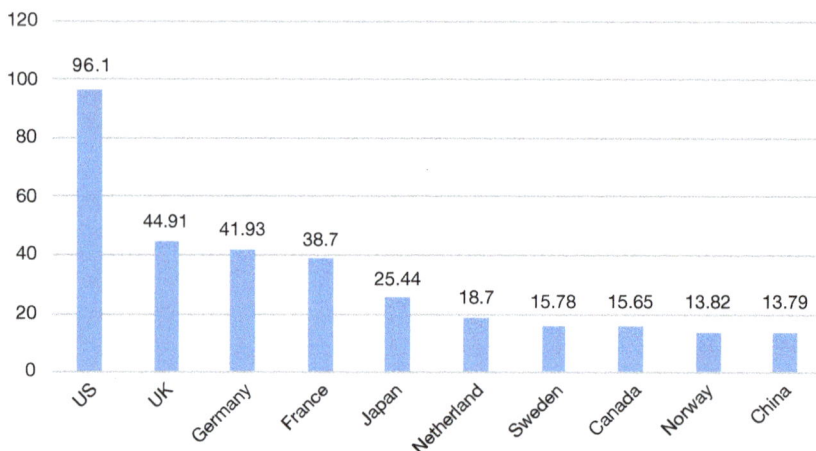

Figure 1. Top 10 donors globally, 2010–2012, USD billion[10]
Source. Compiled by author.

---

10   The Chinese aid data is from its 2014 white paper on foreign aid. The data for traditional donors is from the OECD online database (see OECD, 2016b).

Chinese aid to Africa and Oceania is representative of its increasing magnitude and structure. From 2013 to 2015, more than half of Chinese foreign aid was directed to the African continent, and Chinese concessional loans that were committed to Africa during this period exceeded $17 billion (MOFCOM, 2015b, para. 2). At the summit of the forum on China–Africa cooperation in Johannesburg in December 2015, Chinese President Xi Jinping pledged an enormous aid package that was to be rolled out in Africa over the following three years. The announcement included $5 billion in grants and interest-free loans, $35 billion in concessional loans and export credit,[11] 30,000 government scholarships and 40,000 training opportunities (Xi, 2015a). Though small in land size and population, the Pacific Island countries[12] had received $1.45 billion (RMB 9.4 billion) of Chinese aid by November 2013. In the same month, at the second China–Pacific Island countries economic development and cooperation forum, an additional $1 billion in concessional loans was pledged for the next four years (Wang, 2013). During his meeting with Pacific Islands leaders in Fiji in November 2014, President Xi announced that China would provide further assistance to these countries, including 2,000 scholarships and 5,000 training opportunities, over the following five years (Du & Yan, 2014, p. 1).

Chinese Aid Concerns

The rapid growth of China's aid worldwide has raised concerns for some traditional donors and analysts regarding its motivations and modes of delivery, which are not shared by some of China's aid partners in the developing world. The lack of understanding regarding China's aid approach has greatly contributed to these concerns. As will be further elaborated in Chapter 2, there is growing literature on China's motivations for providing foreign aid bilaterally and on these concerns for Chinese aid; however, China's motivations for trilateral aid cooperation are under-researched. This partially justifies the creation of this book, as it challenges these misperceptions.

---

11   Export credit is not calculated as Chinese aid. A separate figure for concessional loans was not provided by China.
12   In principle, China provides aid to countries with whom it has diplomatic relations. As of September 2019, 10 of the 14 Pacific Island countries have such relations with China, including Cook Islands, the Federated States of Micronesia, Fiji, Kiribati, Niue, Papua New Guinea, Samoa, Solomon Islands, Tonga and Vanuatu. Some Pacific Island countries have swayed their diplomatic recognitions between China and Taiwan.

Clemens Six (2009) argued that China's rise as an emerging donor complicates the traditional aid regime because it introduces new norms and practices, and that the normative dimension of China's rise demands further analysis. Zimmermann and Smith (2011, p. 732–733) argued that the rise of emerging donors has intensified the 'legitimacy crisis' of the current aid system. Kragelund (2011, p. 598) argued that China delivers aid primarily in the form of projects that produce tangible results more quickly than aid programs and that China favours 'prestige projects'. Some researchers from the Centre for Global Development have argued that although China claims that its aid has no conditionalities, in reality, it is tied aid that requires the use of Chinese companies, labour and materials (Walz & Ramachandran, 2011, p. 18). Laura Savage and Rosalind Eyben followed the arduous negotiation process at the Busan fourth high-level forum in 2011. They argued that China behaved defensively during the conference, refusing to be held accountable to the principles that it believes apply to traditional donors. China thus rejected several draft versions of the conference document (Savage & Eyben, 2013). To these scholars, China's behaviour hindered the conference from reaching a binding commitment for all stakeholders in global aid cooperation (Savage & Eyben, 2013).

Richard Manning, former chairman of the OECD DAC, called attention to the main risks that were caused by emerging donors—including the rising debt among recipient nations and the low levels of conditionality that are attached to development finance—and emphasised that DAC norms should continue to be observed (Manning, 2006, p. 1). In November 2011 and August 2012, US Secretary of State Hillary Clinton warned developing countries against cooperating with emerging donors like China, who are more interested in exploiting natural resources than in promoting real development (Bland & Dyer, 2011; Ghosh, 2012). The Trump administration adopted the Indo-Pacific strategy in November 2017 and pledged to compete with China in the region by funding infrastructure projects that are 'physically secure, financially viable and socially responsible' (Pompeo, 2018, para. 38). A report produced by the Danish Institute for International Studies examined the challenges that emerging economies caused for the European Union in development cooperation. It argued that:

> If China continues to attract the attention of African leaders [through means including investment and foreign aid], the EU will have to downplay the role of governance and human rights conditionalities in the partnership [with Africa] or they will have no one to cooperate with. (Fejerskov, 2013, p. 42)

Moisés Naim is among the most vocal critics of Chinese foreign aid and its threat to the regional and global order. He explicitly labelled donor countries such as Venezuela and China as 'rogue' because they egoistically chase self-interest at the expense of recipient countries; he also warned that this situation must be redressed before it creates a development landscape that is characterised by corruption and chaos (Moisés, 2007).

Some analysts express concerns regarding certain aspects of Chinese aid. Anabela Lemos and Daniel Ribeiro believe that some African regimes, including Mozambique, have taken advantage of China's non-interference policy to obtain Chinese aid while avoiding local and international pressure to combat corruption (Lemos & Ribeiro, 2007). Ian Taylor (2006, p. 952) expressed his concerns with issues such as human rights and governance that arises from China's oil diplomacy in Africa. Yiagadeesen Samy (2010, pp. 85–86) argued that although most African leaders welcome Chinese aid, civil society in Africa is concerned with this aid, including with the support of corrupted regimes, rising debt levels and inappropriate use of local workers.

China's influence as an increasingly prominent donor has also been felt in the Pacific Islands. In addition to the US, leaders of traditional donors in the region have expressed concern regarding the transparency, accountability and debt risks that are associated with Chinese aid. Prime Minister John Key warned in September 2011 that Pacific Island states must consider their ability to repay loans when accepting finance from China (Trevett, 2011). During the sixth Japan–Pacific Islands states summit in May 2012, Japanese Prime Minister Yoshihiko Noda called on China and other emerging donors to increase their aid transparency (Zhang, 2012). In April 2013, then Australian Prime Minister Julia Gillard told the media that although Australia welcomes more aid from emerging donors to the Pacific, more accountability and transparency is needed (Australian Associated Press, 2013). More recently, in response to China's rise, both the coalition government and the opposition Labor Party in Australia pledged to establish loan facilities to support infrastructure development in Pacific Island countries. Similarly, the New Zealand government is re-energising its regional approach and increasing its technical and financial assistance to Pacific states.

The Theoretical Significance of Studying Foreign Aid

Research on foreign aid has theoretical significance. Foreign aid is an interesting issue because it has been 'a microcosm of donor states' foreign policies' since its birth after World War II (Hook, 1995, p. 16). Donors' motivations are complicated. Hans Morgenthau (1962, p. 301), a leading twentieth-century expert of international politics, lamented half a century ago that:

> Of the seeming and real innovations which the modern age has introduced into the practice of foreign policy, none has proven more baffling to both understanding and action than foreign aid.

Different schools of international relations have offered competing explanations for the motivations of states in providing aid. Realists treat aid as a tool that donors use to strengthen their power and security; liberals consider aid an instrument to promote cooperation and settle collective problems in an era of growing interdependence; Marxists and many structuralists regard aid as a tool that donors can use to exploit and control poor recipient countries; and constructivists focus on the norm that rich nations should provide foreign aid to poor nations to reduce poverty (Hook, 1995, pp. 34–40; Lancaster, 2007b, pp. 3–5; Pankaj, 2005, pp. 118–119). Maurits van der Veen (2011, pp. 210–211), a US scholar on international relations and politics, argued that no single theoretical model has been successful in explaining foreign aid; he vividly described the nature of aid as a 'Swiss Army knife' with multiple functions.

Some development specialists argued that 'aid is a moral issue' and that rich countries bear an obligation to assist the poor (Riddell, 1987, p. 74). However, Tanweer Akram (2003) from Columbia University used statistical models to test the relations between aid allocation and human needs in recipient countries from 1960 to 2000 and found that the aid that was delivered had little relationship to the basic needs of these countries. Economists Alberto Alesina and David Dollar argued that colonial history and political alliances are the major determinants of the direction and amount of foreign aid (Alesina & Dollar, 2000). Ilyana Kuziemko and Eric Werker from Harvard University discussed the vote-buying dimensions of foreign aid, arguing that nations winning the rotating seats in the UN Security Council received more aid from the US and the UN (Kuziemko & Werker, 2006). Despite a long-running discourse on good governance among Western donors, Alberto Alesina and Beatrice Weder (2002) have argued that corrupt governments do not receive less aid from donors.

Chinese foreign aid has triggered similar debate regarding its motivations, which range from strategic ambitions to economic interests and soft power building. For example, David Lampton (2008) analysed what he considered to be the three faces of Chinese power: might, money and minds. He argued that Chinese economic power (money), including the provision of development and humanitarian assistance, has three objectives: 'Keeping the regime in power, promoting human welfare at home, and bringing China the international status it has so long sought' (Lampton, 2008, p. 115). As will be elaborated in subsequent chapters (including Chapter 2), scholars have used different schools of international relations theories—including neorealism, neoliberalism and constructivism—to analyse China's foreign aid program.

Research Question: Chinese Trilateral Aid Cooperation

A close examination of Chinese foreign aid over the past decade reveals a conundrum: China takes a strongly defensive position regarding its unique mode of foreign aid in the international aid regime while, in practice, it engages in increasingly more aid cooperation with traditional donors.

To many Chinese aid officials and scholars, Chinese foreign aid has several distinguishing features—notably, having no political strings attached, respecting the principles of non-interference in the internal affairs of recipient countries, focusing on equality and mutual benefits and following a preference for 'hardware' (infrastructure) rather than 'software' projects (He, 2010, pp. 12–14; Shi, 1989, pp. 15–18; Zhang, 2010; Zhang & Huang, 2012, pp. 43–44; Zhou & Xiong, 2013, pp. 1–3). For example, having 'no strings attached'[13] is not a recent rhetorical development: it is one of the eight defining principles of Chinese aid as announced by

---

13 This term has been modified by the Chinese government from 'no strings attached' in the 1950s to 'no political strings attached' since 1983, during Premier Zhao Ziyang's visit to Africa, which reserves room for China's emphasis of mutual benefits later on in its aid provision to recipient countries. By adhering to this principle of 'no political strings attached', the Chinese government argues that it will not establish conditions for recipient countries, such as them needing to enact political reforms before or when they receive Chinese aid.

Premier Zhou Enlai in 1964 (Zhou, 2008, p. 34). In contrast, traditional donors spend a large amount of aid on 'software' projects, including on democracy promotion and good governance programs, attaching conditionalities to promote accountability and transparency in decision-making, and preferring aid to be delivered through programs rather than projects. It is worth noting that some analysts take issue with the above differences, arguing that many characteristics of Chinese aid are similar to those of traditional donors, such as preferring to use the language of cooperation rather than aid (de Haan, 2011, p. 888).

Laurence Chandy and Homi Kharas, researchers from the US Brookings Institution, presented an interesting argument regarding the relationship between south–south development cooperation providers, such as China and India, and traditional donors (Chandy & Kharas, 2011): according to them, the two types of donors differ not in aid principles, but in the interpretations of these principles (Chandy & Kharas, 2011).

While questioning the effectiveness of traditional donors' ODA, the Chinese government and many Chinese senior aid scholars have expressed their pride for China's unique aid practices. They proudly articulate that China has successfully created a new aid model with Chinese characteristics (State Council, 2011d; Zhou, 2010).[14] According to Wang Cheng'an (1996, p. 7), former deputy director-general of the Department of Foreign Aid from China's Ministry of Commerce (MOFCOM), China has created a new approach to foreign aid that not only meets the demands of recipient countries, but also complies with China's domestic situation. This point is repeated in China's two white papers on foreign aid. Professor He Wenping has argued that China enjoys the natural advantage of being a link between traditional and emerging donors, northern and southern countries and donors and recipients because of its experiences as a recipient country, a fast-growing economy and an emerging donor (He, 2011, pp. 127–134).

Professor Li Anshan, a leading Chinese expert on Africa from Peking University, has taken a more critical approach to traditional ODA. He argued that although traditional donors have benefited by providing aid to Africa (e.g. promoting their diplomatic and economic interest),

---

14 'Chinese characteristics' is a popular term in Chinese official documents. Examples include socialism with Chinese characteristics, foreign policy with Chinese characteristics and foreign aid with Chinese characteristics. The goal of this kind of term is to highlight China's own features and for China to distance itself from Western countries.

they have failed to honour their aid commitments, including reaching the target of spending 0.7 per cent of their gross national product on development assistance (Li, 2014, 2015). Another senior Chinese aid scholar, Li Xiaoyun, and his colleague, Wu Jin, have objected to the critiques from Western donors and commentators that most China-aided infrastructure projects are built by Chinese contractors rather than local companies; they argued instead that this could reduce the incidence of corruption in recipient countries, as the project funds would not go through the recipient governments (Li & Wu, 2009, p. 51).

China takes a strongly defensive position over its aid practice in the international aid regime. Despite ranking as the second-largest economy in 2010, the Chinese government has repeatedly insisted that China is still a developing country and that its foreign aid falls within south–south cooperation. China believes it signed the 2005 Paris Declaration on Aid Effectiveness in its capacity as an aid recipient rather than as a donor (Zhang, Gu & Chen, 2015, p. 17). It is reluctant to align itself with traditional donors and be bound by their aid norms. For example, China refused to join the Cairns Compact,[15] which is an initiative arising from the 2009 Pacific Islands forum that intends to boost aid coordination in the Pacific. China has made it clear that it will not be bound by the Cairns Compact (Trevett, 2011).

China and traditional donors have even delivered foreign aid within different contexts in history. For example, there is a strong connection between DAC aid flows and decolonisation in the 1960s and 1970s. Decolonisation hastened the spread of aid in the 1960s, and most colonial powers rushed to assist former colonies after their independence. Aid went where it would maintain the political influence and economic connections of the aid giver—Dutch aid to Indonesia, British aid to Britain's former colonies in Africa and Asia (especially India), Australian aid to Papua New Guinea, and French aid to the French-speaking countries of West Africa (e.g. the Ivory Coast, Senegal, Mali, Morocco and Cameroon). However, China's foreign aid has been driven by similar motives to those of traditional donors, though in a completely different context. It does not involve decolonisation or maintaining influence in former colonies, though it does entail an expansion of China's influence in the developing world under the name of south–south cooperation.

---

15 Based on the author's casual conversation with Chinese Ministry of Foreign Affairs officials, one possible explanation for China's refusal to join the Cairns Compact is that Beijing does not want its use of foreign aid to be monitored by traditional donors.

In light of these differences, China has demonstrated a strong preference for channelling aid bilaterally. As He (2010, p. 14) explained, China has favoured bilateral aid to Africa for four reasons:

- China has historically gained rich experiences in conducting its diplomacy, including providing aid to African countries bilaterally.
- Chinese aid is the 'mutual assistance among poor countries' that does not belong to ODA.
- Bilateral aid is more efficient than multilateral aid in terms of delivery efficiency.
- African regional integration is still in the process of development, and multilateral and bilateral cooperation is mutually complementary rather than exclusive.

From the above discourse, we would expect China to engage more in bilateral aid delivery and to shy away from cooperation with Western donors; however, we instead observe a growing trend away from this expectation.

Trilateral Aid Cooperation

Despite the considerable differences between China and traditional donors, China has signalled its growing willingness to work with traditional donors in the past decade. It has engaged in discussions and has performed trilateral aid cooperation[16] with traditional donor states and multilateral development agencies, such as the US, UK, Australia, New Zealand, the United Nations Development Programme (UNDP) and the United Nations Industrial Development Organization (UNIDO) (see Table 1).[17] This cooperation covers diverse areas, such as agriculture, food security, public health, environmental protection and technical training. Trilateral aid cooperation has been increasingly acknowledged

---

16   Countries such as China and the US use the term 'trilateral cooperation' while many other countries and international organisations use the term 'triangular cooperation'. For the latter, triangular cooperation involves both a traditional donor (donor state/multilateral development organisation) and an emerging donor, while trilateral cooperation refers to three countries in one project, not necessarily one traditional donor and one emerging donor. To follow China's practice, the term 'trilateral cooperation' is used in this book.

17   Although China and UN agencies began piloting some small trilateral aid projects in the 1980s, China's trilateral aid cooperation with traditional donor states did not start until the last decade. China has also conducted trilateral cooperation with other multilateral development organisations, such as the World Bank, UNESCO and the International Monetary Fund over the last decade. Table 1 includes most Chinese trilateral aid projects.

in China's aid documents (State Council, 2010, 2011d, 2013). China's second white paper on foreign aid (released in 2014) highlighted the China–UNDP–Cambodia trilateral cassava project and the China–New Zealand–Cook Islands water supply project as examples of trilateral cooperation (State Council, 2014, p. 22).

Table 1. Chinese trilateral aid projects

Traditional donor/ UN agencies	Recipient country	Area	Duration
UK	Malawi/Uganda	Agricultural technology transfer	2012–2016
	African countries	Training of African peacekeeping police (3 sessions)	2009–2010
UK/UNDP	Bangladesh Nepal	Disaster risk management	2012–2015
US	Liberia	Facility improvement of the University of Liberia	2008–2010
	Timor-Leste	Agriculture	Phase One: 2013–2014 Phase Two: Cancelled
	Afghanistan	Training of Afghan diplomats	2013–2017
Japan	ASEAN countries	Environmental protection (3 sessions)	2010–2013
Australia	Papua New Guinea	Malaria control	2016–2018
	Cambodia	Irrigation dialogue	2013–2014
New Zealand	Cook Islands	Water supply	2014–2020
UNDP	Cambodia	Agriculture (cassava)	2011–2015
	Ghana/Zambia	Renewable energy	2014–2019
	Malawi	Disaster risk management	2016–2018
FAO	12 from Africa, 2 from Asia, 7 from South Pacific and 4 from the Caribbean	Agriculture and food security under the $30 million donation from China in 2008	Since 2008
UNIDO	African countries	Lighten up Africa project (small hydro stations)	Since 2008

Source. Compiled by author from various resources.[18]

---

18   Data for this table is from mixed sources, including the author's interviews, MOFCOM website, Chinese media reports, public documents, media reports from traditional donors and recipient countries and existing literature. Data from these sources have been compared and contrasted to ensure their accuracy.

It is thus important to understand why China is conducting an increasing number of trilateral projects along with its bilateral aid projects. Is it a signal of real change in Chinese foreign aid policy or merely an expedient to detach China from external criticism? Are different donors really able to coexist and cooperate? Or do we, as Kenneth Kaunda (1966), then President of Zambia, lamented in March 1966, 'end up with a mixture of various explosive gasses [aid from various sources] in one bottle, and inevitably, explosions follow'? Addressing China's motivations for engaging in trilateral aid cooperation will partially answer these questions.

To help shed light on the puzzle, this book will focus on the following research question: What are the main factors that drive the growing Chinese trilateral aid cooperation?

It is worth briefly examining global trilateral aid cooperation as a background here. As a new form of aid distribution, trilateral cooperation has attracted more attention with the rise of emerging donors. This new aid modality can be traced back to the 'Buenos Aires plan of action', which was adopted by the UN in 1978 to push for developed nations' support to pursue south–south technical cooperation (Fordelone, 2013b, p. 13). This aid has been rapidly growing in recent years, with over 40 agreements signed by 2010 (Economic and Social Council, 2008, p. 23) and with two-thirds of traditional donors participating (McEwan & Mawdsley, 2012, p. 1193). There has also been a growing number of international and regional conferences on trilateral cooperation (Heiligendamm Process, 2009; OECD, 2012a; Pantoja, 2009; Portugese MFA, 2013; Schulz, 2010).

Trilateral cooperation entails benefits to international aid practice, including promoting mutual learning among all partners, sharing experiences from developing countries and increasing aid cooperation (Economic and Social Council, 2008; Fordelone, 2013a, 2013b; Mehta & Nanda, 2005; OECD, 2012c; Task Team on South–South Cooperation, 2011; UNDP, 2009a; Yamashiro Fordelone, 2011; OECD, 2016a). Documented disadvantages include increasing coordination difficulties among numerous donors and high transaction costs in comparison to bilateral aid (Fordelone, 2013b; OECD, 2012c).

The Research Gap and this Book's Contributions

China's rise as an emerging donor has far-reaching implications. Chinese foreign aid prompts an important opportunity for the developing world and provides another model of aid in addition to that established by traditional donors. Moreover, as the Chinese government does not release annual country-based aid data, the motivations underlying Chinese aid remain unclear. Analysing China's motivations for trilateral aid cooperation could also provide a new perspective on China's foreign policy.

Compared to bilateral aid, trilateral aid cooperation is a new phenomenon, especially for China. It has begun attracting global attention from aid officials and analysts. As will be elaborated in Chapter 2, traditional donors and multilateral development agencies have convened an increasing number of trilateral workshops and conferences to exchange views and explore this modality. In particular, Japan, Spain, Germany and the UNDP have been pioneers in experimenting with trilateral aid partnerships. Emerging donors, especially those from Latin America (e.g. Brazil), also have positive attitudes towards trilateral cooperation.

Although the influence of the rise of emerging donors on the traditional aid system remains unclear, the problem of aid fragmentation in recipient countries is becoming worse as emerging donors join the donors' camp. As Homi Kharas (2007, pp. 15–16) noted, 'The new reality of aid is one of enormous fragmentation and volatility' and 'information, coordination and planning are becoming harder, yet are more important for development effectiveness'. As such, trilateral aid cooperation is receiving more attention from donors and recipients alike, including at a recent high-level forum on aid effectiveness in Accra and Busan. It is expected to play a bridging role between traditional and emerging donors and to promote aid effectiveness. For example, the first high-level meeting of the global partnership for effective development cooperation in Mexico in 2014 concluded that trilateral aid cooperation has the following strengths:

> Triangular cooperation is an innovative way of inclusive partnering, which puts the role and will of the recipient countries at the core and provides an opportunity to bring together the diversity and richness of the experiences, lessons learned and different assets of Northern and Southern partners, as well as multilateral, regional and bilateral development and financial institutions, by

maximizing, through well-supported cooperation schemes, the use of effective, locally owned solutions that are appropriate to specific country contexts. (Global Partnership for Effective Development Cooperation, 2014, p. 5)

Although it has substantial potential, trilateral aid cooperation is still largely under-researched due to its novelty. This can be partly attributed to the limited number of trilateral projects. The empirical data on trilateral cooperation, in general and on Chinese aid in particular, is extremely limited (OECD, 2012c, p. 3). Reports and conference proceedings on trilateral aid cooperation are increasing in number, but most of them focus on trilateral cooperation's 'static' aspects, such as the history, features, and 'expected' strengths and weaknesses. In-depth critical analysis of other aspects, including the motivations of donors and recipient countries, based on field work is extremely thin. This is why the UNDP argued that trilateral aid cooperation is an 'underutilized tool' (UNDP, 2009a, p. 141). Further, as trilateral aid cooperation is a more recent phenomenon in China and access to aid data is limited, in-depth research on Chinese trilateral aid cooperation is almost non-existent.

Contributions

This research project contributes to the disciplines of development studies and international relations in three aspects: theory testing, methodological rigour and substantive content. It seeks to enrich the debate mainly on Chinese foreign aid, especially on trilateral aid cooperation and China's role in the Asia-Pacific region.

Theoretically, this research is timely and important because it is closely linked to mainstream theoretical debates in international relations regarding the influence of emerging powers, especially China, on global governance. As China is continually transforming itself and global governance architecture, this research uses foreign aid as a portal to illustrate China's global influence and its position towards cooperation with traditional donors and UN agencies. It will facilitate our understanding of whether China, as a leading emerging donor, will be able to coexist with traditional donors in peace and it will offer unique insights into Chinese foreign policymaking and aid policymaking. It will also trace in detail the process of three trilateral projects in which China has been involved (to be elaborated in Chapters 4, 5 and 6). This book additionally analyses the evolution of Chinese foreign aid policy. As will be discussed in Chapter 2, the constructivist and cognitive learning theories on identity, interest and ideas will be adopted for analysis. The book will focus on China's identity, interests and ideas, with regard to development cooperation. It will investigate whether China's identities, interests and ideas have changed over time during its engagement with traditional donors and UN development agencies. If they have, why? And what is the causal relationship between identity, interests and ideas? How have the changes informed China's endorsement of trilateral aid cooperation? These analyses will have implications for the wider theoretical debate regarding identity, interests and ideas in international relations and politics, economics and soft power in Chinese foreign policy.

Methodologically, this research has taken multiple measures to ensure its analytical validity. As the motivations behind China's foreign aid are complex, it is difficult to adequately analyse using a single approach. Therefore, to analyse Chinese trilateral aid cooperation, this research provides a three-layered approach that amasses national interests, international engagement and domestic institutions. This will help readers understand the roles that are played by external players in this process—including traditional donor states, UN agencies and Chinese domestic–vested interest groups. In addition, 'process tracing' is used as a tool to collect the details and investigate the whole notion of the selected trilateral aid projects. During the interview process, the views from three sides of the trilateral aid projects are compared and triangulated to maximise their reliability.

In terms of its substantive contribution, this research fills an important gap in the existing literature, as Chinese trilateral aid cooperation is new and relevant research is extremely limited. It is a pioneering research project on China's trilateral aid cooperation, especially in terms of identifying why Chinese actors are motivated to pursue trilateral development cooperation. This research also enriches the existing limited research on Chinese foreign aid in the Asia-Pacific region (particularly the Pacific), which in turn contributes to our knowledge of China's role in the region. As the existing literature on the Asia-Pacific region focuses on Chinese bilateral aid, this research expands the debate by ushering in China's trilateral aid cooperation in the region, which has increasingly become an important testing ground, as will be demonstrated in Chapters 4 to 6. Moreover, it gathers valuable data on Chinese trilateral aid projects and enriches the aid database for future research. It also draws implications for aid policymakers regarding how to best engage in trilateral aid cooperation with China in the future.

This research collects extensive firsthand data on Chinese trilateral aid cooperation and analyses three of China's trilateral aid projects in the case study chapters in-depth: the China–UNDP–Cambodia trilateral cassava project, the China–Australia–Papua New Guinea trilateral cooperation on malaria control and the China–US–Timor-Leste trilateral cooperation on food security. Research is also conducted on China's other trilateral projects, including the China–New Zealand–Cook Islands trilateral project on water supply and the China–Australia–Cambodia trilateral project on irrigation dialogue. This book also closely follows China's trilateral cooperation with the UNDP, UK and other donors in Africa. Most of the interviewees during my field work were senior aid officials from China, traditional donors, multilateral development agencies and recipient countries; they were also officials and aid experts who were deeply involved in these projects. This has enhanced the quality of the research findings by making the voice of these main players prominent and, in doing so, reducing the risk of analytical speculation that can arise from over-reliance on secondary sources.

Main Argument

The main argument of this book is that China's adoption of trilateral aid cooperation is the result of its stronger desire for building its global image as a responsible great power and for cognitive learning to improve its aid performance. The Chinese government has strategically used trilateral aid cooperation to build its global image as a responsible rising power since the early 2000s. Technically, China has aimed to learn selectively from traditional donor states and international development organisations so it can improve its aid delivery via trilateral aid cooperation.

These two perspectives are analytically distinct from each other so that mutual disturbance can be avoided. To elaborate, they focus on China's interest calculations and international engagement, respectively. As will be argued later, China is emphasising global image–building more as part of its interest calculation, which somewhat relates to the pressure arising from traditional donors and multilateral agencies. However, external pressure is not the decisive factor for China's global image–building. The deep-rooted reason relates to China's adjustment of its identity and national interest calculation during shifting international and domestic circumstances.

As an example, China officially adopted the reform and opening-up policy in 1978 due to its changing identity and national interest calculations. China began to highlight its identity as a developing country rather than as a socialist country and prioritised economic development over ideological considerations. The improved relationship with Western nations in the 1970s is a supporting, rather than decisive, factor for China's reform and opening up. Similarly, external pressure is also a supporting rather than defining reason for China's emphasis on global image–building, as China can choose to take or reject the pressure. The first perspective thus differs from the second perspective.

Book Structure

The current chapter, Chapter 1, provides the introduction to the book. It sets the broad analytical background for this research, including its theoretical and policy relevance. It introduces the research question, identifies the research gap and explains the study's main contributions. The entire structure of the book can be briefly summarised as follows.

Chapter 2 outlines the conceptual framework for the research. It begins with a brief discussion of China's motivations behind bilateral aid and then introduces the three analytical perspectives on Chinese trilateral aid cooperation, including China's interest calculations, international engagement in foreign aid and domestic aid management institutions. Constructivist theories of international relations and knowledge-based cognitive learning regime theories of identity, interests and ideas—which will be tested in the book—are introduced. What follows is a brief explanation of the research methods and of the three Chinese trilateral aid projects in Cambodia, Papua New Guinea and Timor-Leste.

Chapter 3 outlines the adoption of the conceptual framework in China's context. It approaches Chinese trilateral aid cooperation from three perspectives. First, this chapter explains how changes to China's identity have affected its interest calculations and preferences for development cooperation in terms of the Chinese government's interest calculations. Second, in terms of international engagement, the chapter categorises and reviews the interaction between China and external donors, especially UN agencies and traditional donor states from 1950 onwards. It further explains how the cognitive learning process during interaction has influenced China's attitude towards development cooperation with these partners. Third, in terms of domestic institutions, the chapter examines China's complicated aid management system and explores the diversified positions of China's different ministries and interest groups regarding trilateral aid cooperation. These three perspectives will be discussed in detail in the case study chapters.

The next three chapters aim to test the aforementioned theories and my central argument by tracing China's three trilateral aid projects in the Asia-Pacific region. Chapter 4 analyses China's trilateral aid cooperation with the UNDP—especially the China–UNDP cassava project in Cambodia, which is the first trilateral project between the two donors. Chapter 5 redirects to the Pacific region, a place of small island countries and a relatively limited number of donors, which facilitates the comparison of donors. The chapter focuses on China's development cooperation with Australia, the leading traditional donor in the Pacific, which is an excellent example of China's engagement with a donor who enjoys regional dominance. Similarly, Chapter 5 starts by analysing the China–Australia engagement on foreign aid since 1979, as Australia is the first Western state to provide aid to China. What follows is an in-depth analysis of the China–Australia–Papua New Guinea trilateral aid project on malaria control, the first trilateral project between China and Australia. Chapter 6 discusses trilateral aid cooperation between China and the US; the two are the contemporary world's largest traditional donor and emerging donor, respectively. The chapter also traces the process of the China–US trilateral project in Timor-Leste, which is the first such project between China and the US in Asia.

While testing constructivism and cognitive theories on identity, interests and ideas, this book will also engage with alternative explanations from international relations theories regarding China's adoption of trilateral aid cooperation. For example, it will discuss whether the neorealist perspective could explain the growing trilateral aid cooperation between China and the US—who are potential rivals, as foreign aid is ultimately believed to be about serving respective national interests. As Kenneth Lieberthal and Wang Jisi argued, 'the US-China strategic distrust is growing, is potentially very corrosive' (Lieberthal & Wang, 2012, p. 49). As such, the China–US trilateral aid cooperation is a least likely case with strong analytical power. At a time when these two great powers are caught in an atmosphere of growing strategic rivalry, their continued commitment to trilateral aid cooperation deserves our further attention.

Chapter 7 builds upon the three case study chapters and extends further by providing an overview of China's trilateral aid cooperation, including the main features, China's official position and the bureaucratic arrangement for this modality. It will then discuss the future prospects of China's trilateral aid cooperation. The chapter will also examine China's foreign aid reform, in which trilateral aid cooperation is situated, and the newly created China International Development Cooperation Agency.

Chapter 8 is my reflection on this research. It will revisit the broad question: what are the most appropriate international relations theories that can interpret China's trilateral aid cooperation and overall foreign aid? A second question to be discussed is, what is the relationship between China's growing willingness to undertake trilateral aid cooperation and its seemingly assertive diplomacy? The scope for future research on China's triangular aid cooperation will also be examined.

2

Conceptualising Chinese Aid Motivations

Chinese aid motivations are heatedly debated. As China has different norms and practices, traditional donors, recipient countries and researchers are curious about the objectives and aspirations of Chinese aid. Some are concerned that China is reluctant to ally with traditional donors and that it is providing an alternative to foreign aid from traditional donors, thus challenging the traditional aid regime.

China's growing readiness for trilateral cooperation amplifies the curiosity of traditional donors, recipient countries and researchers. They are unsure why China is shifting from merely providing bilateral aid to conducting an increasing number of trilateral aid projects, given the considerable differences between China and traditional donors regarding foreign aid. Nor do they understand whether this change is expedient or whether it truly signals a change in China's foreign aid policy.

This chapter is divided into two main parts. The first briefly examines China's motivations for providing bilateral aid and the second presents the conceptual framework that will guide this research. It includes the constructivist and cognitive learning theories of identity, interests, ideas and social interaction, as well as my research design and my data collection methods, especially case studies and process tracing.

The Three Dimensions of China's Bilateral Aid Motivations

Politics Takes Command

The political/strategic factor is a distinctive feature of socialist China that permeates many government policies and bureaucratic norms. During the long period from 1949 to 1978 in the Cold War context, 'Politics took command' (*zhengzhi gua shuai*)[1] and Chinese foreign policy and aid worked to consolidate relations with other socialist countries and build a united front with other developing countries. A great amount of aid was provided to other developing countries, even though China itself was poor. China's foreign aid accounted for 5.88 per cent of the government's total fiscal outlay between 1971 and 1975, and the figure was as high as 6.92 per cent in 1973 (Shi, 1989, p. 68). Alan Hutchison (1975) argued that China used aid as a weapon to combat the influence of the Soviet Union and the West in Africa, as well as to promote its status in the developing world. US scholar John Copper (1976) echoed the view that Chinese leaders considered foreign aid an effective method of promoting international status. From the late 1970s, especially after the reform and opening-up policy was introduced in 1978, the influence of ideology on foreign aid faded.

Some scholars perceive China as a potential threat, one with strategic ambitions to alter the status quo that underpins international order. From this perspective, Chinese bilateral aid is simply another tool to woo recipient countries and achieve strategic ambitions. Taking the Pacific as an example, some analysts argue that China regards the region as a strategic asset and that China intends to replace the US as the dominant power in the long run (Henderson & Reilly, 2003; Lum & Vaughn, 2007; Shie, 2007; Windybank, 2005). Anne-Marie Brady (2010) has argued that China aims to become a leading power in the Pacific.

---

1   This was a popular term from the 1950s to the late 1970s in China and it highlighted the dominant role of politics in relation to other aspects of work. It appeared frequently in state media such as the *People's Daily*, particularly on 27 March 1958 and 22 April 1966.

The Taiwan issue is widely recognised as a core component of Chinese foreign policy. China has invested significant resources to prevent other countries from establishing diplomatic ties with Taiwan and to prevent Taiwan from joining international organisations in which statehood is a requirement. This is understandable from the Chinese side, which maintains that Taiwan is merely a renegade province of China that will eventually be reunited with the mainland. Therefore, isolating Taiwan and promoting the 'one China' policy are frequently cited as the important strategic motivations of Chinese bilateral aid (Atkinson, 2010; Wesley-Smith, 2007; Yang, 2011). The Taiwan issue sometimes becomes a bargaining chip for countries to acquire more aid from both mainland China and Taiwan (Hanson, 2008b; Stringer, 2006; Yang, 2009).

As China is moving towards being a superpower, the strategic element of its foreign policy and aid becomes increasingly important to the outside world and deserves greater attention. The Chinese government and some Chinese scholars maintain that Chinese aid is selfless and that it aims to help other developing countries improve their development capacity and fulfil China's due international obligations (State Council, 2011d; Zhang & Huang, 2012; Zhou, 2010); however, suspicions persist. Because foreign aid mirrors Chinese foreign policy, an in-depth analysis of the subtle changes of Chinese aid preference for cooperation is much needed to explain how strategic factors influence China's aid cooperation.

An Economic Explanation

Since the late 1970s, domestic economic development has become the top priority of China's national policy. Rod Wye (2011) argued that the Chinese Communist Party is obliged to deliver continued economic growth in exchange for public support of its dominant position. Substantial efforts have been dedicated to improving China's foreign relations with other countries to facilitate economic cooperation. This has become more prominent since 1992, when China officially announced its objective of establishing a socialist market economy, and was reinforced when China became a net importer of oil in 1993. Foreign aid has been offered as a tool to strengthen China's foreign relations in exchange for much-needed natural resources to fuel its fast-running economic engine and to expand the markets for its manufactured goods and investment. This became more evident in 1999, when the Chinese government enacted the 'go global strategy' (*zouchuqu zhanlue*), supporting its enterprises to pursue an international strategy. Since 2000, Chinese leadership has stressed the importance of leveraging foreign policy to support China's economic development in the first two decades of the twenty-first century—which China has labelled the 'period of strategic opportunities' (*zhanlue jiyuqi*).[2]

Much literature has focused on the economic aspects of Chinese bilateral aid. Some scholars argue that economic and resource concerns dominate China's Africa policy. To these scholars, the main drivers of China's aid to Africa are to open up overseas markets for its goods and investment and to help Chinese companies obtain energy and resource assets to reduce the risks of rising energy prices and long-term energy supply shortages (Lancaster, 2007a; Davies, Edinger, Tay & Naidu, 2008; Lum, Fischer, Gomez-Granger & Leland, 2009). Christopher Alden (2012) agrees with this economic-centred view and argued that the 'Angola mode' has become China's favourite approach in Africa: providing aid to access energy and resources in resource-rich countries and use resources as collateral for debt payment.[3]

In terms of China's growing bilateral aid in the Pacific, Jenny Hayward-Jones (2013) stressed that it is inappropriate to observe China's presence in the Pacific from a geo-strategic perspective and further argued that China's main purpose is to seek commercial gains and promote south–south cooperation. Zhang Yongjin (2007) argued that China has limited strategic intentions in the Pacific and that Chinese aid provides new opportunities for regional economic development. Michael Powles (2007, p. 50) believed that Pacific seabed mineral resources have enormous potential and that they could dramatically change the region. China has already noted this opportunity, as its ocean mineral resources research and development association has completed research surveying the Pacific Ocean's mineral resources and has suggested that the Chinese government should use its aid to promote the cooperative exploration of seabed minerals in the Pacific (Mo & Liu, 2009).

---

2   In July 2009, Chinese President Hu Jintao mentioned at the 11th conference of ambassadors that the first two decades of the twenty-first century remain a strategic opportunity for China. This has been reaffirmed by his successor, President Xi Jinping (see Wu, 2009b; Xinhua, 2015b).
3   It is worth noting that the majority of Chinese finance to Angola is not ODA.

Aid as Soft Power

China's rapid development has given rise to numerous 'China threat' discourses. As a countermeasure, the Chinese government has enacted the 'peaceful development' concept, which was adopted in 2004 and linked to the promotion of a 'harmonious world' announced by former President Hu Jintao at the 2005 UN summit. According to Joseph Nye (1990, p. 166), a state's soft power is different from coercive power because it attracts another country to 'want what it wants' rather than 'order others to do what it wants'. Compared to economic expansion and military modernisation, the soft power approach has caught the attention of the Chinese leadership by providing a less sensitive alternative to strengthening China's global influence and reducing the resistance from other powers.

Some scholars have analysed Chinese foreign aid in terms of the 'peaceful development' and 'harmonious world' concepts. Bates Gill and James Reilly argued that China's engagement with Africa, including its provision of foreign aid, serves its global strategy of promoting its image as 'a peacefully developing and responsible rising power seeking a harmonious world' (Gill & Reilly, 2007, p. 38). Wei Xuemei (2011) argued that soft power has been incorporated into China's national strategy on foreign aid, including in Africa. Some scholars noted that the Chinese government proposed the 'harmonious world' concept to mute 'China threat' criticism and expand its influence through aid provision to avoid the 'new imperialism' or 'neo-colonialism' labels that are sometimes used to describe China's recent engagement with Africa (Guo & Blanchard, 2008).

Some analysts examined the soft power aspect of Chinese aid in China's diplomacy. Zhu Zhiqun (2010b) argued that China has been building its soft power in Southeast Asia and the South Pacific by providing bilateral aid and treating the countries in the region as equal partners. Joshua Kurlantzick (2007) argued that China has upgraded its public diplomacy in Southeast Asia through means such as aid and trade to sell the idea that China will not be a threat to its neighbours. Some scholars emphasised the notion that China is promoting its soft power through economic and cultural diplomacy, such as establishing over 400 Confucius institutes worldwide by 2010, providing aid through human resource training and providing Chinese-language teaching to project a benign global image (Lai & Lu, 2012; He, 2010). Yanzhong Huang and Sheng Ding argued that China is skilful in using foreign aid to 'communicate favourable intentions or evoke a sense of gratitude' from African states (Huang & Ding, 2006, p. 37).

The three dimensions discussed in the paragraphs above have largely explained the motivations behind China's bilateral aid. However, little attention has been given to the main factors that have driven Chinese growing trilateral aid cooperation in recent years. The existing literature fails to explore how Chinese aid preferences are influenced by others—traditional donors, multilateral development agencies and recipient countries—in a dynamic process of interaction. Nor does the existing literature place due attention to Chinese domestic bureaucratic power structures and state and non-state interest groups that directly affect Chinese aid preferences for trilateral cooperation. Many questions remain. For example, why is China, with its rapidly growing economic clout and aid budget, conducting more cooperation with traditional donors instead of flexing its muscles and working unilaterally? Why is China conducting trilateral aid projects with the US if it intends to replace them? Discussions in the following chapters aim to fill this knowledge gap by analysing China's motivations in conducting trilateral aid cooperation.

Conceptual Framework

This section outlines the rationale of my research design. It will begin with a brief explanation of the complexity of China's foreign aid. Three analytical perspectives will be presented to address this complexity and justify my use of constructivist theories on identity, interests and ideas, and of cognitive learning theories as the main theoretical threads to explain the expansion of China's trilateral aid cooperation. What follows is an introduction to my research design and data collection methods that focuses on case studies and process tracing.

Three Analytical Perspectives

The diversity of Chinese aid motivations means that no single factor can supply a satisfactory explanation. Given its growing economic and global influence, Chinese aid receives scrutiny and pressure from the outside world, and its multilateral aid cooperation is inevitably exposed to outside influence through a dynamic process of interaction. This outside influence will not automatically translate into aid policy changes in China, but it must undergo a complex internal 'translation' process that is shaped by several domestic stakeholders and interest groups. Moreover, China's foreign aid policy is generated through a dynamic rather than static process. Past aid policy reform exerts influence on the current aid policy reform, which in turn will inform changes in the future.

As will be explained, I will draw upon constructivist and cognitive learning theories to address my research question, while remaining cognisant of the relevance of other theories relating to power and material interests. It is not that I am dismissing alternative theories, but rather that I am identifying the limitations of neorealism and neoliberalism in explaining Chinese aid behaviour. I will use a three-layered approach that brings together national interests, social interactions and domestic institutions. These three perspectives include:

- the interest calculations of the Chinese government
- international engagement in foreign aid
- China's domestic institutions.

Interest Calculations

As foreign aid is intertwined with China's political, economic and global image interests, it is an integral part of China's foreign policy. It is also closely linked to China's overseas economic activities. This perspective focuses on the potential domestic reasons for China's adoption of trilateral cooperation and will analyse China's diplomatic strategy and calculations of national interest. A thorough analysis of China's interest calculations in its foreign aid program will facilitate the understanding of China's recent adoption of trilateral aid cooperation. The findings that are outlined in the following chapters will examine how China's changing identity leads to changing calculations of what constitutes its national interest, as well as the changing ideas on which aid modalities are suitable. It will explore how China measures global image–building and other factors, such as political and economic interest in aid delivery and how China adopts trilateral aid cooperation to promote its global image.

International Engagement

China's engagement with traditional donors and multilateral development agencies has expanded rapidly. This process does not merely produce functional pressures for China's compliance with international aid norms; it also redefines China's understanding of its interests, ideas and practices regarding aid cooperation. This perspective aims to identify potential external reasons for China to engage in trilateral cooperation. It will trace China's historical engagement with traditional donors and multilateral development agencies, especially since 2000. From this historical basis, it will investigate how international engagement has affected China's perceptions of identity, interest calculations and ideas to improve aid effectiveness, which leads to China's experimentation with a new aid modality—trilateral cooperation.

Domestic Institutions

Kenneth Waltz (1979, p. 81) argued that 'domestic political structure has to be examined in order to draw a distinction between expectations about behaviour and outcomes in internal and external realms'. Lancaster (2009, p. 808) highlighted that 'the impact of domestic politics on aid giving is often overlooked by scholars'. The heterogeneity of Chinese aid policymaking allows room for China's aid agencies to compete, cooperate and coordinate with each other in pursuit of their own interests. This domestic interaction directly shapes the decisions regarding cooperation under different circumstances. Changing the aid modality from bilateral to trilateral will inevitably affect the vested interests of these stakeholders, who can either support the Chinese government's tendency to cooperate within the international aid regime or create resistance. Given that the research on the influence of Chinese domestic aid institutions is inadequate, this perspective will be integrated into an overall analysis of the motivations behind China's trilateral aid cooperation; it will compare the attitudes of China's various aid agencies towards trilateral modality. The influence of China's new aid agency on trilateral cooperation will also be discussed.

Theories on Identity, Interests, Ideas and Social Interaction

International Relations Theories

Why do states cooperate? Rationalist theories and constructivism offer different answers to this question. Based on a brief introduction to these theories, I will justify why constructivist theories of identity, interests and ideas have greater analytical power to address my research question.

Neorealism and neoliberalism are rationalist theories. Neorealist scholars perceive power as the essence of international relations. They assume that states are egoists who are primarily concerned with the pursuit of material self-interest in the anarchical world (Gilpin, 1981; Mearsheimer, 2010; Waltz, 1979). Neoliberalism shares the materialist assumptions that underpin neorealism, though this school of thought argues that self-interested states can cooperate in some circumstances with a view to absolute gains. Robert O. Keohane (1984, p. 107) analysed how international regimes facilitate cooperation among states by 'reducing the costs of legitimate transactions … and of reducing uncertainty'.

Constructivist theories share a critique of the static material assumptions that rational analysts hold, and they emphasise the process of interaction (Fierke, 2010, pp. 178–180). These theories focus on the roles of norms, identity, interests and social interactions. Alexander Wendt (1992, pp. 394–395) challenged the assumptions of rationalist theories, arguing that 'identities and interests are endogenous to interaction, rather than a rationalist-behavioural one in which they are exogenous … Anarchy is what states make of it'. Constructivists do not deny the importance of interests—but they argue that social interactions can reshape states' perceptions of identities and interests, while identities can inform interests and political actions (Finnemore, 1996; Reus-Smit, 2013; Wendt, 1992, 1999).

Rationalists believe that states may cooperate in some circumstances to maximise their interests, but that their interests and preferences are treated as inherent. Jeffrey Checkel (2001, p. 561) argued that rational choice scholars believe that actors may acquire new information through simple learning to alter their strategies during interaction, but that their given preferences will not change. This differs from constructivist theories, which hold that the identities, preferences and interests of actors are all open to change through the course of interactions (Checkel, 2001, p. 561).

When analysing the European identity, Jeffrey Checkel and Peter Katzenstein argued that 'identities flow through multiple networks and create new patterns of identification … identity matters' (Checkel & Katzenstein, 2009, pp. 213, 216). Amitav Acharya investigated the development of multilateralism in the Asia-Pacific region and argued that 'the emergence of Asia-Pacific multilateral institutions is not just (material) interest-driven, but identity-driven' (Acharya, 1997, p. 343). In an influential study, Martha Finnemore detailed how international organisations such as the UN Educational, Scientific and Cultural Organization, the International Committee of the Red Cross and the World Bank socialise states to accept new norms, values and perceptions of interests (Finnemore, 1996).

In contrast to Finnemore's analysis of how external factors influence states' identities, some constructivists examine the role of domestic factors in this identity-shaping process. Alastair Johnston explored how China's realpolitik strategic culture shapes its security policy, and Peter Katzenstein highlighted the importance of culture and identity in defining actors' interests (Jackson & Sørensen, 2007, pp. 171–172).

Cognitive Learning Theory

Cognitive learning originates from regime theory, a branch of international relations theory. Cognitive learning and constructivist theories share much in common regarding the importance of identity, interests, ideas and interactions. Many constructivist scholars have actually developed their theories through the empirical analysis of international regimes. As such, cognitive learning theories will be introduced and used in my research to examine China's learning processes through its interaction with the traditional aid regime.

Regime theory became popular after World War II as a means of explaining why states still sought ways of cooperating in an anarchical world. Realism failed to explain why states became enmeshed in international organisations and why they supported regional integration (Haggard & Simmons, 1987, pp. 491–492). However, the idea of regimes remains a contentious issue in international relations, and scholars have failed to reach a consensus regarding whether it really matters. The Grotian school of scholars, including Oran Young, Raymond Hopkins and Donald Puchala, insist that regimes are pervasive within the international system. In contrast, Susan Strange and Kenneth Waltz contended that regimes have little to no effect because power or interests are the dominant factors that determine state behaviour (Krasner, 1983). Many other scholars take a middle path. For example, Arthur Stein, Robert Keohane, Robert Jervis, John Ruggie, Charles Lipson and Benjamin J. Cohen argued that regimes are needed in an anarchical world to help coordinate state behaviour for collective gains (Krasner, 1983).

Stephan Krasner's widely used definition of an international regime remains dominant in the literature:

> Regimes can be defined as sets of implicit or explicit principles, norms, rules, and decision-making procedures around which actors' expectations converge in a given area of international relations. Principles are beliefs of fact, causation, and rectitude. Norms are standards of behaviour defined in terms of rights and obligations. Rules are specific prescriptions or proscriptions for action. Decision-making procedures are prevailing practices for making and implementing collective choices. (Krasner, 1983, p. 2)

Three main approaches to regime studies are recognised in the literature (Haggard & Simmons, 1987; Hasenclever, Mayer & Rittberger, 1997, 2000; Krasner, 1983; Rittberger & Mayer, 1993; Tarzi, 2003). The first is power-based neorealism, which emphasises the dominant role of power in regime development and highlights the relative gains among actors. Hegemonic stability theory suggests that the rise and fall of a hegemon leads to a regime's evolution. The second is an interest-based neoliberal approach that shares assumptions with neorealism: that states pursue self-interest and that they care about definite gains. Both neorealist and neoliberal scholars embrace a rationalist explanation for cooperation: states accept the existence of the regime because only through cooperation can they achieve common interests in an anarchical world (Hasenclever et al., 1997).

A third approach is knowledge-based cognitive theory, which will be applied to analysing China's trilateral aid cooperation in this book. It emphasises the importance of beliefs, knowledge and identity in regime development. According to this theory, the beliefs of decision-makers can shape the interactions among states and lead to policy changes. Learning is a process that creates new knowledge, helps form ideas and affects cooperation between states. Shared ideas or beliefs are conducive for cooperation and the formation of norms, while norms in turn reinforce shared ideas.

Identity is a central concept in cognitive theory, and cognitivists argue that the identities of states change in response to social interaction. Identities are affected by both the structure of the regime and by the interactions among states (Hasenclever et al., 1997, pp. 137–192). Compared to the rationalist approaches of neorealism and neoliberalism, cognitivism is an important analytical tool for explaining the evolution of regimes, as it utilises the vital role of learning. It sheds light on a dynamic that the other two approaches do not consider (Haggard & Simmons, 1987, p. 510). Ernst Haas provided an in-depth analysis of the learning process and categorised two kinds of learning processes: adaptation and learning. While adaptation includes the use of new means to achieve the same goal, learning signifies the changing of both goals and means; it is a process of redefining actors' interests in light of new knowledge and information to seek collective gains' (Haas, 1990, pp. 3–4).

Theoretical Justification

This research will apply constructivist theories and cognitive learning theories to examine the evolution of China's identity, interests and ideas from the three perspectives of interest calculation, international engagement and domestic institutions. Specifically, constructivist theories will be used to analyse China's interest calculations and domestic aid institutions. Cognitive learning theory will be used to explore China's external engagement with the international aid regime.

Constructivist theories are preferred because they explain the relations between identity, interests and ideas. This book will examine how and why China's identities, interests and ideas regarding aid norms are changing. It will also demonstrate how China's changing identities inform its calculations of national interest and its adoption of specific aid modalities.

Similarly, cognitive learning theory is chosen because of its explanatory power in regard to the learning process that occurs during social interactions. This relates closely to my research of trilateral aid cooperation, as 'knowledge sharing, mutual learning and capacity development are at the heart of triangular cooperation' (OECD, 2012c, p. 1). The theory will explain the ways that, and the extent to which, the social dynamics between China and traditional donors and multilateral development organisations affect China's preferences for trilateral cooperation. Another reason to emphasise cognitive learning is that, as China is not an OECD DAC member, OECD aid norms are not binding to China. The cognitive learning approach is thus used to test the constitutive effect of external interactions on China's changing aid preferences. During the analysis, I will pay attention to two levels of learning: the first is due to the functional needs, including external pressure, on China to learn; and the second relates to the changes in thinking among China's aid policymakers.

I will take a critical approach to theories in my analysis. The first point involves a selection of constructivism theories and cognitive learning theories that is based on my comprehensive background study of China's existing trilateral aid projects before analysis. This provides me with empirically based assumptions that the above two theories might have more strengths than some other international relations theories to explain China's trilateral aid cooperation. The material interest-based rationalist theories (including neorealism and neoliberalism) seemingly have weak analytical power in explaining China's willingness to engage in trilateral aid cooperation. For example, neorealism argues persuasively that material power determines an actor's behaviour, yet there are clear challenges to this assumption in my book: why did China provide large amounts of foreign aid in the first three decades of the People's Republic (1950s–1970s), even when its own economy was weak? As the following chapters will demonstrate, identity matters. Another example is how China's economic capacity has been strengthened greatly after more than three decades of reform and opening up. China could be more assertive in its foreign aid; it could emphasise the singularity of its aid practice more and remain with bilateral aid. However, reality points to the opposite. China is showing more readiness for trilateral aid cooperation. These observations are difficult to explain using rationalist theories.

The second point is that even though I will borrow some constructivism and cognitive theories in my analysis, this does not entail that I take them as revealed truth. They have the potential to explain my research question, but these theories will be rigorously tested through my research for their validity, especially in my three case studies. I am also aware of the criticism that constructivism faces—especially from neorealism, the main theoretical opponent for most constructivists. Neorealism scholars are sceptical about the roles of norms and social interaction among states, arguing that states routinely disregard the norms that are not in their interest and that they cannot easily become friends during social interaction (Jackson & Sørensen, 2007, pp. 172–173). Consequently, in addition to constructivism and cognitive theories, international relations theories such as neorealism, neoliberalism and alternative explanations that are engendered for my research question will also be discussed in my analysis (in Chapters 4, 5, 6 and 8).

Research Methods

This study is mainly based on qualitative research, and case study and process tracing are the two main research methods.

Case Study Method

The case study method has its distinctive advantages. It can strengthen conceptual validity through contextualised comparisons and draw contingent generalisations. An in-depth analysis of selected cases can discover new hypotheses, and well-designed case studies can also explore causal mechanisms, by modelling and assessing complex causal relations (George & Bennett, 2005, pp. 19–22). I am also mindful of the disadvantages of the case study method, such as case bias, the cherry-picking problem of selecting cases intentionally to confirm the hypothesis, the under-representation of cases and the related generalisation issue (George & Bennett, 2005, pp. 22–34). Measures have been taken to minimise the negative effects of these disadvantages.

Case Selection Criterion

It would be useful to combine large-number cases with small-number case studies, which could reduce the risk of case bias and address the generalisation issue. However, the reality is that China's trilateral aid cooperation is still in its infancy and that the number of projects is limited, which makes a large-N study impossible. Additionally, I do not include Chinese bilateral projects in my case study for two reasons. First, selecting an appropriate bilateral project for comparison is difficult, as China has numerous bilateral aid projects: the danger of cherry picking is apparent. Choosing a bilateral project also carries the risk of bias, as many projects are subject to case-specific technical factors (e.g. an individual official's personal preferences or connections), which will reduce the validity of the analysis. Second, comparing a Chinese bilateral aid project with a trilateral project is not a good fit for my research question. Such a comparison is perfect for answering a different question: under what conditions will China deliver its aid bilaterally or trilaterally? It is not suitable for explaining my research question: why is China conducting trilateral aid cooperation?

I have selected cases that range across regions, project fields, the importance of the recipient countries in China's foreign aid landscape and the importance of the traditional donor partners to China. As Table 2 reveals, typical cases, diverse cases, most different cases and least likely cases are chosen, which can compensate for the absence of a bilateral aid project in my case study. These criteria tease out any unimportant technical factors and allow us to test China's interest calculations, international engagement and domestic institutions in a wider context.

Table 2. Case selection variables in this research

Variable	Case one	Case two	Case three
	China–UNDP–Cambodia trilateral project on cassava	China–US–Timor-Leste trilateral agricultural project	China–Australia–Papua New Guinea trilateral project on malaria control
Case type	**Typical case** **Diverse case** **Most different case**	**Least likely case** **Diverse case** **Most different case**	**Typical case** **Diverse case** **Least likely case**
Donor partner	UNDP	The US	Australia
Importance of donor partner	The largest UN development agency	The largest traditional donor	The largest traditional donor in the Pacific region
Recipient country	Cambodia	Timor-Leste	Papua New Guinea
Recipient country in China's foreign policy	Strategic	Normal	Normal
Recipient country in China's aid landscape	Main recipient of China's aid	Small recipient of China's aid	Main recipient of China's aid in the Pacific
Geography	Southeast Asia	Southeast Asia	South Pacific
Project field	Agriculture	Agriculture	Health
Population[1]	15.32 million (2014)	1.21 million (2014)	7.94 million (2014)
Land area	176,520 km²	14,870 km²	452,860 km²
Project execution	2011–2014	2013–2014	2015–2017
Project value[2]	$610,000	$400,000 (China side) $5 million (US side)	AU$4 million

[1] The data on population and land area is derived from the World Bank's database.

[2] The project value on the China–US–Timor-Leste trilateral agricultural project is an estimate from the author's interviews. While the Chinese side affirmed that China's spending on the project was $400,000, according to the Timor-Leste government, Chinese disbursement was $210,000.

Source. Compiled by author from own analysis and based on John Gerring's categories of case selection (Gerring, 2007, pp. 89–90).

China–UNDP–Cambodia Trilateral Aid Project on Cassava

International organisations are significant partners of Chinese multilateral aid cooperation projects and could be the catalyst for the evolution of Chinese aid preferences. The UNDP is the largest UN agency that focuses on development. It is also among the earliest and most active of the international organisations to promote multilateral partnership with China. In 1979, not long after the end of the Maoist era, the UNDP established an aid cooperation partnership with China, though the early focus was on aid to China. In 2010, the two sides signed a new memorandum of understanding (MOU) and pledged to promote trilateral aid cooperation, which marked the commencement of their second phase of cooperation (Wang, 2013). Cambodia is one of the main recipients of Chinese aid in Asia. Due to historical and strategic reasons, Cambodia enjoys close diplomatic relations with China. The country is also a major recipient of international development assistance. Nearly 90 per cent of the Cambodian government's expenditure has relied on foreign assistance since 2005 (Council for the Development of Cambodia, 2008, p. 1). In addition, this cassava project is the first trilateral project between the UNDP and China.

These reasons render this trilateral project a typical case in China's trilateral cooperation. This research will examine China's identity, interest calculations and ideas in the process of China–UNDP's engagement on development cooperation. This project can illuminate China's trilateral aid cooperation with multilateral aid agencies, especially UN agencies, and how these agencies differ from China's interaction with traditional donor states.

China–Australia–Papua New Guinea Trilateral Project on Malaria Control

Australia is the leading traditional donor in the Pacific and enjoys close relations with Melanesian countries. Papua New Guinea (PNG) is the largest and one of the most influential countries in the region. Australia–PNG relations are among the top priorities of Australia's foreign policy. From 2018 to 2019, Australia's total aid budget to PNG reached $379.2 million (AU$519.5 million),[4] accounting for 49.6 per cent of Australian aid to the Pacific (DFAT, 2018). PNG is also China's leading partner for

---

4   US$1 is equal to approximately AU$1.37 (as of 31 December 2015).

economic cooperation in the Pacific region and an important recipient of China's foreign aid. However, PNG is plagued by a weak institutional capacity in its aid management.

On one side, China–Australia trilateral aid cooperation in PNG is a typical case of cooperation between China and traditional donors on the regional level. Conversely, it is a least likely case, given the chaotic aid coordination in PNG in comparison to other Pacific Island countries (especially Samoa) that have a stronger institutional capacity in aid management and a stronger desire to observe aid coordination among donors, as will be discussed in Chapter 7. Similarly, this research will analyse China's identity, interest calculations and idea changes in the process of China–Australia's engagement on development cooperation. It will also examine the particularities of this China–Australian–PNG trilateral aid project on malaria control.

China–US–Timor-Leste Trilateral Project on Agriculture

China and the US are important in developing global aid norms, with the former being the largest emerging donor and the latter the largest traditional donor. Their aid cooperation in Timor-Leste—though little known, even in policymaking circles—has significant implications for the evolution of the international aid regime. In recent years, China and the US have exhibited a growing interest in conducting trilateral aid cooperation and they have begun turning their ideas into practice. The US is the main priority of China's foreign policy. It is also the most vocal critic of China's foreign aid practices.

According to the neorealist approach, China and the US are potential rivals, and foreign aid serves their respective national interests. It appears that they will be the least likely to cooperate in delivering foreign aid. As China's national economic and military capacity grows, it gains the strength to act more assertively through bilateral means. Further, Timor-Leste is not a focal point in terms of foreign aid or foreign policy for either China or the US.

These reasons signify that this trilateral cooperation project is a valuable least likely case. This study will analyse China's identity, interest calculations and ideas through the lens of China–US engagement on development cooperation, in the specific context of a trilateral agricultural project in Timor-Leste. It will attempt to explain which causal factors rendered this least likely case a reality.

Considering the numerous variations of indicators in Table 2, we can note that the three cases are diverse in nature. Case one and case two, in particular, are the most different cases in many aspects. A comparative analysis of the three cases will be conducted in the following chapters to strengthen this research.

Focus on the Asia-Pacific Region

My case studies will concentrate on China's trilateral aid cooperation in the Asia-Pacific region for four reasons.

- This region is an important focus of Chinese foreign aid policy.
- The Asia-Pacific region is defined as China's 'great periphery'[5] in foreign relations, which is critically linked to its stability and development. This diplomatic position directly shapes Chinese aid policy in the region.
- Pacific Island countries depend heavily on foreign aid and are traditionally located within the spheres of influence of the US, France, Australia and New Zealand. This signifies that the Pacific is an ideal place to review the dynamic interactions between China and traditional donors.
- Far less attention has been given to the Pacific region compared to Africa and Asia.[6]

Though the case studies focus on the Asia-Pacific region, this research covers China's foreign aid policy as a whole. The research's timeframe will cover Chinese foreign aid in the relatively long period from 1950 to 2018. This is necessary not just because China's engagement in development cooperation dates back to the 1950s, but because constructivist theories are best applied to research subjects that can be examined longitudinally. As Wendt (1999, p. 367) argued, the analytical division of labour is 'rationalism for today and tomorrow, constructivism for the *longue durée*'. China's foreign aid since 2000 will be particularly highlighted because China's development assistance has increased significantly over the past decade and because China's trilateral aid cooperation emerged during this period.

---

5   The definition of 'great periphery' comes from the speeches of Chinese President Hu Jintao at the 10th and 11th conferences of Chinese ambassadors in 2004 and 2009, respectively (see Chen, 2009).
6   A topic search combining the key words 'Chinese aid' plus 'region' in the ProQuest Database dated 19 April 2016 finds 2,028 items (including books, journal articles, news reports, etc.) on Chinese aid to Africa, 2,399 on Asia, 706 on Latin America and 147 on the South Pacific.

Process Tracing Method

As Figure 2 illustrates, the causal process that links causal factors and China's adoption of trilateral aid cooperation is sealed in a black box and remains unknown. An analysis of this process will greatly facilitate the understanding of this black box and the whole causal process.

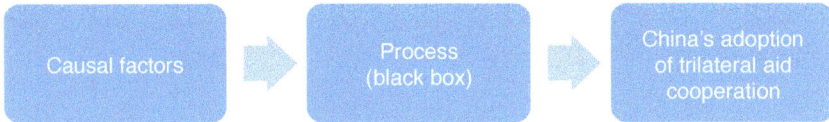

Figure 2. Process: Tracing Chinese trilateral aid cooperation
Source. Compiled by author from own analysis.

Process tracing is tasked with identifying the causal mechanisms as:

> Ultimately unobservable physical, social, or psychological processes through which agents with causal capacities operate, but only in specific contexts or conditions, to transfer energy, information, or matter to other entities. In doing so, the causal agent changes the affected agencies' characteristics, capacities, or propensities. (Bennett & Checkel, 2015, p. 12)

Process tracing is employed in this research for its strengths. It can address the issue of equifinality-multiple paths to the same outcome by confirming or disconfirming particular causal mechanisms as viable explanations in individual cases. It can also reduce the risk of omitting important causal factors (Bennett & Checkel, 2015, p. 20). I have also taken measures to minimise the weakness of process tracing, including the resource problem, the measure-of-fit problem, the storytelling problem and the problem of generalisation (Schimmelfennig, 2015, pp. 102–104). For example, while using process tracing in case studies, if one must select case studies, Frank Schimmelfennig (2015, p. 105) suggested that one should select typical cases, conduct two to three diverse cases and make use of least likely cases. This coincides with my case selections above.

In my case studies, I will use process tracing to examine the whole process of China's trilateral aid cooperation—from the initiation of the project idea, to the idea flow, the coordination among the three countries in each project and the coordination among China's domestic aid institutions, to the final execution of the project on the ground. In particular, critical junctures and the sequence of decision-making will be highlighted.

Data Collection Techniques

Data for this research is mainly collected through interviews and documentation, which includes primary and secondary sources. Primary sources include government policy papers and media reports, while secondary sources include the literature on Chinese foreign aid. Although my cases focus on China's trilateral cooperation in the Asia-Pacific region, some sources on China's aid cooperation in Africa will be referred to as well, as Africa is the largest recipient of China's foreign aid.

Taking into consideration that one great obstacle to studying China's foreign aid is the lack of available data, especially from the Chinese side, I have taken advantage of my language skills as a native speaker of Chinese and have based my analysis on a large number of China's public documents—including white papers, speeches of state leaders and aid officials and media releases. Careful content analysis of these documents has revealed much about Chinese decision-makers' views of foreign aid. I have also enriched this research by widely surveying the literature that Chinese researchers have produced. This book aims to enrich the existing research on Chinese foreign aid by interpreting China's aid through the lens of Chinese decision-makers. It also builds from extensive interviews with the main participants in each of the three partner countries (see Table 3), which has increased the validity of the research.

Table 3. A breakdown of interviews

	Government aid officials	Research institutes	Non-Chinese diplomats, multilaterals	Chinese officials, companies	Business, media, civil society	Total
China	13	12	14			39
Australia	1	7		5		13
New Zealand	6	1				7
Papua New Guinea	15	4	8	6	1	34
Timor-Leste	12	1	11	1	2	27
Cambodia	5	4	4	1	1	15
Samoa	2		2			4
Cook Islands	1					1
Total	55	29	39	13	4	140

Source. Compiled by author from own analysis.

Table 4 demonstrates the research transparency, which includes data access, collection techniques and process methods.

Table 4. Research transparency in project

China's trilateral aid cooperation	Perspective one: Interest calculations	Perspective two: International engagement	Perspective three: Domestic aid institutions
Main concepts	China's identity, interest and ideas on aid modalities.	Learning from international engagement on aid issues.	Impact of trilateral aid cooperation on China's aid agencies.
Sub-questions	What are the changes of China's identity, interest and ideas on aid modality? Why and how have they occurred?	How is the learning process? What are the results?	What are the portfolios of China's aid agencies? What are their attitudes towards trilateral aid cooperation? Why?
Data acquired	China is placing growing emphasis on its identity as a rising great power and its global image–building in diplomacy.	International engagement has led to China's changing views on Western aid and cooperation with traditional/multilateral donors. China has been learning to reform its aid policies.	China's aid agencies have demonstrated diversified positions on trilateral aid cooperation.
Research methods	Three case studies; process tracing.		
Data collection techniques	Interviews: aid officials, participants of China's trilateral aid projects, scholars from China, traditional donors, multilateral aid agencies and recipient countries. Documentation: official documents, speeches, media reports from China, traditional donors, multilateral aid agencies and recipient countries; existing literature.		
Data processing	Triangulation is applied to increase data reliability; comparative analysis of the three cases.		

Source. Compiled by author from own analysis.[7]

---

7   The idea for this table stemmed from *Field Research in Political Science—Practices and Principles*, a book by Diana Kapiszewski, Lauren M. Maclean and Benjamin L. Read (2015).

Triangulation

As China does not release country-based figures for its aid data, I have accounted for the possibility of bias in my data and have used triangulation to reduce this risk when possible. Because much of the data is derived from interviews with aid officials and trilateral project participants, I have been cautious of their answers to the interview questions and have considered the context behind their views. For example, it is common that government officials tend to exaggerate the positive aspects of the projects and that they conceal their real motivations. To address this issue, I have asked the same question during my interviews with officials and stakeholders from the three countries involved in each trilateral project and I compared these views to increase the reliability of data. I have also compared the views of aid officials from these countries with relevant government documents.

In terms of interviews, the selection of interviewees depended on their availability; however, I also considered the hierarchical nature of the policymaking system, particularly in China. Low-level officials do not have decision-making authority, but they do have a better understanding of the background information; it is opposite for the high-level officials. Interviews with these two types of aid officials have both advantages and disadvantages. Therefore, I chose to interview these two types of aid officials with certain questions and to triangulate their answers.

Conclusion

This chapter has studied the main motivations behind Chinese bilateral aid. It also introduced the main theories of international relations regarding identity, interests, ideas and social interaction. Constructivist theories and cognitive learning theories are foregrounded because of their potential to explain China's adoption of trilateral aid cooperation. In addition, the research methods of case studies, process tracing and data collection methods are explained to demonstrate the transparency of this research.

Allow me to conclude by citing the metaphor from Professor Li Anshan, a senior Chinese expert on China–Africa relations and Chinese foreign aid from Peking University, on the gradual evolution of China's aid policies:

> A US expert on Chinese affairs [Denis Waitley] wrote a book *Dragon and Eagle*. He described China as a dragon. As a giant, the dragon will not feel a single gentle touch from outside at all. Similarly, China is a huge country and receives a lot of information from different perspectives. It will only pay attention when different sources [forces] touch it on the same place … China's diplomacy will take into considerations factors from all aspects. It will not be influenced easily by an individual Chinese scholar. (Interview, Beijing, 30 August 2015)

Though he referred to the limited role of Chinese think tanks in the policy circle, the metaphor suggests that the Chinese government considers numerous factors before adjusting its policies. An inclusive analysis of both domestic and international factors is thus valuable for examining China's adoption of trilateral aid cooperation.

3

China's Foreign Aid and Trilateral Cooperation: Interest Calculations, International Engagement and Domestic Institutions

Introduction

Building on the three theoretical dimensions of my conceptual framework that was outlined in Chapter 2, this chapter[1] will further elucidate them in China's context. It will examine China's political, economic and global image interest calculations in its provision of overseas assistance, China's international engagement in development assistance and China's domestic bureaucratic institutions of foreign aid management. These three dimensions will help explain the rationale of China's foreign aid policy and its evolution. They will particularly provide insights into China's adoption of trilateral cooperation as a new modality of aid delivery amid its seemingly immutable aid practice with Chinese characteristics.

This chapter is organised into four sections. The first two elaborate on China's interest calculations and international engagement; section three introduces Chinese aid agencies and their reactions to trilateral aid cooperation; and the final section summarises the findings—that China's

---

1   This chapter is derived in part from an article published in *Pacific Review* on 2 March 2017, doi. org/10.1080/09512748.2017.1296886; and an article published in *Third World Quarterly* on 12 June 2017, doi.org/10.1080/01436597.2017.1333419.

adoption of trilateral aid cooperation is the result of its stronger desire to build its global image as a responsible great power and for cognitive learning to improve its aid performance.

China's trilateral aid cooperation will be analysed against the broad backdrop of the evolution of Chinese development assistance. The rationale is threefold. First, as ideas and norms seldom change over the short term, a long period is needed to test whether China's aid policies have changed, which have changed and whether the changes are caused by a change of ideas or one of material power. This will offer us insights regarding the extent to which China's adoption of trilateral cooperation is instrumental or otherwise. Second, China's trilateral aid cooperation remains in its infancy. The numbers of projects and scholarly research are limited, so examining the historical reasons for the shifts in China's aid policies will help us understand China's current involvement in trilateral aid cooperation. A final, but methodologically important, reason for doing so is that China's aid projects are occasionally subject to the influence of case-specific factors (e.g. an individual official's personal preferences or connections). These cases cannot fully reflect the actual reasons for China's trilateral cooperation. If this research focuses only on recent years in its examining of China's trilateral cooperation, it could miss the longer-term setting for China's evolving approach and changing motivations. Situating China's trilateral aid cooperation in historical context reduces this risk.

Interest Calculations and China's Trilateral Aid Cooperation

This section attempts to analyse whether China's identity and calculations of its political, economic and global image–building interest have changed. If so, how have these changes related to China's participation in trilateral aid cooperation?

Before proceeding, the relationship between China's foreign aid and its foreign policy must be explained to understand Chinese aid evolution. The Chinese government has repeatedly emphasised that the provision of foreign aid is an integral part of China's foreign policy. In October 2010, China's Minister of Commerce, Chen Deming (2010, p. 1), stated that 'the foreign aid of our country is an important part of our external work'.

As China's foreign policy serves its national development, the study of China's foreign aid should be juxtaposed against the broader backdrop of China's development.

The pursuit for prosperity has been China's core focus after suffering the invasion and piecemeal occupation of Western powers and Japan from the 1840s. A belief that strong societies survive while the weaker ones perish has formed the core philosophy of the Chinese leadership (Waley-Cohen, 1999, p. 209). The 'century of humiliation' has tremendously influenced Chinese nationalism, which features a strong sense of insecurity in regard to China's international position (Callahan, 2010; Gries, 2004, pp. 43–53). Domestic development and economic growth have consequently become the top priority of China's national policy since its adoption of 'reform and opening up' in 1978—and substantial progress has been achieved. Susan Shirk (2007, p. 17) argued that 'China's dramatic economic transformation has revived it as a regional and global power after over a century of humiliating weakness'.

China has been a beneficiary of engagement with other nations in the past four decades. It has changed from being 'a revolutionary to a stakeholder' of the international system (Wang & Rosenau, 2009, p. 11). Beijing has realised that it must continue opening itself to the outside world. Chinese leadership has emphasised the need to consider both the circumstances within China and abroad and China's domestic and overseas markets (Hu, 2007, p. 1). China has looked outward to secure resources for maintaining its growth trajectory and protecting its interests 'by all means necessary' (Economy & Levi, 2014). The Chinese government considers development assistance a useful tool in the service of these objectives. In 1989, then Vice Minister of MOFCOM and later Vice Premier Li Lanqing highlighted that:

> Providing foreign aid is a serious political task and has been under the direct leadership of the Chinese Communist Party Central Committee and the State Council. It is China's global obligation and an important component of its diplomacy to provide economic and technical assistance to friendly countries from the Third World. This is very necessary in order to strengthen China's solidarity and cooperation with the Third World and to create a peaceful and stable global environment to serve China's socialist modernisation. It also plays an important role in raising China's global position and influence. (Shu, 1989, p. 3)

Since 2000, the Chinese leadership has stressed the importance of leveraging foreign policy to better use the period of strategic opportunity (*zhanlüe jiyuqi*) in supporting China's economic development in the first two decades of this century (Wu, 2009a, p. 1). The main objective of Chinese diplomacy is to secure a sound international environment for facilitating China's domestic economic development over this 20-year period. As a part of China's foreign policy, its foreign aid is provided to serve this main objective. It is helpful to bear this context in mind when interpreting China's foreign aid.

1949–1978: As a Socialist Country

From 1949, when the People's Republic of China (PRC) was founded, until 1978, when China officially adopted its reform and opening-up policy,[2] China was isolated by US-led Western countries and later by the Soviet Union when relations deteriorated in the late 1950s. During this period, China's identity as a socialist country was more visible in its foreign aid provision than in other aspects of its identity. China provided foreign aid to other socialist and developing countries to construct an extensive united front against Western countries and, later, the Soviet Union.

In October 1958, the Chinese government issued an official document stating that:

> Foreign economic and technical assistance work is a serious political task. Any mistake in foreign aid work may have an unfavourable political impact, to which the whole party must pay high attention. (Xinhua, 2005, para. 2).

The eighth National Congress of the Communist Party of China (CPC) concluded that the growth and solidarity among socialist countries was the most favourable international condition for building socialism in China (Liu, 1956). Chairman Mao Zedong told African delegates in 1963 that 'it is our international obligation as a nation that has achieved revolutionary success to help those countries who are still fighting for their revolutionary success' (Xinhua, 1963, p. 1).

---

2 Some scholars, including Warren Sun and Frederick Teiwes, argued that many reforms had started during Hua Guofeng's administration before 1978—but 1978 has become an easy shorthand period. For more information, see Teiwes and Sun (2010).

When Somali Prime Minister Abdirashid Ali Sharmarke expressed his gratitude to China for an aid of 80 million Swiss francs, China's Premier Zhou Enlai replied that China is obligated to provide aid to other countries that achieved victory at a later stage because China had achieved revolutionary victory earlier than them (Ministry of Foreign Affairs [China], 1993, p. 216). Premier Zhou highlighted in his report to the third National People's Congress in December 1964 that:

> The basic point of departure of China's foreign aid policy is to provide aid to support socialist construction in fraternal countries and increase the strength of the socialist camp based on the spirit of proletarian internationalism. China's aid to fraternal countries and newly independent countries increases the strength of the socialist camp and reduces the strength of imperialism, which means great support to China in return. (Xinhua, 1964, p. 1)

Though the flavour of ideology has faded since 1978, China still formally maintains this obligation. In March 1983, Chinese leaders at the sixth national conference on work relating to foreign aid emphasised that China as a socialist country must provide aid to other countries even though China itself is poor, because this is determined by China's identity as a socialist country (Shi, 1989, p. 70).

To China, the importance of developing beneficial political relations with other developing countries can never be downgraded because it needs their support in its international affairs. Chinese leaders repeatedly emphasise at the CPC National Congress that it is China's fundamental standing point to strengthen its solidarity and cooperation with Third World countries.[3] The support from developing countries for the PRC's admission into the UN Security Council in 1971 remains fresh in the minds of the Chinese leadership. Among the 23 developing countries who initiated the supportive proposal, 22 were recipients of China's foreign aid, with Yugoslavia as the only exception. Forging relations with developing countries has formed the basis of China's political interest when it provides foreign aid. It explains why political interests prevail over short-term economic interests during times of conflict.

---

3   For example, see Xinhua (2002).

1978–1999: As a Developing Country

Since China formally adopted the reform and opening-up policy in 1978, its identity as a developing country was emphasised and domestic economic development became its top priority. To facilitate its engagement with the outside world, China became an ardent supporter of the existing global economic order—which is in stark contrast to Mao's opposition in the 1950s and 1960s (Lampton, 2007). The Chinese government amended the ideology-based foreign policies and used a more pragmatic approach to its foreign aid provision. Although China continued to provide aid to Third World countries, guided by the principle of 'being practical and acting within one's capacity' (*shishi qiushi, liangli erxing*), it tightened its control on its aid budget, which accounted for as high as 6–7 per cent of government expenditure in the early 1970s (Zhou & Xiong, 2013, p. 19).

In 1996, Yan Xuetong, dean of the Institute of Modern International Relations at Tsinghua University, ranked China's national interests according to the urgency and importance of four factors: external environment, national strength, levels of science and technology, and subjective understanding. He argued that China's prime national interest is its economic interest, followed by its political, security and cultural interests (Yan, 1996, p. 111).

Advertising its identity as a developing country elicits benefits for China. It places China in an advantageous position to focus on domestic development and to guard against pressures from traditional donors and recipient countries who push China to provide more aid. Mao Xiaojing, division chief from the China Academy of International Trade and Economic Cooperation (CAITEC), argued that as Western donors try to pressure China's foreign aid, shape China's aid delivery and integrate China's foreign aid into the Western-dominated aid regime, China can repel the pressure by insisting that its aid is a south–south cooperation and that it differs from Western aid (Mao, 2010, p. 60).

Compared to traditional donors, China's identity as a developing country offers it the natural advantage of partnering with other developing countries and of gaining their support on global issues. As China's then Premier Zhao Ziyang reaffirmed at the conference on south–south cooperation in Beijing in April 1983, the Chinese government will unswervingly use its solidarity and cooperation with Third World countries as China's fundamental standing point for its foreign policy (Zhao, 1983, p. 261). The Chinese government highlights this even in the present day.

By maintaining its identity as a developing country, China does not consider itself a 'donor'. China regards its foreign aid as being south–south cooperation and believes that it differs significantly from Western aid or north–south cooperation. This justifies the way that China uses its aid to promote mutual benefit. While assisting other countries, China believes that it is understandable to secure access to natural resources in recipient countries and to support Chinese companies in exploring markets in these countries (Interview with Chinese contractors, Port Moresby, November 2014). China believes that it is appropriate to use Chinese contractors, workers and building materials for its aid projects because it must create employment opportunities for its citizens at home (Interview with Chinese contractors, Port Moresby, November 2014). This explains why Zhu Hong—deputy director-general of the Department of International Trade and Economic Affairs (DITEA) of MOFCOM—highlighted the 'common but differentiated responsibilities' between traditional and emerging donors (MOFCOM, 2011a) when he attended the fourth high-level aid effectiveness forum in Busan in April 2011.

The benefits of identifying as a developing country also explain why— when the international community began to debate whether traditional donors should still provide aid to China—MOFCOM hosted a policy coordination conference for donors and international organisations in December 2004 to quell the debate. MOFCOM's then Assistant Minister Yi Xiaozhun told the conference that although China's economy has been growing fast, the per capita GDP is still low and that China is far from graduating from poverty. He insisted that China still needed full support from the international society and that foreign aid to China would continue to play an irreplaceable role in China's development (Shi, 2004, p. 1).

It should be noted that China's experience of domestic economic development has informed its foreign aid program. For example, Merriden Varrall (2013) argued that this experience has underpinned Chinese elite views of 'what is "developed"', 'how development should be achieved' and 'how should China play a role in international development' (pp. 243–253). From 1978 to 1999, China was preoccupied with its economic development task at home as a developing country. It did not have any incentive to promote trilateral cooperation with traditional donors. Although it continued providing overseas assistance, it was not central to China's foreign policy.

Since 2000: As a Rising Great Power

China's identity as a rising great power has received growing attention from the Chinese government since 2000. China's growing economy paves the way for regaining its lost position as a global great power. As David Lampton argued, China's growing capacity that was built over the past four decades has transformed its global role and has strengthened its power projection—including not only military might, but also other means, such as overseas financing and development assistance (Lampton, 2014, pp. 51–52). Being recognised as a global great power requires not only a growing economy, but also a positive global image to earn respect from other nations. This explains why the Chinese government places an increasing emphasis on global image–building.

Is China using foreign aid provision as a tool to amplify its global image as a responsible leader? If so, we should expect to see China fulfil its moral duty by continuing to deliver foreign aid and by becoming more responsive to the increasing demands for more aid from recipient countries and to the demands from traditional donors and recipients to improve aid delivery in areas such as social responsibility and environmental protection. Evidence indicates that the Chinese government is becoming more conscious of external criticism regarding its foreign aid, whether from recipient countries or from traditional donors. It is aware of traditional donors' demands for more cooperation in development assistance.

The emphasis on moral duty can be traced back to the early years of the PRC. Chairman Mao Zedong (1956, p. 1) said in 1956 that 'China, a country with an area of 9.6 million km^2 and a population of 600 million people, needs to make a fairly big contribution to mankind'. China's leader, Deng Xiaoping, also said in 1979 that:

> Though China faces economic difficulties, we still need to allocate a certain amount of money for foreign aid. When China is fully developed, it needs to allocate a substantial amount of money for foreign aid. China should not forget about this when it is fully developed. (Shi, 1989, p. 70)

President Jiang Zemin stated in 1990s that 'we cannot forget about our poor friends just because our economy is developed, or because our economic development only needs the funds and technologies from the developed countries' (Cui, 2010, p. 6).

Recently, the moral imperative of China's foreign aid was further highlighted with increasing attention being drawn to China's foreign aid and with growing pressure on the Chinese government to increase aid transparency and accountability. After the release of China's second white paper on foreign aid in July 2014, searches for 'China's foreign aid' on Baidu (China's largest search engine) increased by 81 per cent in the first month (Song, 2015, p. 81). Figures 3 and 4 illustrate the rapid growth of international[4] and domestic[5] attention to China's foreign aid.

Since 2000, the Chinese government enacted a series of new concepts intended to mute the 'China threat' discourse and improve China's global image. In September 2005, Chinese President Hu Jintao officially raised the concept of 'building a harmonious world' (*jianshe hexie shijie*) when he addressed the 60th session of the UN. He announced substantial aid measures and pledged that China was willing to collaborate with the international community to promote a twenty-first century that benefits everyone (Hu, 2005, p. 3). MOFCOM Minister Chen Deming highlighted that providing foreign aid and honouring its global obligation is an important way for China to present its image as a responsible great power[6] and make its contribution to building a harmonious world visible (Chen, 2010, p. 44).

4　The key searching words are 'China's aid' OR 'Chinese aid' OR 'China's foreign aid' OR 'China's foreign aid' OR 'China's assistance' OR 'Chinese assistance' OR 'China's foreign assistance' OR 'China's foreign assistance' OR 'Chinese overseas assistance'. All these phrases are typed in one search to maximise searching results.

5　The key searching terms are '中国援助' (*Zhongguo yuanzhu*, China's aid/Chinese aid) OR '中国对外援助' (*Zhongguo duiwai yuanzhu*, China's foreign aid/Chinese foreign aid) OR '中国援外' (*Zhongguo yuanwai*, China's aid overseas/Chinese aid overseas) OR '中国外援' (*Zhongguo waiyuan*, China's aid overseas/Chinese aid overseas). All these phrases are typed in one search to maximise searching results.

6　This point could also be supported by China's rapidly growing humanitarian assistance overseas in recent years.

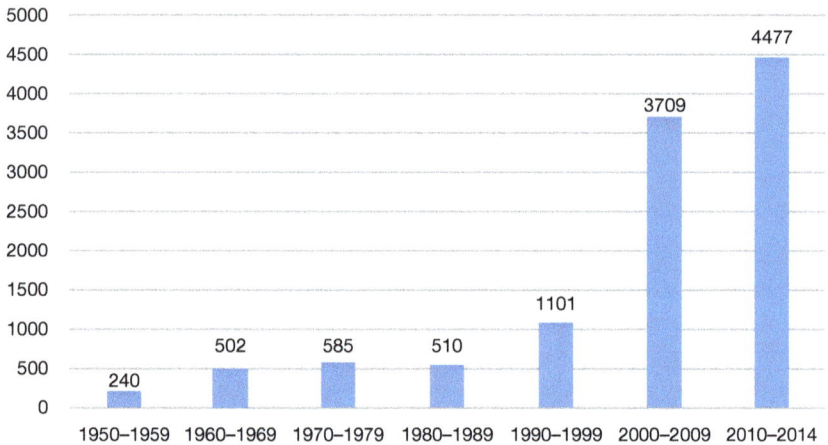

Figure 3. International reports on China's foreign aid

Source. Compiled by the author from the ANU Library ProQuest database.

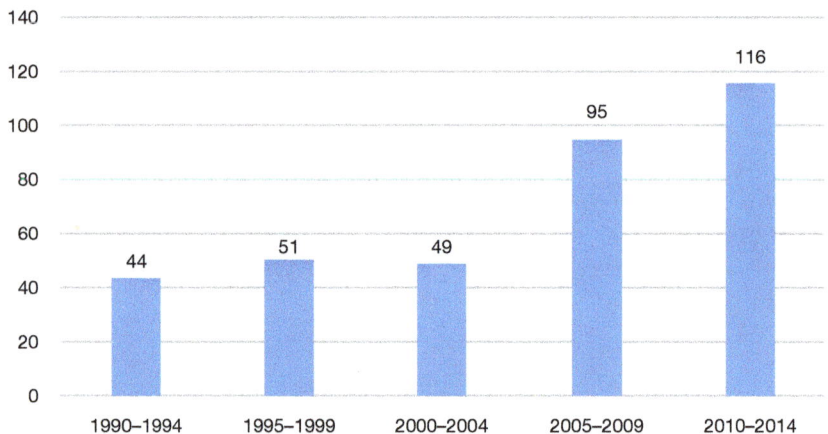

Figure 4. Domestic reports on China's foreign aid

Source. Compiled by the author from the ANU Library People's Daily database.

China released its white paper on peaceful development in September 2011 and promised to follow a path of peaceful, cooperative and common development (State Council, 2011c). A senior official from MOFCOM's Department of Foreign Aid (DFA) explained that the release of China's first white paper on foreign aid in 2011 was to respond to the longstanding concerns of Chinese citizens and the international community regarding China's foreign aid (Zhao & Wang, 2014).

At the central conference on work relating to foreign affairs held in November 2014, China's President Xi Jinping emphasised that China had to perform good work on foreign aid to uphold justice and to pursue shared interests (*hongyi rongli*) (Xinhua, 2014b). In February 2015, President Xi and Premier Li Keqiang attended the conference on the work of economic offices in China's diplomatic missions overseas, which reiterated the importance of upholding the right concepts of justice and interests in China's foreign aid (*zhengque yiliguan*) (Xinhua, 2015d).

At the UN sustainable development summit in September 2015, President Xi stressed that China will continue taking a right approach to justice and interests by prioritising justice over interests (*yili xiangjian, yili weixian*) (MFA, 2015a). He pledged that China would provide an initial contribution of $2 billion[7] to establish a south–south cooperation assistance fund and that China would waive the debt of the outstanding intergovernmental interest-free loans that were due by 2015 and owed by the least developed, landlocked and small-island developing countries (MFA, 2015a). This provides some evidence to suggest that China considers its obligations as a rising great power seriously.

The Chinese government has dedicated greater efforts to improving its image by providing better aid. One example is that China is improving the quality assurance of its foreign aid projects in the 2014 'Measures for the Administration of Foreign Aid', a document that outlines long-term quality assurance and technical support for China's complete aid projects.[8] As MOFCOM Assistant Minister Zhang Xiangchen explained, the emphasis on the quality assurance of China's aid projects is a main feature of China's aid management reform. He stated that 'the work of foreign aid relates to China's image. We cannot tolerate any negligence or project of poor quality' (MOFCOM, 2014b).

To improve its global image, China has even begun softening its position on some of the defining principles of its foreign aid. Deborah Bräutigam provided an example of how China's non-interference policy experienced changes in Darfur. She described how, at first, China refused to support the UN in pressuring the Sudanese government to accept the deployment of UN peacekeepers in Darfur. As the international pressure increased

---

7   An additional $1 billion was committed in May 2017.
8   Complete aid projects refer to those that are conducted by China from designing to completion. Most of them are infrastructure projects.

and campaigns surfaced to boycott the 2008 Beijing Olympic Games in protest of China's role in Darfur, China's position began to change. Chinese President Hu Jintao persuaded Sudan's President Bashar to agree to the UN proposal. China appointed a special envoy to continue the dialogue and later dispatched 300 peacekeepers to join the mission. Bräutigam argued that 'without the threat to the Olympics, Hu Jintao may not have been so keen to ensure that Khartoum "got the message" [China wants Khartoum to accept the deployment of the UN peacekeeping mission]' (Bräutigam, 2009, pp. 281–284).

Interest Calculations and China's Growing Trilateral Aid Cooperation

The change of China's identity focus has informed China's interest calculations and foreign aid policy changes. Since 2000, China's identity as a rising great power is receiving more attention from the Chinese government. This signifies that the Chinese government is seemingly willing to pilot more trilateral cooperation projects to improve its global image as a responsible global power—although, as will be demonstrated, the attitudes of China's aid agencies towards trilateral partnership vary. While continuing to retain its identity as a developing country, China is becoming economically stronger and can afford to sacrifice some short-term economic interests for the benefit of its global image. The remarks of then Chinese President Hu Jintao further evidence that the Chinese government is firm in regard to using foreign aid to serve its national interests, including global image–building. In regard to the relations between commercial and public interests, the market and the government in China's foreign aid, President Hu emphasised, 'The government cannot be held hostage to the market. On the contrary, it should guide the market' (Zhou & Xiong, 2013, p. 28).

The Chinese government considers trilateral aid cooperation a new method of pacifying traditional donors and improving China's global image. It wants to be regarded as a responsible stakeholder who is willing to honour its obligations as an emerging donor in certain areas, including aid coordination. It wants to convey the message that China has no intent to challenge the traditional donors' leadership in the international aid regime or alter the status quo. During meetings at the sideline of the fourth World Trade Organization (WTO) aid for trade global review conference in Geneva in July 2013, MOFCOM Vice Minister Li Jinzao noted that China would continue increasing its foreign aid, but that south–south cooperation would complement north–south cooperation, which remains the main channel of development assistance (MOFCOM, 2013b). Compared to some other areas, foreign aid is a less sensitive area to pilot cooperation between China and traditional donor nations. In the context of China's rise as an emerging donor and the substantial differences between China and traditional donors in its bilateral aid, trilateral aid cooperation, if it proceeds well, can potentially become a new modality for these two types of donor configuration to find common ground in development cooperation. More than that, trilateral aid cooperation will also enrich broader bilateral relations between China and traditional donors. Xu Weizhong, director of the African Research Institute of China Institute of Contemporary International Relations said:

> Trilateral aid cooperation is a new area for emerging donors and developed countries to learn to live with each other. If China and traditional donors such as European countries cannot cooperate on aid issues, how can we expect them to cooperate in other areas that are more sensitive? (Interview, Beijing, 24 August 2015)

Further evidence for this shift came when President Xi announced a generous aid plan at the UN sustainable development summit on 26 September 2015, which triggered a heated debate among Chinese citizens. To counter the negative reactions, the *People's Daily* published a long article two days later that listed five benefits justifying China's overseas assistance:

> History has proven that moral conduct and efforts to safeguard justice will be paid off at the international arena. Regarding China's forgiveness of debts owned by the least developing countries, let's listen to what Xi Jinping has said, 'We need to pay more attention to big gains rather than small gains. Especially we need to pay more attention to political and strategic gains rather than economic and short-term gains'. (Wang, Li & Li, 2015, para. 15)

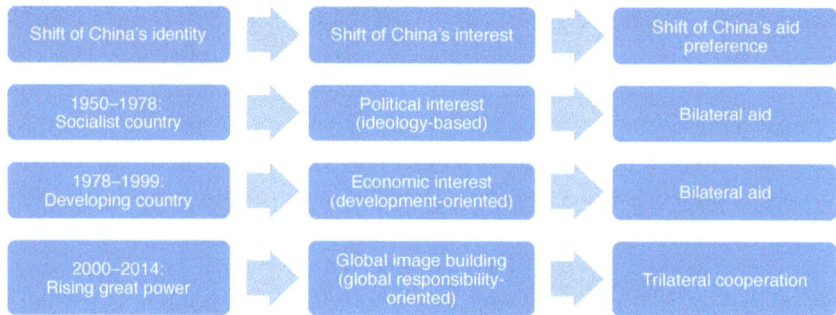

Shift of China's identity		Shift of China's interest		Shift of China's aid preference
1950–1978: Socialist country		Political interest (ideology-based)		Bilateral aid
1978–1999: Developing country		Economic interest (development-oriented)		Bilateral aid
2000–2014: Rising great power		Global image building (global responsibility-oriented)		Trilateral cooperation

Figure 5. China's changing identity, interest calculations and aid modality preferences

Source. Compiled by the author from own analysis.

To summarise, as Figure 5 illustrates, China's shifting focus among its three identities—socialist country, development country and rising great power—has informed its shifting interest calculations and aid modality preferences. Professor Gilbert Rozman from Princeton University argued that 'China's identity has changed more rapidly than that of other states' (Rozman, 2012, p. 95). Although these three identities exist concurrently in China, the focus of China's identity has shifted due to the changes in its domestic and international circumstances. In the first stage of China's foreign aid (1950–1978), China focused on its identity as a socialist country. This drove China to use foreign aid bilaterally to promote the construction of a revolutionary united front against Western capitalist nations. In the second stage (1978–1999), China focused on its identity as a developing country, concentrating on its domestic economic development and reducing its foreign aid. Since 2000, China has focused on its identity as a rising global power and has used foreign aid to promote the building of its global image as a responsible and leading global power. Although bilateral aid continues to dominate Chinese aid program, China pilots trilateral aid cooperation as a new means of benefiting its global image.

It should be noted that a state's identities and interests are always multifaceted and that they cannot simply be reduced to single formulations over a set time (see Shambaugh, 2013). Similarly, the boundaries of China's three identities, as analysed above, are not clear-cut, but blurred; China's emphasis on one particular identity within a specific period does not exclude the presence of the other two. It signifies that this identity is more visible and that it receives more attention from China's policymakers. The other two identities remain, along with their influences and norms. It is equally important to recognise that, internally, China is far from a monolithic entity (see Kelly, 2006, p. 429). For example, China's aid agencies have divergent interests and compete acutely for influence in decision-making, as will be discussed in the next section.

International Engagement

This section will examine the influence of China's growing international engagement—especially with traditional donors and UN agencies—on its conduct of trilateral cooperation. It will discuss whether and how this interaction has contributed to mutual learning and to the mindset changes of Chinese policymakers regarding foreign aid, as well as whether and how this interaction led to China's gradual acceptance of trilateral cooperation as an acceptable aid modality. The analysis will concentrate on five periods within the trajectory of Chinese aid policy evolution (see Figure 6) and it will test the role of engagement and mutual learning in triggering changes. The fifth period will be highlighted because it relates to China's adoption of trilateral aid cooperation.

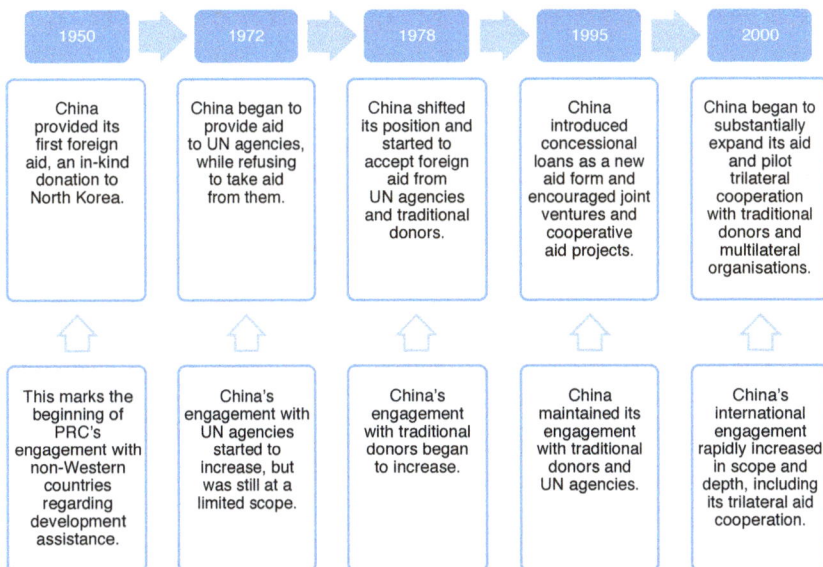

1950	1972	1978	1995	2000
China provided its first foreign aid, an in-kind donation to North Korea.	China began to provide aid to UN agencies, while refusing to take aid from them.	China shifted its position and started to accept foreign aid from UN agencies and traditional donors.	China introduced concessional loans as a new aid form and encouraged joint ventures and cooperative aid projects.	China began to substantially expand its aid and pilot trilateral cooperation with traditional donors and multilateral organisations.
This marks the beginning of PRC's engagement with non-Western countries regarding development assistance.	China's engagement with UN agencies started to increase, but was still at a limited scope.	China's engagement with traditional donors began to increase.	China maintained its engagement with traditional donors and UN agencies.	China's international engagement rapidly increased in scope and depth, including its trilateral aid cooperation.

Figure 6. China's foreign aid evolution and five crucial time points[9]
Source. Compiled by the author from own analysis.

---

9   There are different ways of demarcating China's aid history. For example, former MOFCOM Deputy Minister Fu Ziying divides China's aid history into five periods: 1950s, 1960s–1970s, 1980s, 1990s and 2000s. Professor Zhou Hong from the China Academy of Social Sciences (CASS) merges these into three periods: 1950–1970s, 1980–1990s and 2000s. See Zhou and Xiong (2013).

The focus on the learning process also arises from the Chinese government's own claim that it is a firm supporter of international exchanges and that it has effectively learned from international engagement in development assistance. As China has been exposed to the outside world in diversified areas—including foreign aid—since late 1970s, its learning claim will be tested.

Learning from Non-Western Countries (1950–1971)

The Kuomintang regime did not provide aid in the period from 1928 to 1949, a time of domestic disturbance. The PRC's international engagement on development assistance began as early as 1950, when it provided in-kind donations to the Democratic People's Republic of Korea and marked the beginning of the PRC's foreign aid. China later provided foreign aid to other socialist and developing countries.

At that time, China received aid from the Soviet Union and socialist countries in Eastern Europe (Wu, 2010). China initiated the aid from the Soviet Union to obtain capital, equipment, knowledge and development experience to support industrialisation. China proposed the aid projects, machinery equipment and list of experts to the Soviets (Zhou, 2015, p. 17). In the 1950s, China received around $1.4 billion aid in loans from the Soviet Union for the construction and upgrading of 156 industrial projects in China (Wei, 1992, p. 5).[10] These included military and economic loans, most of which had an annual interest rate of 2 per cent for two to 10 years (Shi, 1989, p. 318).

The process of China learning from the Soviet Union is apparent. In the early 1950s, the Chinese government realised that it had to fully rely on learning from the Soviets to build modern factories in China—including using Soviet design, technologies, machinery and experts—which was a realisation that was put into practice (Shen, 2001, pp. 58–59). Zhou Hong reinforced this point:

---

10 According to Shen Zhihua, China received $300 million aid in loans from the Soviet Union in the early 1950s. The loans had a duration of five years, with an annual interest rate of 1 per cent. They were provided to China in the form of machinery, equipment and materials. One condition for the loans was that China had to supply strategic metals (e.g. tungsten, antimony, lead and tin) to the Soviets. See Shen (2001).

The Soviet Union's planning and management methods were solidified into the systems and mechanisms of China's planned economy … Aid projects [from the Soviet Union] brought not only hard-ware and equipment to China, but also technology, ideas, management methods, behaviours, and a whole set of management system for planning. These factors, together with Soviet aid to China's heavy industrial machinery, continued to influence China's development path and development model between the cessation of Soviet aid and the beginning of aid from the West. (Zhou, 2015, p. 18)

From 1950 to 1971, China's international engagement on foreign aid was restricted to socialist and developing countries because China was isolated by US-led Western nations who recognised the Republic of China (Taiwan) at the UN. In this period, China's foreign aid provision was dominated by ideology, which reflected the broader Cold War context. The objective was to construct beneficial relations with other socialist and developing countries and improve China's political status and national security. However, even during this period, China's foreign aid yielded lessons to support China's own economic development.

China's then Premier Zhou Enlai stressed that providing foreign aid to other countries could spur China into making greater progress in economic and technological development. To Zhou, the wishes of recipient countries forced China to work harder and be more innovative; he urged Chinese aid technicians to learn the latest technologies from other countries, such as desert road-building skills from the United Arab Emirates and Morocco (Xue, 2013, pp. 72–73). Foreign aid also provided an opportunity for testing new technologies. The technology of building light, steel-structured factory buildings was successfully tested in the China-aided construction of the matches and cigarette factory in Guinea, and it was later applied to buildings in southern China (Xue, 2013, p. 73). Similarly, China tested and produced a second-generation diesel locomotive for the Tanzania–Zambia railway, China's largest foreign aid project at the time (Chen, 2011, p. 5).

Limited Engagement with UN Agencies (1972–1978)

China's engagement with UN agencies on foreign aid officially began in 1972. In October 1971, the PRC won China's seat at the UN, including a permanent membership of the UN Security Council from the Republic of China (Taiwan). This paved the way for China's economic and technical cooperation with UN agencies. China established cooperative relations with UN agencies, including the UNDP, UNIDO and the UN Department of Technical Cooperation for Development (Shi, 1989, p. 496). China began attending international conferences on development issues, voicing its official positions and being involved in the policymaking processes of these UN agencies and the review of their financial and administrative work (Shi, 1989, pp. 496–497). In addition, China began providing voluntary donations to UN agencies, which were used to arrange visits, technical training and international conferences in China for other developing countries. From 1972 to 1978, China donated a total of RMB 16.2 million and $400,000 to the UNDP, UNIDO and the UN Capital Development Fund (Shi, 1989, p. 498).[11]

China itself was poor in this period and required foreign assistance. UN agencies were enthusiastic about including China in their aid programs, but they were rebuffed by China. In that ideology-based era, China equated the concept of 'self-reliance' (zili gengsheng)[12] with rejecting external assistance. Even after a 7.8-magnitude earthquake that levelled Tangshan city in 1976 and that claimed 240,000 lives, the Chinese government refuted offers of humanitarian aid from the international community (Han & Ren, 2008, p. 26). In this period, when China was experiencing the final years of the Cultural Revolution, the people remained conservative and the influence of ideology remained strong. Consequently, although the door was open, China's engagement with UN agencies remained limited in scope and restricted to voluntary donations to the UN, conference participation and involvement in some UN activities. China began obtaining fresh knowledge of the UN system, but the potential for

---

11 The donations were made in RMB and US dollars, respectively. Consequently, I did not convert them into the same currency.

12 The Chinese government has been emphasising the concept of 'self-reliance' (zili gengsheng) since the founding of the PRC in 1949. The concept was included in China's official documents, such as the government report of 1964. The Chinese government drew this conclusion from the bitter experience of China's 'century of humiliation' (1840–1949): that the help of foreign countries in nation building was not reliable. In 2018, the Xi Jinping administration re-emphasised this concept of 'self-reliance', as the trade war with the US escalated.

learning was outweighed by ideological considerations, as China refused aid offers from the UN and missed opportunities for further engagement and mutual learning.

Active Engagement with UN Agencies and Traditional Donors (1978–1994)

The year 1978 was a turning point in China's foreign policy. The third plenary session of the 11th CPC central committee in December 1978 elected a new leadership that was led by Deng Xiaoping and that endorsed the reform and opening-up policy. Under the new leadership team, peace and development were endorsed as the two central themes of the era, and domestic economic development was prioritised as the paramount task. Ideology-based policies began to weaken.

The mindset of China's policymakers subsequently changed. They believed that China should use all possible opportunities, including accepting external assistance, to facilitate economic development. China's permanent mission to the UN produced a report in 1970s that recommended China make good use of the UN's $25 billion annual aid budget, including around $5 billion in grants—and this report caught the attention of Chinese high-level officials (Wang, 2001, p. 172). China began adopting a new aid principle—'to take while giving' (*you ji you qu*)—which allowed it to receive foreign aid while providing aid overseas.

Guided by this principle, China opened its doors to UN agencies and traditional donors and began accepting their aid. This marks a significant shift in China's foreign aid policy. In 1978, China began approaching the UNDP for economic and technical assistance for the first time and it received a positive response (Shi, 1989, pp. 498–499). In 1979, China commenced receiving aid from the UNDP and, later on, from other UN agencies, including the UN population fund, UNICEF and UNIDO. From 1979 to 1985, China received $210.8 million in grants from UN agencies (Shi, 1989, p. 500). The country received more external aid than it gave in aid overseas, becoming a net recipient in 1986. Taking the UN system as an example, China donated RMB 29.11 million and $23.41 million[13] in total to UN agencies over the period from 1972 to 1987, while it received over $300 million aid from the UN from 1979 to 1987 (Zhang, 1989, p. 1).

---

13 The donations were made in RMB and US dollars, respectively.

The Chinese government felt more comfortable working with UN agencies on development cooperation, regarding them as politically neutral compared to Western countries.[14] China was also attracted to the UN agencies' advanced technologies, strong fundraising capacity and established information network that could be used to support China's own development. For example, the UN population fund provided high-performance computers that could not be purchased from commercial channels to assist China in conducting its third national census (Wang, 2005, p. 3). China learned many new ideas and concepts, including 'baby-friendly hospitals', 'child-friendly learning environments' and 'happy learning methods' from UN aid (Wang, 2005, p. 3).

While beginning to receive aid from UN agencies, China continued working collaboratively with UN agencies to provide aid to other developing nations. In 1986 alone, China pledged and subsequently undertook 121 technical cooperation projects at a UNIDO conference in New Delhi and at a conference of technical cooperation among developing countries in Beijing (Chen, 1987, p. 3).

Similar to China's growing engagement with UN agencies, the warming of China's foreign relations with the US, Japan and other developed countries facilitated their engagement on development assistance. Along with UN agencies, traditional donors were keen to extend an olive branch to China and commence aid cooperation. Providing aid to China would broaden the agencies, and traditional donors' aid programs and boost their understanding of China. It would also strengthen their bilateral relations with China and facilitate access to the growing economic opportunities of one of the world's fastest-growing economies.

The engagement with Western donors was also rewarding for China, as it desperately needed Western capital, advanced technologies and management skills to fill the gaps. China increased its engagement with traditional donors such as Japan, Australia, West Germany, Canada, Belgium and European Community, and began receiving bilateral aid from these donors after 1979. The total aid amount that was pledged by these six donors to China reached $278 million (RMB 892 million) from 1979 to 1985 (Shi, 1989, p. 549). Aid from traditional donors

---

14　This point was repeatedly highlighted by Chinese officials and scholars during the author's interviews (Beijing, August–September, 2015).

covered areas such as agriculture, forestry and technical training. Similar to the aid from UN agencies, this has been aligned with China's domestic development plans.

In addition to extra financial resources, foreign aid substantially contributed to the transfer of technologies and skills to China. For example, China learned from Canada and improved its research skills in the areas of computerisation, electrical operations, testing and environmental protection in power plants (Shi, 1989, p. 556). In the area of patent promotion, China dispatched 150 technicians to study in West Germany in the early 1980s. With the resulting improved institutional capacity, 4,452 patent applications were processed in the first two years after the patent law was promulgated in China in 1984 (Shi, 1989, p. 557).

These tangible benefits reinforced the perception among China's policymakers that aid from traditional donors and UN agencies could be of great assistance to China's development. For example, the UNDP funded a $1.65 million research project in December 1992 to improve China's planning and macro-economic management capacity. The Chinese government credited this project, as Fang Weizhong, deputy director of the state planning commission stated:

> This project provides an opportunity for China to learn more about the experiences of western countries on developing their market economy. It will be of great assistance to China in developing its market economy, accelerating its concept updating on the planned economy and improving its planning methods. (People's Daily, 1992, p. 2)

On 30 October 1998, the *People's Daily*, China's official newspaper, published an article praising the EU's aid to China as an example of successful cooperation (Zheng, 1998, p. 6). This is another example that demonstrates the Chinese government's increasingly positive view of Western donors, at least of their skills and technologies. According to the report, the EU provided substantial aid to support China's agriculture, especially to the dairy industry. It contributed to the average rapid growth rate of 13.2 per cent of China's dairy production after 1978. The article also acknowledged the EU's contribution to combating AIDS in China— which was the first AIDS program between China and other countries.

International engagement with UN development agencies and traditional donors triggered new ideas from the Chinese government for development cooperation. Sun Guangxiang, director-general of the DFA of the Ministry of Foreign Trade and Economic Cooperation,[15] stated that from 1978, China began exploring new modalities of foreign aid delivery. Among these was the notion that China and recipient countries would jointly contribute funds for China's companies to enact aid projects in recipient countries and that China could work together with international financial organisations or other donors to deliver aid to recipient countries for projects that Chinese companies implemented (Sun, 1993, p. 10). Guangxiang suggested that China should learn from internationally recognised aid norms, common practices and advanced management skills to align with these effective international standards (Sun, 1993, p. 11).

Wang Xitao, director of the academic committee on development assistance from the China Association for International Economic Cooperation[16] proposed in 1988 that China should learn international common practices and effective management experience in aid from UN agencies (Wang, 1988, p. 5). He suggested that China increase multilateral aid cooperation with the UN and international financial organisations and that it conduct aid projects that were funded by these organisations in Third World countries (Wang, 1988, p. 6).

China, traditional donors and UN agencies began exploring trilateral development cooperation as far back as the 1980s. China built a small brick factory in Gambia with the UN capital development fund and a maternity clinic with the UN family planning association (Bräutigam, 2009, pp. 59–60). In November 1987, China, West Germany and the UNDP co-hosted a symposium on foreign aid and cooperation. Delegates from West Germany argued that China could become a partner of development cooperation and a 'transfer station' when West Germany and other traditional donors provided aid to other developing countries (Lin, 1987, p. 20). They suggested that West Germany and China conduct trilateral cooperation with West Germany contributing funds and China providing technicians and technologies—and these suggestions won

---

15   The Ministry of Foreign Trade and Economic Cooperation was the predecessor of MOFCOM.
16   This association was established in Beijing in 1983. It is a nation-wide organisation under the leadership of MOFCOM. The main task is to conduct policy research and exchange regarding China's participation in international economic cooperation. It has acted as a bridge between the Chinese government and enterprises, universities, research institutes and overseas organisations.

support from the Chinese delegates (Lin, 1987, p. 20). This was one of the earliest occasions in which China and traditional donor states discussed trilateral cooperation.

Introducing Concessional Loans (1995–1999)

The year 1995 marked another turning point in China's foreign aid, as China hosted a national conference on foreign aid reform and decided to make two significant adjustments to its foreign aid in October. China would first introduce concessional loans as a new form of aid delivery, which could increase China's foreign aid by combining the government aid budget with bank funds. It could also assist Chinese companies in exporting equipment and building materials for aid projects in recipient countries. Second, China would promote foreign aid projects in the form of joint ventures and cooperative projects. This was to complement its aid budget with finance from companies and deepen the cooperation on project management and technological exchanges between China and recipient countries.

To implement the reform measures, the Export–Import Bank of China (China Exim Bank), the China Development Bank and the Agricultural Development Bank of China were established in 1994 as China's three policy banks. Among them, the China Exim Bank is the only one to manage China's concessional loans, though most of its loans are commercial. The Exim Bank's concessional loan portfolio has grown rapidly. After the first concessional loans framework agreement was signed with Zimbabwe in July 1995,[17] China had signed 56 such agreements with 43 countries by 1998 (Wei, 1999, p. 4), among which 14 agreements were signed with 14 different recipient countries in 1997 alone (International Economic Cooperation, 1998, p. 1).

The overhaul of China's foreign aid in the mid-1990s has roots in domestic policy adjustment and international engagement. China was domestically searching to further deepen its economic reform to overcome the economic stagnation of the early 1990s. In November 1993, the third plenary session of the 14th central committee of the CPC

---

17   For China's concessional loans, the Chinese government will sign a framework agreement with the recipient government. China Exim Bank will then sign an agreement with their counterpart in recipient countries regarding how to use the loans for the aid project.

pledged to develop China's socialist market economy. China's foreign aid was accordingly adjusted to support its economic reform by facilitating Chinese companies to extend overseas.

China was externally influenced by traditional donors to enact foreign aid reform. As MOFCOM Minister Wu Yi stated at the aid reform meeting in 1995, the introduction of concessional loans was to align with common international practice, and China would encourage companies from within itself and recipient countries to play a more significant role in its foreign aid delivery, as well as promote direct interaction and cooperation between these companies (Qi, 1995, p. 5). One reason was because recipient countries were pressured by traditional donors to implement economic liberalisation and privatisation, and they were keen to attract more investment from foreign companies and reduce the debt burden on their governments (Qi, 1995, p. 5). This point was echoed by African delegates at the conference on development in Africa that was held in Tokyo in October 1993 (Wang, 1994, p. 7).

Expanding International Engagement on Development Assistance (2000–2014)

From 2000, China's foreign aid exhibited new features. Its foreign aid has increased substantially and it has experienced an annual increase of 29.4 per cent from 2004 to 2009 (State Council, 2011d, p. 22). The forms of China's foreign aid have also diversified greatly. From 2010 to 2012, concessional loans accounted for more than half of China's total aid. China has increased its aid projects that are related to poverty reduction, human resources training and global issues such as climate change. China dispatched its first teams of youth volunteers and Mandarin-language teachers in 2002 and 2003, respectively (Mao, 2012, p. 90). It established regionally specific initiatives such as the Forum on China–Africa Cooperation (FOCAC) and the China–Arab States cooperation forum.

China's engagement with traditional donors and multilateral development organisations continues, but at a faster pace and with a broader scope. China participated in the high-level aid effectiveness fora in Paris, Accra and Busan. It attended the first and second high-level meetings of the global partnership for effective development cooperation in 2014 and 2016, and the country has been actively involved in the international aid for trade efforts. From 2008, China began providing $200,000 annually to support the WTO aid for trade initiative and doubled the volume since 2011 (State Council, 2014, p. 22). Since 2008, China has also actively involved itself in working group discussions on development in the Heiligendamm process, joining G8 members and major emerging economies to examine issues such as aid effectiveness, aid to Africa and trilateral aid cooperation (MOFCOM 2009b).

The growing interest in engagement also arises from traditional donors. Their purposes include gaining a better understanding of China's foreign aid, seeking opportunities for cooperation and influencing Chinese aid practice. A researcher from CAITEC, the think tank involved in developing Chinese aid policies, echoes this point:

> The international community did not pay much attention to China's foreign aid before 2006. We [CAITEC] had almost no exchanges with foreign countries at that time. The 2006 Summit of the Forum of China–Africa Cooperation had a tremendous influence. After that, the governments and research institutes of foreign countries began to approach us to learn about China's foreign aid. Later, some Western scholars put up suggestions to strengthen exchanges and cooperation with China on foreign aid. They used many terms including 'engage China'. These Western scholars realised that criticising China [for its aid practice] could not solve the problem. Therefore, they suggested traditional donors conduct trilateral aid cooperation with China to promote mutual understanding. (Interview, Beijing, 4 August 2015)

Attitude towards Learning

China has recently demonstrated a more eager attitude towards aid reform and learning. Shen Danyang—then deputy director of CAITEC and later director-general of MOFCOM's Department of Policy Research—highlighted in 2005 that China must strengthen its research on ODA. He argued that while maintaining its principles of foreign aid, China must emphasise learning effective aid practices from other donors more—and that it is an urgent task for China to establish innovative aid concepts and strategies and conduct aid reforms by learning from other donors (Shen, 2005, p. 32). To Shen, it could even be an option for China to join the Paris Club—a group of OECD DAC member nations who are traditional donors—in the future, and China should be more open to development cooperation with other donors (Shen, 2005, p. 32). By examining China's growing role in the global governance of food security, Professor Katherine Morton argued that China has greatly emphasised the 'learning by doing' process (Morton, 2012).

China's engagement with UN agencies is an example of its cognitive learning and of the mindset changes. Professor Zhang Qingmin, chair of the Department of Diplomacy at Peking University, argued that by participating in multilateral diplomacy—including with the UN—China's attitude towards the international system has changed from high levels of suspicion, through gradual acceptance, to active participation (Zhang, 2006, p. 58). To him, the change of ideas occurs because Chinese leaders have begun regarding international relations as mutually beneficial rather than viewing them merely through a security or a strategic prism (Zhang, 2006, pp. 58–59). More importantly, ideational change is attributable to the adaptation and learning process that are provided by China's participation in the global system (Zhang, 2006, p. 59). Ideational change has been an incremental rather than sudden process (Carstensen, 2011).

At the national conference on work relating to foreign aid in August 2010, Chinese Premier Wen Jiabao emphasised that based on consolidating China's traditional foreign aid methods, China should actively promote the innovation of its foreign aid methods, build a more dynamic, efficient and open foreign aid system, and strengthen engagement and cooperation in an active and prudent spirit with the international community regarding aid issues (People's Daily, 2010, p. 1). Remarks made by MOFCOM Deputy Minister Yi Xiaozhun at the high-level segment development cooperation forum of the UN Economic and Social Council in New York in June 2010 offered insights into the psyche of China's aid decision-makers regarding the role of development cooperation. This insight can also apply to China's desire to learn from traditional donors in trilateral partnership. This rhetoric has also been supported by China's growing engagement with traditional donor states and organisations, such as the OECD, in recent years.

> China is a beneficiary of international development cooperation … China's own development experience shows that international cooperation, effective utilization of resources and international best practices will help developing countries to accelerate the development process … Here are some examples. In the 1980s, with UNICEF's support, China developed the 'cold chain' system for the Expanded Program of Immunization and met the target of 85 per cent child immunization coverage ahead of schedule; since the 1990s, China has cooperated with UNDP on microcredit schemes in 17 provinces, cities and autonomous regions covering one million poor people … Clearly, China's efforts in reform and

opening-up were greatly facilitated by international development cooperation, without which its pursuit of poverty alleviation would not have been possible. (Yi, 2010, paras 3–5)

At the press release of China's first white paper on foreign aid in July 2011, Vice Minister Fu Ziying of MOFCOM stressed that China's foreign aid is open to change, reform and innovation. He claimed this was an important reason for the success of China's foreign aid in the past six decades (State Council, 2011b). In November 2014, MOFCOM issued 'Measures for the Administration of Foreign Aid', the first comprehensive regulation on China's foreign aid management. This document states that China will create a medium- to long-term aid plan, establish the reserve of aid projects and generate country-based aid plans (MOFCOM, 2014a). A Chinese aid official explained that 'these new measures originated from China's learning from traditional donors' (Interview, Beijing, 4 August 2015).

At the subsequent media briefing that was hosted by MOFCOM in December 2014, Wang Shengwen, director-general of MOFCOM's DFA, stressed that China is learning from other donor countries to improve its foreign aid delivery and that it is paying more attention to the needs of recipient countries (MOFCOM, 2014b). For example, China is increasing its number of aid projects to improve people's livelihood and human resources training, which supports regional interconnection and communication and strengthens environmental protection (MOFCOM, 2014b). Yu Zirong, deputy director-general of the same department, highlighted that aid evaluation remains a weak link in China's foreign aid management, as China traditionally emphasises project implementation; he also considered Western donors' aid practices useful references for China (MOFCOM, 2014b). This could be one major area for reform in the near future.[18]

There is evidence to suggest that mutual learning has been an important factor in China's growing engagement with traditional donors. As a Chinese aid official commented:

> When we do research on China's foreign aid, we will check how traditional donors deliver their foreign aid and make policy recommendations referring to some foreign aid projects conducted by the Western donors in China. In terms of China's trilateral aid cooperation, we are also learning how other donors such as

---

18   This point was repeatedly mentioned by Chinese aid officials and scholars during the author's interviews (Beijing, August–September 2015).

Germany, Japan and Brazil are doing their trilateral projects. So, this is a process of mutual influence. Though China's [fundamental] aid policies are hard to change because of China's emphasis on South-South cooperation, we can still learn from each other on many specific aid practices. In areas where we believe the Western countries are doing better, we will absorb their good practices. China has kept on learning some specific aid practices from the West at the micro-level. For instance, we learned from Western countries to combine foreign aid with trade and investment. The aid from Japan and many European countries to China was mixed with their economic activities. (Interview, Beijing, 4 August 2015)

Learning by Doing in Controversial Areas

The learning process has reached into divisive issues in which China is facing criticism. An example concerns the environmental standards in China's overseas projects, which were high on the list of the US's and Japan's objections to the establishment of the China-sponsored AIIB. In February 2013, China promulgated the 'Guidelines for Environmental Protection in Overseas Investment and Cooperation', China's first specialised guideline on environmental protection for overseas projects. Bie Tao, deputy director-general from China's Ministry of Environmental Protection, explained that China encourages its companies to research and learn the principles, standards and common practices of environmental protection from international organisations and multilateral financial institutions such as the UN and OECD agencies (MOFCOM, 2013c).

Debt relief is another example. In 2000, China began to write off debts for heavily indebted and least developed countries, which was the first time that China had forgiven debts based on initiatives from international development organisations and that it had used a country list that was drafted by Western organisations (Wang, 2009, p. 42). Chinese leaders made similar efforts at high-profile international events, including debt relief measures that were announced by Xi Jinping at the 2015 UN development summit.

The Chinese government is also softening its position on aid coordination— another sign of its gradual integration with the international community due to learning and its desire for image building. Not being a member of the OECD DAC, China refused to adopt the Paris Declaration on aid effectiveness and some regional aid effectiveness agreements, including the Cairns Compact in the Pacific. However, it became a signatory to other agreements on aid effectiveness that were initiated by developing nations. China signed the Vientiane Declaration on aid effectiveness in 2006 and the Kavieng Declaration on aid effectiveness in 2008, which are local versions of the Paris Declaration in Laos and PNG. China and seven traditional donors signed the Kavieng Declaration that pledged to:

> Conduct more and make greater use of joint missions and analytical work … rationalise their systems and procedures by implementing common arrangements for planning, design, implementation, monitoring and evaluation … make full use of respective comparative advantage at sector level by aligning support and deciding, where appropriate, which development partner will lead the co-ordination of programs, activities and tasks … enhance the predictability of future aid through joint decision making processes with the GoPNG. (PNG Department of National Planning and Monitoring, 2008, pp. 5–6)

This demonstrates that China is revealing more readiness to engage and coordinate with traditional donors on aid delivery in selected countries such as PNG.

Learning from the OECD

The OECD has become another source of learning of aid knowledge and skills. China has increased its efforts to engage with the OECD in recent years. The China–DAC study group was established in 2009, with the aim of promoting knowledge sharing and experience exchanges between China and the OECD, as well as the aim of introducing China's development experience to Africa (OECD, 2011). China participated in DAC high-level meetings, the OECD global forum on development and the OECD–WTO's work on tracking aid for trade.

China is increasingly involved in the substantive work of the OECD's specialised committees. In November 2013, the OECD and MOFCOM co-hosted a symposium on cooperation that was attended by 26 Chinese ministries, 18 OECD member states and the EU (OECD, 2014, p. 4). China stated that it valued the mutual learning process between China and the OECD in facilitating China's development. As Wang Shouwen, assistant minister of MOFCOM, stated, 'It's [the OECD's] research results, along with the experiences of its member countries, [that] provide valuable references for China in deepening reform, further opening up and participating in global economic governance' (OECD, 2014, p. 4).

Growing Trilateral Aid Cooperation

In recognition of China's growing economic strength, traditional donors began reducing their aid to China. Japan was comfortably the largest donor to China. From 1979 to 2004, cumulative aid from Japan to China exceeded 3.3 trillion Yen (RMB 164.9 billion in contract value), which accounted for more than 60 per cent of the total external aid to China (Pei, 2004, p. 1). From 2001 to 2004, the annual reduction of Japan's aid to China exceeded 20 per cent (Pei, 2004, p. 1). The World Food Programme had ceased its food assistance to China by the end of 2005. Traditional donors have also shifted their aid to China from providing hardware aid to soft areas, such as training for Chinese staff, providing consultancy, targeting sectors such as poverty reduction, environmental conservation, public health and governance.

Although reducing their aid to China, traditional donors and multilateral development organisations have growing interests in inviting China to jointly provide aid to other developing countries. To them, China is no longer in need of external aid, as it has achieved remarkable economic development over the past three decades, and it has become a major emerging donor with a different modality. It thus becomes imperative for traditional donors and multilateral development organisations to promote coordination and cooperation with China through trilateral cooperation. Traditional donors expect that increased coordination and cooperation will facilitate their understanding of China's foreign aid, as well as leverage and influence China's foreign aid delivery (Interviews, Beijing, 29 July, 4 and 26 August 2015). As an OECD report highlighted:

> How to engage with China in a manner that contributes to the international aid effectiveness agenda and the achievement of the Millennium Development Goals has been an issue of great concern for DAC donors. (OECD, 2012b, p. 4)

Strengthening cooperation with traditional donors and multilateral development organisations is also attractive to China. As China has substantially expanded its foreign aid in recent years, the desire to learn useful aid policies and practices from traditional donors has grown even stronger. A former senior Chinese aid official explained that 'China wants to learn from traditional donors in areas including aid procedures, feasibility study, evaluation and monitoring. China is weak in these aspects' (Interview, Beijing, 1 September 2015). Consequently, China, traditional donors and multilateral development organisations have improved their engagement in exploring trilateral cooperation as an innovative method of partnership.

In 2005, the China Institutes of Contemporary International Relations (CICIR) and the US–China Relations Council co-hosted the China–US aid workshop in Beijing—the first of its kind in China. Officials and experts from the two countries, as well as other traditional donors, proposed ideas for aid cooperation (Glosny, 2006). In July 2013, MOFCOM's Vice Minister Li Jinzao met with DAC Chair Erik Solheim and responded positively to the OECD's call for development cooperation in Africa. Li suggested that the two sides choose an African country who had an interest in trilateral aid cooperation to initiate such a plan and that they gradually expand it later on (MOFCOM, 2013b).

The diversified engagement has boosted China's understanding of traditional aid and has led to the change of ideas regarding external aid and cooperation in the mindset of Chinese policymakers. To these policymakers, engagement and cooperation with donors and organisations in trilateral cooperation is attractive to China. Therefore, the Chinese government has agreed to pilot trilateral aid cooperation.

Domestic Institutions

The first two sections of this chapter have explained China's calculations of interests and its growing international engagement in development cooperation. However, this kind of external interaction is filtered through a complicated domestic process that involves a cluster of China's aid agencies before it can wield influence on China's foreign aid. This section will explore four aspects of this domestic process: China's aid management structure; the decision-making procedure of China's foreign aid; two channels to influence Chinese officials' perceptions of aid; and the diversified positions of China's aid agencies on trilateral cooperation.

China's Aid Management Structure

A clear understanding of the identities and interests of China's main aid agencies will be the basis for exploring these agencies' attitudes towards trilateral aid cooperation. It should be noted that the following discussions in this chapter will examine China's aid management system prior to the establishment of the China International Development Cooperation Agency (CIDCA) in April 2018, which will be discussed in Chapter 7 as a new development. Three reasons suffice. First, China's pilot trilateral aid projects were conducted under the old aid system. Second, the main players in the old aid system will continue playing highly significant roles in Chinese aid management, even though CIDCA was created. Third, as CIDCA is new, its influence on Chinese aid management is yet to be observed.

China did not have a single aid agency until April 2018. Instead, it established an inter-agency liaison mechanism in October 2008 that was upgraded to a coordination mechanism in 2011. Members meet regularly to discuss aid-related issues and to coordinate aid policies. This coordination mechanism on foreign aid consists of over 40 agencies that are chaired by the MOFCOM (chair), MFA (deputy chair) and MoF (deputy chair) as the three core players. The three ministries and the China Exim Bank play the most important roles in China's foreign aid. China's state-owned enterprises (SOEs) enjoy much influence in this process as project contractors. In addition to the coordination mechanism, China has held nine national conferences on foreign aid work that were attended by Chinese premiers or vice premiers.

I use the variables of 'personnel' and 'interest-based alliance propensity' to illustrate approximately how different aid agencies wield influence on China's foreign aid (see Table 5). 'Personnel' refers to the power of the aid agencies in China's domestic politics and their human resource capacity to manage aid. 'Interest' refers to material benefits. The 'interest-based alliance propensity' refers to the tendency of aid agencies to form alliances that are based on their respective material interests.

Table 5. Interest-based alliance propensity of Chinese aid agencies

Interest-based alliance propensity Personnel	Weak	Strong
Weak	MoF Other ministries	SOEs China Exim Bank
Strong	MFA	MOFCOM

Source. Compiled by the author from own analysis.

MOFCOM

MOFCOM is tasked with managing China's foreign aid and thus plays the most important role. Other line ministries are required to support MOFCOM in delivering aid. MOFCOM's DFA is the organisation responsible for managing Chinese foreign aid, including drafting China's foreign aid policies, aid regulations[19] and aid plans (including the annual plan) and approving and managing aid projects (Zhang & Smith, 2017, p. 2332). The department has a team of around 70 staff, making it the largest concentration of aid technocrats relative to other aid agencies in China.[20]

In combining the number of staff from this department and the three executing aid agencies that are affiliated to MOFCOM—including from the Executive Bureau of International Economic Cooperation (96 staff), the China International Centre for Economic and Technical Exchanges (140 staff) and the Academy for International Business Officials (over 200 staff)—the total number of MOFCOM aid officials is around 500.[21] However, excluding support staff, the number of foreign aid officials in China is between 200 and 300.[22] This is in stark contrast to the 1,652 employees of the Australian aid program in the financial year of 2012–2013 and the 3,797 employees of the US aid program in 2015 (excluding an even larger number of their local employees in recipient countries) (Australian Public Service Commission, 2013, p. 253; USAID, 2015a, p. 4).

Additionally, there is one division within MOFCOM's DITEA that traditionally focuses on inbound grant aid that is provided to China by traditional donors and UN agencies. With experience that has been gleaned from over more than three decades of dealing with traditional donors and UN agencies, this department is also involved in China's foreign aid.

---

19 China does not have a comprehensive law outlining its foreign aid regulations. Its foreign aid is mainly governed by a handful of regulations that are drafted by MOFCOM. Important regulations include *Measures for the Administration of Foreign Aid (trial)* in 2014; *Measures for the Administration of Complete Foreign Aid Projects (trial)* in 2008; *Measures for Accreditation of Qualifications of the Enterprises Undertaking Foreign Aid Projects* in 2015; and eight regulations covering areas such as the inspection, construction management and project design of complete projects.
20 This figure originates from the author's interviews. It also matches the figure that Zhou Hong and Xiong Hou provide. According to them, in 1998, MOFCOM's Department of Foreign Aid had 64 staff (Zhou & Xiong, 2013, p. 29).
21 Figures from the websites of these agencies (MOFCOM, 2011b, 2011c, 2011d).
22 Based on author's interviews (Beijing, August 2015). It also matches the finding of Song Wei from CAITEC. See Song (2015).

MOFCOM is also the point of contact (*guikou danwei*) designated by the Chinese government to liaise with traditional donors and UN development agencies on their aid to China.[23] In terms of providing bilateral aid in grants to China or of conducting trilateral aid cooperation with China in a Third World country, traditional donors and UN agencies must go through MOFCOM regardless of their inclination to do so. Once approved by MOFCOM, they can continue with contacting other line ministries in China.

In terms of MOFCOM's domestic influence, it plays a prominent role in Chinese politics. As economic development has been regarded as the top priority of the Chinese government, MOFCOM naturally enjoys high political status, and many MOFCOM ministers have been promoted to high positions as state leaders. This can have a decisive influence when controversial issues surface, including whether MOFCOM or the MFA should assume control of China's foreign aid. Table 6 presents a brief comparison of the political promotions of former ministers from MOFCOM, the MFA and the MoF that testifies to the status of these ministries in China's political system.[24]

Table 6. Status of three ministries in China's political system

	Number of ministers	Number of ministers becoming state leaders
MOFCOM	8 (1982–2013)	4 (Deputy Chair of National People's Congress: 1; Vice Premier: 2; member of Chinese Communist Party Politburo: 1)
MFA	5 (1982–2013)	4 (Vice Premier: 2; State Councillor: 2)
MoF	5 (1980–2013)	1 (Deputy Chair of National People's Congress)

Source. Compiled by the author from online data.

---

23   The responsible agency for the World Bank and Asian Development Bank is China's MoF. Similar matching relations are China's Ministry of Agriculture with the Food and Agriculture Organization, and the World Food Programme and the People's Bank of China with the International Monetary Fund.

24   There are several vice premiers in the Chinese government. The positions held by former MOFCOM ministers in the graph are ranked more highly than those held by former MFA ministers. For example, former MOFCOM Minister Li Lanqing and his successor, Wu Yi, were the highest-ranked vice premiers in the State Council. Li was also a member of the standing committee of the politburo, the core decision-making organ in China.

Economic and Commercial Counsellor's Offices

Unlike China's other aid agencies, MOFCOM enjoys the privilege of sending its staff to the economic and commercial counsellor's offices in almost all of China's diplomatic missions overseas, including embassies and consulates. Due to the shortage of staff in MOFCOM, it is common for MOFCOM to select commercial officials from the provincial and city level to staff some economic and commercial counsellor's office— particularly smaller and more remote postings, such as those in the South Pacific.

One duty of these offices is to take care of aid projects on behalf of MOFCOM in China's diplomatic missions, though aid is not a priority in the department's daily work compared to trade and investment. These offices have the advantage of obtaining firsthand information on Chinese aid projects in the field and of reporting to MOFCOM promptly, which offers MOFCOM the advantage of access to information that it may or may not choose to share with the MFA or the MoF. Economic and commercial counsellor's offices will represent MOFCOM and the Chinese government in liaising with recipient governments, receiving aid proposals from them and reporting back to MOFCOM. They are involved in the negotiations between China and recipient governments and they supervise the implementation of Chinese aid projects.

However, due to the lack of aid expertise, officials from the economic and commercial counsellor's offices are mainly involved from the political perspective as representatives of MOFCOM, but not from the technical perspective (Zhang & Smith, 2017, p. 2333). Technical experts appointed by Chinese contractors oversee the technical issues for each aid project (Zhang & Smith, 2017, p. 2333). Although the economic and commercial counsellor's offices can offer advice on aid projects, they are constrained by MOFCOM's policy instructions. They are executing agents rather than decision-makers in essence.

Executing Aid Agencies

MOFCOM has three affiliations as implementation arms of Chinese aid projects. The Executive Bureau of International Economic Cooperation was created in 2003. Once MOFCOM's DFA has completed the internal procedures to approve the proposed aid project (both complete projects and technical cooperation projects), it is then passed to this bureau to manage the implementation—including the designing of the project, signing of the implementation agreement/contract with the recipient country, performing of the pre-qualification of Chinese bidding contractors,[25] overseeing of the bidding process, signing of the internal contract with Chinese companies, monitoring of the project management, performing of the project acceptance after completion and passing of it to the recipient country (MOFCOM, 2016).[26]

The China International Center for Economic and Technical Exchanges (CICETE) and the Academy for International Business Officials (AIBO)—which were established in 1983 and 1980 respectively—as two more executing agencies were tasked by MOFCOM in 2008 to manage foreign aid. CICETE was tasked with managing China's in-kind donations, including the bidding arrangements and project management after MOFCOM's DFA had conducted internal checks on a given project. Similarly, AIBO implements China's aid training, including organising, managing and evaluating the training after MOFCOM's DFA has completed internal procedures to approve the projects.

MOFCOM's Relations with Chinese Companies

As MOFCOM is the statutory body on economic development and the caretaker of Chinese companies overseas, the consideration of economic interests plays a prominent role when MOFCOM makes decisions on foreign aid. China adopted the 'go global strategy' (*zouchuqu zhanlue*) in October 2000 and encouraged its companies to explore economic and trade opportunities in overseas markets (China Council for the Promotion of International Trade, 2007). Guided by the principles of mutual benefit in providing foreign aid and this 'go global strategy', MOFCOM has been actively assisting Chinese companies to travel overseas and deliver foreign aid, to explore overseas markets for Chinese products and to satisfy the resource needs of China's fast-growing economy. In contrast to the MFA or MoF, it is easier for MOFCOM to form alliances with Chinese companies in circumstances in which a conflict between economics, diplomacy and global image arises (Zhang & Smith, 2017, p. 2334).

---

25 Bidding can take the form of open or negotiated bids. Negotiated bidding is used in circumstances such as when the aid project is urgent, when there are fewer than three qualified bidding companies or when the potential contractors have to be appointed due to patent or other reasons.

26 Please also note that the Executive Bureau of International Economic Cooperation has recently been renamed as the Agency for International Economic Cooperation in English.

The MFA

The MFA is the statutory body of China's foreign relations with other countries. Its overarching task is to construct positive external relations and to create a favourable environment for China's domestic development and stability. Foreign aid has been used as a diplomatic tool for such purposes and has served as an integral part of China's diplomacy.

Central to understanding the MFA's role is the term *zhengzhi* (politics) in China's foreign policy, including economic diplomacy and foreign aid policy. Chinese leadership and official documents consistently highlight three terms: *jiang zhengzhi* (talk politics), *zhengjing jiehe* (combine politics and economics) and *yijing cuzheng* (use economics to promote politics) (Zhang & Smith, 2017). For example, China's then Premier Wen Jiabao said at the national conference relating to central economic and diplomatic work towards developing countries in 2004 that 'China … needs to be good at combining economic and political work, and using economic work to promote the political relations between China and other countries' (Gong, 2004, p. 2).

China's diplomacy always emphasises the political relations between China and other countries. From the MFA's perspective, the importance of political relations prevails over the importance of short-term economic gains because, in China's philosophy, it is not possible to develop beneficial economic relations without the establishment of excellent political relations. This explains why when economic and political interests are in conflict, the Chinese government chooses to safeguard long-term political interests at the expense of short-term economic gain in some circumstances. To the Chinese government, if the loss of an economic benefit leads to the improvement of political interests, this will create more economic opportunities for China in the future: a loss in the short term signifies a profit in the long run.

This explains why the Chinese government has kept focusing on the importance of 'talking politics', as well as why it has instructed Chinese aid agencies to implement China's foreign aid projects 'from the height of talking about politics', 'combining the strengths of political relations and economic benefits' and 'using economic benefits to promote better political relations' between China and recipient countries (Zhang & Smith, 2017). An example of the MFA's role in China's foreign aid is that the MFA minister co-chairs the Chinese follow-up committee of

FOCAC with his or her counterpart in MOFCOM. The secretariat of the committee is located in the MFA's Department of African Affairs, with the director-general of this department acting as the secretary-general (MFA, 2013).

As a generalisation, the MFA strongly supports providing foreign aid because this will help enhance China's diplomatic relations with other countries and ease life for the MFA. It values China's diplomatic and strategic interests above short-term economic interests. Bilateral relations between China and recipient countries play an important role in China's foreign aid provision. It is the precondition that the recipient country must enjoy beneficial relations with China and fully support the 'one China' policy before China provides a single *fen* of aid to this country, though exceptions exist in circumstances including humanitarian disasters. Foreign aid in turn will be used by China to improve relations with recipient countries.

Ambassadors and the Economic and Commercial Counsellor's Office

Compared with the economic and commercial counsellor's office, Chinese ambassadors exert influences in China's foreign aid in different ways. In regions such as the Pacific (where the Taiwan issue is still in play) in which small island nations occasionally sway their diplomatic recognition between China and Taiwan, each Chinese ambassador controls a small amount of discretionary funds (around $50,000) that is used for some small aid projects (Smith et al., 2014, p. 10). Moreover, in small nations, the economic and commercial counsellor's office is part of the embassy.[27] Foreign aid reports that the economic and commercial counsellor's office prepared are subject to the approval of the ambassador before they are sent to MOFCOM and the MFA through the embassy (Zhang & Smith, 2017).

In terms of proposing aid projects, there could be divisions between the ambassador and the economic and commercial counsellor's office. The ambassador, in most cases a career diplomat from the MFA, represents the MFA's interests and emphasises China's diplomatic interests in determining aid spending more. In contrast, the economic

---

27   In countries such as PNG, the economic and commercial counsellor's office is separate from the embassy.

and commercial counsellor's office is a branch of MOFCOM and it is inclined to offer more considerations to China's economic interests when the country creates aid proposals. For the sake of diplomacy, the ambassador sometimes suggests new aid projects directly to MOFCOM. However, the amount of influence that the ambassador wields over the aid projects that were provided to his or her country is debatable, as the final say is delivered by MOFCOM. It is fair to state that the economic and commercial counsellor's office has a more direct influence than the ambassador on aid in the country.

Why Does MOFCOM Oversee China's Foreign Aid?

Some background information will help frame the question. As mentioned earlier, China's foreign aid began as early as the 1950s, when China provided aid—mostly in the form of in-kind donations that were supplemented by occasional money transfers—to other socialist and developing countries, such as North Korea and Vietnam. China's Ministry of Foreign Trade, established in August 1952 (the predecessor of MOFCOM),[28] was tasked with managing China's foreign aid by instructing its subordinate export and import companies to purchase the materials and then provide them to the recipient countries. Since then, MOFCOM and its predecessors have remained the custodians of China's foreign aid.

Some Chinese officials and aid scholars have long questioned MOFCOM's leadership of Chinese aid program, suggesting that the MFA should assume control, as foreign aid is closely linked to China's foreign policy and the Taiwan issue is central to the Chinese foreign aid program (Interviews, Beijing, 30 August, 1 September 2015). To these officials, MOFCOM's focus on seeking economic gains and promoting the interests of Chinese companies could negatively affect China's management of foreign aid, whose purpose is to support China's strategic and diplomatic interests.

---

28   China's ministry in charge of foreign aid has experienced several restructures. In 1949, China's Ministry of Trade was established and was soon renamed the Ministry of Foreign Trade in 1952. In 1961, a new agency was created to manage aid: the General Bureau for Economic Relations with Foreign Countries. It was upgraded to the Commission for Economic Relations with Foreign Countries in 1964, and then upgraded again in 1970 to become the Ministry of Foreign Economic Liaison. In 1982, the Ministry of Foreign Trade, the Ministry of Foreign Economic Liaison, the State Import Export Regulation Commission and the State Foreign Investment Regulation Commission merged into the Ministry of Foreign Economic Relations and Trade, which was renamed in 1993 to the Ministry of Foreign Trade and Economic Cooperation. Since 2003, it finally became the Ministry of Commerce.

For example, Yan Xuetong from Tsinghua University has called on the Chinese government to consider whether Chinese foreign policy should continue to be economically centred, questioning:

> Should China's rise serve the goal of increasing its economic benefits or improving its global image? My personal answer is clear. The latter goal is more urgent than the former. (Yan, 2006, p. 14)

The State Council had occasionally been called on to deliberate this question, but it decided in favour of MOFCOM until the establishment of China's new aid agency.

The MoF

The MoF is responsible for drafting and managing China's budget. Being the keeper of purse strings, the MoF will review and approve the aid plan that is MOFCOM drafts and integrate it to China's annual national budget. After approval, the MoF will allocate aid funding to be disbursed by MOFCOM and other line ministries. This is also a process of budget monitoring. The gap between the commercial and concessional interest rate of the concessional loans that the China Exim Bank provide is included in the annual aid budget overseen by the MoF.

The MoF also manages China's multilateral aid, including donations to the World Bank and UN agencies. In terms of bureaucratic interests, the MoF's role in China's foreign aid is relatively neutral compared to MOFCOM and the MFA. In addition, the MoF is concerned with the bilateral loans from traditional donors and loans from multilateral agencies to China.[29] The MoF's Department of International Economic and Financial Cooperation is tasked with managing these loans, including from the World Bank, the ADB, the International Fund for Agricultural Development and the European Investment Bank. Some grants mixed with loans projects in China are also within the MoF's purview. The MoF also manages grant aid from the global environmental facility to China (Ministry of Finance (China), 2016).[30]

---

29   MOFCOM previously managed bilateral loans from traditional donors in China.

30   The MoF's Department of International Economic and Financial Cooperation was established in 2014 by merging the original Department of Finance (managing bilateral loans coming in to China) and the Department of International Cooperation (managing loans received from multilateral organisations).

China Exim Bank

The China Exim Bank—its concessional loan department, to be specific—is responsible for China's expanding concessional loan portfolio. At the policy level, it is still subject to the supervision of MOFCOM. As discussed above, it was created in 1994 to manage China's concessional loans, which have increased tremendously in recent years, exceeding the 30 per cent growth rate annually since 2005 (China Exim Bank, 2014, p. 10). The loans have facilitated Chinese companies moving overseas. The China Exim Bank consequently enjoys an important status in the politics of Chinese aid.

Another reason for the importance of the China Exim Bank is that, in addition to providing concessional loans, it also provides preferential buyer's credit to support economic and trade cooperation between China and other developing countries. This kind of credit is not counted as China's foreign aid.

Concessional loans target large infrastructure projects and involve large amounts of aid money. They are implemented by Chinese companies, typically powerful SOEs. With support from the China Exim Bank, several of China's companies—such as the China Road and Bridge Corporation, China Harbour Engineering Company, Sinohydro Corporation, Shanghai Construction Group and Gezhouba Group—have rapidly expanded their overseas operations (China Exim Bank, 2014, p. 11). The China Exim Bank has supported nearly 1,700 'going out' projects that were conducted by Chinese companies. The contract value of these projects accounted for more than 20 per cent of China's foreign direct investment and its overseas project contract value combined (Jin, 2014). Therefore, the tendency to form alliances between the China Exim Bank and China's SOEs is high. Because of their shared interest in safeguarding the economic interests of Chinese companies, the China Exim Bank and MOFCOM have also a high propensity for interest alliance. Lucy Corkin argued that although the MFA regards China's concessional loans in Africa as a diplomatic tool, MOFCOM 'sees them as principally a market-entry tool for Chinese companies' goods and services' (Corkin, 2011, p. 73).

Other Line Ministries

China's other line ministries—such as the Ministry of Agriculture, National Health Commission, Ministry of Education, Ministry of Science and Technology and Ministry of Civil Affairs—are also involved in providing foreign aid. They compete for a share of the growing foreign aid budget. Their mandate is to provide foreign aid within their specialised areas. For example, the Ministry of Agriculture provides agricultural support overseas, sending agricultural technicians to almost every developing country that recognises the PRC. These teams are often in the field in unstable regions, where aid contractors from developed nations would be reluctant to work (Zhang & Smith, 2017). Following a similar modality, the Ministry of Health is responsible for China's foreign aid in the health sector, including the donation of medical equipment and medicine and the dispatching of medical teams overseas. Since China sent its first medical team overseas to Algeria in April 1963, 21,000 Chinese medical staff had been sent to 69 developing countries by 2010 (MOFCOM, 2010), and the number is growing in recent years. Compared with MOFCOM, the MFA and the MoF, these line ministries concentrate more on technical issues in their areas rather than on political and economic issues.

Not all aid projects in specialised fields will be conducted by line agencies. As an example, the Ministry of Agriculture will not enact all agricultural aid projects. This is because nearly all of China's aid projects are sent to MOFCOM, who have the option to conduct any given project by themselves (Interviews with Chinese aid officials and scholars, Beijing, August–September 2015). In the process of implementation, MOFCOM may approach other line ministries for technical support in specialised areas. If MOFCOM does not want to take on the project, it may ask other line ministries instead, and the project budget will be allocated to these line ministries. However, the State Council has delegated some line ministries the responsibility of dealing directly with some donor organisations. These aid projects do not need to go through MOFCOM or seek its approval. China's Ministry of Agriculture deals directly with the FAO and the World Food Programme. The Ministry of Agriculture can directly approve aid from these multilateral agencies for projects inside China or with them in Third World countries. In addition, many line ministries have an annual budget for promoting international cooperation, which are typically about half to two-thirds used for aid projects (Zhang & Smith, 2017). These projects do not need to be approved by MOFCOM.

China's SOEs

China's large SOEs are powerful players in domestic politics. The state controls the majority of large economic entities in China to ensure that it remains a socialist country with a high level of state ownership. SOEs produce a large percentage of China's annual GDP, create employment for Chinese citizens and generate revenue for the government. Barry Naughton (2011, p. 315) argued that China's SOEs accounted for 26.7 per cent of industrial output and for 20.4 per cent of industrial employment in 2009. SOEs still accounted for over half of China's industrial output in six sectors, such as electrical and heat power, mining and the washing of coal in 2011 (Lardy, 2014, pp. 76–77).

Most Chinese SOEs have their origins in China's ministries, which explains why they enjoy close relations. The China Road and Bridge Corporation was formed on the basis of the foreign aid office of China's Ministry of Transport in 1979, as required by the reform efforts to separate the government from companies. Similarly, the predecessor of the China railway engineering corporation is the General Bureau of Capital Construction of the Ministry of Railways, which was established in 1950. The China nuclear engineering and construction corporation—a military industrial corporation—was established in 1999 based on the former China national nuclear corporation. Several international economic and technical cooperation companies were also established in China's provinces to conduct foreign aid projects. They enjoy close relations with their provincial governments. In China's political system, the directors of large SOEs are interchangeable with high-ranking political positions such as ministers and provincial governors.[31] This illustrates how important they are in China's domestic politics. Chinese SOEs are also often chosen to implement Chinese aid projects, including concessional loan projects, because they are state companies and have resources, including technologies, skills and qualified staff.

---

31 Secretary of the Chinese Communist Party's political and legal affairs commission, Guo Shengkun, Minister of Industry and Information Technology Miao Wei, Director of State-owned Assets Supervision and Administration Commission Xiao Yaqing, former Governor of Shangdong province Guo Shuqing, Minister of Transport Li Xiaopeng, former Governor of Hebei province Zhang Qingwei are all former heads of Chinese SOEs.

The strategy developed for China's agricultural aid in Africa illustrates how SOEs are favoured in China's aid delivery. China's agricultural demonstration centres have been widely piloted in Africa since 2006. These centres will operate for 15 years. For the first three years, China's SOEs are contracted to construct the centre with grants that are provided by the Chinese government; for the second 12-year phase, a Chinese SOE will take over the centre and run it on a commercial basis (Gabas & Tang, 2014; Nzikou-Massala, 2014, p. 19).

Being the implementer of China's economic diplomacy and the 'go global strategy', China's SOEs receive much support from the Chinese leadership. Xu Weizhong, a Chinese aid expert from CICIR, explained:

> When Chinese leaders visit Africa, they often hold meetings with China's SOEs working in these countries and listen to their views on economic issues. Chinese SOEs are often consulted by MFA and MOFCOM for advice before the conferences of the Forum on China-Africa Cooperation are held. (Interview, Beijing, 24 August 2015)

Another way that SOEs wield influence on China's foreign aid is proposing aid projects to the economic and commercial counsellor's office at China's diplomatic missions, and even to MOFCOM directly. As these SOEs have previously enacted aid projects in the recipient countries and become established, they have close relations with both the Chinese government (including MOFCOM, the MFA and the economic and commercial counsellor's office) and the governments of recipient countries. They are familiar with China's foreign aid policies and the bilateral relations between China and recipient countries.

Due to their close relations with aid officials and some politicians in recipient countries, China's SOEs also have easy access to information related to recipient countries' demands for aid projects from China. The SOEs are keen to lobby China and the recipient countries for new aid projects because once both countries agree on a given project, the SOE that initiated the project will typically win the contract to enact it. This explains why, in some circumstances, Chinese SOEs and recipient governments form an informal alliance, in which China's SOEs persuade recipient governments to raise new aid projects with Beijing and promise to help behind the scenes to secure financing (Zhang & Smith, 2017). In return, recipient governments will propose to Beijing that they want these SOEs to implement the projects (Zhang & Smith, 2017). It becomes a win–win situation for China's SOEs and their partners in recipient countries. Some Chinese SOEs subcontract the project to other contractors from China or another country, while taking a commission.[32]

In comparison with MOFCOM, the MFA and the MoF, China's companies seemingly care less about China's political interests and focus more on their commercial interest. The principal–agent dilemma is observed in many cases. While the Chinese government hopes to create high-quality aid projects that will serve China's long-term political and economic interests, China's companies are driven by economic gain. They are keen to immediately complete the aid projects and move on— sometimes at the expense of project quality, environmental obligations, social responsibilities and the relations between the Chinese management team and local workforce (Zhang & Smith, 2017). In many instances, short-term economic interest has the upper hand over China's long-term geopolitical interests.

Another reason for some companies' ignorance of the Chinese government's requirements is that these companies consider aid projects to be merely a first step towards establishing themselves in the market of recipient countries. Over time, they move on to commercial projects that are usually more profitable than aid projects. However, things are more complicated than that. These companies realise that if they have a poor record and reputation for their aid projects, it becomes difficult for them to win commercial contracts, especially in smaller countries where news spreads quickly. Therefore, companies that manage to become established in the recipient countries begin caring more about establishing a good name for themselves, though they may still spare little thought to China's national interest.

Think Tanks

The role of think tanks in China's foreign aid is limited. In the Chinese government system, the shifting of personnel between government and academic posts is rare. This is different from Western countries such as the US, where it is relatively common for government officials and academic

---

32   One example is how the China civil engineering and construction corporation subcontracted the Palace renovation and wharf projects in Tonga to Fletcher Royco (Tongan Ministry of Information and Communications, 2010).

researchers to switch roles. However, it should be noted that many of China's ministries, particularly the more influential ones, have affiliated research academies that provide information to these ministries and that conduct research on selected topics for their paymasters (Zhang & Smith, 2017). Some think tanks have more influence than the others.

CAITEC, which has over 140 staff and conducts research work on behalf of MOFCOM, is one of the most important affiliated think tanks. MOFCOM's DFA has only about 70 staff to manage China's global aid program. Unsurprisingly, the department is overwhelmed by its rapidly growing workload. To compensate, CAITEC has been tasked with numerous research projects on behalf of MOFCOM, such as drafting Chinese white papers on foreign aid and conducting research on trilateral aid cooperation. Some CAITEC officials have been promoted to senior positions within MOFCOM and thus influence Chinese aid management. As a typical example, Shen Danyang—former deputy director of CAITEC (March 2003 – November 2008)—served as the director-general of MOFCOM's Department of Policy Research (April 2014 – July 2018) until he was further promoted to be vice governor of the Hainan province.

The MFA's affiliates, such as the China Foreign Affairs University and the China Institute of International Studies, conduct limited research on Chinese foreign aid because they devote more attention to diplomacy and security-related global issues. The situation at the MoF is similar. Its research institute for fiscal science has conducted sparse research on China's foreign aid.

China's Aid Decision-Making Procedure

Figure 7 summarises China's aid formal decision-making procedure—from project initiation, to international coordination to its implementation.[33]

---

33 This flow chart draws on the following references: MOFCOM (2014a); China Exim Bank (2014); and Zhou (2008).

Project proposal The recipient country will submit the proposal to the Economic Counsellor's Office at the Chinese Embassy.	**Concessional loans** For concessional loans, the two governments will sign a framework agreement. China Exim Bank and the borrower in the recipient country will then sign a detailed agreement on loan use.	**Project implemenation** MOFCOM will instruct its selected executing agency to implement the project, including designing the project, selecting the Chinese contractor and monitoring the project.
Information flow to China The Economic Counsellor's Office will report back to MOFCOM and MFA and relevant line agencies in China. Loan projects will also be cc'ed to China Exim Bank.	**Sign the formal agreement** If the aid proposal is approved, the Chinese government, often represented by the Ambassador, will sign a formal agreement with the recipient government.	**Sign the implementation and internal contracts** MOFCOM or its selected executing agency will sign the implementation contract with the recipient country and the internal contract with the Chinese contractor.
Project approval Based on available information and the feasibility of the study report, MOFCOM will make a decision and pass it on to MFA, MoF and other relevant line agencies for advice.	**Notify if the project is declined** If the proposal is declined, the Economic Counsellor's office will be instructed to notify the recipient country.	**Project monitoring** The Economic Counsellor's Office will assist MOFCOM in overseeing project implementation and the Chinese contractor, and it will liaise with the recipient country and MOFCOM.
Concessional loans For concessional loans, MOFCOM will seek advice from China Exim Bank before making the decision.	**Endorsement from the State Council** Large-scale projects and projects of particular significance will be submitted to the State Council for approval.	**Project completion** MOFCOM's selected executing agency will perform project acceptance after completion, pass it to the recipient country and provide necessary maintenance/support.

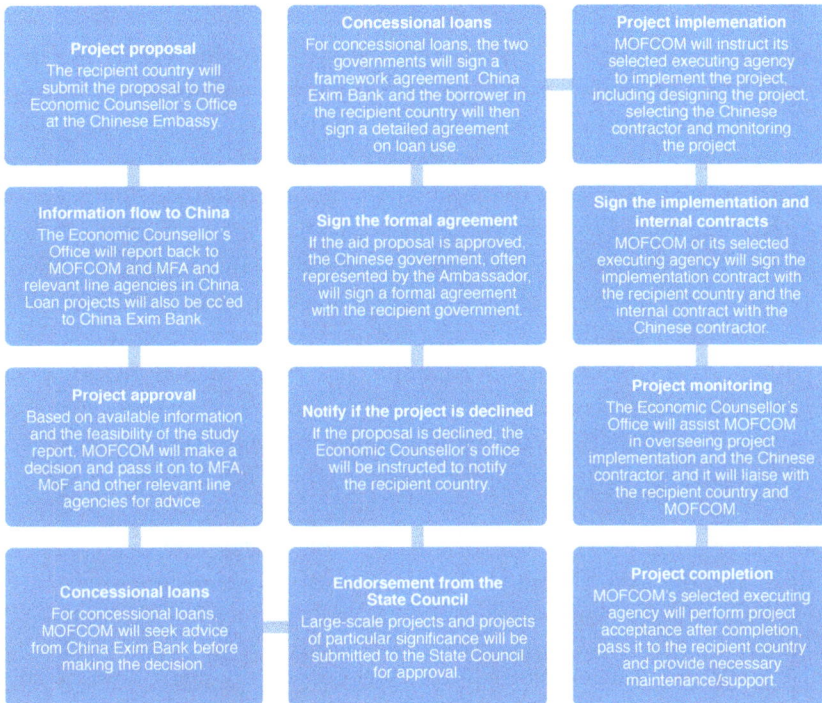

Figure 7. China's aid decision-making procedure
Source. Compiled by the author from own analysis.

Two Ways of Promoting New Information Flow

Taking the case of MOFCOM, this section will illustrate two ways that new ideas about foreign aid are promoted, even though other ways may also exist. Most university graduates who are recruited into MOFCOM's DFA do not major in foreign aid and development, as these courses themselves are rare. Instead they originate from diverse fields, such as foreign languages (especially English), business and law. Their knowledge of foreign aid is derived from daily practical work in MOFCOM and their senior colleagues. One major source of new ideas on foreign aid is the exchange with traditional donors and multilateral development organisations.

Take the exchange between China and the OECD as an example. China's officials have benefited from the OECD's training programs, which introduce new ideas. Xue Hong, then a CAITEC senior aid official, visited OECD DAC in 1992 for three months—the first

Chinese aid official to be posted there; he was exposed to the DAC's aid policies and practices (Interview, Beijing, 1 September 2015). Later, Mao Xiaojing, division director of international cooperation from CAITEC, participated in the same exchange program (Interview, Beijing, 1 September 2015). At the end of 2012, the OECD and the German federal enterprise for international cooperation co-funded the program of temporary assignments for Chinese officials in the OECD, which offered opportunities for mid-level Chinese officials to work at OECD headquarters in their specialised areas for a few months (OECD, 2014, p. 7). This boosted the level of China's learning from the OECD. From 2012 to 2013, 11 mid-level Chinese officials from ministries including the National Development and Reform Commission, Development Research Centre of the State Council, MOFCOM, MoF and Ministry of Science and Technology participated in this program which focuses on China's 12th Five-Year Plan covering areas including aid effectiveness (OECD, 2014, p. 7). This program contributed not only to closer relations between China and the OECD, but also to the flow of new ideas among Chinese officials and policy reforms.

In July 2015, China's Premier Li Keqiang became the first Chinese leader to visit the OECD headquarters in Paris. During the visit, China agreed to join the OECD development centre—a platform to discover solutions for stimulating growth in developing countries. OECD Secretary-General Angel Gurría credited this agreement as 'a historical and transformative opportunity for mutually beneficial knowledge-sharing [between China, OECD, and other developing countries]' (OECD, 2015b, para. 4). China has also agreed to accept the OECD policy coherence for sustainable development—a policy tool for integrating the various dimensions of sustainable development into policymaking and for ensuring that they are mutually supportive (OECD, 2015a, p. 24). This can potentially improve the development coordination between China and OECD members in other developing countries.

The movement of aid officials within the Chinese government system has further spread new ideas about aid. Officials sometimes have the opportunity of moving to positions in other departments. This movement carries with it knowledge from the old department to the new workplace. It is common for aid officials to shift between MOFCOM's DFA and their DITEA. As they oversee China's outgoing foreign aid and development assistance that comes into China respectively, this movement of aid officials could promote knowledge sharing of the practices that are associated with these two types of aid flow. The promotion of aid officials to higher positions in new departments facilitates information flow. As mentioned earlier, Shen Danyang, former deputy director of CAITEC, was promoted to the position of director-general of the Department of Policy Research and MOFCOM's chief spokesperson. Clearly, new aid ideas from CAITEC can easily obtain his attention and, with his support, it is more likely that these new ideas will become aid policies.

Reactions of China's Main Aid Agencies to Trilateral Aid Cooperation

As China's trilateral aid cooperation is yet quite new, the attitudes of China's aid agencies towards trilateral aid cooperation are not entirely clear at this stage. Based on my interviews and inferences from the interests of these aid agencies, the following conclusions can be drawn (see Table 7).

Table 7. Attitudes of China's aid agencies towards trilateral cooperation

Aid agencies	MFA MoF Other line ministries	MOFCOM China Exim Bank	SOEs
Attitude	Positive	Cautiously positive	Ambiguous

Source. Compiled by the author from own analysis.

The MFA

The MFA is the most active Chinese agency in promoting trilateral aid cooperation. As the MFA's primary concern is China's diplomatic relations with foreign countries, trilateral aid cooperation has appealed to MFA as a new method for China to promote new partnerships with traditional donors and multilateral development organisations. For example, trilateral aid cooperation has become an important new component of China's partnership with traditional donors, including the US, UK, Australia and New Zealand. From this perspective, the MFA supports this new modality of aid delivery. Merriden Varrall, a former UNDP senior representative in Beijing, confirmed this appoint and argued that the MFA is pressuring MOFCOM to undertake trilateral cooperation and that the MFA believes that trilateral cooperation could also ease China's troubled relations with developed nations such as the US (Varrall, 2016, p. 30).

MOFCOM

MOFCOM's attitude towards trilateral aid cooperation is more cautious compared to that of the MFA. MOFCOM is tasked with improving the effectiveness and efficiency of China's foreign aid. In this sense, it is interested in new aid modalities, such as pilot trilateral aid projects. MOFCOM also faces pressures from other line ministries to pilot trilateral aid cooperation for their political and technical benefits. However, MOFCOM is mindful of obstacles for advancing trilateral aid cooperation, including its unfamiliarity with this aid modality, the wide gulf that its officials perceive between Chinese and Western foreign aid practices and norms, the increasing cost of aid coordination when more donors are involved and the ambiguous attitude of Chinese aid contractors and their partners in recipient countries towards trilateral cooperation.

In this complicated situation, MOFCOM—as the custodian of aid management on behalf of the Chinese government and Communist Party—takes a cautious attitude towards trilateral cooperation. We can expect that China will be stubborn in maintaining its core aid principles and the independence of its foreign aid delivery rather than being bound by Western aid norms. Based on this precondition, China will be open to more international engagement and pilot trilateral aid cooperation, so it can learn from traditional donors and multilateral development organisations. MOFCOM has been observing these pilot projects closely and has been gaining experience for the future expansion of trilateral cooperation. This reflects the wisdom of 'crossing the river by feeling for stones',[34] which is gained from China's reform and the opening-up process (Chen, 1980, p. 279).

The MoF and Other Line Ministries

Being the caretaker of China's annual budget, including the aid budget, the MoF's position on foreign aid is detached to a certain extent. It does not stand to lose much from trilateral cooperation, but it has the opportunity to promote mutual learning with its counterparts, such as

---

34 'To cross the river by feeling for stones' is a concept raised by Chen Yun in December 1980—and endorsed by Deng Xiaoping, the architect of China's reform process. In Chen's thinking, as China had no experience in reform, it had to be careful and move slowly. One useful way was to conduct pilot projects and accumulate experience for later projects, which is a practice that can be traced back to the Maoist era. After the benefits were found to outweigh the risks—or in Deng's terminology, the 'flies'—the experiment was expanded to the whole country.

the World Bank and the ADB. Therefore, their overall attitude towards trilateral cooperation is more positive than that of MOFCOM (Interview, Beijing, 6 August 2015).

Other line ministries, including the Ministry of Agriculture and the Ministry of Health, are active in promoting trilateral cooperation. Line ministries, especially those with technical expertise, are more interested in the exchange of skills in foreign aid provision, and they are keen to use trilateral cooperation as an opportunity for learning from their Western counterparts. A Chinese aid expert involved in the China–Australia–Cambodia irrigation dialogue—a trilateral project on knowledge sharing—applauded this project. He stated that 'Australia has very advanced theories and practices in areas such as legislation, well-defined users' rights, trading and monitoring of water resources. This is a good learning opportunity for China' (Interview, Beijing, 24 August 2015).

Line ministries are also keen to apply and test their technologies in unfamiliar environments. In the case of agriculture, there is also a profit motive and access to new markets for China's agricultural expertise and products, such as agricultural machinery. Other sectors (e.g. the health and disaster relief sectors) are similar. For example, one motivation of China's Ministry of Civil Affairs (MCA) in joining the trilateral project with the UK's Department for International Development (DFID) on disaster relief in Bangladesh and Nepal was to expand the influence of China's disaster relief experience (Interview, Beijing, 4 August 2015). This in turn can add value to the MCA's portfolio and expand its influence.

In addition, every line ministry has its department of international cooperation, which is tasked with liaising with foreign countries. These departments were mainly responsible for managing traditional donors and receiving their aid to China. As traditional donors reduce their aid to China, these departments are strongly motivated to explore new markets for their work, so they can maintain staffing and funding levels. Conducting trilateral cooperation with traditional donors in Third World countries is such a market. This explains why these departments in various ministries are actively pushing for trilateral cooperation.

The China Exim Bank

The China Exim Bank's attitude is ambiguous. It is seemingly cautious about undertaking trilateral projects due to concerns regarding the coordination costs. As the bank's large proportion of concessional loan projects are large-scale infrastructure projects, the work of coordination in potential trilateral cooperation could be daunting (Interview with MOFCOM aid official, Canberra, 19 July 2016). Another possible reason is that it could be difficult to divide the dividends in concessional loan projects that have substantial commercial interests. However, as concessional loans now account for more than half of China's total foreign aid, it is natural for the China Exim Bank to become involved in trilateral aid cooperation. At this stage, the China Exim Bank is trying to bypass the difficulty of dividing its commercial interests by conducting trilateral aid projects in which China and traditional donors are each responsible for their own part of the project, under the broad umbrella of trilateral cooperation. The China–New Zealand–Cook Islands trilateral project on water supply in Rarotonga is a suitable example. In effect, this is parallel rather than trilateral cooperation.

Chinese Companies

The attitudes of China's aid contractors towards trilateral cooperation are similar to those of the China Exim Bank. They are not accustomed to working jointly on aid projects with traditional donors and construction companies from developing nations, nor are they keen to divide the economic benefits of these projects or take direction from foreign project managers. Yet, an increasing number of Chinese companies is gaining this kind of experience by winning commercial contracts from traditional donors. Chinese companies are also keen to learn from traditional donor skills and management expertise in areas such as social responsibility and environmental protection, with which Chinese companies are less familiar (Interview with Chinese companies, Port Moresby, 10 and 11 November 2014). To some Chinese resident managers, promoting partnerships with their Western counterparts might also help move their businesses up the value chain and even access markets in developed nations.

In short, identities and material interests influence China's aid agencies' attitudes towards China's foreign aid and trilateral aid cooperation. The MFA is the most supportive of trilateral cooperation, while

MOFCOM cautiously welcomes it. The MoF is more positive because it has less 'skin in the game' than MOFCOM, and other line agencies also welcome this new aid modality. The China Exim Bank and Chinese companies have ambiguous or conflicted attitudes.

Conclusion

This chapter has analysed the evolution of China's foreign aid policy and practices—especially its adoption of trilateral aid cooperation—from both external and domestic perspectives, as well as the interest calculations by the Chinese government. This triangulation reduces the research bias and errors that might occur if the research focuses solely on one perspective.

From the perspective of the Chinese government's interest calculations, China's leaders continue to emphasise their three identities as a socialist country, a developing country and a rising great power. The shift in identity over time has led to the shift in China's interest calculations. From 1950 to 1978, the Chinese government focused on its identity as a socialist country and thus foreign aid was used to promote its political interests by building a revolutionary united front against Western countries. From 1978 to 1999, China enacted the reform and opening-up policy to rejuvenate its moribund economy. China's identity as a developing country received more attention and foreign aid was regarded as promoting mutual benefits for China and the recipient countries rather than revolution. To China, the provision of foreign aid could help Chinese companies gain access to overseas markets for their products and investment, as well as obtain resources to support domestic economic development.

Since 2000, China's economy has continued to grow, and its economic strength has been significantly boosted. In the area of development cooperation, the Chinese government has focused more on its identity as a rising global power. The importance of global image–building has thus begun to prevail over short-term economic benefits. Foreign aid serves this purpose. China's policymakers, looking to promote China's global image as a responsive, responsible and respectable global power, have come to accept trilateral aid cooperation, albeit to differing degrees.

From the perspective of international engagement, the PRC government has been engaging with the outside world since 1950, when it began providing development assistance. China's engagement with traditional donors and multilateral development organisations has increased since 1978, after which China agreed to accept their assistance. Since 2000, this engagement has diversified and expanded substantially; the influence of China as an emerging donor is growing rapidly. The focus of Western donors and multilateral development organisations on development cooperation with China is shifting from providing aid to China to aid coordination and the joint provision of assistance to other developing countries. Trilateral aid cooperation is consequently discussed and piloted between China and traditional donors and multilateral development organisations.

From the perspective of China's domestic foreign aid bureaucracy, China's aid agencies differ in their human resources capacity to manage foreign aid. Based on their own interests, the objectives they seek to achieve by providing foreign aid are also different, which defines their differing propensities for interest-based alliances. This point applies to their attitudes towards trilateral aid cooperation. Among these agencies, the MFA, with its diplomatic focus, is an enthusiastic supporter of trilateral cooperation, while MOFCOM welcomes it with some reservations. The China Exim Bank is piloting 'parallel' aid cooperation, in which China and traditional donors separately conduct their own part of the project under the umbrella of a trilateral project. China's other ministries show more interest in the opportunities of learning technical and management skills in their areas of specialisation, and they largely support trilateral aid cooperation. China's aid contractors have conflicted attitudes towards aid cooperation, as they oppose cooperation on projects with substantial commercial interests while being keen to learn useful aid practices and skills from their Western counterparts.

Based on the above discussion, and with the hindsight of empirical support from the following three case study chapters, I argue that China's adoption of trilateral aid cooperation reflects its stronger desire to be globally considered a responsible great power, as well as its stronger desire to learn through growing international engagement with traditional donor states and multilateral development agencies on aid delivery. Professor Zhou Qi from the China Academy of Social Sciences provided another example of China's aid evolution as a result of cognitive learning and global image–building. She traced the process of China's changing position on participating in global peacekeeping from outright opposition (1949–1980), to acquiescence (1981–1988) and to active support (since 1989) (Zhou, 2010). In explaining this evolution, she argued that China has become actively involved in global peacekeeping for reasons including global image–building as a responsible great power and is learning advanced technologies and management skills from the peacekeepers of other countries (Zhou, 2010, p. 59).

How will China reform its foreign aid in the future? MOFCOM Vice Minister Fu Ziying's remarks are instructive:

> There will be no big changes to China's foreign aid policies, but changes may happen regarding its foreign aid structure and in some areas due to the new circumstances and changes in global development … China will further promote its external engagement on development assistance, to learn some advantageous and effective ways of aid delivery from international multilateral organizations and other countries, so as to improve China's foreign aid system, ways of delivery, policies and measures. (State Council, 2011b, para. 20, 33)

4

The UNDP as a Catalyst for China's Development Cooperation: The Case of the China–UNDP–Cambodia Trilateral Cassava Project

Introduction

The devil, as they say, is in the details. The following three case study chapters will test whether the proposed theories and argument in Chapters 2 and 3 can pass the test on the ground. These cases are not simply reduced to an analysis of trilateral aid projects. They are much broader thematic case studies that concern China's evolving approach towards developing aid cooperation with a micro-study on trilateral cooperation. As such, these chapters will analyse China's interest calculation and the cognitive learning process with regard to its trilateral aid cooperation in three different project settings. The subtle reactions of China's diversified aid agencies in each trilateral aid project will also be discussed.

UN agencies have played a significant role in spurring economic and social development in developing countries. Among them, the UNDP is one of the most active players. The UNDP works in more than 170 countries and territories to promote poverty alleviation and development. It has been pushing hard to achieve the millennium development goals (MDGs), strengthen the post-2015 development agenda and adopt the new sustainable development goals (SDGs) in September 2015 (UNDP, 2015d).

China seemingly values its cooperative relations with UN agencies. Its international engagement on development cooperation started with UN agencies in the 1970s. As will be elaborated, the Chinese government has placed more trust in cooperating with UN agencies relative to Western sovereign states. In terms of trilateral aid cooperation, China has been actively conducting pilot projects with the UNDP, FAO and UNIDO. Through a detailed examination of the China–UNDP–Cambodia trilateral cassava project, this chapter will investigate the catalytic role of the UNDP in the evolution of China's trilateral aid cooperation engagements.

The chapter is structured as follows. It will begin with an examination of China–UNDP interactions from the 1970s and their effect on China's trilateral aid cooperation. Then, an overview of the evolving trends in aid to Cambodia, especially China's foreign aid, will be provided as background. What follows is an in-depth discussion of the recent China–UNDP–Cambodia trilateral project on cassava, the first trilateral project between China and UNDP. Finally, the effect of this project on future cooperation between China and UNDP will also be discussed.

China–UNDP Engagement on Development Cooperation

This section will review the engagement between China and the UNDP on development cooperation since the 1970s, with a focus on recent events. To follow the theoretical thread of this book, it will analyse how China's changing identities and interests have informed its ideas on cooperating with the UNDP in the area of foreign aid during the course of their interactions. It argues that China's growing desire for global image–building and learning from the UNDP has led to its deepening trilateral aid cooperation with the UNDP.

Multilateral Diplomacy at the UN

According to the Chinese government, a basic principle guiding China's economic and technical cooperation with the UN since the 1970s has been 'supporting the third world countries' and 'supporting their just positions and requirements on important economic and social development issues' (Shi, 1989, p. 504). At a time when the Western developed countries isolated China in the early 1970s, the Chinese government perceived the UN as an ideal platform for consolidating with other developing countries. Pu Ping from the Remmin University of China argued that in the early 1970s, China viewed the UN as a diplomatic platform and worked on behalf of the Third World countries (Pu, 2009, p. 83). China's participation in UN activities has evolved from being passive in the early and mid-1970s, due to a lack of understanding of the UN and the domestic Cultural Revolution, to becoming increasingly active from the late 1970s (Zhang & Feng, 2011).

In recent years, multilateral diplomacy, especially at the UN, has received further endorsement from China's leadership. At the 10th conference of China's ambassadors in April 2004, multilateral diplomacy was prioritised as 'a significant platform' in China's diplomacy (Chen, 2009). In his address at the 70th UN general assembly, President Xi Jinping referred to the UN as 'the most universal, representative and authoritative inter-governmental organization' (Xi, 2015b, para. 2).

Working on multilateral diplomacy is even linked to the fast promotion of officials within China's Ministry of Foreign Affairs (MFA). Many officials from the MFA's Department of International Organizations and Conferences (the main agency in charge of China's multilateral diplomacy) have been appointed as senior ministers, such as current first highest-ranking Vice Minister Zhang Yesui and former Vice Minister Liu Jieyi (current Minister of the Taiwan Affairs Office).

Chinese scholars have also highlighted China's multilateral diplomacy at the UN. Wang Yizhou, deputy dean of the School of International Studies at Peking University, argued that while focusing on its own development, China must also consider its global responsibility and image (Wang, 2001, p. 7). He noted that 'carrying out multilateral diplomacy is the path China must follow in order to become a global power' (Wang, 2001, p. 8). Vice Professor Su Changhe from Fudan University argued that China has developed a new thinking in its diplomacy, believing that global and regional public issues should be settled based on multilateral institutions (Su, 2005, p. 13). His colleague, Professor Wei Zongyou, from Fudan University argued that in response to the 'China threat' and 'China pride' discourses, China has used multilateral venues, including the UN, to propose policy initiatives such as 'peaceful development' and 'building a harmonious world' to project its image as a responsible power (Wei, 2014, p. 20).

Professor Shi Yinhong from the Renmin University of China introduces two main concepts to explain China's foreign policy. The first is that economic development is the top priority and the second relates to China's increasing integration into the global system. He argued that China's foreign policy is tightly linked to these two concepts and that China's perception of its identity has evolved from 'a country out of the global system' to 'a country in the global system' (Shi, 2006, pp. 34–35). Following Professor Shi's logic, it is natural for China to promote multilateral diplomacy to play its role in the global system.

China's diplomacy towards the UNDP is also reflected in its aid policy alongside its changing identity and interest calculations. In the 1970s, China began engaging with the UNDP, but great suspicion lingered, based on China's isolation by and mistrust of Western countries and the UN. By emphasising its identity as a socialist country of self-reliance, China refused to receive aid from the UNDP. As China began emphasising its identity as a developing country and shifting its priority to economic development from the late 1970s, it increased its cooperation with the UNDP and began accepting its aid. China adopted a more positive perspective of the UNDP and believed that the UNDP's aid was conducive to China's development. China has recently highlighted its identity as a responsible growing power. It has begun piloting trilateral aid cooperation—starting with the UNDP—as a method of promoting its global image and of learning to improve its own aid performance, as the following discussion illustrates.

Cognitive Learning

The following section will analyse how four decades of engagement between China and UNDP have influenced China's ideas on foreign aid and trilateral cooperation.

1970s: Tentative Engagement

China's engagement with the UNDP started in the early 1970s, and a mutual understanding began to increase. In October 1972, China pledged to donate $400,000 and RMB 3.2 million to the UNDP, which was China's first donation to the organisation (Shi, 1989, p. 510). In January 1973, China was an observer at the 15th UNDP governing council meeting for the first time (Shi, 1989, p. 649). In October of the same year, UNDP administrator, Rudolph A. Peterson, visited China and exchanged views with the Chinese government regarding the use of Chinese donations and the dispatching of Chinese staff to work at UNDP headquarters (Shi, 1989, p. 511). For the first time in its capacity as a full member, China attended the 19th UNDP governing council meeting in New York in February 1975 (Shi, 1989, p. 653).

During this period, China refused to receive development assistance from the UNDP; its involvement with the UNDP was restricted to conference participation and voluntary donations. Though limited in scope, this engagement between China and the UNDP increased their mutual understanding and trust and it paved the way for greater cooperation in the following years.

The Chinese government officially divides its engagement with the UNDP into two main periods. According to Ambassador Wang Min— deputy representative of China's permanent mission to the UN—the first period of cooperation (1979–2009) focused on the UNDP's development assistance for China's domestic development, while the second period started in 2010 when the two sides signed an MOU to promote trilateral aid cooperation in Third World countries (Wang, 2013).

Following the formal adoption of China's reform and opening-up policy in 1978, the mindsets of the Chinese leadership towards cooperating with the UNDP began to change. The Chinese government became aware that in addition to its donations to the UNDP, China could benefit by receiving aid from the UNDP to support its domestic development. In September 1978, a Chinese delegation led by Wei Yuming, vice minister of China's Ministry of Foreign Economic Liaison,[1] visited the UNDP headquarters in New York. They discussed the issue of receiving aid from the UNDP with UNDP administrator Bradford Morse, and received positive feedback (Shi, 1989, pp. 498–499). According to then interpreter of the meeting Long Yongtu—who later became vice minister of MOFCOM and chief WTO negotiator—the UNDP side was shocked by China's dramatic change of policy when Minister Wei said that China had decided to accept aid from the UNDP, and it double-checked the change with interpreter Long (Long, 2015, p. 46). In the following month, Vice Minister Wei wrote a formal letter to Morse, stating that

---

1   The predecessor of MOFTEC (1993–2003) and MOFCOM (2003 to present).

'the Chinese government would welcome UNDP's technical assistance to assist China in learning from the advanced external technologies and managerial experiences' (Shi, 1989, p. 499).

On 29 June 1979, Morse and China's ambassador to the UN, Lai Yali, signed the 'Agreement between the government of the People's Republic of China and the United Nations Development Programme' (United Nations, 1979, pp. 16–25). This document marked the beginning of the cooperation between the two sides and opened the door for the flow of the UNDP's aid to China. Administrator Morse opened the UNDP China office during his visit to China in September 1979 (Shi, 1989, p. 511). After that, engagement between China and the UNDP in the development sector began to increase substantially, which has had a threefold effect on China.

Financial Support

The UNDP has provided substantial financial and technical assistance to support China's economic development since the 1970s. The UNDP's aid has provided 'seed money' and been 'a catalyst', as it also mobilises substantial aid funds from the Chinese government and other UN agencies.

Table 8 provides an overview of the UNDP's aid to China between 1979 and 2015. The UNDP conducted 328 aid projects in China, with an allocation of $15 million in the period 1979–1981 (CICETE, 2014a).[2] Its first country plan for China in the period 1981–1985 coincided with China's sixth five-year plan and China received aid of $134 million from the UNDP (CICETE, 2014e). In the following years, the UNDP provided $122 million (1986–1990), $189.9 million (1991–1995), $76.3 million (1996–2000) and $39 million (2001–2005), respectively (CICETE, 2014b, 2014c, 2014d; United Nations Development Programme, 2001).[3] The UNDP aimed to mobilise $133 million and $136.5 million for China over the periods 2006–2010 and 2011–2015, respectively (UNDP China, 2005; UNDP, 2010).[4]

2   The UNDP's country plan usually has a lifespan of five years. The UNDP did not draft its country plan for China from 1979–1981 because its program cycle (1977–1981) had already started in 1977. According to MOFCOM, there is some convergence of UNDP's aid to China in the year 1981, as illustrated in Table 8.
3   According to a report from the Department of Commerce in China's Hunan Province, the UNDP provided about USD 50 million to China in the period 2001–2005.
4   The final figures for the period 2006–2010 and 2011–2015 are not available.

Table 8. UNDP's development assistance to China, 1979–2015

Time	Aid volume (USD)
1979–1981	15 million
1981–1985	134 million
1986–1990	122 million
1991–1995	189.9 million
1996–2000	76.3 million
2001–2005	39 million
2006–2010	133 million
2011–2015	136.5 million

Source. Compiled by the author from the CICETE and UNDP website data.

One significant feature of the UNDP's aid to China is that it aligns with China's own five-year plan, and China has demonstrated strong ownership in the process. The China International Center for Economic and Technical Exchanges, an aid implementation agency affiliated to MOFCOM, is designated by MOFCOM to draft plans for UNDP's aid in China (CICETE, 2014f). As China's 11th five-year plan (2006–2010) highlighted the vision of building 'a moderately prosperous society' (*xiaokang shehui*)—a concept of Confucian origin and one that is best known during President Hu Jintao's administration (2002–2012)—the UNDP together with other UN agencies helped China develop economic and social policies to operationalise the 'moderately prosperous society' vision in the UN development assistance framework for China (2006–2010) (UNDP China, 2005).

Technological Support

In terms of new technologies, China has benefited greatly from its interaction with the UNDP. As the *International Business Daily*, a newspaper run by MOFCOM, noted, 'To solve development challenges, China not only needs to make great efforts by itself, but also to learn from good external experiences and practices through international cooperation' (Wang, 2005). To assist China achieve the target of tripling its agricultural and industrial outputs by 2000, the UNDP's aid to China from 1986 to 1990 listed technological development as a main area of cooperation, such as introducing advanced technologies in the areas of energy efficiency fuel, building nuclear power stations and developing solar power (CICETE, 2014b).

The UNDP funded the establishment of China's first laser parameter testing centre at the Beijing Institute of Opto-Electronic Technology in the 1980s. With the UNDP's support of technical training and research, this testing centre adopted the crucial technology of producing a helium-neon laser (Shi, 1989, p. 541). In April 1991, the UNDP and China signed an aid agreement to conduct an industrial modification program of machine tools for the Beijing no. 2 Machine Tool Works Co. Ltd. With funding of more than $12 million, this cooperation was the UNDP's first aid program rather than a project in China (Zhou, 1991).

Over the period 1991–1996, the UNDP assisted China in establishing a management and surveillance system for forestry resources to achieve a target of increasing China's forestry coverage rate from 13 to 17 per cent (CICETE, 2014c). From the 1990s, the UNDP also introduced microcredit projects to assist low-income families in rural western provinces such as Gansu, Guizhou and Sichuan, which facilitated the Chinese government's understanding of microcredit and the promulgation of related policies (CICETE, 2009).

With the technical assistance of the UNDP, the IRICO Colour Picture Tube company in China's Xianyang city completed a technical innovation project in climate and stratospheric ozone protection, and the project manager, Ma Mingqing, received the 2004 Climate Protection Award from the US Environmental Protection Agency (Wu, 2004). Through the UNDP, China also learned the concept of a 'human development index' and, by October 2005, the UNDP introduced nearly 1,000 technologies to support China's industrial modernisation (Wang, 2005).

China paid tribute to the substantial support from UNDP China's development achievements (International Poverty Reduction Center in China, 2007; MOFCOM and UNDP, 2010). As early as 1989, Shi Lin, former vice minister of China's Ministry of Foreign Economic Liaison, stated:

> The UN's multilateral economic and technical cooperation has a history of nearly four decades. It has a good financing channel, advanced technical know-how and an excellent information network. By making a full use of the UN system to conduct various forms of international cooperation, it will be beneficial for the self-reliance of developing countries and for socialist modernization in China. (Shi, 1989, p. 506)

Sources of Ideational Change

With a rapidly growing aid budget and footprint overseas, China is increasingly aware of the weakness in its foreign aid performance.[5] The desire to learn from traditional donors and UN agencies has grown accordingly. China is keen to improve its foreign aid efficiency by learning from the UNDP's experience (UNDP China, 2014b, p. 9). In the process of learning, the UNDP has played an important advisory role to the Chinese government regarding foreign aid and has facilitated the change of ideas in the latter.

The UNDP has seized opportunities as an advisor to introduce new ideas on foreign aid to MOFCOM, China's leading aid agency. The UNDP has recently been frequently approached by MOFCOM to conduct joint projects or to provide policy advice. For example, China has been increasingly depended on to provide policy advice on south–south cooperation and global development issues (UNDP China, 2012, p. 3). As requested by MOFCOM, UNDP China submitted a policy report in April 2011 and provided advice on the evolution of the G20 working group and the role that China could play within it (UNDP China, 2012, p. 3). In 2012, the UNDP conducted two research projects on behalf of CAITEC, the think tank under MOFCOM, regarding the roles of civil society and think tanks in foreign aid (UNDP China, 2013a, p. 6).

UNDP China was also approached for advice on China's first white paper on foreign aid (Interview with Napoleon Navarro, Deputy Country Director, UNDP Cambodia, Phnom Penh, 15 July 2015). At the request of MOFCOM, the UNDP discussed the draft of China's second white paper on foreign aid with MOFCOM and provided advice in July 2013 (UNDP China, 2014b, p. 11). The UNDP suggested that MOFCOM clearly demonstrate the benefits of China's foreign aid (UNDP China, 2015f, p. 5). A former UNDP senior official recalled the engagement at that time:

> They [MOFCOM] came to us informally and said, 'Look, we've got a draft of the second white paper here. Could you have a look at it and see what you think the traditional donors or the Western world will criticise; will they think it is not good enough? Are we communicating well in the way that our Western readers will

---

5   This point is also supported by the author's interviews with Chinese aid officials and scholars (Beijing, August–September, 2015).

> understand it?' We had very frank conversations with them, very informal. We talked about things that maybe would have some criticism, things that looked good, things that they could expand a little bit more. They re-drafted it many times after that, and some of the things we suggested were in the final version. (Interview with a former senior UNDP official, Canberra, 28 June 2016)

The UNDP also developed the English version for China's 'Measures for the Administration of Foreign Aid', which was released in late 2014 (UNDP China, 2015f, p. 5). This umbrella document introduces Chinese foreign aid management, including project set-up procedures and monitoring principles.

Second to UNDP headquarters and regional offices is another source of ideational change for China's aid policymakers. In September 2013, two senior aid officials from MOFCOM's DFA were seconded to UNDP headquarters in New York for six months, with the stated aim of increasing their understanding of UNDP's aid policies (UNDP China, 2014b, p. 9). Later on, another three division/deputy division directors from the DFA participated in this exchange program and chose to work in the UNDP offices in Bangladesh, Zambia and New York to diversify their experiences of the UNDP's aid practices (Interview with UNDP official, Seoul, 10 December 2015). This exchange has greatly contributed to the DFA officials' support for trilateral aid cooperation with the UNDP (Interview with UNDP official, Canberra, 29 June 2016), as will be elaborated later on. It also reinforces the argument that this kind of exchange program has been a major source of new ideas regarding aid cooperation within MOFCOM.

The UNDP and China jointly reviewed various approaches to foreign aid and their effects on China's aid reform (UNDP, 2015c). The Chinese government invited the UNDP to present papers on several occasions, such as at the global think tank summit (June 2011), the first MOFCOM capacity development seminar (August 2011) and the conference on the economic outlook for Sub-Saharan Africa (October 2011) (UNDP China, 2012, pp. 4–5). Joint research between the UNDP and MOFCOM has even extended to the Pacific region. In 2014, the UNDP and China CAITEC launched a joint research project chaired by Dr Graeme Smith from ANU. The research team assessed the demands from Pacific Island countries and identified numerous potential areas for trilateral aid cooperation between traditional donors and China in these countries

(Smith et al., 2014). As a follow-up, the UNDP undertook research on China–Pacific Island countries' south–south cooperation in the context of the post-2015 sustainable development agenda (Zhang, 2017a).

In addition to MOFCOM, the UNDP has also provided support to the MFA and China's think tanks on the topic of development assistance. In preparation for the fifth ministerial conference of the forum on China–Africa cooperation to be held in Beijing in July 2012, the MFA requested advice from the UNDP on the potential areas of cooperation between China and Africa in the area of development; this advice was accepted with appreciation (UNDP China, 2013a, p. 7). In June 2014, the UNDP and MFA's Department of International Economic Affairs[6] discussed issues of post-2015 process (UNDP China, 2015f, p. 17). Four months later in October, the UNDP and the China Center for International Economic Exchanges (the think tank under the China National Development and Reform Commission) convened the first and second high-level policy fora on global governance and discussed global economic governance and sustainable development financing for the post-2015 agenda (China Centre for International Economic Exchange and United Nations Development Programme China, 2013; UNDP China, 2015f). The UNDP produced a paper in 2011 for the China Development Research Foundation, a non-profit organisation under the State Council Development Research Center, based on the effect of China's WTO accession on other developing countries (Bhattacharya & Misha, 2015). In October 2011, UNDP China conducted a joint assessment with the Peking University and Edinburgh University of the development effect of China's scholarships on recipient countries, especially in Africa (UNDP China, 2012, p. 3).

The UNDP has also been assisting China to participate substantially in regional and global dialogues, negotiations and development initiatives (UNDP China, 2005; UNDP, 2015c). In preparation for the upcoming Mexico high-level meeting on global partnership for effective development cooperation in April 2014, the UNDP and CAITEC co-hosted a workshop in April in Beijing, in which government and civil society representatives from 11 emerging donors exchanged views for the

---

6   This is a new department created in October 2012 due to the growing workload in global governance. It was born out of the existing Department of International Organisations and Conferences.

Mexico meeting and agreed that trilateral aid cooperation can draw on the comparative advantages of different stakeholders and contribute to an increased understanding among them (UNDP China, 2014c).

The UNDP's support for the sensitive areas of Chinese aid is also apparent. It is lending support to the Chinese government in the area of corporate social responsibility, a weakness of China's aid providers overseas. In 2013, China's State-owned Assets Supervision and Administration Commission (SASAC) requested that the UNDP develop a CSR framework to guide Chinese companies abroad (UNDP China, 2014b, p. 16). The UNDP is optimistic that its dialogue with SASAC and CAITEC on this issue 'can yield considerable influence on policies and guidelines for Chinese companies' overseas investments and bring about a transformational change' (UNDP China, 2015f, p. 13). The three sides co-produced the 2015 report on the sustainable development of Chinese companies overseas, which assessed the performance of Chinese companies overseas and provided policy advice (UNDP China, 2015a).

The UNDP is also partnering with China's private sector and pushing it to abide by internationally recognised norms overseas with regard to environmental and labour standards (UNDP, 2015c), as most—but not all—of China's aid providers are SOEs. It is also assisting China in improving its aid evaluation mechanisms, another 'soft rib' of Chinese foreign aid. It is supporting CAITEC to conduct research on the approaches of traditional and emerging donors, including Japan, Australia, India, Mexico and Brazil, and on international development evaluation (UNDP China, 2014b, p. 11).

International Poverty Reduction Centre in China

The establishment of the International Poverty Reduction Centre in China (IPRCC) is an important example of the UNDP's support to the Chinese government on south–south cooperation. At the sideline of the global poverty reduction conference in Shanghai in May 2004, the UNDP and the Chinese government, represented by MOFCOM and the State Council leading group office of poverty alleviation and development, signed an MOU on the establishment of IPRCC, the only organisation of its kind in China (International Poverty Reduction Center in China, 2007).[7] The purpose is to use this centre as a platform

---

7   IPRCC has closed links with the Chinese government. For example, the first director of IPRCC, Zhang Lei, was a senior official (director general level) from the State Council leading group office of poverty alleviation and development.

for promoting the sharing of China's development experiences with other developing countries. The Chinese government is aware of the differences between its foreign aid—part of south–south cooperation—and the ODA of traditional donors. It is not shy to feature its distinct aid practices globally and is thus using cooperation with partners, including the UNDP, to promote China's experiences in the developing world.

With the support of the UNDP and other partners, the IPRCC has hosted 74 workshops on poverty reduction for 1,798 trainees from 104 developing countries (UNDP China, 2015d). The UNDP and the IPRCC have co-convened high-level conferences on poverty alleviation, including China's annual international poverty reduction forum. In December 2008, MOFCOM, CICETE and UNDP China agreed to launch a four-year project of $4 million for strengthening the capacity of the IPRCC (CICETE and UNDP, 2008). In November 2010, China and the UNDP co-hosted the first China–Africa poverty reduction and development conference in Addis Ababa with Ethiopia and signed the letter of intent to expand the scope of sharing China's development experience with African countries (UNDP China, 2015d).

In January 2012, the UNDP and IPRCC co-hosted a symposium at Shenzhen University and discussed how Africa could learn from China's experience in establishing special economic zones (SEZs) (UNDP China, 2013a, p. 14). This was a reaction to the sensitive issue—some of these SEZs, such as in Ethiopia, had run into trouble (Bräutigam & Tang, 2011). A main achievement of UNDP–IPRCC cooperation in 2014 was the testing of a new model for the training of government officials by using the pilot China–Bangladesh Urban Solution Lab (UNDP China, 2015f, p. 7). The project aimed to learn from China's 'one-stop' urban service centres—which are meant to deliver social safety nets to the poor—and adapt it to Bangladesh.

The close engagement between China and the UNDP can be attributed to the accumulated trust that the Chinese government has in the UNDP, which in turn paves the way for future cooperation. As UNDP China noted, 'this [providing policy advice to China on South–South cooperation and global development issues] is a highly strategic area of work that UNDP is opening that are sometimes less available to others' (UNDP China, 2012, p. 3). One reason for the Chinese government's trust in the UNDP is that, compared with traditional donor states, China regards the UNDP as a multilateral agency that is relatively politically neutral and that does not pose a threat to the Chinese government.[8] Similarly, in contrast to some other multilateral agencies, including the World Bank and the International Monetary Fund that are dominated by Western nations, China believes that the UNDP is more trustworthy and that China can exert influence on the UNDP more easily as an important member. Another reason for the trust relates to the UNDP's cautious approach: trying not to take a judgmental attitude but to provide objective and helpful advice when approached by Chinese ministries (Interview with former senior UNDP official, Canberra, 28 June 2016). In terms of staff, in a way that differs from these multilateral agencies, the UNDP China office has around 75 per cent of its staff as Chinese nationals, which could also help the UNDP earn trust from the Chinese government.[9]

Trilateral Cooperation: A New Focus

UNDP administrator Helen Clark's visit to China in November 2009 was an important event in the evolution of UNDP–China trilateral aid cooperation. She met with China's Premier Wen Jiabao and his senior ministers of commerce, foreign affairs, finance and environmental protection. The two sides discussed the upgrade of their three-decade-long cooperation to a new strategic level, including piloting trilateral aid cooperation in Third World countries, which China's ministers agreed to (UNDP, 2009b). MOFCOM minister, Chen Deming, noted that the planned trilateral partnership would greatly support development in Third World countries, and that China's minister of environmental protection, Zhou Shengxian, expressed his willingness to share China's environment-friendly technologies with other developing countries through trilateral cooperation with the UNDP (UNDP, 2009b).

With Premier Wen and Administrator Clark as witnesses, MOFCOM Vice Minister Wang Chao[10] and UN Assistant Secretary-General and UNDP Assistant Administrator Ajay Chhibber signed an MOU on

---

8　This point is supported by the author's interview with Chinese aid officials (Beijing, August 2015). It also builds on the author's observations during his decade-long career as a diplomat.

9　This point is also supported by the author's interview with a UNDP official (Canberra, 29 June 2016).

10　Wang has been a career MOFCOM official since 1982. He was appointed as vice foreign minister (third-highest-ranking vice minister) in January 2014. This is a rare movement, as most MFA senior officials have been appointed from within rather than outside. The other exemption is Vice Foreign Minister Xie Hangsheng, who used to work in the People's Bank of China. To some extent, Wang's appointment as vice foreign minister could be interpreted as Xi Jinping administration's emphasis on the economic diplomacy in its foreign policy.

strengthened cooperation between China and UNDP in New York in September 2010, the first of its kind that China had signed with a multilateral organisation (UNDP China, 2015e). The two sides pledged to focus their partnership on five main areas: 1) trilateral cooperation; 2) experience sharing on foreign aid systems; 3) global and regional issues; 4) private sector engagement and south–south cooperation; and 5) sharing development experiences and lessons through south–south dialogue (UNDP China, 2013a, p. 1).

The signing of this MOU further reflects China's trust of the UNDP. As the MOU stated, 'The trilateral cooperation (between China and UNDP in the future) should be built on an existing long standing, trusted and strong base of cooperation in the past thirty years' (UNDP and MOFCOM, 2010). The stated aims were, in addition to bringing greater benefits for the recipient countries, that China and the UNDP would strengthen their understanding of each other's foreign aid modalities through trilateral aid cooperation (UNDP, 2015c).

In its development assistance framework for China (2011–2015), the UNDP aims to encourage China's greater participation in the global community to cause wider mutual benefits. To achieve this target, the UNDP pledged to further facilitate the sharing of China's development experience with other developing countries through ways including the UN–China south–south trilateral development partnership (UNDP, 2010, p. 19). In November 2010, the UNDP and China's Ministry of Science and Technology signed a letter of intent to conduct trilateral cooperation in Africa in the areas of food security and poverty alleviation in rural areas (UNDP China, 2015d). The two sides also signed a letter of intent to share the experience of their UNDP–China program on technical extension services for rural development with other developing countries.

From 27 August to 3 September 2013, UNDP administrator Helen Clark paid her second visit to China and exchanged views with senior Chinese officials on issues including south–south cooperation and trilateral partnership. During the meeting, China's Vice President Li Yuanchao expressed his support for China–UNDP south–south and trilateral cooperation (Dai & Li, 2013; UNDP China, 2013b). He also commended the UNDP's three major contributions to China's development as follows.

Although some analysts regard the UNDP as an ineffective aid provider, Vice President Li's remarks sent a signal that the Chinese government is supportive of China's continued cooperative relations with the UNDP:

> 1. Bringing in and spreading advanced ideas and concepts, such as sustainable human development. 2. Helping to train Chinese Government officials, including officials from central to local levels. 3. Piloting new approaches to solving China's development challenges in poverty reduction, governance and environmental protection. (UNDP China, 2013b)

Table 9 is an overview of China–UNDP trilateral aid projects. In addition to the recipient countries involved, more countries have expressed interest in cooperation (UNDP China, 2014b, p. 5). The UNDP is optimistic that its trilateral cooperation with China will be extended to new countries and sectors (UNDP China, 2015f, p. 10).

Table 9. China–UNDP trilateral aid projects

Recipient country	Area	Partner in China	Funding (USD)	Status
Cambodia	Agriculture (cassava cultivation and exporting)	MOFCOM	Phase one China: 210,000	2011–2012
			Phase two China: 400,000	2013–2015
Ghana	Renewable energy	Ministry of Science and Technology	Denmark: 2,720,000 China provides expertise	2014–2019
Zambia	Renewable energy	Ministry of Science and Technology	Denmark: 2,624,400 China provides expertise	2014–2019
Bangladesh Nepal	Disaster risk management	Ministry of Civil Affairs	Phase one DFID (UK): 4.2 million China provides expertise	2012–2015
			Phase two DFID (UK): 6.1 million China provides expertise	2015–2017
Malawi	Disaster risk management	MOFCOM	MOFCOM: 500,000 UNDP Malawi: 400,000	2016–2018

Source. Compiled by the author from online data and interviews.[11]

---

11 The China–UNDP–Burundi project on renewable energy, which was included in UNDP's website, has been suspended due to the civil war in Burundi.

China's Domestic Structure on Working with the UNDP

As mentioned in Chapter 3, MOFCOM is designated by the Chinese government as the point of contact for the UNDP's activities in China. This signifies that the UNDP must go through MOFCOM before it can contact other line ministries in China—such as agriculture, health, science and technology—no matter whether the issue of discussion is within MOFCOM's portfolio or not (Interviews with Chinese aid officials and scholars, Beijing, August–September 2015). This is a tricky issue that often confuses aid officials and analysts of other countries and even Chinese scholars.

Here are two examples. Though agricultural cooperation is within the portfolio of China's Ministry of Agriculture, the China–UNDP–Cambodia trilateral project on cassava is completed by MOFCOM because it provided the funding and it had interest in doing so. Dr Prum Somany, then deputy director of the Department of International Cooperation from the Cambodia Ministry of Agriculture, Forestry and Fisheries (MAFF) and the main participant of the trilateral cassava project from the MAFF, said that 'I really want to include China MOA in this project, but Chinese policy is that foreign aid has to go through MOFCOM' (Interview with Dr Prum Somany, Phnom Penh, 15 July 2015). For the China–UNDP trilateral projects on renewable energies in Ghana and Zambia, although MOFCOM provided the funding from the Chinese side, MOFCOM does not want to manage the projects, so they passed to China's Ministry of Science and Technology (MOST). Another reason for MOFCOM's involvement in the Cambodia project and MOST's involvement in the Ghana and Zambia projects is that the Cambodia project, being explorative in nature, was the first pilot project between China and the UNDP, and MOFCOM was cautious. The UNDP also aimed to promote MOFCOM's understanding of trilateral partnership through this project. In contrast, the Ghana and Zambia projects are more technical in nature. They relate to the transfer of Chinese technical expertise through MOST to Ghana and Zambia (Interview with UNDP official, Canberra, 29 June 2016).

More specifically, MOFCOM's DITEA has historically taken responsibility for receiving the UNDP's aid to China. Benefiting from its established network with the UNDP, DITEA remains the liaison contact for UNDP China regardless of whether the issues are about the UNDP's aid to China or trilateral aid projects with China in Third World countries. This arrangement becomes 'the structural constraint in the first place' for the UNDP to seek cooperation directly with MOFCOM's DFA, which overlooks Chinese aid overseas (Interview with former senior UNDP official, Canberra, 28 June 2016).

A latest shift in China–UNDP trilateral aid cooperation is that the DFA has, since September 2015, started to actively approach the UNDP for trilateral partnerships. This is in stark contrast to the tradition that DITEA rather than the DFA is the main partner for UNDP China. One main reason, according to UNDP officials, is that the DFA is eagerly searching for appropriate trilateral projects to materialise part of the $2 billion south–south cooperation fund pledged by Chinese President Xi Jinping at the UN sustainable development summit in September 2015 (Interview with UNDP officials, Canberra, 29 June and 4 July 2016). UNDP China is now consequently conducting two streams of trilateral projects with MOFCOM, one with DITEA and one with the DFA.

Evolving Trends in Aid to Cambodia

Cambodia is one of the most aid-dependent countries in Asia. Foreign aid has accounted for nearly 90 per cent of the Cambodian government's expenditure since 2005 (Council for the Development of Cambodia, 2008, p. 1). The total amount of foreign aid to Cambodia reached about $5.5 billion over the period 1998 to 2007 (Sato, Shiga, Kobayashi & Kondoh, 2011, p. 2093). Between 1990 and 2018, Cambodia received aid from about 40 bilateral and multilateral donors, including Australia, Canada, China, France, Japan, South Korea, the US, the World Bank and the ADB for 3,140 aid projects (CDC, 2018).[12] In 2018, total disbursements for aid projects in Cambodia exceeded $1.1 billion (CDC, 2018).

---

12   The database of the council for the development of Cambodia includes the completed, ongoing, suspended and pipeline projects. Most of them fall under the category of completed or ongoing projects.

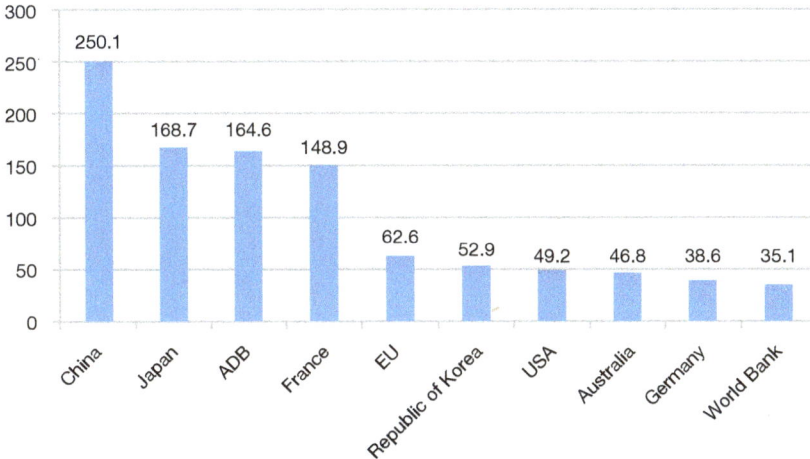

Figure 8. Top 10 donors in Cambodia in 2018, USD million
Source. Compiled by the author from the CDC aid database.

Figure 8 lists the top 10 donors in Cambodia in 2018 in terms of aid disbursement. By 2018, the UNDP had a total of 75 aid projects in Cambodia (CDC, 2018). With an aid of $10.8 million, the UNDP was the 15th largest donor in 2018 (CDC, 2018). Some notable evolving trends in aid to Cambodia in the last two decades include that 1) foreign aid to Cambodia has increased over time, rising from $555.4 million in 2004 to over $1.1 billion in 2018 (Council for the Development of Cambodia, p. ii; CDC, 2018); 2) countries such as Kuwait and Qatar have joined the donor camp to provide aid to Cambodia; and 3) aid from China to Cambodia has grown rapidly and this trend continues. In particular, Chinese aid to the infrastructure sector in Cambodia has been prominent, as will be discussed.

Chinese Aid to Cambodia

China began developing close relations with Cambodia since the latter's independence from France in 1953. China's leadership, including that of the late Chairman Mao Zedong and Premier Zhou Enlai, established a strong friendship with Cambodia's late King-Father, Norodom Sihanouk, on certain occasions, including at the Bandung Conference, the first Asian-African conference that was held in Bandung, Indonesia in April 1955. Cambodia has lent persistent support to the 'one China policy', a most important and sensitive issue in China's diplomacy. Sophie Richardson (2010, p. 48) argued that 'without Cambodia's help, China's battle to regain the UN seat (from Taiwan in October 1971) would likely have taken far longer than a decade', though most of the Chinese discourse tends to give the credit to Africa.

Chinese foreign aid to Cambodia dates back to 1956. On 21 June 1956, the two countries signed an agreement on economic assistance, making Cambodia the first non-socialist country in Asia, Africa and Latin America to receive Chinese aid. Based on the agreement, China provided a grant of £8 million for in-kind assistance and infrastructure projects, including textile, plywood, paper making and cement plants (Shi, 1989, pp. 37–38). The four factories produced around half of Cambodia's gross industrial output at the time and they laid the foundation for the earliest modern enterprises in Cambodia (Zhou & Xiong, 2013, p. 216). This aid agreement was credited by the Chinese government as 'a concrete result of China and Cambodia's implementation of the resolution of the Bandung Conference, and another good example of the peaceful coexistence and friendly cooperation among Asian countries' (People's Daily, 1956, p. 1).

Chinese aid to Cambodia is divided into two main periods by Xue Li from China Academy of Social Sciences and Xiao Huanrong from the Communication University of China (Xue & Xiao, 2011). China mainly provided grants and military support to Cambodia in the period 1953–1989. Chinese aid was strongly ideology-based and gave scant consideration to economic return. Since 1990, and especially in recent years, China has emphasised a mutual benefit in its aid to Cambodia: concessional loans rather than grants became the main form of assistance. For example, among the $600 million in aid pledged by visiting Premier Wen Jiabao in 2006, the overwhelming majority was in the form of concessional loans (Xue & Xiao, 2011, p. 27).

China's influence and aid to Cambodia has grown rapidly over the past two decades. The Cambodian government led by Prime Minister Hun Sun turned to Beijing for diplomatic and financial support after 1997, when it faced considerable pressure from Western donors after the coup to oust co-premier Prince Norodom Ranariddh. An important reason for the peak of Chinese aid to Cambodia in 2012, as shown in Figure 9, also relates to President Hu Jintao's state visit to Cambodia from late March to early April in 2012. As a common practice in China's diplomacy, China signed numerous projects, including aid projects with Cambodia during this high-level visit. In addition, China's largesse in 2012 could also be attributed to China's seeking diplomatic support on sensitive regional issues, especially the South China Sea when Cambodia chaired ASEAN in 2012.

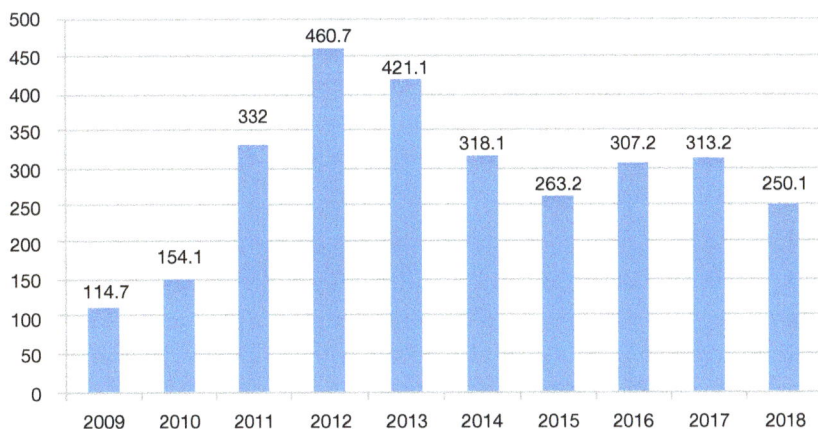

Figure 9. Chinese aid to Cambodia, 2009–2018, USD million

Source. Compiled by the author from the CDC aid database.[13]

Table 10. Summary of China's aid projects in Cambodia by 2018

	Grant aid projects	Concessional loan projects
Total number	18	62
Total value	$309.5 million	$4,316.5 million
Percentage of project value	6.7%	93.3%

Source. Compiled by the author from the CDC aid database.[14]

Table 10 provides an overview of China's aid projects in Cambodia. According to the aid database of the council for the development of Cambodia—the government agency in charge of aid in Cambodia— China provided a total budget value of around $4,626 million for 80 aid projects in Cambodia by December 2018 (CDC, 2018).[15] Large infrastructure projects with China's concessional loans are visible across Cambodia. Among the 62 concessional loan projects in Table 10, 60 are infrastructure projects that include roads, bridges, agricultural irrigation and electricity transmission. Though the workload of China's foreign aid

---

13   As some Chinese aid projects take a few years to complete, especially large infrastructure projects, yearly disbursements may differ. To some extent, this explains the fluctuations in the figure.
14   This graph is made by the author based on the aid database from the council for the development of Cambodia.
15   The database includes most Chinese concessional loans projects in Cambodia, but grants and interest-free loans are incomplete. For example, it does not include the Cambodia Senate building project ($7.7 million, grants), the Cambodia agricultural laboratory building ($9.26 million, grants) and two MA 60 aircraft to the Cambodian military (interest-free loan). The date of access to DCD database was 20 December 2018.

in Cambodia is heavy and growing, there are only two staff working on aid from the economic and commercial counsellor's office from the Chinese Embassy in Cambodia. This makes it extremely difficult for the embassy to effectively manage its aid program. It could also partially explain why the embassy's involvement in the China–UNDP–Cambodia trilateral cassava project is limited.

In addition to infrastructure, China has provided a large quantity of aid to the Cambodian military, such as donating helicopters, trucks, aircraft, uniforms and providing military training. For example, Cambodia purchased two MA 60 aircraft from China in 2012 with Chinese interest-free loans (MOFCOM, 2012).

China–UNDP–Cambodia Trilateral Project on Cassava

| Initiation and signing MOU Sept 2010 | First phase Dec 2011 – Jan 2012 | Second phase Jan 2013 – Mar 2015 | Monitoring and assessment Dec 2014 |

Figure 10. Timeframe of the China–UNDP–Cambodia trilateral project
Source. Compiled by the author from own analysis.

Phase One: Capacity Building (December 2011 – January 2012)

The trilateral cassava project is the first trilateral project since China and the UNDP signed their MOU on strengthened cooperation in 2010. Discussions occurred between China and the UNDP regarding the possibility of exploring trilateral cooperation. According to Napoleon Navarro, then deputy country director of UNDP China, UNDP initiated this trilateral cassava project. China agreed to 'experiment' with trilateral cooperation, but 'there was some caution of what we will do and how we can do it' (Interview with Napoleon Navarro, Phnom Penh, 15 July 2015).

In 2011, a scoping mission from UNDP China visited Cambodia to flesh out this project. Officials from UNDP China and UNDP Cambodia discussed issues with the Cambodian MAFF. An episode occurred during discussion. Prum Somany from the MAFF at first mistook the trilateral cooperation proposal as another China–Cambodia south–south cooperation project. He explained that he was concerned, because south–south cooperation is difficult to implement in Cambodia because it requires Cambodia to pay for the accommodation of international experts and local transport, which MAFF could not afford due to its limited budget (Interview with Dr Prum Somany, Phnom Penh, 15 July 2015). He was later briefed that it would be a new type of initiative.

According to Dr Somany, the proposal for trilateral cooperation came at the right time because although China had signed two bilateral agreements with Cambodia in agriculture,[16] Cambodia did not have the capacity to produce good-quality and large volumes of cassava for export to China. As such, Dr Somany proposed the cassava sector to the visiting UNDP delegation for a potential project (Interview with Dr Prum Somany, Phnom Penh, 15 July 2015). This proposal was also supported by MOFCOM.

The first phase of the project was undertaken by UNDP China and MOFCOM from 27 December 2011 to 16 January 2012. Thirty trainees were selected from Cambodia, including the general directorate of agriculture, the provincial departments of agriculture, the Royal University of Agriculture, Cambodian Agricultural Research and Development Institute, Prek Leap and Kampong Cham National Schools of Agriculture (UNDP Cambodia, 2012). They attended three weeks of training on cassava cultivation techniques at the China Academy of Tropical Agricultural Sciences (CATAS) in Haikou (China Academy of Tropical Agricultural Sciences, 2012).

The training combined classroom lecturing, visits to CATAS cassava laboratories and field experimentation. The training covered numerous topics, including soil preparation, variety selection, breeding and genetic transplantation, planting techniques, pest control, weeding, harvesting and processing (UNDP Cambodia, 2012). Deputy Division Director Cai Fang from MOFCOM's DFA addressed the opening ceremony on behalf of the Chinese government (China Academy of Tropical Agricultural Sciences, 2012, p. 13). Zhu Hong, deputy director-general from MOFCOM's DITEA, and Christophe Bahuet, UNDP country

---

16 They include an MOU on strengthening agricultural cooperation (March 2010), and the MOU on sanitary and phytosanitary (SPS) cooperation in the field of animal and plant inspection and quarantine; the protocol of phyto-sanitary requirement for Cambodia's milled rice export to China; and cooperation relating to the working plan of the quarantine market access of tapioca chips from Cambodia to China (October 2010).

representative in China, officiated at the conclusion of the training and promised to provide further support (UNDP Cambodia, 2012). Their commitment materialised in the second phase of the project.

MOFCOM contributed $210,000 (RMB 1.3 million) to this first phase (Mo, 2013). It provided training facilities, experts, accommodation and related expenses. UNDP offices in China and Cambodia conducted a comprehensive assessment of Cambodia's training demands. They also contributed to the training agenda and fielded an international expert on cassava and a Chinese-speaking staff member from UNDP Cambodia to facilitate during the training. The government of Cambodia, mainly through MAFF, set forth the demands for training and selected the trainees (UNDP China, 2012, p. 2).

Phase Two: Cassava Cultivation and Trading (January 2013 – March 2015)

Phase Two was designed to be an extension and expansion of Phase One. While the first phase focused on capacity building for cassava cultivation, the second phase extended the scope of cooperation to cassava cultivation and trading. It aimed to assist Cambodian cassava growers to cultivate high-quality products and move up the trade chain while minimising the environmental influence (UNDP China, 2015f, p. 9).

Due to a lack of technical support and market information, Cambodia is incapable of exporting its cassava products directly to the international market. In 2012, it had to export half of its fresh cassava, 40 per cent of its dried cassava and 10 per cent of its cassava starch to traders in Vietnam and Thailand (Mo, 2013). By exploring the route to market, the project aimed to improve farmers' livelihoods by promoting direct export of cassava products to China, rather than by having profits be captured by middlemen in Vietnam and Thailand.

This project had a project steering committee that was comprised of the Department of International Cooperation from Cambodia MAFF, the Cambodia Agricultural Research Development Institute, the Trade Promotion Department of Cambodia Ministry of Commerce, the Cambodia Association of Cassava Exporters and Producers, MOFCOM, UNDP Cambodia and UNDP China (Cambodia MAFF and UNDP Cambodia, 2013, p. 10). Cambodia MAFF was the project implementer responsible for overall daily activities. Benefiting from its familiarity with China, UNDP China assumed the role of a 'strategic liaison partner', responsible for coordinating with UNDP Cambodia, MOFCOM and Chinese institutions and technical experts. MOFCOM played a role as the financial and technical partner. It contributed $400,000 to finance the project (Cambodia MAFF and UNDP Cambodia, 2013), making China's total contribution to the two phases $610,000. It also maintained close contact with UNDP China regarding the progress of the project, including monitoring and assessment. Through UNDP China, Chinese agricultural experts were also hired to provide technical input for the environmental impact report and technical solutions during project implementation.

The second phase of the project claims achievements, including:

> The completion of need assessment study, environmental impact study, development of the training materials, ad hoc training, training of trainers, business matching mission to Guangxi, and joint monitoring mission from China. (UNDP, 2015a)

To meet the targets that were set out in the project document, the project team completed a 'needs assessment study' in consultation with Cambodian cassava farmers, processors and exporters (Cambodia MAFF and UNDP Cambodia, 2013; UNDP, 2015a). In addition, as cassava growth has been expanding rapidly in Cambodia while its environmental impact and related mitigation solutions are unknown (Interview with Dr Prum Somany, Phnom Penh, 15 July 2015), an 'environmental impact study' was conducted that examined the potential short- and long-term effects of cassava cultivation on the environment, such as soil degradation/ erosion and water pollution (UNDP, 2015a). The research found that cassava production in Cambodia would not necessarily have a negative environmental impact, which is contrary to some people's presumption (Interview with UNDP Cambodia officials, Phnom Penh, 15 July 2015).

Based on the abovementioned 'needs assessment study' and 'environmental impact study', the project team tailored training manuals for trainers, farmers, processors and exporters, as sampled in Figure 11 (Cambodia MAFF and UNDP Cambodia, 2015). One training program was provided to agricultural extension workers, who later acted as trainers for cassava farmers. Two sessions of training were conducted to the selected farmers in the cassava provinces of Tbaung Khnum and Kampong Cham. The training covered theoretical lecturing, interactive discussion and field demonstration (UNDP, 2015a). In total, the trilateral project has provided technical training to 114 beneficiaries (UNDP China, 2015b).

Accounting for the small scale of this trilateral project ($610,000) and the huge challenges that Cambodia's agricultural extension system faces, the final effect of the above technical training on Cambodia's cassava industry should not be overestimated.

In addition to the improvement of cassava production, market exploration was another major task of the trilateral project. In September 2014, a 17-member Cambodian business-matching mission visited Guangxi, the largest cassava growing and trading province in China (UNDP China, 2015f, p. 9). The mission was composed of Cambodian MAFF officials, UNDP staff, cassava farmers, processors and traders and it was led by He Mom Thany, Under Secretary of State from MAFF. By meeting with the Chinese hosts—including the vice governor of Guangxi, MOFCOM officials, private business and research institutes—the delegation improved its understanding of the cassava demands and technical requirements of the Chinese markets and increased its business links with Chinese businesspeople, which paved the way for the direct export of Cambodian cassava to China. An example is that in November 2014, the Cambodian company, Advanced Glory Logistics, was contracted to export 150,000 tons of cassava directly to the Chinese biofuel firm Henan Tianguan Group, and the first shipment occurred in January 2015 (Styllis & Sony, 2015).

Figure 11. Project training manual for farmers (pp. 1 and 5)
Source. Cambodian MAFF and UNDP Cambodia (2015).

China's Motivations

As China's foreign aid has increased dramatically since 2000, traditional donors and UN agencies have either phased out or reduced their aid programs in China. They have concurrently approached China to explore new types of cooperation, including trilateral aid cooperation. Similarly, UNDP China has been actively promoting trilateral partnership with China in Third World countries. In this circumstance, China has agreed to test trilateral cooperation as a response to increasing calls for cooperation from the UNDP. What is visible is that China hopes to project an image that it is ready to work together with the UNDP to deliver better foreign aid to the Third World countries. As one of China's agricultural experts who was heavily involved in the cassava project emphasised, 'Working with UNDP on this trilateral project will help project China's image globally and in Cambodia as a responsible power' (Interview, Beijing, 25 August 2015). MOFCOM former Vice Minister Long Yongtu also believed that cooperating with the UN in foreign aid is beneficial for China's global image:

> China was poor in the past. When China provided aid to other countries at that time, it was appreciated because China was poor. But nowadays (as China becomes rich), Chinese aid is not appreciated that much because the recipient countries tend to suspect some hidden agenda behind it. In this case, I believe the UN system provides a new channel and good framework for China's foreign aid and South–South cooperation, and will help improve the effectiveness of China's foreign aid. (Long, 2015, p. 47)

In addition, China feels more comfortable in piloting trilateral cooperation with the UNDP because of the UNDP's political neutrality,[17] China's membership of the UNDP and the trust that has been accumulated over the past four decades. Long Yongtu emphasised that the UNDP's political neutrality was a main reason for China's acceptance of its aid in the late 1970s, as China believed that the UNDP would not interfere in its sovereignty and impose pressures on its policies (Long, 2015, p. 46). While China suspects a 'hidden agenda' behind traditional donor states' push for trilateral cooperation, it feels more relaxed working with the UNDP. That is also why China insists that the UN should

---

17   This point is also supported by the author's interview with a UNDP official (Beijing, 18 August 2015).

play a central role in global governance, including in the post-2015 development agenda. Li Baodong, China's deputy foreign minister in charge of multilateral affairs argued that:

> The UN system has played a key coordinating role in advancing the MDGs, and the UNDP in particular deserves much of the credit. China always believes that it is important to establish and improve an international development architecture centred on the United Nations and supported by other multilateral institutions. (Li, 2014, para. 17)

The trust of the UN and the desire to burnish China's global image by supporting the UN system also explains China's recent agreement to a substantial increase of its UN membership fee (7.9 per cent) and contribution to UN peacekeeping (10.2 per cent) over the period 2016–2018. According to Ambassador Wang Min, deputy representative of China's permanent mission to the UN, this increase reflects China's responsibility and obligation as a UN member (China's Permanent Mission to UN, 2015).

Geo-strategic Considerations

It would be valuable to analyse the China–Cambodia bilateral relationship here, which is characterised by complex historical and geo-strategic considerations. There is a compelling alternative argument: China conducts trilateral aid cooperation for its own strategic and geopolitical gain.

China has invested substantial efforts, including through foreign aid, to strengthen its strategic relations with Cambodia. This can be to a great extent attributed to Cambodia's geopolitical position in China's diplomacy in Southeast Asia. This becomes more obvious in recent years, as China faces mounting pressure from some ASEAN countries regarding sensitive issues, such as maritime disputes with countries such as the Philippines and Vietnam over territory in the South China Sea. According to Colonel Veasna Var from the Cambodian Royal Army:

> For China, Cambodia has the strategic importance of its geopolitical location allowing for security and oversight in the South China Sea with Vietnam, Taiwan, and the Philippines, especially to secure its claim on the disputed Spratly Islands and natural resources. (Var, 2011, p. 32)

China's largesse in Cambodia has yielded success. Cambodia has provided open support for China, even at the expense of irritating ASEAN member states. In July 2012, the ASEAN foreign ministers' meeting in Phnom Penh failed to issue a joint communiqué for the first time in its 45-year history. As the rotating chair, Cambodia was blamed for siding with China on the South China Sea disputes (BBC, 2012). Colonel Veasna Var noted that 'Cambodia's foreign policies are heavily influenced by China. Cambodia is playing a strategic[ally] important role for China's political diplomatic interests in the region and the world' (Var, 2014, p. 10). He also argued that the Cambodian government has taken different approaches to the construction of dams by China and Laos along the Mekong River. While expressing strong opposition to the construction of dams in Laos, due to China's massive economic influence in Cambodia, the Cambodian government took a softened stance on Chinese dams and was reluctant to take up this issue directly (Var, 2011, pp. 28–29). In April 2016, Cambodia, along with Laos and Brunei, reached a four-point consensus with China that supported China's position on the settlement of the South China Sea disputes (MFA, 2016b).

Others argue that the Cambodian government acted in China's favour on several sensitive issues, including denying the visa to Dalai Lama, repressing Falun Gong practitioners in Cambodia in 2002 and withdrawing support for Japan's 2005 bid for a permanent UN Security Council seat (Ciorciari, 2015, pp. 261–262). While the US slammed Cambodia's deportation of 20 Uyghur asylum seekers to China in December 2009 (Cable News Network, 2009), China's MFA spokeswoman, Jiang Yu, insisted that 'every country [referring to Cambodia] has its right to make decisions according to its domestic laws' (People's Daily, 2009). She reiterated China's no-strings-attached aid principle amid speculation that this deportation case was linked to China's aid in Cambodia (People's Daily, 2009). In April 2012, China's former ambassador to Cambodia, Hu Qianwen, credited Cambodia's support for China. He said that 'Cambodia has provided a "high-degree" of understanding and support for China's core interests including the Taiwan and Tibet issues, and also maintained a "just" position on the South China Sea issue' (Xinhua, 2012).

It is fair to admit that the geo-strategic factor has dominated China's foreign aid to Cambodia due to its geopolitical importance to China's diplomacy. China has a much stronger strategic interest in Cambodia than in the other two recipient countries—PNG and Timor-Leste, which are my selected cases of trilateral cooperation in Chapters 5 and 6. However, it is evident that this geo-strategic factor alone is insufficient for explaining China's adoption of trilateral cooperation in Cambodia. First, as bilateral aid would better serve China's geo-strategic benefits because China would not need to share the credit with other donors—diluting its influence on the Cambodian regime—why should China agree to conduct this cassava project in a trilateral way? Second, Cambodia, PNG and Timor-Leste have different geo-strategic weights in China's diplomacy, but China has conducted trilateral aid cooperation in each of these countries. This makes the geo-strategic consideration not a necessary and decisive factor in China's trilateral aid cooperation. Conversely, the global image factor has a stronger explanatory strength in analysing this trilateral cassava project in Cambodia.

Learning by Doing

As discussed in Section One of this chapter, China hopes to improve its aid delivery by learning from the UNDP's experiences. For example, China expects its trilateral project with the UNDP on renewable energy in Ghana 'will support the review and updating of South–South cooperation policies and guidelines' and 'contribute to solid capacity building, enabling China to engage more systematically in South–South cooperation' (UNDP China, 2015c). China's learning desire is also evident in this trilateral cassava project. As one Chinese agricultural expert involved in the cassava project suggested, China wanted to learn from the UNDP's expertise and this project has exactly combined China's funding with the UNDP's expertise (Interview, Beijing, 25 August 2015).

China hopes to learn to pilot its aid in soft areas by moving away from over-concentrating on difficult infrastructure projects, which could improve China's aid delivery. This problem has been highlighted by Chinese scholars, such as Song Lianghe from Xiamen University and Wu Yijun from Jilin University (Song & Wu, 2013). Currently, most of Chinese aid projects in Cambodia are supported by concessional loans (see Figures 12 and 13), with fixed interest rates of 1, 1.25 or 2 per cent.

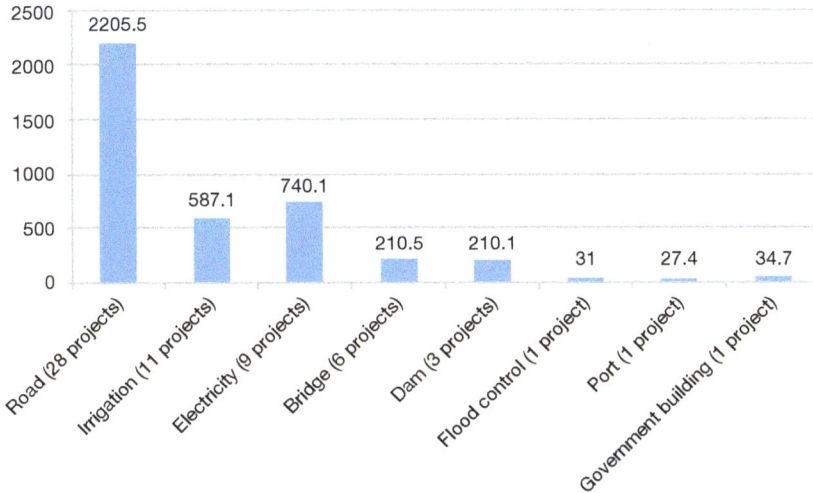

Figure 12. China's infrastructure concessional loans projects in Cambodia by value, USD million

Source. Compiled by the author from the CDC aid database.

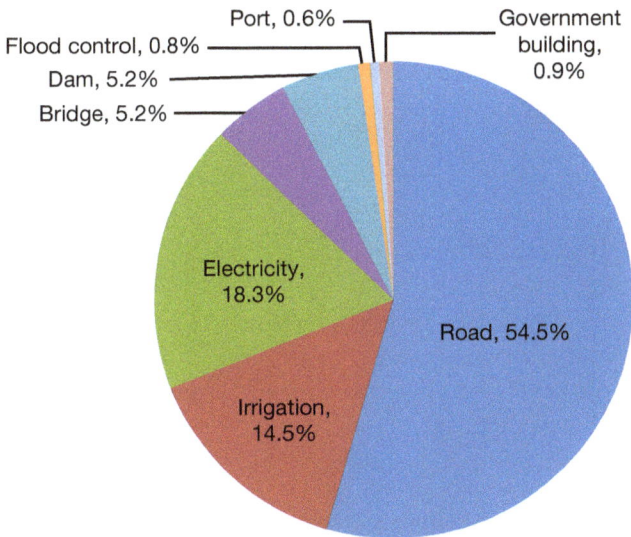

Figure 13. China's infrastructure concessional loans projects in Cambodia by percentage

Source. Compiled by the author from the CDC aid database.

137

Though infrastructure projects are of great significance to Cambodia, China is mindful that it must increase its aid in soft areas such as capacity building to complement the hard projects. As such, China's economic and commercial counsellor's office in Cambodia expressed interest in the trilateral cassava project, noting that '"soft, grassroots-oriented" trilateral cooperation helps shape "hard" bilateral aid and business towards more poverty reducing outcomes' (UNDP China, 2014a). Hannah Ryder, head of the policy and partnership unit of UNDP China, concurs with this view. She elaborated:

> What have we learned about China's south–south cooperation from this project? I think there are two things we have learned. First that China's south–south cooperation at the moment especially is very hard infrastructure focused. We hear about it all the time. But with this project and increasingly so, China is expressing a real interest in more grassroots poverty reduction livelihood-focused type projects. They are harder to implement and harder to get results from but China is really interested. The second thing we have learned is that China really cares about the fact that government (of the recipient country) owns the project. (UNDP China, 2015b)[18]

Facing donors' evolving aid policies, including China's attempt to invest more aid in 'soft' areas, the Cambodian government's position has been detached to a great extent. Some scholars argue that Cambodia welcomes emerging donors' aid as an alternative to aid from traditional donors and that it is reluctant to address aid fragmentation (Sato, Shiga, Kobayashi & Kondoh, 2010, p. 18; Greenhill, Prizzon & Rogerson, 2013, pp. 28–30). As a response, Cambodian senior aid officials argued that their government has been promoting aid coordination and that it has welcomed donors to provide aid to areas of comparative advantage, 'But at the end of the day, donors, especially those who bring in their own grants and own money, they have a lot more say than the Cambodian government' (Interviews with Cambodian officials, Phnom Penh, 3 and 7 July 2015).

In light of this, while the Cambodian government welcomes Chinese aid in the infrastructure in Cambodia, it is also open to China's growing input in aiding 'soft' areas. To elaborate, while appreciating China's no-strings-attached principle and huge contribution to the infrastructure in

---

18   This transcript is derived from a video clip on the UNDP China website regarding the trilateral cassava project.

Cambodia, Cambodian aid officials have also shown interest in improving Chinese aid practices in Cambodia by promoting China's learning from traditional donors. One senior Cambodian aid official revealed his observation of aid projects from China and Japan in his country: while working on the same type of aid, such as road projects, the Japanese aid workers will talk to the local people including the villagers and establish good public relations, while the Chinese workers seldom do this and just focus on their work. This official noted that it would be beneficial for China to learn from their Japanese colleagues (Interview, Phnom Penh, 27 May 2015).

Agriculture is a major sector for Chinese aid in Cambodia. It has been highlighted as one of the three priority areas for bilateral cooperation[19] since 2002 (Li, Ye & Mi, 2002). It is also included in the areas of cooperation under the China–Cambodia 'Strategic Comprehensive Partnership Agreement of 2010', an umbrella document that guides bilateral cooperation. As China's aid to the agricultural sector in Cambodia traditionally focused on individual infrastructure projects and technical training, the second phase of the trilateral cassava project 'brings in a more systematic way of providing support in the form of a longer-term development project' (UNDP, 2015a). The cassava industry is an ideal sector for experimentation as China is the largest importer of cassava products, importing 84 per cent of global import for fresh/dried cassava and 34.5 per cent for cassava starch in 2012 (Cambodian Government, 2014, p. 319). The Cambodian government places high hopes on the Chinese market. Moreover, there is great room for Cambodia's export, as the bilateral trade is in China's favour with a surplus of $2.8 billion in 2014, nearly six times that of Cambodian export to China ($483 million)—though food export accounts for 6.6 per cent (He, 2015).

The UNDP's Motivations

The UNDP has aligned its development assistance with the development priorities that have been set out by the Cambodian government. The UN development assistance framework (2011–2015) for Cambodia has made economic development and sustainable development (including enhancing Cambodia's agricultural sector) as the UNDP's first priority in Cambodia (UN Cambodia and Cambodian Government, 2010).

---

19   The other two areas are human resources development and infrastructure construction.

As the UNDP pledges to scale up its support for south–south and trilateral cooperation in its strategic plan for 2014 to 2017 (UNDP, 2013), it has been enthusiastic to shift from providing aid to China to promoting trilateral partnership in Third World countries. This can potentially promote aid effectiveness in other developing countries by leveraging China's resources and fresh development experiences and UNDP's expertise, management and worldwide networks. Further, as some Chinese and UNDP officials stated, by trilateral cooperation, the UNDP expects to influence the reforms of Chinese aid policies by encouraging China to learn from the UNDP (Interviews, Beijing, 18 and 20 August 2015). Moreover, the UNDP is keen to maintain the networks with the Chinese government.

The UNDP has taken the lead in promoting trilateral partnership with China and has maintained the trust it has earned over the years from MOFCOM. For example, while insisting traditional donor states should provide funding for trilateral projects with China, China is willing to fully underwrite trilateral cooperation projects that are completed with the UNDP, allowing the cash-poor UN agency to bring only technical assistance to the table. Cooperating with the UNDP is appealing to the Chinese government in two main ways. First, it bears plenty of symbolic significance, as the UNDP is the UN's largest development agency. Partnership with the UNDP could strengthen China's image as a responsible member state within the UN system. Second, the Chinese government is keen to benefit from the UNDP's abundant expertise and wide network in development (UNDP and MOFCOM, 2010). However, compared to some other multilateral agencies such as the World Bank, the UNDP's available funding to China is limited, which to some extent limits its influence in China.

The roles of different UNDP offices in this trilateral cassava project must be explained. The UNDP head office was not directly involved in project implementation, but their support, such as through UNDP administrator Helen Clark's two visits to China in 2009 and 2013, set the general tone for trilateral cooperation with China. UNDP China played a major role in the project, such as by liaising with all the relevant actors, selecting Chinese cassava experts and making project assessment. Their main goal was to make this trilateral project a model for the UNDP's trilateral partnership with China. UNDP Cambodia was responsible for liaising with the Cambodian government, jointly selecting Cambodian trainees for the first phase of the project and jointly managing the second phase together with the Cambodian government. UNDP Cambodia's role was more supportive compared to UNDP China. It is helpful to mention that although UNDP China's communication with offices in other countries was blamed for being weak in some cases, its coordinating role in this project has seemingly been successful based on interviews with numerous actors.

Cambodia's Motivations

The Cambodian government is open to trilateral cooperation. Heng Chou, director-general from the Council for the Development of Cambodia noted that 'we welcome trilateral cooperation because of the advantages each partner brings to us' (Interview with Heng Chou, Phnom Penh, 7 July 2015). However, Cambodia's endorsement for this trilateral cassava project was pragmatic. This project was designed as an important part of larger support to the cassava industry under the Cambodia Export Diversification and Expansion Program funded by the Enhanced Integrated Framework under the Cambodia cassava trilateral assistance and diagnostic trade integration strategy enhancement program (Cambodia MAFF and UNDP Cambodia, 2013). Enhancing the agricultural sector has been persistently highlighted as the first side of the 'growth rectangle' in Cambodia's rectangular strategy phase I, II and III (Cambodian Government, 2004, 2008, 2013).

Cassava is the second-most important agricultural crop in Cambodia after rice. It is potentially among the five top global exporters of fresh/dry cassava and a conservative estimate of Cambodian cassava by informal exports was about $200–300 million in recent years (Cambodian Government, 2014, p. 318).[20] The planting area of cassava in Cambodia has increased dramatically from around 16,000 hectares in 2000 to more than 345,000 hectares in 2012 (Cambodian Government, 2014, p. 324).

However, the cassava sector faces serious challenges, such as rare technical support to the sector and limited market information. In addition, the Cambodian government noted that they need a trustworthy report with scientific evidence regarding the environmental impact of cassava cultivation to help them make decisions in the cassava industry (Cambodia MAFF and UNDP Cambodia, 2013, p. 3). Teng Lao, secretary of state

---

20   According to the Cambodia government, most of its cassava export belongs to the informal and unrecorded cross-border trade with Thailand and Vietnam.

from Cambodia MAFF, noted that 'though 80 per cent of Cambodia's population work in the agriculture sector, lack of access to the market information and technology has made the export of Cambodian agricultural products extremely difficult' (Mo, 2013).

For cassava exports to China, one challenge is transport costs and seaport loading capacity. Another hurdle is the inability of Cambodian cassava products (e.g. chips, starch, ethanol and animal feed) to meet stringent sanitary and phyto-sanitary requirements in China (Cambodia MAFF and UNDP Cambodia, 2013, p. 3). Due to technical and information constraints, Cambodian farmers, processors and exporters struggle to compete with their counterparts in other countries for the Chinese market.

To meet the challenges, the Cambodian government has emphasised the application of new technologies and the adding of value to agricultural products (Cambodian Government, 2013, p. 17). The Cambodian national strategic development plan (2014–2018) and the Cambodia trade integration strategy (2014–2018) established targets for enhancing cassava quality to meet sanitary and phyto-sanitary requirements, increase the direct export of cassava to China and Korea and reduce the dependence on exports of unprocessed tubers to Thailand and Vietnam (Cambodia MOP, 2014, pp. 74, 189; Cambodian Government, 2014, p. 24). This trilateral project was initiated and undertaken as a move in this direction.

Project Assessment

Overall, the three participants of the trilateral cassava project credited the project as a success, at least in public (Interviews with UNDP officials, Phnom Penh and Beijing, June–September 2015). In December 2014, a joint monitoring and reviewing mission led by Liang Hong,[21] division director of MOFCOM's DITEA, and Hannah Ryder, deputy country director of UNDP China, assessed the project progress in Cambodia, lauding it as 'a complete success' (UNDP China, 2014a). They have drawn the following lessons:

---

21 Linking this to the previous fact that Deputy Division Director Cai Fang from MOFCOM's DFA and Deputy Director General Zhu Hong from MOFCOM's DITEA were involved in Phase I, we can tell that the two departments were both involved in the trilateral cassava project.

The experience gained thus far shows the crucial importance of strong demand and buy-in from the third country government and participating institutions. These are not only core principles for both UNDP and the Chinese Government, but also the key to project success and sustainability. Work done in 2013 has also shown that trilateral cooperation as an innovative modality requires flexibility, with allowance to be made for a step-by-step process as partners learn about each other's approaches. Mutual learning is a key part of trilateral cooperation: different and complimentary contributions are made by all partners, and different approaches to what 'development' means and how it can best be achieved are seen as strengths. (UNDP China, 2014b, p. 5)

This project has yielded tangible results for the cultivation and export of Cambodian cassava to China's market. For example, in March 2013, the first shipment of 8,000 tons of dried Cambodian cassava left for China, which was the first time that Cambodia had exported cassava to China by shipping in bulk (Mo, 2013). The sanitary and phyto-sanitary issue is also being addressed. With a grant of around $9.26 million (over RMB 60 million), China funded the construction of the Cambodia agricultural laboratory building and donated three whole sets of sanitary and phyto-sanitary equipment for agricultural products (Peng, 2013).

However, although the two phases of the trilateral cassava project have exposed the Cambodian farmers, processors and traders to advanced cultivation technologies and market information in China, this is only a first step in a long journey. Dr Somany from Cambodia MAFF emphasised the need for follow-up. He highlighted that there are 500,000 cassava growers in Cambodia, while fewer than 120 of them have received training through the trilateral project. To test whether the training manuals are effective, the donors and the Cambodian government must provide trainees with more support, such as fertiliser. Otherwise, the farmers could not afford to buy fertiliser and follow the cultivation instructions in the manuals (Interview with Dr Prum Somany, Phnom Penh, 15 July 2015), which suggests to some extent that the training manuals are unrealistic, as they do not match with agricultural conditions and the financial circumstances of farmers. With a top-up of $50,000 from the UNDP, Cambodia MAFF was planning to establish 12 one-hectare family farms and provide inputs that included seeds and fertilisers to test the result of the training manuals (Interview with Dr Prum Somany, Phnom Penh, 15 July 2015). In addition, more work is needed in the long run to integrate different sectors of the cassava value chain, including growth, processing, marketing and exporting, as well as promoting closer coordination among government agencies and the private sector. Improvements in infrastructure, such as expanding seaport loading capacity, is needed. High-level commitment and support from Chinese and Cambodian governments on these issues are also needed.

Reservations exist for this cassava project. As this cassava project was small, some participants think it was set as too ambitious a target from the beginning, in regard to issues such as the environmental study and the link to the Chinese market (Interviews with one Chinese aid official and one UNDP official, Beijing, 4 and 18 August 2015). Niels Knudsen, assistant country director of UNDP China, stated that the UNDP–China joint assessment mission in December 2014 thought that the cassava project had reached the ceiling and faced practical challenges, including infrastructure and transport problems in Cambodia (Interview with Niels Knudsen from UNDP China, Beijing, 30 July 2015). A third phase pilot project apparently cannot help solve these problems. A third phase thus seems unlikely, unless the high-level leadership of MOFCOM and the UNDP wills it.

Conclusion

This trilateral cassava project in Cambodia is a model of China's trilateral cooperation with the UNDP that has played a catalytic role in promoting China's experimentation of this new modality. As the above discussion has demonstrated, China participated in this project for two main reasons. The first is because China values its cooperation with the UNDP and wants to use trilateral aid cooperation to promote its global image as a responsible power. Second, the four-decade-long engagement between China and the UNDP in development cooperation has formed the perception in the mindset of Chinese policymakers that the UNDP could play a positive role in China's development cooperation, and that China could benefit by learning from the UNDP's aid practices and expertise through trilateral cooperation. These findings support the arguments of constructivism and cognitive learning theories regarding a state's identity, interests and ideas, as well as the role of engagement in eliciting idea changes.

While trilateral cooperation with the UNDP has occurred in Cambodia, it could be more difficult for China to conduct trilateral projects with Western donor states. Colonel Veasna Var argued that although Cambodia turns to China for foreign aid and to the US for defence cooperation, the competition between the two superpowers places the Cambodian government's future policymaking in a dilemma, one between the extremely important issues of aid and democracy (Var, 2011, p. 31). It is also sometimes in the Cambodian government's interest to play the superpowers against each other. Therefore, China and the US will readily endorse bilateral rather than trilateral cooperation in Cambodia. However, this does not rule out the potential for trilateral cooperation between the two superpowers in less sensitive areas, such as agriculture and public health. However, as the strategic motivations behind China and the US's aid to Cambodia are strong, the start of a trilateral cooperation will require high-level political commitment from the two governments.

Let me conclude this chapter with a quotation from a Chinese official regarding his view of trilateral aid cooperation. This could illuminate China's future trilateral cooperation with the UNDP, other UN agencies and traditional donor states. Ambassador Wang Min clearly stated China's official position for trilateral cooperation with the UNDP in September 2013:

> While identifying trilateral cooperation projects with the UNDP, the Chinese government mainly has three factors in mind. First, the will of the government of the third country involved in the project should be fully respected. Second, the project should give full play to the synergy of China and the UNDP in terms of experience and resources. Third, the outcome of the project should bring maximum benefit to all three sides. (Wang, 2013, para. 13)

5

Peaceful Coexistence in the Pacific? China–Australia–Papua New Guinea Trilateral Malaria Project

Introduction

This chapter will focus on the Pacific region, which has been a place of experimentation for China's trilateral partnership, though the region is a small recipient of Chinese aid globally. In particular, the chapter will explore China's historical engagement with Australia and their joint trilateral aid project in PNG.

Australia is an established traditional donor and the largest donor to Pacific Island countries. Its aid budget to the region totalled $764.2 million (AU$1,047 million)[1] in the 2018–2019 financial year alone (DFAT, 2018). Though geographically distant from the Pacific region, China's overseas assistance to this area has grown impressively. China's official figures reported an aid of $577.8 million (RMB 3.75 billion) to the Pacific region over the period from 2010 to 2012 (State Council, 2014, p. 22). The Lowy Institute noted that China committed $5.88 billion aid to the Pacific from 2011 onwards, ranking China as the second-largest

---

1   US$1 was equivalent to AU$1.37 on 31 December 2015. This rate is used consistently in the book.

donor behind Australia and ahead of the US, World Bank, Japan and New Zealand (Lowy Institute, 2018). Although $1.26 billion was disbursed, China was also the second-largest donor to the region behind Australia (Lowy Institute, 2018).

While welcoming China's contribution to the development of the Pacific region, traditional donors have shown growing concerns about China's aid growth, the motivations behind Chinese aid and its implications for the traditional aid regime. Against this backdrop, China and traditional donors have embarked on trilateral aid partnerships in the region. As an example, China and New Zealand officially launched their first trilateral aid project on a water supply upgrade in the Cook Islands (Te Mato Vai) in February 2014. The trilateral aid cooperation between China and Australia on malaria control in PNG officially commenced in January 2016.

Taking into consideration that China is the largest emerging donor and that Australia is the largest traditional donor in the Pacific, this chapter will use the China–Australia–PNG trilateral aid malaria project to illustrate the motivations behind the growing engagement and cooperation between China and traditional donors in the region.

The chapter unfolds in four sections. Section one examines the China–Australia engagement on aid and its effect on China's development cooperation. Section two briefly discusses Chinese aid to the Pacific more broadly and the evolving trends in aid to PNG. Section three analyses the China–Australia–PNG trilateral project on malaria control. It examines how the China–Australia engagement has led to changes in China's ideas regarding aid. It also demonstrates how China's change of ideas and interest calculations triggered this trilateral project. The final section discusses the implications of this trilateral project for future cooperation between China and Australia, as well as other traditional donors in the Pacific and Asia-Pacific region at large.

China and Australia Engagement on Development Cooperation

This section will outline China–Australia interactions on development since 1979, shifting from China receiving Australian aid to jointly conducting trilateral cooperation in a Third World country. In particular, this section will examine the effect of the engagement on China's evolving views on Australian aid and cooperation with Australia, which significantly contributed to China's approval for piloting trilateral aid cooperation with Australia.

Australia was the first Western bilateral donor to China. China changed its attitude towards foreign aid and agreed to receive aid from traditional donor states and UN agencies after 1978. The Australian government reacted quickly and expressed its willingness to offer a loan of AU$50 million to China in November 1978 and the Chinese government accepted the loan in April 1979 (Hou, 2006, p. 83). This marked the beginning of Australian aid to China, and it indicated that the Chinese government was abandoning its ideologically oriented thinking and that it was beginning to approach Australian aid as a useful means of promoting China's economic development.

In November 1980, China and Australia signed a meeting minute on conducting development and technical cooperation and discussed ways and procedures for cooperation (Shi, 1989, p. 551). In October 1981, the two governments signed an official agreement on technical cooperation for development and selected areas for cooperation, which include land development, agriculture, fisheries and animal husbandry, natural science, civil engineering, medical science and English-language training (Shi, 1989, p. 551).

In the 1980s, China was receiving AU$20 million in annual aid from Australia (Zhang, 1989, p. 1). In 1988, China and Australia signed an MOU on concessional loans, which greatly boosted the Australian aid volume to China, until these loans were cancelled in 1996 (Hou, 2006, pp. 83–84). By 2011, China had received a total aid of AU$1.2 billion in grants from Australia and 136 aid projects were implemented, covering areas including poverty reduction, health, sanitation, governance and capacity building (MOFCOM, 2013a). Figure 14 depicts the trend of Australian bilateral aid to China from 1997 to 2013.

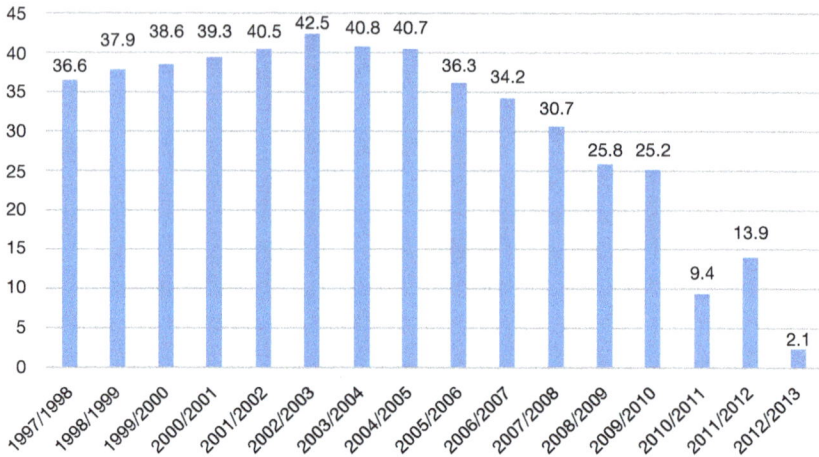

Figure 14. Australian bilateral aid to China, 1997–2013, AUD million
Source. Compiled by the author from AusAID annual reports.

In light of China's expanding influence as an emerging donor globally and especially in the Pacific region since 2000, Australia showed a growing interest in China's overseas assistance program. Greater efforts were made by the Australian government to encourage China to engage with traditional donors and to participate in joint aid projects in other developing countries. In 2003, the Australian Senate's foreign affairs, defence and trade committee produced a report on the implication of China's emergence on Australia. It recommended that Australia encourage China to accept and observe the OECD principles on development assistance and that they jointly conduct aid projects in the Southwest Pacific (Bishop, 2011). In a similar report produced by this committee in 2006, it expressed concerns regarding Chinese aid in the Pacific and suggested:

> Clearly, the political rivalry between China and Taiwan in the Southwest Pacific does not provide an environment conducive for the most effective use of development assistance … funds provided to local politicians or government officials without proper conditions attached can encourage fraudulent behaviour and undermine political stability. Without appropriate safeguards, aid assistance may not be directed to where it is most needed; it may find its way into the hands of local politicians, officials, or other improper beneficiaries. Serious corruption or political unrest can also occur as rival factions bid for increased untied grants in return for promises of diplomatic recognition

... The Australian government, through the Post Pacific Islands Forum, encourage China to adopt, and adhere to, the OECD principles on official development assistance for the islands of the Southwest Pacific ... [The Senate Committee also suggested that] Australia work closely with China to encourage both countries to enter joint ventures designed to assist the development of the island states of the Southwest Pacific. (Australian Senate, 2006, pp. 172–182)

AusAID's launch of the 'China, Australia Country Program Strategy 2006–2010' sent a strong message of change in AusAID's policy towards China. Australia was to shift from providing bilateral aid to China in support of poverty reduction to promoting knowledge sharing, high-level capacity building and policy engagement. To Australia, the change in policy could harness common interests with China, such as 'building government-to-government linkages and seeking ways for both countries to work together on regional issues, as partners, reflecting China's emerging role as a player in global development' (AusAID, 2006b, p. 2).

China observed the change of AusAID aid policy towards China closely. In September 2006, the MOFCOM policy research office interpreted the 'China, Australia Country Program Strategy 2006–2010' as follows: Australia considers China a strategic partner of cooperation and wants China to shoulder greater international obligations; Australia wants to treat China as a donor rather than as a recipient country and share its aid experience with China, which sets a precedent for China's bilateral and multilateral cooperation with traditional donors (MOFCOM, 2006). Based on this analysis, MOFCOM suggested that China prepare to 'graduate' from being an aid recipient and instead build on its experience as an aid recipient to promote its overseas assistance (MOFCOM, 2006). It also emphasised that potential trilateral cooperation in a Third World country in areas of poverty reduction and environmental protection could become a beneficial point in future development cooperation between China and Australia (MOFCOM, 2006).

Australia's new aid approach was also to promote mutual understanding, particularly China's understanding of the aid principles and practices of traditional donors. A better understanding of traditional donors has the potential of increasing China's acceptance of OECD DAC norms and practices. Through growing engagement, Australia sought to influence China's aid evolution. This explains why AusAID stated clearly that it would provide capacity-building opportunities for China's government aid agencies to better understand how AusAID and OECD DAC operate (AusAID, 2006b, p. 7).

In an address to the Brookings Institution in March 2008, then Australian Prime Minister Kevin Rudd explained his thinking on further engagement with China:

> As China makes the transition from development assistance recipient to donor, China should be encouraged to work with other donors to develop appropriate OECD-consistent norms for development assistance delivery. Having made the transition, China's experience would be invaluable to other developing nations. For Australia, getting development assistance to the Pacific island nations on a stable footing is crucial, and we'd be happy to partner with China in some pilot projects. In short, we look to China to make a strong contribution to strengthening the global and regional rules-based order. (Rudd, 2008, p. 35)

He admitted that engaging with China is complicated, 'But one key is to encourage China's active participation efforts to maintain, develop and become integrally engaged in global and regional institutions, structures and norms' (Rudd, 2008, p. 36). This explains the rationale on which Australia has been working hard over the past decade to promote aid coordination and cooperation with China in regard to development assistance. This tone for engagement was clearly reflected in AusAID's 2008–2009 annual report:

> As an international power and driver of regional and global economic growth, China's economic growth is an important catalyst for development in the Asia-Pacific and global achievement of the MDGs. In addition, China's influence on international development, including as a growing donor to the Asia-Pacific, underscores the importance of engaging China on these issues. As such, the China country strategy's goal is to further mutual national interest by supporting China's balanced development policies and working together in the region. (AusAID, 2009, p. 95)

Australian bilateral aid to China was reduced to reflect the above thinking. In July 2011, Rudd, by this time the Australian Foreign Minister, announced that as China has become one of the largest economies in the world, Australia would phase out its bilateral aid program in China. Australian bilateral aid to China ended in June 2013. Promoting trilateral aid cooperation with China became a new focus of Australia.

Moving towards Trilateral Cooperation

Australia and China have recently amplified their efforts in exploring trilateral aid cooperation, which is an important element of the broader shift from China being a recipient of Australian aid to China emerging as a donor in its own right. It is fair to admit that Australia has been more proactive in this process and that China's role has tended to be more reactive. This is similar to other trilateral aid projects between China and traditional donor states, as well as multilateral development agencies. Moreover, new aid modalities (including trilateral cooperation) have been popular in the first decade of this century. Not only are Australia and China exploring this field, but many other donors are doing the same.

Engagement between Australia and China on development cooperation has notably increased, which paved the way for their trilateral cooperation. In March and October 2007, Wang Shichun, director-general of MOFCOM's DFA, met with visiting AusAID Deputy Director-Generals Annmaree O'Keefe and Murray Proctor in Beijing. The two sides exchanged views on aid delivery and expressed their interest in development cooperation (MOFCOM, 2007a, 2007b). In April 2009, Wang and his deputy, Gao Yuanyuan, met with AusAID Deputy Director-General Richard Moore and discussed the potential for aid cooperation in Southeast Asia and the Pacific region (MOFCOM, 2009c).

Australia's capacity-building programs for Chinese aid officials in the last decade cannot be underplayed. According to a former senior AusAID official, although Australia still had its bilateral aid program in the years before it ended in 2013, AusAID began to increase its capacity building to Chinese aid officials in the area of aid management (Interview, Canberra, 5 May 2016). In a sense, this was a crucial transitional moment between the era of Australia providing aid to China and the era of Australia cooperating with China as a fellow donor (Interview, Canberra, 5 May 2016). MOFCOM aid officials attended such training programs that were hosted by AusAID. For example, they attended a training program on aid evaluation that was funded by AusAID in Thailand from 23 February to 1 March 2009 and updated themselves on international aid evaluation theories and practices (MOFCOM, 2009e). From late February to early March 2009, MOFCOM aid officials visited AusAID and learned about AusAID policies, institutions and management practices (MOFCOM, 2009d). In July 2009, China and Australia jointly hosted a symposium on their overseas assistance. Chinese aid officials from MOFCOM's DFA expressed their willingness to conduct feasible aid cooperation with Australia in the Pacific region and agreed to enact working-level negotiations to realise this proposal (Bishop, 2011).

A range of high-level mechanisms between China and Australia have included development cooperation on their agenda. It is frequently discussed on bilateral and multilateral occasions, including the Pacific bilateral official talks, the Pacific Island forum post-forum dialogue and the meetings between the Australian Embassy in Beijing and China's aid agencies such as MOFCOM, MFA and China Exim Bank (Interview with DFAT official, Canberra, 23 September 2014).

MOFCOM's Assistant Minister Yu Jianhua visited Australia in November 2012 and discussed issues of development cooperation with his Australian counterpart, including AusAID Deputy Director-General James Batley. They agreed on three priorities for regional development collaboration between AusAID and China: negotiating a new MOU on regional collaboration; establishing a high-level dialogue mechanism; and joint cooperation in areas such as regional public health and water resources management in the Pacific and Southeast Asia (Chinese Embassy in Australia, 2012). This visit laid the foundation for the two countries to enter into a formal agreement on development cooperation.

In April 2013, China and Australia signed an MOU on development cooperation and pledged to conduct trilateral aid cooperation in Third World countries (DFAT, 2013), which marks a new kind of partnership between the two countries on foreign aid. The two countries noted their common interest in reducing poverty, advancing development and promoting stability in the Asia-Pacific region and in the world at large. The MOU outlines partnership principles and priority areas for cooperation and coordination, which cover global poverty reduction, health, water, environmental sustainability, economic and fiscal reform, food security and humanitarian assistance (DFAT, 2013). It can be expected that trilateral aid cooperation between China and Australia will occur in these areas in future.

In February 2014, Australian Foreign Minister Julie Bishop explained that Australia strengthened its engagement with China on development assistance:

> For not only it [China] is a growing presence in our region, but we should be doing what we can to capitalise on our respective strengths, using our combined weight to bear overcoming some of the development challenges of the Pacific. (Bishop, 2014)

This point was echoed by her top assistant, Peter Varghese, secretary of the Department of Foreign Affairs and Trade in the same month: 'I don't see why they [China] should be inherently incompatible with Australia's interests … there's nothing illegitimate about China also pursuing relationships with the South Pacific' (Varghese, 2014). He mentioned that Australia is searching for opportunities for trilateral aid cooperation with China in the South Pacific (Varghese, 2014).

China and Australia have presently embarked on two trilateral aid projects—one on malaria control in PNG, which will be introduced later in the chapter, and the other on the China–Australia–Cambodia trilateral cooperation on irrigation dialogue. This project consisted of three visits from the officials and experts from the three countries in 2013 and 2014, which aimed to promote knowledge and experience exchange in agricultural irrigation in these countries and strengthen irrigation management in Cambodia (Interview with officials and project participants, Phnom Penh and Beijing, June to September 2015). These two areas—water and health—were already highlighted as areas of priority for cooperation in the new Australian aid policy towards China that was released in 2006 (AusAID, 2006b, p. 4).

Engagement's Influence on China

Growing interaction with Australia has promoted changes in thinking among China's policymakers. In stark contrast to China's indiscriminate refusal of aid from traditional donors up until the late 1970s, China has improved its understanding of Australian aid through the gradual learning process. Australia is accredited by MOFCOM, China's guardian of foreign aid, as 'the most active and distinctive development partner though it is not the largest bilateral donor to China' (MOFCOM, 2006). The engagement has created three roles for Australian aid in the eyes of China.

Economically, Australia is a developed Western country, with advanced technologies and management skills that can be learned by China to support its own modernisation in sectors such as agriculture, iron and steel. For example, AusAID provided over AU$8 million to support a project for the improvement of livestock and grassland in China's Yunnan Province from 1983 to 1991 (Zhao & Jin, 1991, p. 33). This project assisted in the development of human resources from China's side and was lauded by Chinese official media as 'a great success' with remarkable achievements, including that the project cultivated over 20 new species of grass for China; that the grass yield and stock-carrying capacity of the forage legume reached four times the original natural pasture; and that the species of Australian premium beef cattle were introduced to China (Zhao & Jin, 1991, p. 33).

AusAID also funded a freon-free compressor refrigerator project in Jingdezhen city of China's Jiangxi province from 1990 to 1993. This was the first time that China had introduced this technology in the refrigerator industry (Hou, 2006, p. 84). As Australia has rich experience in the iron and steel industry, AusAID provided a technical training program for the Wuhan Iron and Steel Company in China from 1990 to 1995 and improved the production efficiency of the company (Hou, 2006, p. 84).

Politically, as the first Western donor to provide bilateral aid to China, Australia can set an example for other traditional donors, which may encourage them to follow suit and provide foreign aid to China along similar lines. This complies with the trope in Chinese politics and culture that being 'first' carries a significant influence.[2] That is why Professor Hou Minyue argued that the significance of Australian aid to China was not restricted to the economic arena. To him, Australia continued to provide aid to China when some traditional donors such as Japan announced the cessation of their aid programs in China in the early 2000s, which underlined the prominent political role of Australian aid to China (Hou, 2006, p. 84).

From the perspective of foreign aid, China values its engagement with Australia and displays its interest in learning from Australian aid practice. Zhou Taidong, a former MOFCOM official, and Mao Xiaojing from CAITEC argued that China should learn from Australian practices on aid transparency and increase engagement with traditional donors (Zhou & Mao, 2013). Sun Tongquan from the China Academy of Social Sciences and Zhou Taidong recommend that China learn from the Australian regulatory system of foreign aid and adopt reform measures, including formulating a clear foreign aid strategy, reducing

---

2   Another example is Chinese leaders repeatedly mentioning the 'firsts' between China and New Zealand, such as how New Zealand was the first Western nation to recognise China's market-economy status, the first developed nation to being negotiating a free trade agreement and the first to sign the agreement. By highlighting these 'firsts', the Chinese government is demonstrating its satisfaction with the bilateral relations and is signalling to other nations that they may have forgone benefits by not being 'first'.

aid fragmentation, strengthening inter-agency coordination, establishing inclusive partnerships with different actors and focusing on the results of aid projects (Sun & Zhou, 2015, p. 137).

The Chinese government has appreciated Australia's development cooperation with China. An example is that AusAID was nominated by the Chinese government as one of only two nominees from foreign development agencies for the first and second China Poverty Alleviation Awards in 2004 and 2006, though the World Bank and the UNDP eventually won the awards (China Foundation for Poverty Alleviation, 2004; People's Daily, 2006). The Chinese government praised AusAID as follows:

> AusAID's aid to China was not only big in volume, but also focused on poverty alleviation and social development. Among bilateral donors in China, AusAID's performance and contribution to China's opening up and poverty alleviation has been outstanding.
> (People's Daily, 2006)

Capacity Building: A Good Way to Promote Idea Changes

Building institutional links with China's government ministries and agencies is a main strategic objective of AusAID's new approach towards China (AusAID, 2006b). AusAID stated that its aid practice in China has lifted Australian engagement with China to 'a strategic policy and institutional level' (AusAID, 2010a, p. 86).

Providing capacity-building programs has become an important component of Australian aid to China, as well as a method of promoting idea changes among Chinese aid officials. In the 1990s, as China was moving from a planned economy to embracing a market economy and preparing for its accession to the WTO, AusAID provided aid to strengthen China's capacity building in this direction. In 1997 to 1998, Australia and China reached an agreement on a four-year capacity-building program in China, with a budget of AU$20 million. The objective of the program was to introduce Australian expertise to China to facilitate the latter's transition to a market economy (DFAT, 1998). In the same year, with AusAID support, a trade policy library was established in China's Ministry of Foreign Trade and Economic Cooperation, the predecessor of MOFCOM (DFAT, 1998).

Official training programs are another component of AusAID's engagement with China. From 1997 to 1998, 12 Chinese officials completed a graduate diploma in international economics in Australia under AusAID scholarships (DFAT, 1998). In 2000 to 2001, AusAID funded capacity-building programs for 650 Chinese officials in liberalised foreign trade policy and procedures and for over 840 Chinese officials in China's transition to a market economy (AusAID, 2001, p. 48). In 2003 to 2004, 1,718 Chinese officials attended AusAID training on China's entry into the WTO and more than 600 officials across China's 20-plus ministries and agencies benefited from AusAID's capacity-building program (AusAID, 2004, p. 72).

These official training programs have forged close links between Australia and China at a policy level, which boosted China's understanding of Australian foreign aid and paved the way for cooperation in the future. In 1998 to 1999, Australia provided aid to China's Ministry of Labor and Social Security, National Audit Office and State Administration of Taxation on capacity building in their respective areas (Australian Agency for International Development, 1999, p. 57). In 2004 to 2005, AusAID initiated a program of events with China's Central Party School and mobilised a major governance program that aimed to help China implement governance reforms in areas of fiscal management and trade-related and social security, and that aimed to improve strategic links between the government agencies of the two countries (AusAID, 2005, p. 72; 2010b, p. 5). In 2005 to 2006, Australia provided training to China's MoF on fiscal policy and management practices (AusAID, 2006a, p. 79).

These training programs have had a far-reaching influence. They have exposed China to Australian technologies and skills and have triggered idea changes from Chinese officials on foreign aid, which is a source of aid reforms in China. Based on her research on foreign aid in China, Zhou Hong from the China Academy of Social Sciences argued that foreign aid training programs in China:

> Have a subtle effect on the ideas and practices of Chinese project workers. These changes can also penetrate into the deeper levels of "identity" that is to change the identity held in the mind of the participant. (Zhou, 2015, p. 296)

One example is that a Chinese official participated in a health aid project[3] and realised that he needed to shift his identity from a 'government official or health technician' to a 'social worker' to do the project well (Zhou, 2015, p. 296).

Evolving Trends in Aid to PNG

This section will provide an overview of Chinese aid to the Pacific region and the evolving trends in aid to PNG, the largest and most populous country in the region. As Chinese aid to the Pacific is growing fast and this region is crucial to Australian policy, this section will serve as necessary background to understanding China's and Australia's enthusiasm for engagement, which led to their trilateral project in PNG.

Chinese Aid to the Pacific

China began providing foreign aid to Pacific Island countries in the 1970s, when it established diplomatic relations with countries such as Fiji and Samoa. As China's international aid began to grow substantially after 2000, its aid to the Pacific region also expanded. The inaugural China–Pacific economic development and cooperation forum meeting held in Nadi, Fiji, in May 2006 was a landmark event in China–Pacific relations. China's Premier Wen Jiabao attended the conference and pledged a significant aid package for Pacific Island countries. The most significant part relates to $463.1 million (RMB 3 billion) concessional loans that were pledged to the region over the following three years (Wen, 2006, p. 11). Wen also promised that China would waive the debts that matured by 2005 for the least developed Pacific countries and granted an extension of 10 years for mature debts of the other Pacific countries (Wen, 2006, p. 11).

These concessional loans have funded the construction of several major infrastructure projects in the Pacific. A typical example is the rebuilding of the Central Business District in Nuku'alofa, the capital city of Tonga, after the old area was destroyed during a riot on 16 November 2006. However, China's concessional loans were criticised by some traditional donors and researchers for leading to the spiralling external debt in these financially fragile Pacific states (Dornan & Brant, 2014, pp. 353–355).

---

3   Although this is an aid project from the UK rather than Australia, according to Zhou Hong, these projects have had a similar effect on changing the attitudes of Chinese officials.

In November 2013, the second conference of the China–Pacific economic and development cooperation forum was held in Guangzhou, China. Similarly, China made new pledges of aid, including $1 billion in concessional loans to the Pacific over the next four years (Wang, 2013). For the first time, Australia was invited to attend the conference as an observer and testify to the growing engagement between China and Australia since the signing of the 2013 MOU on development cooperation (Interview with Australian diplomat, Port Moresby, 5 November 2014).

In November 2014, Chinese President Xi Jinping visited Fiji and met with state leaders of the eight Pacific Island countries that have diplomatic relations with China. This was the first time in history a Chinese president visited the Pacific region. In addition to standard pledges to establish strategic relations of mutual respect and common development, Xi announced new aid to these countries, including granting zero tariff for 97 per cent of exports to China from the least developed Pacific Island countries, and providing 2,000 scholarships and 5,000 short-term training opportunities. He also invited these countries to participate in the China-initiated '21st Century Maritime Silk Road imitative' (Du & Yan, 2014, p. 1). Similar meetings occurred in November 2018 on the sidelines of the Asia-Pacific Economic Cooperation summit held in Port Moresby. Xi pledged that China would enhance development cooperation with Pacific states under the BRI initiative. He also announced that China would provide $300 million worth of concessional loans to PNG and extend Tonga's repayment of Chinese loans for another five years.

Traditional donors are concerned by the largesse of Chinese aid and China's inflexibility in its way of aid delivery. In August 2012, Cui Tiankai, deputy foreign minister of China and in charge of Pacific affairs, briefed the media that 'China's foreign aid to Pacific Islands countries belongs to South–South cooperation which is the mutual assistance among developing countries and differs totally from South–North cooperation' (Liu & Huang, 2012). Although Australia and New Zealand approached China to join the Cairns Compact, which was initiated at the 2009 Pacific Islands forum meeting in Cairns, China declined the invitation. This remains an important point between traditional donors and China in the region (Interview with former senior AusAID official, Canberra, 5 May 2016). It also underpins the differences between China and traditional donors.

However, positive occurrences have happened from China's side on the ground. In 2008, China signed the PNG declaration on aid effectiveness, a local version of the Paris Declaration in PNG (PNG Department of National Planning and Monitoring, 2008). For the first time, China and the US attended the Heptagon group of donors meeting in Auckland in October 2014 as observers, together with current Heptagon members that included Australia, New Zealand, Japan, the European Union, the World Bank, the ADB and the International Monetary Fund (Interview with DFAT official, Canberra, 23 September 2014).

Reasons behind China's Aid in the Pacific

As discussed in Chapter 3, China is under the influence of three identities: a socialist country, a developing country and a rising great power. Consequently, China provides overseas assistance to other developing countries to serve its triple interest of safeguarding its political interest as a socialist country, advancing its domestic economic development and building a favourable global image as a responsible partner. This applies to China's aid efforts in the Pacific.

Politically, China needs support from Pacific countries at international and regional fora. A typical issue is the 'one China' policy, which relates directly to China's national unification. Among the 15 countries that recognise Taiwan diplomatically, four are small Pacific countries: Nauru, Marshall Islands, Palau and Tuvalu (see Table 11). As the following graph clearly demonstrates, the diplomatic tug-of-war between mainland China and Taiwan had been tense in the past three decades, as quite a few small Pacific countries swung between the two sides. China extended invitations to Taiwan's Pacific allies to attend the 2006 China–Pacific economic development and cooperation forum meeting in Fiji, though they did not attend due to pressure from Taiwan (Interview with Chinese scholar, Beijing, 19 August 2015).

Tension eased in 2008, when the two sides reached a diplomatic truce. It is reported that for the sake of cross-strait relations, mainland China even refused requests from at least five countries, including El Salvador and Panama, to switch their diplomatic allegiance from Taiwan to mainland China after 2008 (The Economist, 2009). However, in light of the changing politics in Taiwan and the cross-strait relations, the 'one China' issue will remain an important and sensitive issue for China in the long run. In his statement published in the *Fiji Times* and the *Fiji Sun* in November 2014, President Xi Jinping said that 'we are so grateful to the long-term precious support from the Pacific islands countries on issues relating to our core interest' (Xinhua, 2014c), which includes the Taiwan issue. Moreover, the cross-strait rivalry was revitalised after the pro-independence Progressive Democratic Party won the presidential election in Taiwan in January 2016. Since then, eight countries that used to recognise Taiwan— including Gambia, Sao Tome and Principe, Panama, the Dominican Republic, Burkina Faso, EI Salvador, Solomon Islands and Kiribati—have established diplomatic relations with China. China is also using aid to pressure recipient countries to shut down or restrict Taiwan's unofficial representatives, with Nigeria ordering Taiwan's trade office to move out of the capital city in January 2017.

In addition to the Taiwan issue, China looks to Pacific countries for support on issues such as the reform of the UN Security Council, as well as domestic issues. For example, President Xi lauded Fiji's efforts in chasing corrupt Chinese officials abroad when he met with Bainimarama in November 2014. With the help of Fijian officials, a Chinese economic crime suspect and a drug smuggler were seized in Fiji (Beijing Youth Daily, 2014b, p. A03).

Table 11. Diplomatic landscapes of mainland China and Taiwan in the Pacific region

Pacific country	ROC/Taiwan	PRC	ROC/Taiwan	PRC
PNG		12 Oct 1976	5 Jul 1999	21 Jul 1999
Fiji		5 Nov 1975		
Samoa	29 May 1972	6 Nov 1975		
Cook Islands		25 July 1997		
Federated States of Micronesia		11 Sep 1989		
Niue		12 Dec 2007		
Tonga	10 April 1972	2 Nov 1998		
Vanuatu		26 Mar 1982	3 Nov 2004	11 Nov 2004
Solomon Islands	24 Mar 1983	21 Sept 2019		
Kiribati		25 Jun 1980	7 Nov 2003	28 Sept 2019
Palau			29 Dec 1999	
Marshall Islands		16 Nov 1990	20 Nov 1998	
Nauru	4 May 1980	21 July 2002	14 May 2005	
Tuvalu	19 Sep 1979			

Source. Compiled by the author from online data.

Economically, China has approached the Pacific region for raw materials and natural resources to support its national development (see Wesley-Smith, 2010, pp. 31–32). The $1.4 billion Ramu Nickel mine in PNG is China's largest single investment project in the Pacific (Smith, 2013, p. 180). In 2018, China committed an additional $1.5 billion to expand the project. The China Exim Bank provided substantial financial support to the PNG LNG (liquefied natural gas) project, which is listed as one of the most important projects in the history of the China Export–Import Bank (Jin, 2014). In December 2014, China Sinopec began purchasing 2 million tons of LNG annually from PNG for 30 years (MFA, 2014c).

China's fishing fleet has been expanding in the Pacific Ocean. The China Overseas Fisheries Corporation has been in the Fijian exclusive economic zone since 1998. It owns 43 tuna-long liners and operates in the waters of Fiji, Vanuatu, Solomon Islands and Tuvalu (China Overseas Fisheries Corporation, 2013, p. D4). The Pacific region has also provided economic opportunities for Chinese companies. China's bilateral trade with the Pacific Island nations grew at an average annual rate of 27 per cent over 2006–2013 and reached $4.5 billion in 2013 (Wang, 2013). Nearly 150 Chinese companies have established businesses in the Pacific region, with a total investment of nearly $1 billion, and the contract value of projects by Chinese companies exceeded $5 billion (Wang, 2013). Based on available data, Figure 15 demonstrates the rapid growth of China–PNG trade, though it was in PNG's favour in the period 2001–2006 and it has been in China's favour since 2007. It is important to note that many Chinese companies, especially state-owned ones, have played an active role in China–Pacific commercial and aid engagement (see also Smith & D'Arcy, 2013).

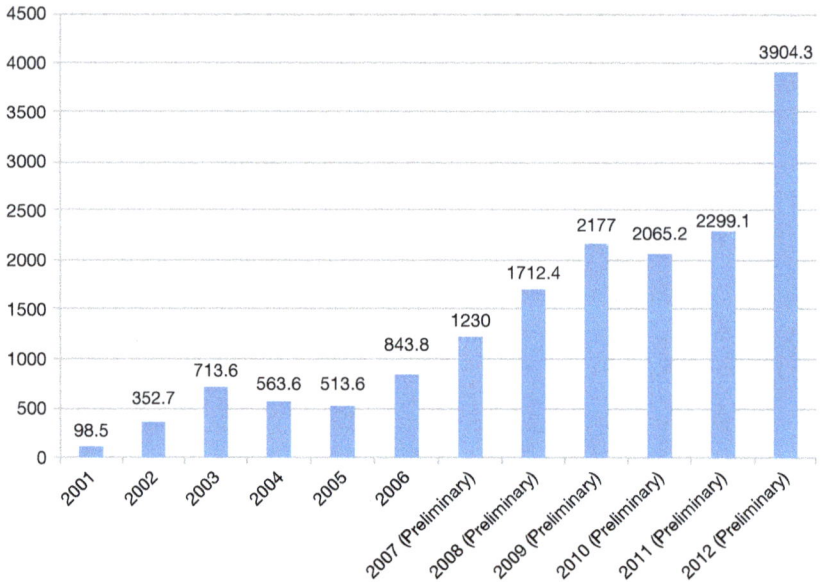

Figure 15. Trade between PNG and China, 2001–2012, Kina million
Source. Compiled by the author from PNG government data.[4]

In terms of global image–building, the support from these small Pacific Islands countries is also important. Chen Mingming, a member of China's MFA's public diplomacy advisory committee and former ambassador to New Zealand, Cook Islands and Niue, explained in November 2014 that 'establishing excellent bilateral relations with the Pacific islands countries is conducive to China's global image as a growing power, and helps China "win hearts"' (Beijing Youth Daily, 2014a, p. A03). As China has been promoting initiatives such as 'peaceful development' and 'the China dream', support from Pacific countries is much needed. It also explains why China has been increasing its aid to the Pacific in regard to climate change. The second China–Pacific economic development and cooperation forum meeting coincided with the China international green innovation products and technology show. In November 2014, President Xi Jinping reaffirmed China's support for the Pacific's efforts on climate change (Du & Yan, 2014, p. 1), placing them at odds with the Australian government.

---

4   The data was kindly provided by an official from PNG Department of Trade, Commerce and Industry.

Moreover, image building in the Pacific region and other regions, such as Asia and Africa, has realistic significance for China. As China's economic presence is growing rapidly, negative aspects of China's engagement—such as the poor quality of some Chinese products and construction projects, the low environmental standards and political lobbying, coupled with biased media reports—have complicated China's diplomacy in the region. For example, the Ramu Nickel mine project in PNG was delayed for years as a result of local concerns of its environmental impact. To some extent, Beijing expects Chinese foreign aid to play a role of image building in the Pacific Island countries and mitigate the negative effects of its economic engagement.

Although China provides foreign aid to the Pacific to further its political, economic and global image interests, global image–building has been a more significant motivation in recent years. First, with the exception of the 'Taiwan issue', the Pacific is not a priority in Chinese diplomacy according to China's leading Pacific experts, such as Yu Changsen and Guo Chunmei (Interviews, Beijing, 6 and 26 August 2015; Yu, 2016). Compared to other regions, the Pacific also ranks low in China's economic priorities due to the small size of its markets and the lack of natural resources other than fisheries. The political and economic motivations do not provide adequate explanations for China's involvement in trilateral aid cooperation in the Pacific region.

The Fiji Issue

China's aid to Fiji is an issue with which traditional donors such as Australia and New Zealand have concerns. While Australia and New Zealand imposed sanctions on the military regime in Fiji after the 2006 coup, China forged closer relations with Fiji and provided large amounts of assistance to the country. This has further increased China's profile in the 'backyard' of Australia and New Zealand. It is reported that the Australian and New Zealand governments protested against then Chinese Vice President Xi Jinping's stopover visit to Fiji in 2009, in fear of compromising their sanctions on the Fiji military regime (Field, 2011). Fergus Hanson (2008a), then research associate at the Lowy Institute and author of several reports on China's rising influence in the Pacific, criticised Chinese aid support to the Bainimarama regime in Fiji as a double standard, questioning 'how can Beijing complain about other countries interfering in its internal affairs when it interferes so dramatically to prop up a dictatorship [in Fiji]?'

In terms of Chinese aid to Fiji, with a total committed aid of $339.78 million and spent aid of $291.9 million since 2011, China was the second-largest donor in Fiji after Australia (Lowy Institute, 2018). The year 2014 is another example that illustrates the magnitude of China's aid commitment. In addition to a grant aid of $12.3 million (RMB 80 million) to Fiji when Fiji President Epeli Nailatikau attended the Youth Olympic Games hosted by China in Nanjing in August, Chinese President Xi announced an additional grant aid of $10.8 million (RMB 70 million) to Fiji during his visit to the country in November (Devi, 2014), meaning that China's total pledged grant aid from the 2014 visits exceeded $23 million. As China's influence is increasing so rapidly, it is understandable that Australia and New Zealand become more eager to increase their engagement with China to promote coordination on regional issues, with the view of influencing China's policies or, at least, of increasing their understanding of China in the Pacific.

China's Aid to PNG

Since the establishment of diplomatic relations on 12 October 1976, Chinese aid began to flow into PNG. One caveat is that as China does not release country-based and annual figures for its aid data, it is extremely difficult to find accurate data on Chinese aid to PNG. However, by triangulating sources—including official reports of China MOFCOM, the MFA, mainstream media, the PNG government departments and some existing literature—we are able to grasp the main features of Chinese aid to PNG.

Most notable is China's fast-growing concessional loan program, as China was eager to materialise $643.1 million (RMB 3 billion) in concessional loans that were pledged by Premier Wen Jiabao in 2006. Table 12 and Figure 16 outline examples of Chinese large-scale concessional loan projects.

Table 12. Examples of Chinese concessional loan projects in PNG

Project	Value	Chinese contractors	Status
University of Goroka dormitory construction, phase 2–4	$45.3 million (RMB 294 million)	Guangdong Foreign Construction Company	Completed
National electronic identity card project	$55.4 million (RMB 359 million)	Huawei	Completed
Integrated government information system	$109 million	Huawei	Completed
NCDC road upgrade in Port Moresby	$109.6 million (RMB 710 million)	China Harbour Engineering Company	Ongoing
Pacific marine industrial zone project	$95 million	China Shenyang International Economic and Technical Cooperation Corporation	Ongoing

Source. Compiled by the author from the China Embassy in PNG website.

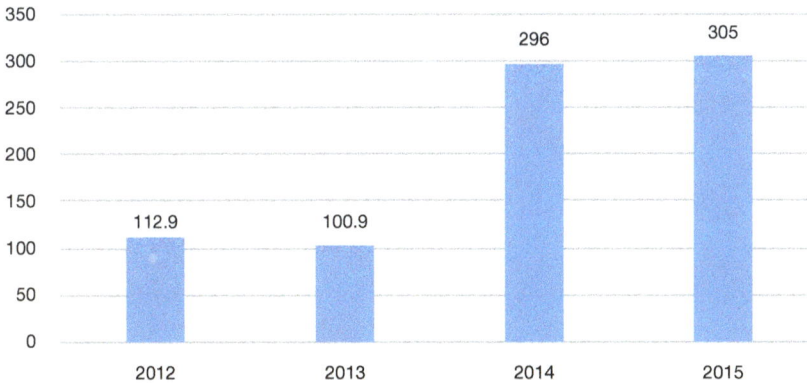

Figure 16. Chinese concessional loans to PNG, 2012–2015, Kina million
Source. Compiled by the author from PNG Treasury annual reports.

The University of Goroka dormitory project was China's first concessional loan project in PNG. As a Chinese company representative noted, this project was hailed as a success and changed the reluctance of the PNG government towards accepting China's concessional loan. It has become a bargaining chip in demonstrating the PNG government's capacity to manage China's soft loan projects when the PNG government lobbies for more Chinese loans (Interview, Port Moresby, 10 November 2014). Figures 16 and 17 summarise Chinese concessional loans and grant aid to PNG in recent years.[5]

---

5   The aid data is not available for some financial years in PNG Treasury annual reports.

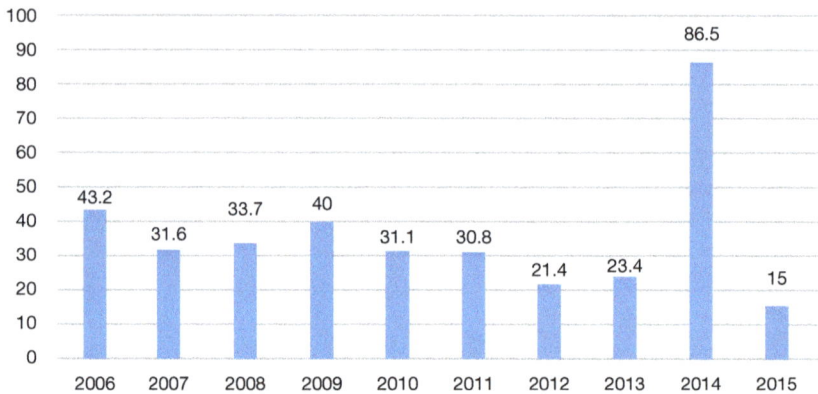

Figure 17. Chinese grant aid to PNG, 2006–2015, Kina million

Source. Compiled by the author from PNG Treasury annual reports.

Australian Aid to PNG

As PNG is a former Australian colony and near neighbour, the two countries enjoy close political, economic and strategic relations. Australia has been providing aid to PNG since decolonisation in 1975 and Australia is easily the largest donor to PNG. In the 2018–2019 financial year, total Australian aid to PNG reached $379.2 million (AU$519.5 million), accounting for 12.5 per cent of the total of Australia's overseas aid and nearly half of Australian aid to the Pacific (DFAT, 2018, pp. 7–9).

Figure 18 is an overview of Australian aid to PNG between 2001 and 2015.[6] Australian aid to PNG is focused on priority areas, including education, health and HIV/AIDS, transport infrastructure, law and justice. Australia has invested great efforts into the improvement of aid effectiveness in PNG. The two countries have entered into a new aid partnership that aims to be better aligned with the priorities of the two governments and to unlock PNG's economic potential (DFAT, 2014).

---

6   To facilitate a comparison with Chinese aid, the data covers recent financial years until 2015.

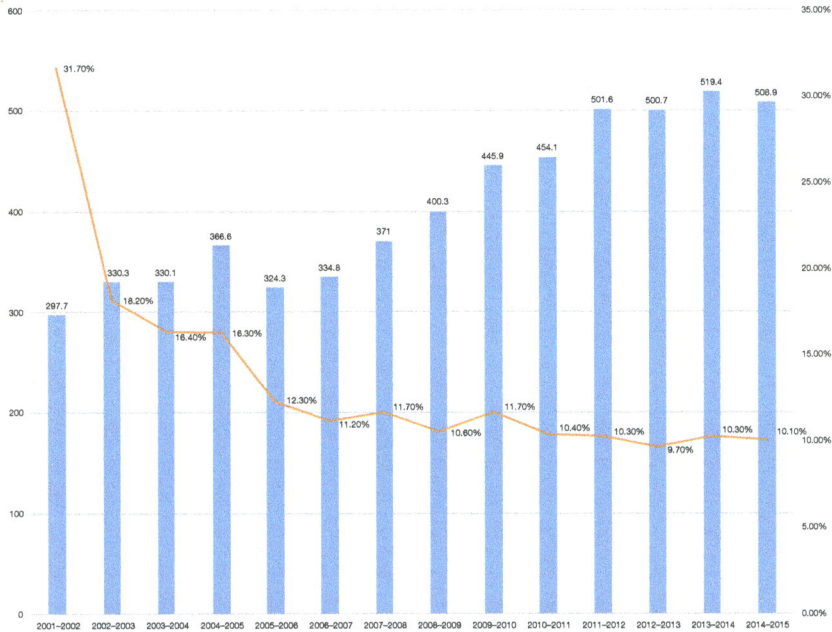

Figure 18. Australian aid to PNG, 2001–2015, AUD million
Source. Compiled by the author from AusAID/DFAT annual reports.

Foreign Aid to PNG

With a landmass of 452,800 square kilometres and a population of around 7.7 million, PNG is the largest and most populous Pacific island nation, dwarfing the other 13 island nations. Though it is blessed with an endowment of natural resources, poverty and development remain intractable challenges. For example, PNG ranked 158 out of 188 countries in the UNDP 2015 human development index (UNDP, 2015b, p. 49). PNG has consequently been a major aid recipient in the Pacific. More than a dozen bilateral and multilateral donors, including Australia, New Zealand, China, Japan, the ADB, the European Union, the World Bank and the UN operate in PNG.

The trends in aid to PNG are evolving. The increasing number of donors has compounded aid coordination difficulties in PNG. China is a typical example amid the expanding footprint of emerging donors. Internally, the PNG government is constrained by its limited capacity to manage foreign aid. The PNG Department of National Planning and Monitoring

(DNPM) is entrusted by law to coordinate foreign aid in the country, including identifying and appraising aid projects and programs. In reality, due to factors such as political corruption and governance challenges, the DNPM is frequently bypassed by donors who go straight to politicians and line agencies in PNG to lobby for support (Interview with DNPM official, Port Moresby, 11 November 2014). The PNG Department of Foreign Affairs and Trade is the custodian of all bilateral agreements with foreign countries. However, it does not have the decisive stance on aid projects. It provides only political endorsement for foreign aid and offers advice to the DNPM, which is often largely symbolic. It is not always kept up to date with the latest developments on aid projects in the country.

Further, continuous economic growth in PNG has given the government more capacity to direct its own money to domestic development rather than relying on external assistance, thus making it more confident in increasing its voice on aid management. For example, donor grants accounted for nearly 20 per cent of total expenditure in PNG in 2004, and this figure was reduced to 16 per cent in 2009 and 10.2 per cent in 2014 (PNG Department of Treasury, 2014, p. 47). This change has the potential to strengthen the PNG government's ownership of foreign aid. It is worth noting that PNG has also been an aid donor since 1997, with donations to the Solomon Islands, Fiji and some other Pacific nations (Batley, 2015). However, changes have occurred since 2015. PNG's economy is now facing difficulties due to falling natural gas prices. PNG has been short of foreign exchange and the government made major cuts to its 2016 budget.

While welcoming the addition of new donors, PNG aid officials insisted that donors must follow PNG aid processes and procurement procedures and that they show respect for the PNG government as a recipient, as well as promote greater cooperation with other donors (Interview with DNPM official, Port Moresby, 6 November 2014). In July 2015, PNG Prime Minister Peter O'Neil even announced a ban on foreign advisors working in PNG government agencies—for two concerns: PNG staff's over-dependence on foreign advisors and spying (Cochrane, 2015). The influence on foreign advisors—especially those from Australia, who are working under the aid program—is unclear and deserves more attention in the future.

PNG Development Plans and Foreign Aid

The PNG government has drawn up plans to address aid effectiveness issues, though there is always a large gap between plans and implementation. In July 2008, the Rt Hon. Paul Tiensten, PNG minister for national planning and district development, signed 'The PNG Commitment on Aid Effectiveness' with its main donors, including Australia, the EU, Japan, New Zealand, the World Bank, the ADB, the UN and China (PNG Department of National Planning and Monitoring, 2008).

The PNG medium-term development plan 2010–2015 emphasises that all foreign aid must fully comply with the PNG development strategic plan. Based on this development plan, the PNG government expects to achieve certain targets, such as establishing and operationalising national and sectoral dialogue for development partners; encouraging PNG central and line agencies to meet global principles on aid effectiveness; achieving significant reduction in aid fragmentation; adopting new modalities of aid and technical support (e.g. co-financing schemes); and promoting south–south cooperation with proper monitoring and evaluation procedures (DNPM, 2010b, p. 122).

The PNG development strategic plan 2010–2030 outlines the broad objectives and strategies for PNG foreign policy and foreign aid. The PNG government aims to move from depending on aid to being a donor in the Pacific region in the period 2011–2030, through measures that include guiding donors to areas of infrastructure building, skills training and education (Department of National Planning and Monitoring, 2010a, p. 129). A typical concern of the PNG government relates to its dependence on donors for providing skilled personnel—which is something that the PNG government aims to address by 2020 (Department of National Planning and Monitoring, 2010a, p. 129). The PNG government is keen to achieve development objectives by abiding by the Paris Declaration principles of ownership, alignment, harmonisation, managing for results and mutual accountability (Department of National Planning and Monitoring, 2010a, pp. 129–130). The Papua New Guinea vision 2050— the long-term development plan—reaffirmed PNG's commitment to directing all foreign aid to priority impact projects (PNG Government, 2011, p. 47).

PNG's View of Chinese Aid

Chinese aid in PNG receives a mixed reaction from the PNG government. PNG aid officials positively view the contribution of Chinese aid to areas that include infrastructure and education, as well as its quick delivery (Interview with PNG officials, Port Moresby, 6 and 12 November 2014). As one PNG aid official said:

> A good thing about Chinese programs is once you want something and you request them, they don't have much lengthy processes to go. They just advise their government and they say it's good, and get it funded. It is very quick response. (Interview with DNPM official, Port Moresby, 6 November 2014)

PNG aid officials also concurrently expressed frustrations with Chinese aid practices:

> You know the Chinese way of doing business. They are very good with our politicians … That is how they get most of the projects. Frankly speaking, our coordinating roles sometimes become very difficult. Because some of the process has been bypassed, we have to find some rules to accommodate them. It makes our facilitation difficult. But sometimes you have to allow them to go through because it has to. (Interview with PNG official, Port Moresby, 6 November 2014)

To summarise, deep historical and strategic interests in PNG render Australia the single largest donor to PNG. As China has substantially increased its foreign aid to PNG in recent years, Australia's interest in China's influence has grown accordingly (Interview with a former senior AusAID official, Canberra, 5 May 2016). From the PNG government's perspective, to meet the challenges of aid effectiveness, the need for aid coordination is rising, as is its confidence in aid management. Promoting aid cooperation, including through trilateral partnership, becomes a possibility within such a context.

China–Australia–PNG Trilateral Project on Malaria Control

This section offers an in-depth analysis of the China–Australia–PNG trilateral aid project on malaria control in PNG. Based on my field work interviews and archival research, process tracing will be employed to uncover the 'black box': the background and negotiation process behind the project. In particular, the motivations of the three countries will be studied.

This China–Australia–PNG trilateral malaria project was officially launched in January 2016, with a duration of three years. PNG Deputy Secretary of Health Dr Paison Dakulala explained the two main objectives of the project (Interview, Port Moresby, 14 November 2014):

1. Malaria diagnosis. This part aims to strengthen the capacity of PNG's health system for malaria control. It will be achieved by improving PNG central public health laboratory (CPHL) services, with a focus on:

   i. upgrading lab infrastructure, improving capacity for malaria diagnosis (e.g. microscopy) and monitoring drug efficacy

   ii. building the capacity of the labs and technology

   iii. training in microscopy

   iv. upgrading lab equipment.

2. Malaria operational research. This part aims to strengthen PNG malaria operational research by assisting the PNG Institute of Medical Research (IMR) in Goroka. This trilateral project will align with the PNG national malaria strategic plan 2014–2018 to strengthen malaria research.

This project is a combined effort that involves the following main stakeholders from Australia, China and PNG (see Table 13). The division of labour is as follows:

Table 13. Main stakeholders in the China–Australia–PNG trilateral malaria project

Australia	Department of Foreign Affairs and Trade (DFAT); Some Australian universities may become involved in a later stage.
China	MOFCOM; National Health and Family Planning Commission (NHFPC);[1] National Institute of Parasitic Diseases (NIPD) of the National Centre for Diseases Control and Prevention.
PNG	National Department of Health (including national malaria control program unit); PNG IMR; CPHL.

[1] China NHFPC was created in 2013 by combining the former Ministry of Health and the National Population and Family Planning Commission. It was renamed the National Health Commission in March 2018.

Source. Compiled by the author from own analysis.

DFAT represents the Australian government in both the policy setting and in the operation of the project. It has pledged to provide AU\$4 million to fund the project, including paying for the secure accommodation of Chinese experts in PNG—which is a major concern of the Chinese side due to the notoriously bad security situation in Port Moresby. Australia provides logistical support because of its long establishment and knowledge of PNG. Australian universities may join the project at a later stage to conduct joint research projects with PNG IMR (Interview with Australian aid official, Port Moresby, 4 November 2014).

China contributes experts and applicable technology for malaria control in the project (MOFCOM, 2015d). MOFCOM represents the Chinese government's participation in the project on a policy level and its signing of the project documents. It also leads the coordination of other Chinese stakeholders in the project at the policy level. MOFCOM's role is more symbolic compared to that of the NHFPC in terms of project implementation. The NHFPC concentrates on the technical aspect of the project and oversees the performance of the NIPD—who, based in Shanghai, dispatches technical experts to work at PNG IMR headquarters in Goroka and the CPHL at Port Moresby General Hospital. The NIDP was chosen because it has similar functions to PNG CPHL as a reference and quality assurance laboratory. It is also a research body, which renders it a suitable partner for the PNG Institute of Malaria Research (at least on paper).

In addition, the NIDP also has the advantage of drawing on an extensive network of provincial institutes in China to support its work in this trilateral project. China pays the salaries of Chinese experts, in a similar way to that of the Chinese medical teams, youth volunteers and Chinese-language teachers who are supported by the Chinese aid program. China may also offer some training opportunities for PNG staff in China.

As the host country, the PNG government will facilitate the operation of the project. It will provide staff and facilities as required and oversee the project. The daily management of the project is contracted with the health and HIV implementation services provider (HHISP), which is managed by Abt JTA in association with the Burnet Institute.[7] The HHISP has been supporting the health and HIV program on behalf of AusAID and the PNG government since it commenced in April 2012. It is required to report to the DFAT counsellor for the development and cooperation in PNG, China's NIPD and the PNG National Department of Health (Devex Corporation, 2014).

Why Malaria Matters?

Why have China, Australia and PNG chosen to focus on malaria in their first trilateral aid cooperation? The reason for the PNG side is relatively simple: malaria was chosen because PNG has a large burden of malaria, which will be elaborated in another section.

China supports this malaria project because it has an impressive record on malaria control and elimination at home, which should enable China to significantly contribute to malaria control in PNG. According to Qian Huilin, associate chief physician at China NIPD, China used to be a victim of malaria, which was prevalent across 1,829 counties (around 80 per cent of counties in China) in the 1950s—and 5.97 million malaria cases were reported in 1955 with an incidence rate of 102.8 per 10,000 (Qian & Tang, 2000, p. 225). By 1998, the malaria cases and incidence rates were reduced by over 99 per cent, with only 31,300 identified cases across China; the incidence rate was also lowered to 0.25 per 10,000 (Qian & Tang, 2000, p. 225). Malaria cases were further reduced to fewer than 3,000 in 2013 and the WHO accredited most parts of China as

---

7   Abt JTA is an international consulting firm on health and the social sector operating in Australia and the Asia-Pacific region. The Burnet Institute is an Australian not-for-profit organisation that links medical research with public health action.

malaria free (WHO, 2014). Presently, China has reached the stage of near elimination of malaria. Although China and PNG differ remarkably in certain areas, including health systems and human resources, China's experience can be borrowed and applied to PNG, such as its laboratory expertise.

Australia has taken the lead in supporting malaria control and elimination in the Asia-Pacific region; it has proposed several new initiatives. AusAID initiated and supported a joint assessment of the response to artemisinin resistance in the greater Mekong subregion from November 2011 to February 2012 (Tulloch et al., 2012). From 31 October to 2 November 2012, the Australian government hosted a major conference—Malaria 2012: Saving lives in the Asia-Pacific—in Sydney, which brought together ministers of health and foreign affairs, as well as regional and international partners from around the region. During the meeting, the Australian government pledged more than $73 million (AU$100 million) to help eliminate malaria in the Asia-Pacific region (Asia Pacific Malaria Elimination Network, 2012). In October 2013, the prime ministers of Australia and Vietnam jointly initiated the establishment of the Asia-Pacific Leaders Malaria Alliance, which was endorsed by 18 leaders from the region (WHO, 2013). This initiative aims to strengthen the political commitment and efforts of combating malaria regionally and globally. During these meetings, Australia, China and PNG officials discussed potential development cooperation on malaria.

A Lengthy Negotiation

As discussed above, Australia and China have been involved in growing engagement opportunities of development cooperation in recent years. This broad engagement has paved the way for the two donor countries to reach an agreement on this trilateral project.

Figure 19. China–Australia–PNG trilateral malaria project timeline
Source. Compiled by the author from own analysis.

This trilateral arrangement was based on a request from PNG's Secretary of Health Pascoe Kase for China and Australia's assistance in combating malaria in PNG in August 2012 (Interview with PNG Deputy Secretary of Health Paison Dakulala, Port Moresby, 14 November 2014). This was after a previous visit of PNG government delegates to China in the same month when PNG and Chinese officials discussed possible collaboration, including in malaria control (Interview with PNG Deputy Secretary of Health Paison Dakulala, Port Moresby, 14 November 2014). The MOU on development cooperation signed by China and Australia in April 2013 stands as a milestone umbrella agreement between China and Australia on development cooperation. Once this high-level decision was made, bureaucrats from China, Australia and PNG set out to determine specific projects for cooperation. Later, the three countries held several rounds of discussions and malaria control was identified as a specific area for cooperation.

In late April 2013, a joint scoping mission that comprised Australian and Chinese officials and experts led by AusAID consultant Dr Jim Tulloch visited PNG to explore possibilities for collaboration on malaria control. This visit coincided with a review of the PNG national malaria control program. During the trip, the delegation held discussions with officials from AusAID, the National Department of Health, the CPHL, the IMR, the Chinese medical team based in Port Moresby and other stakeholders. They made enquiries about PNG's needs and learned that the country needs quality assurance in malaria control and related capacity building. After assessing the situation of malaria control in PNG, the delegation identified possible areas of development cooperation for further discussion. Supporting malaria research at PNG IMR and laboratory services at CPHL were included in these further discussions (Interviews with Australian aid official and PNG Deputy Secretary of Health Paison Dakulala, Porte Moresby, 4 and 14 November 2014).

In November 2013, Dr Geoff Clark, AusAID counsellor for development cooperation (health and HIV) in PNG, and Dr Justin Pulford from PNG IMR visited China to follow up on the malaria project options that were proposed by the exploratory delegation in April 2013 (Interview with Australian aid official, Port Moresby, 4 November 2014). The delegation had discussions with officials from China MOFCOM, the NHFPC and the NIPD in Shanghai and agreed in principle that the three countries would enact the malaria project (Interview with Australian aid official,

Port Moresby, 4 November 2014). From March to April 2014, AusAID consultant Jim Tulloch led a second visit to PNG and China, which consisted of officials and experts from Australia, China and PNG. This visit fleshed out the design and details of the trilateral aid project (Interview with participant of the trilateral project, Canberra, 30 March 201). On 19 October 2015, the three countries finally signed the project agreement (MOFCOM, 2015d). The project was officially launched in January 2016 in Port Moresby.

This malaria project is a drop in the bucket in terms of project value compared to Australia's annual aid outlay of approximately AU$500 million to PNG. However, as illustrated in Figure 19, it has taken the three countries a year and a half to finalise the project agreement. Trilateral cooperation is a new aid modality to Chinese officials, and they want to understand it clearly before the project starts. As one Australian interviewee revealed, 'A MOFCOM aid official said, for China, this is a new thing. So, it takes a long time. This is already quite quick [in Chinese terms]. They [Chinese] are very careful about wording' (Interview, Port Moresby, 4 November 2014).

Based on my interviews with officials and experts from Australia, China and PNG, there is a strong impression that Australia and China (especially Australia) have played a more proactive role in the negotiation and promotion of this trilateral project. From the Chinese side, most of the preparation and negotiation work was performed by MOFCOM, the NHFPC and NIPD at their headquarters in Beijing. The involvement of the Chinese Embassy and the economic and commercial counsellor's office in PNG were limited compared to their Australian counterparts. MOFCOM and the NHFPC's direct involvement demonstrates the significance that China has placed on this pilot project.

The role of the PNG government is limited, if not minimal, and it failed to demonstrate sufficient ownership in the process. Most officials from the main PNG aid agencies—including the DNPM, National Department of Health and DFAT—were not aware of the project, let alone the details. Leo Makita, Director of Malaria and Vector control from the PNG National Department of Health, noted that 'the project was involved at high-level of the three governments and filtered to me [and other bureaucrats]' (Interview, Port Moresby, 12 November 2014).

Motivations of the Three Countries

Although my research question asks what factors drive China's trilateral aid cooperation, in addition to analysing China's motivations, the motivations of the other two countries in the trilateral project must also be examined. Providing a comprehensive view of the trilateral project will help readers better understand the project. More importantly, it takes three to tango in a trilateral project. China's motivations do not stand alone: they are subject to the influence of the other two partner countries in the project and they evolve through the process of interaction.

China

There are two main reasons for China's participation in this trilateral project. First, the Chinese government has regarded its aid in the health sector as an important method for demonstrating China's moral duty and for improving its global image. China has recently increased its foreign aid in public goods, such as in health and climate change. Malaria control is a significant component of China's health aid. As China's first white paper on foreign aid highlighted, health is an important sector of Chinese development assistance; China established 30 malaria prevention and treatment centres in Africa and donated artemisinin anti-malaria medicines that were worth $29.3 million (RMB 190 million) to African countries from 2006 to 2009 (State Council, 2011d, p. 22). China has also provided anti-malaria medicines to the Pacific, as pledged by Chinese Premier Wen Jiabao in 2006 (Wen, 2006, p. 11).

As discussed earlier, China additionally has a strong technical capacity in malaria control. Artemisinin (*qinghaoSu*) was first discovered and extracted by Chinese medical experts from sweet wormwood (*qinghao*), a traditional Chinese medical plant in the 1960s; it was then widely used in the treatment of malaria, which has saved millions of lives worldwide (Miller & Su, 2011). Tu Youyou, a Chinese researcher who was heavily involved in the discovery of artemisinin, was awarded the 2015 Nobel Prize in medicine. The extracted medicine is widely used in PNG.

With regard to PNG, China has been providing assistance to the PNG health sector since 2002, including dispatching medical teams and donating medical equipment. China is well placed to share its experiences in malaria control and elimination with PNG. However, China's experience in delivering aid to the wider public domain in PNG is limited

(Interview with PNG Deputy Secretary of Health Paison Dakulala, Port Moresby, 14 November 2014; Wang & Yu, 2017). This gap can be filled by Australia's rich experience in PNG that has developed over the years. PNG also offers a challenging site for Chinese scientists to conduct applied research in malaria.

A second main motivation relates to China's desire to learn from Australia's aid practices and thus improve its aid effectiveness. Broadly speaking, the interaction between China and traditional donors, including Australia, has increased in the last decade. Engagement provides the spark to experiment with new ideas, including trilateral cooperation. Trilateral cooperation, at least in theory, is an effective way of making use of each donor's comparative advantages and promoting mutual learning. There is genuine interest on the Chinese side to learn how traditional donors deliver their aid. A former Chinese senior aid official said, 'Through trilateral aid cooperation, China hopes to learn and improve its aid practices in the areas of feasibility study, institutions, project evaluation and supervision' (Interview, Beijing, 1 September 2015). Australia's willingness to cover the costs strengthens China's interest in the project. We must clarify that China's learning desire does not contradict its official discourse that Chinese aid is different from the aid of traditional donors. China's purpose is to selectively learn from some aspects of traditional donors, such as aid monitoring, to improve Chinese aid delivery rather than accept all of them.

Another Chinese aid official on health who participated in the trilateral project explained China's learning imperative as follows:

> China can learn through trilateral aid cooperation with western countries. China can learn from their advanced practices in design, management and evaluation of aid projects. Western aid, what they call 'aid programs', has a whole set of management models and frameworks covering areas such as impact assessment and outcome management. In contrast, many of China's foreign aid projects such as providing medical training and dispatching medical teams are not programs. They can only be called 'aid activities' (*huodong*). (Interview, Beijing, 26 August 2015)

China values Australia's broad knowledge of PNG, which has been built over many decades. As China's foreign aid prompts concern from traditional donors, trilateral cooperation is a test case for future cooperation with the potential of not only promoting aid effectiveness, but also improving China's global image as a beneficial international citizen. As two Chinese participants in this trilateral project explained, 'This project can uplift our global influence and visibility, and the Chinese government is willing to shoulder greater international responsibility' (Interviews, Beijing, 24 and 31 August 2015). Guo Chunmei and Tian Jingling, scholars on Oceania from the China Institute of Contemporary International Relations, argued that by working in trilateral partnerships with regional donors such as Australia, China wants to present the image of a cooperative partner in the Pacific rather than one of a state who seeks to dominate the region (Interview, Beijing, 6 August 2015).

MOFCOM and the NHFPC are two of China's government agencies who are most deeply involved in this project. MOFCOM cares about the improvement of China's aid effectiveness by attempting to learn from Australia regarding aid policies and on-the-ground management. The NHFPC has dual interests. From the technical perspective, this project provides the NHFPC with an excellent opportunity to test and apply malaria technologies in a totally new environment. This is beneficial for China's malaria research and application, as malaria cases in China have been rare in recent years. Another benefit for the NHFPC is, as one project participant explained, 'This cooperation offers MOH [NHFPC] officials and experts another opportunity to walk out of their office and travel to an exotic place: PNG' (Interview, Canberra, 30 March 2015).

Lu Guoping, division director of NHFPC's Department of International Cooperation, is deeply involved in this project on behalf of the NHFPC. At the seventh China health communication conference in July 2012, she used the China–UK global health support program, a trilateral initiative signed in September 2012, as an example to explain the benefits that China expects to reap from trilateral cooperation:

> It [trilateral aid cooperation] provides opportunities for the Chinese government and academic institutes to learn about the latest global developments in health and the best practices, and to learn how other donors deliver aid, how international organizations conduct cooperative projects and participate in global health activities. It will also strengthen our capacity, including the capacity of the Chinese government and academic institutes. It will train Chinese experts and help them participate in global health activities. (Finance China Web, 2012)

The bureaucratic imperative is another important factor. There is a growing number of professionalised aid officials and experts in China. As Professor Stephen Howes from the Development Policy Centre of ANU argued, this new generation of Chinese officials wants to conduct good aid projects and be supportive of learning from traditional donors, including through trilateral aid cooperation (Interview, Port Moresby, 2 November 2014).

China has demonstrated its changes of aid practices in this trilateral project. As an AusAID official stressed:

> This trilateral malaria project is the first time that this is not their [Chinese] plan. They are supporting another country's (PNG) plan. The hardest thing we have to do to get over to them is that they [China] keep designing their own plan, and we (Australians) keep saying no … The recipient country [PNG] knows their country. So, it is better we support them implementing their own plans instead of writing our own plan … What we want China to do is to support the PNG government implementing their own plan. PNG has its own national malaria plan … It is a very big shift from how China has done cooperation in the past. (Interview, Port Moresby, 4 November 2014)

Australia

Australia has been seeking a different kind of relationship with China regarding development cooperation in recent years. From a global perspective, China's economy is maturing, and the country is moving away from being an aid recipient, even though intractable poverty remains in many rural areas. The Australian government is encouraging China to play a more active role in global development. As the first Western donor to China, Australia's aid cooperation with China is shifting from providing aid to China to jointly providing aid to other developing countries, with a focus on the Asia-Pacific region. This serves Australia's broader strategic and diplomatic objective of strengthening its relations with China— Australia's largest trading partner and a potential global superpower, though the element of geopolitical competition is becoming more notable in the past two years. In practical terms, through this trilateral malaria project, Australia also expects to wield influence on China's aid delivery and to use China's expertise in malaria control—particularly the development of effective artemisinin-based treatments, though this point is less prominent when compared to Australia's strategic and diplomatic objectives as mentioned above.

Jointly providing aid with China to the PNG health sector also serves Australian interests. Australia is the largest external contributor to the PNG health sector. Due to geographical proximity, helping the PNG government improve its capacity in the health sector, particularly its control of communicable diseases, is also in Australia's interests. As Grant Muddle, chief executive officer of Port Moresby General Hospital, commented, 'The Australian government will accept help from anybody that is going to help improve health in PNG because health in PNG is Australian largest bio risk' (Interview, Port Moresby, 3 November 2014).

In February 2014, then Australian Foreign Minister Julie Bishop credited the complementary roles of Australia and China in this trilateral aid project and lauded it as 'a positive concrete example of China's active engagement in international development and Australia's responses to the realities of the global economy' (Bishop, 2014). This perception is echoed by an Australian aid expert: 'This trilateral project on malaria is something of a natural synergy and partnership' (Interview, Port Moresby, 4 November 2014).

PNG

Foremost, malaria control is a priority task for the PNG government in the health sector. According to the PNG national malaria strategic plan 2014–2018:

> Malaria remains one of the most important public health problems in Papua New Guinea (PNG) and the National Health Plan 2011–2020 identifies reducing malaria-related morbidity and mortality as one of its key objectives. (National Department of Health, 2014, p. 10)

An estimated 94 per cent of PNG's population lives in areas that are classified as highly endemic for malaria; on average, 1.5 to 1.8 million suspected cases of malaria are reported by PNG health facilities annually (National Department of Health, 2014, p. 26; Australian High Commission, 2016).

This trilateral project focuses on both research and operations in which there is a significant capacity gap in PNG. Microscopic examination of the blood of patients with suspected malaria has been the mainstay of malaria diagnosis. However, there is only one PNG expert in the whole country who knows how to use microscopy (Interview with Chinese health expert in the project, Beijing, 31 August 2015). This project aligns closely with the objectives in the PNG national malaria strategic plan 2014–2018, including strengthening 'the capacity of the CPHL to manage microscopy quality assurance and training services' and improving 'surveillance, monitoring, evaluation and operational research' (National Department of Health, 2014, pp. 35–36). The support from Australia and China has aligned with the PNG national malaria strategic plan 2014–2018.

A well-informed Australian aid expert explained PNG's malaria control situation as follows:

> Although there have been some recent improvements on malaria control in PNG, most cases of suspected malaria are treated without a diagnostic test. This has led to over-treatment, which is not only wasteful but also results in patients not receiving treatment for the real cause of their illness, and may contribute to drug resistance. PNG lacks adequate quality assurance mechanisms for diagnosis with diagnosis often inaccurate. Improving diagnosis is critical to ensure effective treatment and to give confidence to the assessment of the impact of malaria control based on reports of confirmed cases. The emphasis on operational research also aims to link technical research with the malaria policy and programming of PNG National Department of Health. (Anonymous Australian DFAT aid official, Canberra, 1 March 2015)

PNG's weak capacity in health is affirmed by the PNG government itself, who acknowledges that the reported reduction in malaria cases requires careful interpretation due to certain challenges, including the data quality and completeness (National Department of Health, 2014, pp. 24–25). In addition, PNG is arriving at the final global round in terms of addressing malaria. One PNG health official revealed that this trilateral aid project is timely because the global funding for AIDS, tuberculosis and malaria ends in 2014 and PNG will have to search for new funding sources (Interview, Port Moresby, 19 November 2014). PNG Deputy Secretary of Health Dr Paison Dakulala explained the position of his department on trilateral aid cooperation as follows:

> This is a relatively new approach and the benefits of it will be yet to be determined. However, in principle, a trilateral agreement will provide an additional broad support from three different countries compared to only two in a bilateral arrangement … It opens new horizons for donor funding in PNG. (Interview, Port Moresby, 19 November 2014)

The potential of trilateral aid cooperation to promote aid coordination and reduce duplication is another motivation from the PNG side, though it is less obvious compared to the pressing needs of malaria control. Aid fragmentation has remained a headache for PNG and it has become a burden on PNG's limited institutional capacity. Many PNG officials stressed that they were keen to guide donors in providing aid in areas of their comparative advantage to promote better results and increase aid efficiency. By guiding donors to align with PNG priorities rather than imposing aid projects on PNG, the central government hopes to strengthen its ownership of aid management. A high-level official from the PNG Department of Foreign Affairs stated that this project utilises Australian, PNG and Chinese funding and resources and that it will address the aid accountability issue, as more actors are involved (Interview, Port Moresby, 14 November 2014).

A senior aid official from the PNG DNPM explained her vision for improved aid coordination:

> Currently we have four to five donors in one sector. You can imagine the person coordinating and satisfying them. We are thinking of putting the money [from donors] in the basket. We want to have aid more coordinated rather than allowing them to run to agencies and coming to us … If they have the same goal, why not put their money in a basket and drive forward? … Donors have to align to our priorities and harmonise into our system. If you think my system is not working, please help us build our system. We are a step forward in localising aid effectiveness agenda … The current aid policy we are drafting now will try to push their aid to areas of their comparative advantages, areas we feel they are better at because they have been with us for these longer years. We trust them in areas which we believe they can deliver best and give us the value for money. (Interview, Port Moresby, 6 November 2014)

Strengthening bilateral relations with China is another motivation for PNG's involvement in this trilateral project. China is becoming one of PNG's most important trading and investment partners, as the PNG government acknowledged: 'Robust growth in China is particularly important for PNG as the revenues received for PNG's mineral exports will increasingly become dependent on the dominant China market' (DNPM, 2010b, p. 118). Ray Anere, senior research fellow at the

PNG National Research Institute, argued that entering into a trilateral partnership with Australia and China in this project 'signifies the maturity in PNG's bilateral relations with China and with Australia' (Interview, Port Moresby, 10 November 2014).

Reactions towards Trilateral Cooperation

Based on my interviews, most interviewees from the PNG government departments, donor community, international and regional organisations, aid implementation companies, business sector and think tanks in PNG and Australia in 2014 and 2015 thought positively in regard to the future for trilateral cooperation. Figures 20 and 21 outline their attitudes towards trilateral aid cooperation. There are two caveats. First, the number of interviews is insufficient for generalisation, but it does indicate the reaction of donors and relevant stakeholders to trilateral aid cooperation as a new aid modality to a certain extent. Second, some analysts believe that trilateral aid cooperation might have been fashionable for a time, especially while the Australian aid program was growing strongly, but it is no longer considered important (Interview with former senior AusAID official, Canberra, 5 May 2016).

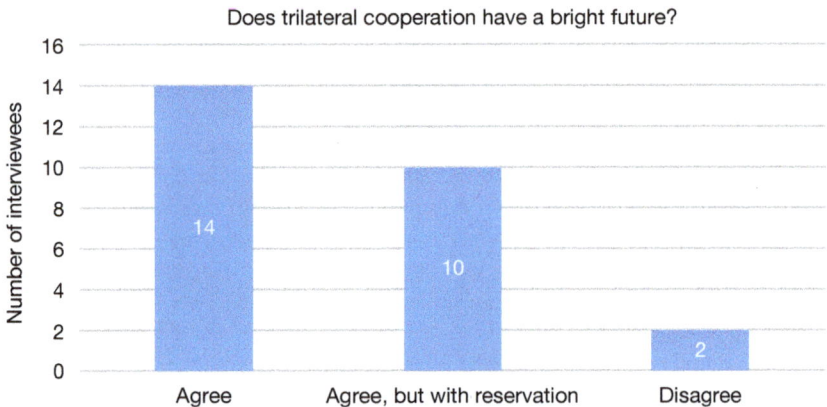

Figure 20. Interviewees' reactions to trilateral aid cooperation
Source. Compiled by the author from interview data.

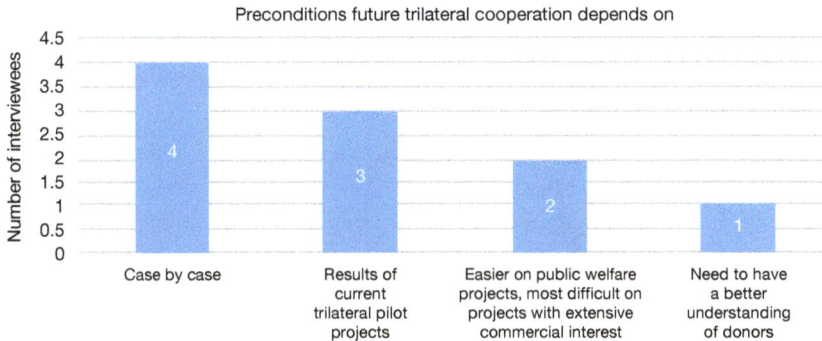

Figure 21. Interviewees' perceptions regarding the preconditions for trilateral cooperation

Source. Compiled by the author from interview data.

Conclusion

This chapter has traced the process of China's engagement with Australia in regard to development cooperation since 1979, especially during the last decade. Against the background of a changing aid landscape in PNG and China's growing inroad in the region, the first trilateral aid project between China, Australia and PNG was explored.

Similar to China's engagement with the UNDP as analysed in Chapter 4, the growing interaction between China and Australia—including through capacity-building aid projects—has led to changes in how Chinese policymakers manage foreign aid and how they improved their understanding of Australian aid delivery. Their attitude to aid from Australia as a traditional donor is not hostile, as depicted before 1970s. On the contrary, they believe that Australian aid can play an important role, such as facilitating China's adoption of advanced technologies and management skills in aid delivery. Moreover, although China has increased its aid to strengthen its political and economic interests in the Pacific, the factor of global image–building is more prominent. China is keen to diplomatically promote its image building in the region as a responsible power. This concurs with the finding of China's trilateral aid cooperation with the UNDP in Cambodia in Chapter 4.

The trilateral aid project on malaria control in PNG supports the above analysis. From the Chinese side, malaria control is China's strength in its foreign medical aid delivery. The Chinese government considers it an effective method for demonstrating its moral duty in providing global public goods and a means of improving its global image. Further, through this pilot trilateral project, China is keen to make use of Australia's comparative advantage in PNG and learn how Australia conducts its foreign aid in the Pacific.

Implications for Australia–China Future Cooperation

This trilateral project, though small, carries significant political and symbolic flavour. As it is the first trilateral cooperation project between China and Australia, it has received a great deal of attention from both governments. China MOFCOM characterises this project as 'a complementation of Chinese and Australian strengths' (MOFCOM, 2015d). Australian Foreign Minister Julie Bishop hailed this project as 'ground-breaking' in her press release after the signing of the project agreement (Bishop, 2015). To reaffirm their determination to strengthen development, China and Australia signed a second MOU on development cooperation in March 2017 (MOFCOM, 2017). As this project is still under implementation, lessons and experiences are yet to be obtained.[8]

The project has important implications for the future cooperation of China and Australia in the Pacific. At a time when this region is crowded with a growing number of traditional and emerging donors, trilateral cooperation has the advantage of reducing mutual suspicions among the donor community and relieving the heavy coordination burden on Pacific Island nations. UNDP reports explored the development needs of the Pacific Island countries and identified several options for trilateral partnership between China and traditional donors in the sectors of agriculture, health, education and even the civil society support program (Smith et al., 2014; Zhang, 2017a). To ease Australia's growing concerns of China in the Pacific, China's Minister of Foreign Affairs Wang Yi told his Australian counterpart, Marise Payne, in September 2018 that 'we are willing to conduct trilateral cooperation with Australia based on the needs of Pacific island states, and assist them in achieving the 2030 sustainable development goals without delay' (Xu & Zhu, 2018).

---

8   In April 2018, a group of experts from Australia, China and PNG conducted an internal mid-term evaluation of the project. The results are not available to the public.

Aid officials from China and Australia emphasised that the prospects for increasing cooperation in the future largely depend on the progress of the pilot project, which is exploratory in nature. China MOFCOM has made it clear to Australia that:

> China will not commit to trilateral cooperation in anything else unless they see how this [Australia–China–PNG malaria] project goes. This project is a pilot project. If it is successful, it will pave the way for future cooperation. (Interview with an Australian aid official working on the project, Port Moresby, 4 November 2014)

The final word goes to a voice from the recipient country—who, in theory, is the final beneficiary of cooperation. Regarding PNG's future plans of conducting trilateral cooperation with China and traditional donors in health, PNG Deputy Secretary of Health Paison Dakulala expressed his personal view:

> Traditionally, what we have worked at is bilateral. When we (PNG) talk about Australian and NZ, they are just part of us, within the same Pacific. We are neighbours, we know and understand each other. That relationship is quite clear. When we go down further, outside of the Pacific, our circle of influence becomes tricky. We need partners that have better understanding … At the end of it, the interest of PNG must come first. (Interview, Port Moresby, 14 November 2014)

6

A Tango of Two Superpowers: China–US–Timor-Leste Trilateral Cooperation on Food Security

Introduction

Chapters 4 and 5 have examined China's engagement in development cooperation with the UNDP and with Australia in the Asia-Pacific region. By tracing the process of the China–UNDP–Cambodia trilateral cassava project and the China–Australia–PNG trilateral malaria project, the analysis concluded that China endorsed these projects for two main reasons. First, China is keen to use development cooperation to project its image as a responsible cooperative partner in the eyes of the UNDP and Australia, which is significant to China's multilateral diplomacy and to diplomacy in the Pacific region. Second, thanks to the decades-long interaction with the UNDP and Australia regarding aid, China has realised that cooperating with these two partners through a trilateral aid partnership would be beneficial for learning how to improve its aid delivery.

This chapter[1] will continue to test China's trilateral aid cooperation in Asia. It will discuss China's trilateral aid cooperation with the US, which is the earliest provider of development assistance. The modern concept of foreign aid started when the US initiated the Marshall Plan to provide aid to Western Europe after World War II in 1947 (Marshall Foundation,

---

1   This chapter is derived in part from an article published in *Asian Journal of Political Science* on 9 April 2018, doi.org/10.1080/02185377.2018.1462218.

2015). The US is also the largest traditional donor; in 2017, its net aid volume reached $35.26 billion, accounting for 24 per cent of the total aid from the OECD DAC (OECD, 2018).

China, the leading emerging donor, has been providing a growing amount of foreign assistance overseas. With its unique features in foreign aid, China has significantly influenced the traditional aid regime. The US has been the most vocal critic of Chinese aid. Then US Secretary of State Hillary Clinton argued that Chinese aid raised serious concerns and that the US wanted to promote common aid standards and approaches (Clinton, 2011). She also warned developing countries against cooperating with emerging donors like China, who are more interested in exploiting natural resources than in promoting real development (Bland & Dyer, 2011; Ghosh, 2012).

More than that, the US has taken actions to offset China's growing influence. This is notable, even in the Pacific Island countries (Firth, 2013, pp. 1–3). In her testimony on foreign aid before the US Senate foreign relations committee in March 2011, Hillary Clinton explicitly stated that 'we are in a competition for influence with China' (Pennington, 2011). In 2012, Hillary Clinton became the first US secretary of state to attend the Pacific Islands forum post-forum dialogue in the Cook Islands. While noting that 'the Pacific is big enough for all of us', she declared that 'the 21st century will be America's Pacific century, with an emphasis on the Pacific' and that the US will stay 'for a long haul' (Clinton, 2012, paras 3–4, 14). She pledged an aid package of $32 million on top of America's annual aid of $330 million to the region (Larsen, 2012), which starkly contrasts the US's aid cut in the past two decades. In addition, USAID opened its office in PNG in 2011 and provided $100 million in military aid to the region (Larsen, 2012). Since 2018, the Trump administration has vowed to implement its Indo-Pacific strategy to compete with China-funded infrastructure projects in the region (Pompeo, 2018).

However, in this context of rivalry, China and the US have begun exploring development cooperation in recent years, bringing hope to the international community that, at least in the development arena, these two superpowers can join hands together to deliver aid to Third World countries. Presently, China and the US have conducted the following trilateral aid projects: the Fendell Campus project of the University of Liberia (2008–2010) (China Embassy in Liberia, 2008; VOA, 2009); peacekeeping in Liberia (2008) (Christensen & Swan, 2008); the project on food security in Timor-Leste (2013–2014) (Zhang, 2015); and the joint training project of Afghan diplomats (since 2012) (Zhang & Ye, 2015).

This chapter is organised as follows. First, it will examine the China–US engagement in development cooperation and conclude that China's perceptions of development cooperation with the US have changed, especially from China's image-building perspective. Second, it will analyse the evolving trends in aid to Timor-Leste, including China's footprint. Section three will provide a detailed case study of the China–US–Timor-Leste trilateral project on food security and it will reveal the motivations of the three countries, especially China. The last section will discuss the prospect of China–US trilateral aid cooperation amid growing uncertainties in the bilateral relations.

China–US Engagement in Development Cooperation

Similar to China's engagement with other traditional donors in trilateral aid cooperation, the US has played a more proactive role in this process. However, the China–US engagement in development cooperation presents distinctive features. First, the US began its aid program in China in 1999, much later than many other traditional donors. This has greatly limited China's engagement in and learning from US aid practices. The second feature is that the diplomatic flavour is more visible during China–US interactions, as they have used aid cooperation as a tool to serve their bilateral relations. However, this does not invalidate my argument that engagement leads to mutual learning and ideational change because the China–US engagement is limited compared to other traditional donors.

Learning from US Aid

The US Congress began authorising funding in 1999 to promote democracy in China[2] (US General Accounting Office, 2004, p. 1). In 2000, the US Act that was granting permanent normal trade relations

---

2   *The Foreign Assistance Act 1961* of the US stipulated that communist nations, including China and its Tibetan region, are ineligible to receive US aid. This clause was repealed in December 1985. However, US aid to China did not start until the late 1990s. One reason relates to the US's sanction on China after the 1989 Tiananmen Square.

treatment to China approved aid programs to foster the rule of law and civil society in China (Lum, 2013, p. 5). According to a US expert on China, the US aid programs started late in China due to the substantial differences between the two countries in areas such as trade, security and human rights. Therefore, the US government felt it was inappropriate to provide aid to China. Additionally, the Chinese government did not accept US aid until some agreements were reached (Email interview, Canberra, 8 December 2015).

US aid to China is mainly administered by the Department of State and USAID. The funding is mainly channelled through US-based non-governmental organisations (NGOs) and universities rather than the Chinese government (Lawrence, 2013, p. 14; Lum, 2013, p. 1). The US was the fifth-largest donor in China, totalling $63.3 million in 2012, and the largest provider of support for NGOs and civil society programming in China (Lum, 2013, p. 2). Interestingly, the US prefers to call its assistance to China 'international programs' rather than 'aid' (Fish, 2013).

Unlike many other traditional donors, the US focuses its aid programs in China on the following three areas rather than on economic development: promoting employment creation, management of natural resource–based livelihood and the preservation of cultural heritage in Tibet; addressing cross-border challenges, including HIV/AIDS, infectious diseases and wildlife trafficking; and promoting the rule of law and reducing greenhouse gas emissions (USAID, 2015d). For example, the US allocated approximately $62 million between 2002 and 2014 for its programs in Tibet and Tibetan communities in China (Lum, 2013, p. 8).

US aid to China became controversial in 2011, as China overtook Japan as the second-largest economy in 2010; US aid to China peaked to its highest level in 15 years (Fish, 2013). It became an issue in US domestic politics because some politicians used this to attack the government. In November 2011, some members of the US House of Representatives criticised the USAID programs in China, arguing that the US 'borrow[s] money from China to give back to China to help it fix its own domestic problems' and that this demonstrates 'the dysfunction in America's foreign aid spending priorities' (US Government, 2011). This is a parallel with the Chinese government's dilemma in selling its growing aid program to the domestic audience when a large population of poverty remains at home.

Learning Influence

China has expressed its desire to learn from US aid delivery. In 2007, Chinese Ambassador to Ethiopia Lin Lin noted that China would consider technical cooperation between China's telecommunication company ZTE and their US counterparts in Ethiopia, such as subcontracting some US firms because ZTE lacked the technical expertise in areas including fibre optics (Wikileaks, 2007). In 2009, China and the US signed an MOU in regard to agricultural cooperation, which was renewed in September 2015. The two countries agreed to cooperate in areas such as food security, capacity building and personnel exchanges (Ministry of Agriculture, 2015).

John Kamm, the founder of Dui Hua, a US-based non-profit humanitarian organisation, argued that China's engagement with the international community including the US has contributed significantly to criminal justice reform in China. He expected that China would continue the international exchanges while eschewing sensitive areas such as political rights and freedom (Lum, 2013, p. 4).

However, the short history of US aid to China and its focus on sensitive areas in China have led to limited engagement and learning compared to China's engagement with other donors (Zhang, 2018). US aid to China is consequently out of the spotlight in China. For example, the Chinese government allows the US aid program to continue in Tibet because it does not focus on sensitive areas such as democracy and the rule of law; however, it prohibits the US Peace Corps from working in Tibet (Fish, 2013), though they are allowed to operate in Sichuan, Gansu, Guizhou and Chongqing. Mention of US aid to China from Chinese officials and in the media is rare. Related research is also limited, except for a handful of articles focusing on the strategic motivations of US aid (Liu, 2010; Zhou, 2002, 2013).

Global Image–Building

As I have argued in Chapter 3, the learning imperative through long-term interactions and global image–building are the two main driving forces behind China's trilateral aid cooperation. While the learning imperative is less obvious in China–US engagement, global image–building has played a notable role in this process.

To elaborate, global image–building has played three roles in China's trilateral cooperation with the US and recipient countries. First, by engaging in trilateral aid cooperation, China hopes to reduce criticism from the US, which is the largest traditional donor and the most vocal critic of Chinese foreign aid. Second, working with the US in areas of critical importance to the recipient countries such as food security and public health is conducive to China's image as a responsible great power. For example, to improve its aid effectiveness and rebut the accusations of a 'China threat' and 'neo-colonialism', China has increased the number of livelihood-related aid projects, including establishing malaria control centres and agricultural demonstration farms in Africa.

Most importantly, global image–building carries a heavy responsibility in China's diplomacy to project a positive image as a responsible stakeholder to facilitate broad China–US relations. At the 10th conference of ambassadors held in Beijing in 2004, China's President Hu Jintao stressed that relations with the big powers are a priority (*da guo shi guanjian*) in China's diplomacy (Chen, 2009). As the US is the only superpower and the dominant force in international relations, Chinese leaders and working-level officials attribute extreme importance to China–US relations. China's President Xi Jinping emphasised during his visit to the US in September 2015 that 'win–win cooperation is the only right choice for the China–US relations' and that the two countries should cooperate in providing more public goods to the international community (MFA, 2015b; 2015c, para. 14).

Using development cooperation as an example, the Chinese government hopes to convince the US that China is a trustworthy partner and that it is ready to work with the US to improve their bilateral relationship. This feature will be prominent in the following discussion.

Development Cooperation: Serving Broad China–US Relations

To make China a responsible stakeholder was the goal of the Clinton administration in the 1990s, as well as of the following Bush administration (Donnelly & Monaghan, 2007, p. 2). According to Thomas Donnelly and Colin Monaghan, the Clinton administration worked to establish a strategic partnership with China under an engagement policy. During the election campaign and in the early days of his presidency, George W. Bush believed China to be a threat rather than a partner for cooperation.

The terrorist attacks on 11 September 2001 were a turning point. The US worked to seek China's support in the counterterrorism campaign: 'China pledged to play a constructive role in international counterterrorism efforts and the Bush administration pledged to pretend that the Chinese were doing so' (Donnelly & Monaghan, 2007, p. 2; Zhang, 2018).

It remained a primary task of the successive US governments to engage with China and make the country a responsible player in global affairs, until President Trump changed the tone. During her visit to China in March 2005, then US Secretary of State Condoleezza Rice said that the US 'look[ed] forward to a confident and a good partner in China' to address common challenges and that she was quite sure that the two countries would 'be able to manage the many issues before us and we will be able to do so in a spirit of cooperation and respect for one another' (US Department of State, 2005a). The term 'responsible stakeholder' was coined by US Deputy Secretary of State Robert Zoellick in his remarks to the National Committee on US–China relations in September 2005.

> For the United States and the world, the essential question is— how will China use its influence? To answer that question, it is time to take our policy beyond opening doors to China's membership into the international system: We need to urge China to become a *responsible stakeholder* in that system … In its foreign policy, China has many opportunities to be a responsible stakeholder … The US response should be to help foster constructive action by transforming our thirty-year policy of integration: We now need to encourage China to become a responsible stakeholder in the international system. As a responsible stakeholder, China would be more than just a member. It would work with us to sustain the international system that has enabled its success. (US Department of State, 2005b, paras 9, 32, 55)

The Chinese side has approached this term with caution. Xinhua, China's official news agency, cited an article on its website interpreting this term as US willingness to cooperate with China on the one hand and a sense of suspicion towards China on the other. It argued that this reveals the sentiment of engagement and containment from the US in its relations with China (Xinhua, 2006). Then Chinese Minister of Foreign Affairs Li Zhaoxing stated that 'China and the US are not only stakeholders but also should be partners of constructive cooperation' (Xinhua, 2006, para. 6).

The US began dedicating more diplomatic efforts to engage with China. US officials on African affairs initiated a policy of engagement with China in Africa, and the US State Department's African bureau began to focus on China's engagement in Africa since July 2005 (Shinn, 2009, p. 5). Michael Ranneberger, deputy assistant secretary of state for African affairs, encouraged the US side to identify areas of common interests for US–China cooperation (e.g. peacekeeping). He argued that 'the future of US–China relations in Africa has yet to be charted, but a focused, direct dialogue is an essential starting point' (US House of Representatives, 2005).

In December 2005, Steve Tvardek, director of the Office of Trade Finance from the US Department of Treasury, and Piper Starr from the US Export–Import Bank met with Chinese officials from MOFCOM, the China Exim Bank and the China Export and Credit Insurance Cooperation in Beijing and exchanged views on development issues (Wikileaks, 2008e). The engagement policy was further emphasised in 2008. In June of that year, Thomas J. Christensen, deputy assistant secretary for East Asian and Pacific affairs, and James Swan, deputy assistant secretary for African affairs, said before the Senate Foreign Relations Committee that:

> We see China's growing activity on the continent [Africa] as a potentially positive force for economic development there … As President Bush has said, we do not see a 'zero-sum' competition with China for influence in Africa … Our goal is to engage Chinese officials to try to define and expand a common agenda for Africa that ultimately will serve both our national interests and maximize the benefit Africa derives from US and Chinese economic investment in the continent. We are actively looking for areas of complementarity and cooperation with the Chinese. (Christensen & Swan, 2008)

In 2008, the US government created a new position of development counsellor at its embassy in Beijing 'to better understand China's foreign assistance structure and establish a working relationship with key Chinese entities responsible for implementing its foreign assistance programs' (USAID China, 2013, para. 6). The Obama administration continued the engagement policy and announced that the US welcomed China's peaceful rise (Lawrence, 2013, p. 5). To President Obama, it was more useful for the US to increase its engagement with China than to sit back and complain about China's growing influence in Africa (Shinn, 2012b). He made it clear that the US needed to 'draw China into the international system and work with it on shared political, economic, environmental and security objectives' (Jia, 2010, p. 254). Development cooperation is part of this process. It worth noting that the competitive flavour between the two superpowers has become more evident since 2013.

Cooperation in Africa

Africa has been a top recipient of both US and Chinese aid. The Bush administration significantly increased its aid to Africa and the trend continued in the Obama era. The US annual aid budget to Africa has been approximately $8 billion in recent years (Shinn, 2015). Africa has long been strategically regarded as a cooperative partner by the Chinese government, since the PRC was founded in 1949. Africa receives approximately half of China's overseas assistance (State Council, 2011d, 2014).

China's rapidly growing footprint in Africa in recent years, especially after the 2006 summit forum on China–Africa cooperation, has alarmed the US government as a challenge to US influence in Africa. As a response, the US began increasing its engagement with China in development assistance in the late Bush administration (Lu Boynton & Savoy, 2012, p. 8)—which was a move to boost US understanding of China's presence in Africa and to influence Chinese aid practices. It is unsurprising that engagement in development cooperation began in Africa.

The first China–US dialogue on African affairs was convened in 2005. Jendayi Frazer, assistant secretary of state for African affairs, suggested that the two countries cooperate with African countries in the sectors of infrastructure, agriculture and health to avoid overlapping aid projects and to improve the efficient use of resources (Shinn, 2012b). Early in the Obama administration, US embassies in Africa were instructed to report back more analysis on China's activities in Africa (Shinn, 2012b).

David H. Shinn, adjunct professor from George Washington University and former US ambassador to Ethiopia and Burkina Faso, echoed the potential for trilateral development cooperation. Based on his 37-year-long career in the US Foreign Service and his extensive working experience in Africa, he argued that the US and China have surprisingly similar interests in Africa, including ensuring access to natural resources, obtaining political support, expanding export markets and minimising the effects of terrorism, international crime and narcotics; he stated that there are numerous areas for cooperation (Shinn, 2015). He suggested that the two countries cooperate in areas of malaria control, treatment of neglected tropical diseases (including hookworms and schistosomiasis) and pandemic preparedness, arguing that 'Africa is an ideal location for the United States and China to reduce mutual suspicion and benefit African countries at the same time' (Shinn, 2012a, para. 12). The US embassies in Africa have continued to explore trilateral cooperation with Chinese embassies. In December 2015, Joyce Winchel Namde, chargé d'affaires of the US embassy in Chad, met with her counterpart, Nie Bo, from the Chinese embassy and expressed willingness to undertake trilateral aid cooperation with China in Chad (MFA, 2015f).

Track Two Engagements

For cooperation in unfamiliar or sensitive areas, the Chinese government prefers to allow China's semi-official think tanks to test the water. In 2005, the Brenthurst Foundation initiated the Africa–China–US trilateral dialogue mechanism on cooperation in Africa, and China responded affirmatively to the invitation (Brenthurst Foundation, Chinese Academy of Social Sciences, Council on Foreign Relations & Leon H. Sullivan Foundation, 2007). In partnership with the Brenthurst Foundation, the US Council on Foreign Relations and the Leon H. Sullivan Foundation, the China Academy of Social Sciences (CASS) co-hosted three meetings in 2006 and 2007 to continue the discussions.

Delegates from China, the US and African countries exchanged views on numerous areas, including globalisation, democratisation and governance, peace and security and corporate social responsibility. They particularly discussed areas for potential trilateral cooperation (Brenthurst Foundation et al., 2007, pp. 3–4). For example, Witney Schneidman, former deputy assistant secretary of state for African affairs, argued that China and the US could jointly assist African countries in conflict prevention, integration into the global economy, health (malaria and HIV), energy, governance and capacity building (Brenthurst Foundation et al., 2007, p. 15). Chinese delegates suggested that the three sides cooperate in areas such as malaria control and health personnel training (Brenthurst Foundation et al., 2007). A similar trilateral dialogue was held in Washington in 2013. CASS scholars He Wenping and Yang Guan argued that there is potential for China–US–Africa cooperation in education, health, infrastructure and security (Brookings Institute, China CASS & University of Ghana, 2013).

Evolving Position on Development Cooperation with the US

The attitude of China, especially that of MOFCOM, towards trilateral aid cooperation with the US has gradually changed for the positive. As will be elaborated in the following discussion, this is the result of China's high-level support and its diplomatic efforts to engage with the US in building a stable China–US relationship for the sake of China's development and security.

A typical example is the China–US global issues forum—a platform for discussing global issues, such as development cooperation. On 13 April 2005, the first forum meeting was co-chaired by Assistant Foreign Minister Shen Guofang and Under Secretary of State for Global Affairs Paula Dobriansky in Washington DC. During the segment on humanitarian assistance, poverty alleviation and development financing, views were exchanged regarding development financing, the MDGs and the ways of supporting and improving the international response to humanitarian assistance (Boucher, 2005). Officials from China's MFA, Ministry of Public Security, Ministry of Health and State Environmental Protection Administration attended the meeting. In stark contrast, MOFCOM as China's leading aid agency did not attend. This could be perceived as a signal for MOFCOM's lack of interest and confidence in exploring development cooperation with the US in the first place (Zhang, 2018).

MOFCOM attended the second forum meeting in Beijing in August 2006. Although it was represented by officials from DITEA—the agency that oversees foreign aid to China instead of the DFA, which manages Chinese aid overseas—this was progress compared to MOFCOM's absence from the first forum meeting. It demonstrated the importance that MOFCOM attributed to the broad China–US relationship.

China's Assistant Minister of Foreign Affairs Cui Tiankai emphasised at the meeting that it would be in the strategic interests of China and the US to cooperate and address common global challenges. China was open to development cooperation with the US in poverty alleviation, development assistance, development financing, improvement of aid effectiveness and efficiency (MFA, 2006). Norman Nicholson, director for donor coordination at USAID, presented US views on foreign aid and development cooperation. Chinese officials expressed appreciation for this introduction and said that this kind of dialogue on foreign aid issues would yield positive results in the long run (Wikileaks, 2006).

China's MFA has been more active than MOFCOM in piloting trilateral aid cooperation with the US, as analysed in Chapter 3. Nicholson's observations in China provided further evidence. He met with MFA officials at the sidelines of the forum meeting. Deputy Director-General Wang Xiaolong from the MFA Department of International Organizations and Conferences said that China wanted to learn from other donors to improve its own aid delivery (Wikileaks, 2006). Zhang Yiming, division director for Pakistan, Afghanistan and Bangladesh from the MFA Department of Asia, said that China was interested in conducting aid cooperation with the US in Afghanistan, especially in humanitarian assistance in drought-stricken areas (Wikileaks, 2006). However, officials from the MOFCOM DFA did not meet with Nicholson (Wikileaks, 2006).

MFA officials continued highlighting the cooperation between China and the US. During his meeting with US Deputy Secretary of State Negroponte in March 2007, China's Deputy Foreign Minister Dai Bingguo said that the two countries should promote dialogue and cooperation (MFA, 2007). Negroponte discussed a possible dialogue on development assistance with Dai (Wikileaks, 2008b).

The US's engagement with China in development cooperation in Africa began to yield results. In October 2007, Chinese Ambassador to Ethiopia Lin signalled China's willingness to explore trilateral aid cooperation with the US in Ethiopia. He welcomed the suggestion from US Ambassador Yamamoto that the two embassies exchange reciprocal visits to their demonstration farms in Ethiopia and that they explore trilateral cooperation in agriculture and food security in the country (Wikileaks, 2007). China MFA officials and scholars stated that China preferred to start trilateral cooperation with discreet projects and then expand them when mutual trust and benefits had been established between China, traditional donors and recipient countries (Wikileaks, 2007). To these agents, the exchange of views on the demonstration farms of China and the US in Ethiopia could be a suitable first step (Wikileaks, 2007).

In May 2007, facilitated by China's MoF, Director-General Wang Shichun from the MOFCOM DFA met with visiting US Deputy Assistant Secretary of Treasury for International Development Finance and Debt

Kenneth Peel. This was the first meeting of its kind, as aid officials from the MOFCOM DFA previously refused to meet and discuss aid cooperation with US embassy staff (Wikileaks, 2008e). Peel encouraged China to agree to a long-term bilateral dialogue on development assistance under the US–China strategic and economic dialogue. Director-General Wang agreed to exchange ideas on this issue (Wikileaks, 2008e).

In August 2007, Charles Aanenson, counsellor at the US Embassy in Japan, met with MOFCOM's Deputy Director-General Liu Junfeng from the DFA. Liu said that China and the US should explore potential aid cooperation in Africa and that they should start identifying specific aid projects for cooperation in Third World countries (Wikileaks, 2008e). This demonstrates that the attitude of the MOFCOM DFA regarding development cooperation with the US was softening.

From 2008, the US has amplified its engagement with the Chinese government in development cooperation. In addition to setting up the USAID counsellor position in Beijing in 2008, the US began raising the proposal for development cooperation directly with China's top leaders. On 16 January 2008, US Deputy Secretary of State Negroponte visited China for the bilateral senior dialogue and met with Chinese Premier Wen Jiabao. Negroponte proposed that the two countries should establish a bilateral dialogue on development assistance, and Premier Wen supported the idea (Wikileaks, 2008b). Wen suggested that China and the US enhance mutual understanding and trust through regular mechanisms, such as their bilateral strategic dialogue, and that they should deepen their cooperation for mutual benefits (Xinhua, 2008).

On the margins of this high-level dialogue, USAID Policy Planning Director David Gordon met with MOFCOM Deputy Director-General Wang Hongbo from the Department of American and Oceania Affairs in Beijing on 17 January 2008. Gordon said that the US was not opposed to China's foreign aid and economic activities overseas and that the US shared with China many similar goals in development overseas (Wikileaks, 2008b). He reiterated the US's desire to have a dialogue on foreign aid to improve the understanding of each other's foreign aid goals and strategies. Wang apologised for the unavailability of aid officials from the DFA for the meeting due to their previously determined schedule, but she promised to share the proposal with them and other ministries, stating that the many high-level dialogues between China and the US underscored the importance of this bilateral relationship (Wikileaks, 2008b).

Vice Ministerial–Level Meeting on Development Cooperation

Though MOFCOM began to open the door for dialogue with USAID, it was not a linear process. At the sideline of the G8 development ministerial meeting in Tokyo in April 2008, USAID administrator Henrietta Fore met with MOFCOM Vice Minister Yi Xiaozhun and proposed that the US and China launch a dialogue on development assistance issues, including aid management structures, lessons of aid delivery and the multilateral aid of the two countries. Yi rejected this proposal for a bilateral dialogue and suggested working-level meetings of aid officials as an alternative (Wikileaks, 2008a). Director Liu Junfeng from the MOFCOM DFA and USAID Office of Development Partners Director Karen Turner were then appointed as the point of contact. Yi also rebuffed Fore's proposal to include scholars, non-profit organisations, journalists and the private sector in the aid dialogue, stating that development economics is not yet a popular subject among Chinese academics (Wikileaks, 2008a).

This was the first vice ministerial–level meeting between China and the US on development cooperation. The US regarded Deputy Minister Yi's willingness to meet Fore 'as a positive step in our efforts to engage China and better understand its development goals and strategies' and 'a unique opportunity to lay the groundwork for our bilateral dialogue on foreign assistance' (Wikileaks, 2008e). In July 2009, MOFCOM Vice Minister Fu Ziying had a meeting with Anne-Marie Slaughter, director for policy planning at the US Department of State. The two sides discussed the potential dialogue on development cooperation and agreed to strengthen working-level communications (MOFCOM, 2009a).

China continued to show interest in expanding its development cooperation in Africa. The third China–US dialogue on Africa affairs was co-chaired by China Assistant Foreign Minister Zhai Jun and US Assistant Secretary of State for African Affairs Jendayi Frazer on 14 October 2008. The two sides exchanged views on their African policies and practices and agreed that they have vast common interests in promoting peace, security and development in Africa (MFA, 2008b). Zhai said that the approach of Chinese companies to their work in Africa is imperfect, that their international experience is shallow and that the Chinese government wants to learn from the US's rich experience in Africa and their aid programs to improve China's foreign aid approaches (Wikileaks, 2008d). He suggested that China and the US conduct pilot trilateral aid cooperation in Ethiopia, Ghana and Liberia (Wikileaks, 2008d).

Discussions between China and the US on development cooperation were not restricted to Africa. In November 2008, China and the US held their third dialogue on Latin American affairs in Beijing. The two sides agreed to maintain a dialogue and to explore further cooperation in this region (MFA, 2008a). The director-general from the MFA Department of Latin American Affairs, Yang Wanming, told US Assistant Secretary for Western Hemisphere Affairs Thomas Shannon that China is open to exploring and conducting trilateral aid cooperation with the US, as long as the views of the recipient Latin American countries are respected. He suggested that the two countries 'tackle easy issues before thorny ones' and that they promote development cooperation step by step (Wikileaks, 2008c). The USAID development counsellor at the US embassy in Beijing proposed the areas of potential cooperation, including health, environment, education and youth employment, and Yang asked for concrete project proposals for further considerations (Wikileaks, 2008c). With regard to Asia, China and the US held their fifth China–US consultation on Asian affairs in January 2014 and agreed to explore trilateral cooperation in areas such as the health sector in Myanmar and to continue their joint training of Afghan diplomats (US Department of State, 2014a).

Obstacles for Trilateral Cooperation

Although the US and China have increased engagement in development cooperation, only a small number of trilateral projects have materialised. David H. Shinn argued that this may be caused by a lack of enthusiasm from representatives of US embassies—particularly in African countries—and by the reluctance of China's embassies to become too closely linked to the US in Africa (Shinn, 2012b). For example, although China and the US agreed on a trilateral health assessment project in Liberia in 2010, the US proposal for a similar project in Ghana was rebuffed by the Chinese ambassador there (Lu Boynton & Savoy, 2012, p. 8). The lack of interest from key Chinese and US personnel on the ground could also explain why, near the end of the Bush administration, the China–US discussions on pursing security sector reform in the Democratic Republic of Congo and irrigation cooperation in Ethiopia went nowhere (Shinn, 2011). Another obstacle is the insufficient number of aid officials and specialists that are posted to developing countries, when many Chinese economic and commercial counsellor's offices are understaffed. The aid officials face substantial difficulties in coping with the rapidly growing workload on bilateral aid, let alone in sparing time to manage trilateral cooperation (Interview with MOFCOM officials, Beijing, 4 August 2015).

The US agencies also have different views regarding development cooperation with China. The State Department has tended to focus on the positive aspects of the engagement, while the Treasury Department has emphasised the negative aspects, such as concerns about China's lending practices (Shinn, 2009, p. 7; Zhang, 2018). Moreover, reservations from African countries add to the complexity of trilateral aid cooperation. The proposed China–US–Angola trilateral agricultural project in 2007 failed to materialise, as the Angola side lacked interest in such cooperation (Shinn, 2009, p. 8). Some senior African officials doubted the benefits of trilateral cooperation for African countries (Wikileaks, 2010; Zhang, 2018), while some others also feared China–US cooperation might compromise China's non-interference policy that was strictly practised in China's bilateral aid projects in Africa (Shinn, 2012b). These obstacles could explain why the US's proposal to have a bilateral dialogue with MOFCOM on development cooperation in the autumn of 2008 was delayed until 2014 (Christensen & Swan, 2008).

China–US Global Development Dialogue

Building on growing engagement and mutual understanding, the first China–US global development dialogue was held in Beijing on 29 April 2014. Liu Junfeng, deputy director-general of MOFCOM's DFA, and Alex Thier, assistant to the USAID administrator, co-chaired the dialogue. The two sides discussed potential development cooperation in areas including scholarly exchanges, training, research in science and technology (USAID, 2014; Zhang, 2018).

According to USAID, this global development dialogue, a platform for regular exchanges on development cooperation between the two countries, 'Is a landmark in US–China relations', and it 'provides opportunities for mutual learning through information exchanges' (USAID, 2014). Thier said that China 'exhibited a strong desire to engage with the US Government on global development issues related both to broad international policy as well as practical elements of implementation' (Thier, 2014, para. 5). MOFCOM also credited this inaugural dialogue as a priority achievement in its 2014 annual work review, which indicates its acceptance by senior MOFCOM officials (MOFCOM, 2015a; Zhang, 2018).

Strategic and Economic Dialogue

Trilateral aid cooperation between China and the US has received growing attention from the high-level political leaders of the two countries. It was discussed with an increasing level at the annual China–US strategic and economic dialogue (S&ED), the highest level of regular mechanism between the two countries.

In 2009, then Secretary of State Hillary Clinton added development cooperation to the agenda of the China–US S&ED and encouraged China to cooperate with the US to find 'tangible ways to work together on foreign aid' (Lu Boynton & Savoy, 2012, p. 8; US Department of State, 2009). This discussion on development cooperation was upgraded, as USAID Chief Rajiv Shah and MOFCOM Deputy Minister Fu Ziying held a side meeting on development cooperation at the 2010 S&ED dialogue (Lu Boynton & Savoy, 2012, p. 8).

At the fourth meeting of the China–US S&ED in May 2012, the two countries agreed to move further and conduct feasibility studies on trilateral aid programs and projects that would be 'agreed and selected by all parties, including the host country, in the fields of agriculture, health, and human resources' (US Department of State, 2012; Zhang, 2018). At the fifth meeting of the S&ED in 2013, China and the US were committed to expanding their trilateral partnership from Afghanistan and Timor-Leste to other developing countries. They also identified potential areas for cooperation, such as regional integration, food and nutrition security, financial stability and inclusive and sustainable economic development in Africa, Latin America and Asia (US Department of State, 2013).

At the sixth dialogue meeting in 2014, China and the US agreed to continue their joint training of Afghan diplomats. At the bilateral Asia-Pacific consultation, the two countries pledged to conduct new trilateral projects in the region, such as health cooperation in Burma and Afghanistan, and to continue the trilateral agricultural project in Timor-Leste (US Department of State, 2014b). At the seventh dialogue meeting in 2015, China and the US reaffirmed their commitment to conducting trilateral aid cooperation. They pledged to identify more trilateral aid projects in countries such as Afghanistan, Timor-Leste and other developing countries. They also agreed to strengthen their cooperation in the health sector in post-Ebola Africa (US Department of State, 2015).

At the sidelines of the seventh dialogue, the two countries hosted their first regular vice ministerial–level dialogue on development cooperation, which was co-chaired by Zhang Xiangchen, vice minister of MOFCOM, and Antony Blinken, deputy secretary of state of the US (Zhang, 2018). The two sides discussed issues, including post-Ebola recovery efforts, humanitarian assistance, disaster relief, finance for development and the post-2015 development agenda (USAID, 2015f); they agreed to establish a bilateral exchange and communication mechanism between USAID and MOFCOM (Lin, 2015), which materialised in September of that year. According to USAID, trilateral aid cooperation between the US and China demonstrated that 'in working together, the US and China can make a difference' (USAID, 2015f, p. 1).

MOU on Development Cooperation

Chinese President Xi Jinping's state visit to Washington in late September 2015 was an important diplomatic event in China. It also gave a final push to the China–US MOU on development cooperation and the establishment of an exchange and communication mechanism. As is common practice, China signed numerous agreements on cooperative projects with the US as achievements of President Xi's visit. Among them, the above MOU was signed between MOFCOM Minister Gao Hucheng and USAID Acting Administrator Alfonso Lenhardt (Lin, 2015).

According to the MOU, the two countries pledged to explore trilateral aid cooperation in areas such as poverty reduction, agriculture, education, health, humanitarian assistance and disaster prevention and response (USAID, 2015c). They will jointly establish disease prevention and control centres together with the African Union and its member states, and they will cooperate to improve the public health capacity in West African countries. China and the US will also strengthen their cooperation in the areas of humanitarian assistance, including by improving the disaster relief capacity in Third World countries and by continuing to support the UN international search and rescue advisory group (MOFCOM, 2015c).

MOFCOM hails this MOU on development cooperation as 'a new highlight in China–US relations which has not only lifted their level of development cooperation but also added new substance to the bilateral relationship' (Lin, 2015, p. 2). More broadly, MOFCOM argued that the MOU demonstrated the appropriate ways that states should follow to deal with each other:

> The aid from China and the US belongs to South–South cooperation and North–South Cooperation respectively ... This [the signing of the MOU] has proven strongly that, as long as the two countries respect the core concerns of each other and do not impose their conception and systems on the other, it is definitely possible for them to seek common ground while putting? Aside the differences, reach consensus among them and the recipient countries, and conduct trilateral cooperation in areas of agreement. (MOFCOM, 2015c, paras 15–16)

Evolving Trends in Aid to Timor-Leste

This section will briefly introduce the evolving trends in aid to Timor-Leste, including aid from the US and China. It will serve as the backdrop for the induction of the China–US–Timor-Leste trilateral aid project on food security.

Timor-Leste gained impendence on 20 May 2002, ending 24 years of Indonesian occupation. As a young nation, Timor-Leste has received a large amount of aid from both traditional and emerging donors, totalling to approximately $8 billion (da Costa, 2015, p. 6). As Timor-Leste's MoF noted, 10 bilateral and eight multilateral donors committed aid to Timor-Leste in 2015. Among them, Australia, the European Union, Portugal, Japan, New Zealand, the ADB, Germany and the World Bank are the top donors, who contributed approximately 84.5 per cent of total (grant) aid to the country (Timor-Leste Ministry of Finance, 2014a, p. 7). China, Brazil and Cuba are the three emerging donors in Timor-Leste, focusing on infrastructure, education and vocational training, as well as public health in rural areas (da Costa, 2015).

According to Dr Helder da Costa, secretary-general of the G7+ and senior advisor to the Timor-Leste government on aid effectiveness, the trends in aid to Timor-Leste have changed dramatically in the past decade. The total aid volume to Timor-Leste was about $70 million in 2002. It surged to $300 million in 2003 and then fluctuated between $180 and $250 million in the past five years due to the lack of donors' predictability (Interview, Dili, 3 February 2015). It remained around $250 million per annum from 2011 to 2013, and a total of $165.5 million in aid was committed for 2015 (Timor-Leste MoF 2014a, p. 6). In 2018, development partners committed $181.73 million in grants and $61.6 million in concessional loans to Timor-Leste (Timor-Leste MoF, 2018, p. 9).

Timor-Leste's dependence on foreign aid has been decreasing rapidly due to the influx of oil revenue from its petroleum fund.[3] Timor-Leste has remained highly dependent on this fund, which provides 95 per cent of the national income (Leach, 2016, p. 469). The ratio of foreign aid as a percentage of the state budget has dropped from 86 per cent in 2002 to 16 per cent in 2012, and further down to 12 per cent in 2018 (da Costa, 2015, p. 7; Timor-Leste MoF, 2018, p. 9)—a sharp contrast to the case of Cambodia, as discussed in the previous chapter.

In terms of US aid, the US conducted 54 aid projects through USAID and its embassy in Dili from 2005 to 2015. The actual disbursements of these projects amounted to $125.6 million, as illustrated in Table 14.

Table 14. US aid (grant) projects in Timor-Leste, 2005–2015

Project number	Actual commitments USD	Actual disbursements USD
US (54)	143,581,333	125,605,118
USAID (42)	143,489,998	125,499,233
Embassy of the US (12)	91,335	105,885

Source. Compiled by the author from the Timor-Leste MoF aid transparency portal.

---

3   Timor-Leste Petroleum Fund was set up in 2005. All oil revenues are required to go be included in the fund. They are then used to invest in overseas financial assets and support the state budget.

Chinese Aid in Timor-Leste

China's assistance to Timor-Leste dates back to the resistance period, when Timor-Leste was occupied by Indonesia in the 1970s. China was one of the first countries to recognise the Democratic Republic of Timor-Leste in 1975.[4] China provided diplomatic and financial support to Timor-Leste, even including weaponry, though Indonesian forces intercepted this (Interview with a senior Timor-Leste official, Dili, 6 February 2015). China's presence in Timor-Leste is felt as an emerging non-traditional donor (da Costa, 2015). Figure 22 and Table 15 depict China's foreign aid (grants) to Timor-Leste from 2006 to 2015.[5] During this period, the actual disbursement of China's aid to Timor-Leste reached $60.4 million, $8.9 million more than it committed. This is further evidence of China's growing foreign aid outlay. China announced in November 2013 that it would increase its aid to Timor-Leste to approximately $15.4 million (RMB 100 million) a year (Horta, 2014).

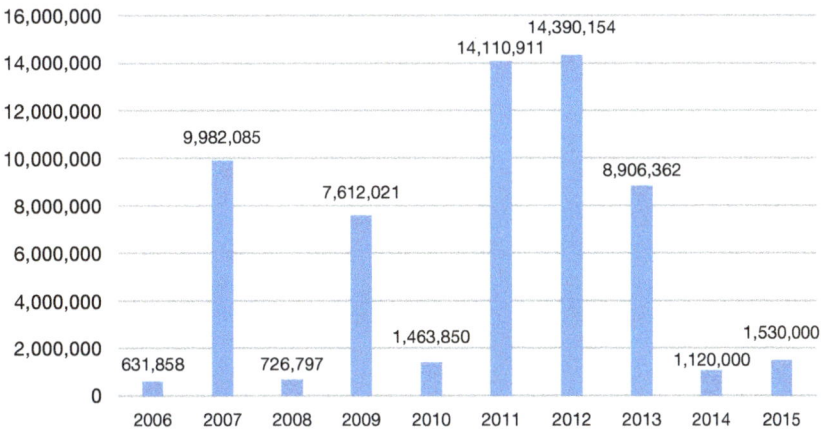

Figure 22. Chinese aid to Timor-Leste, USD

Source. Compiled by the author from the Timor-Leste MoF aid transparency portal.

---

4   On 28 November 1975, the Revolutionary Front for an Independent East Timor (Fretilin) declared the founding of the Democratic Republic of Timor-Leste, 10 days before the Indonesian occupation.

5   Figure 22 and Table 15 are based on data from the Aid Transparency Portal of Timor-Leste Ministry of Finance. The calculations based on actual disbursement lead to the fluctuation in the chart because some Chinese aid projects, especially the large infrastructure projects, will take a few years to complete. The years of project completion usually have high figures. The aid data before 2006 is unavailable.

Table 15. Chinese aid (grant) projects in Timor-Leste, 2006–2015

	Actual commitments	Actual disbursements
17 projects, USD	**51,555,256**	**60,474,039**
X-ray scanner for customs	7,906,763	8,033,419
8,500 tons of rice	7,465,636	7,465,636
Construction of Timor Leste Defence Force (F-FDTL) HQ	6,367,748	6,907,942
MFA Office Building (2)	6,033,430	9,316,613
Chinese medical team	5,731,513	9,769,472
President's office (geological survey, construction and maintenance)	4,063,306	6,880,096
Study centre for diplomats	3,303,861	1,682,692
Construction of flood-control project of 100 quarters for the F-FDTL (2)	2,661,032	2,697,257
Construction of 100 quarters for the F-FDTL	2,488,545	2,654,176
Construction of China-aided medical team dormitory project	2,290,208	2,090,000
Construction of a primary school	731,925	731,925
President's office building technical cooperation	600,179	328,526
50,000 sets of blankets	548,632	512,348
Furniture for the office building of MFA	439,181	470,995
Furniture for the F-FDTL office building	395,908	401,606
Six ambulances for the Ministry of Health	314,980	321,337
Three-party cooperation on agriculture between China, US and Timor-Leste	212,408	210,000

Source. Compiled by the author from the Timor-Leste MoF aid transparency portal.

In the process of advancing south–south cooperation in Timor-Leste, China has been strategic in providing large infrastructure aid projects that are quite visible within the country. The following China-aided buildings stand as landmark architectures in Dili: the MFA building (China's first turnkey project in Timor-Leste); the Presidential Palace; the Ministry of Defence building; and the Headquarters of the Defence Force. Though unpopular with many ordinary people who notice no direct benefits from the projects, these infrastructure projects are needed by the recipient governments and thus draw China and others closer together. Moreover, it seems relatively easy to obtain aid from China than from traditional donors, who require lengthy and stringent procedures. As Vicky Tchong, the Timorese ambassador to China, said: 'We can get almost anything we want from China; all we need to do is to ask' (Horta, 2014).

Technical assistance projects are also conducted by China. A good example is the hybrid rice project that was contracted to the Long Ping High Tech Agriculture Corporation Limited over the period 2008–2015. China provided rice seeds, fertiliser and agrochemicals as well as technical instructions. The experimentation was conducted in districts including Manatuto, Baucau, Lautem, Bobonaro and Viqueque (China Embassy in Timor-Leste, 2011). Timor-Leste has also actively participated in China's short-term training and scholarship programs. More than 600 Timor-Leste public servants attended training in China in 2013 alone, and 1,236 Timor-Leste Students had studied in China by February 2014 (Horta, 2014). China also channels aid to Timor-Leste through the Forum for Economic and Trade Cooperation between China and Portuguese-speaking countries.

In contrast to Cambodia where the majority of Chinese aid projects take the form of concessional loans, Timor-Leste has just started to approach China for concessional loans. In 2009, Timor-Leste Foreign Minister Zacarias da Costa revealed that his country was negotiating a loan from China to finance infrastructure projects (Macao Hub, 2009). In 2010, Timor-Leste President Ramos Horta requested a loan of $3 billion from Chinese Premier Wen Jiabao (Horta, 2014). In December 2015, the China Exim Bank agreed to provide a concessional loan of $50 million to Timor-Leste for the construction of the drainage system in Dili over the next three to five years (Forum Macao, 2015; Timor-Leste MoF, 2014b). This was China's first concessional loan to Timor-Leste.

China–US–Timor-Leste Trilateral Project on Food Security

This trilateral project was initiated by the US and China in close discussion with Timor-Leste Ministry of Agriculture and Fisheries (MAF) (Interview with Lourenco Fontes, Dili, 19 January 2015).[6] In July 2011, US Secretary of State Hillary Clinton and China's Foreign Minister Yang Jiechi announced the two countries' intention to conduct a trilateral agricultural aid project in Timor-Leste (US Department of State, 2011). In September 2012, Hillary Clinton visited Timor-Leste, which was the first trip by a US secretary of state to visit the country. According to the

---

6   Lourenco Fontes, director-general of Timor-Leste MAF.

accompanying US officials, Secretary Clinton had the desire to increase aid coordination with China in Timor-Leste (Lakshmanan, 2012). As discussed earlier, Hillary Clinton and Dai Bingguo, China's state councillor in charge of foreign affairs, agreed at their bilateral S&ED in May 2012 that the two countries would collaborate on development cooperation in the areas of health and agriculture (US Department of State, 2012).

In February 2013, a joint scoping mission of nine Chinese and US experts visited Timor-Leste to realise the above commitment. They assessed local conditions and discussed potential areas for trilateral aid cooperation (USAID, 2013, p. 2). During the visit, the three countries agreed to support the Timor-Leste MAF strategic plan 2014–2020 to build human capacity through training and technical assistance (Email interview with USAID official involved in the trilateral project, Canberra, 14 January 2015). To be more specific, they reached a consensus to focus their first trilateral project on increasing Timorese farmers' knowledge and capacity building to in turn increase the production of selected crops (Interview with Lourenco Fontes, Dili, 19 January 2015).

On 30 October 2013, the formal signing ceremony of the project occurred in Dili. China's Economic and Commercial Counsellor Ding Tian from the embassy in Dili, Acting USAID Director in Dili Sandra Minkel and Director-General Lourenco Borges Fontes from Timor-Leste MAF signed the agreement on behalf of their governments (Interview with Lourenco Fontes, Dili, 19 January 2015).

The core of this project is agricultural technical assistance. The main stakeholders include MOFCOM, USAID and Timor-Leste MAF. China and the US provided short-term training and technical assistance to Timor-Leste participants, targeting selected crops that included staple crops of maize and beans and cash crops of onions and garlic. In terms of labour division, China concentrated on the cultivation of maize, while the US focused on beans, onions and garlic. Timor-Leste MAF provided training facilities and the field side for demonstration plots, and organised participants to attend the training (Interview with Lourenco Fontes, Dili, 19 January 2015). The beneficiaries of the project included smallholder farmers, extension specialists from Timor-Leste MAF, agriculture students from the National University of East Timor and the NGO/donor program staff and lead farmers (Interview with Lourenco Fontes, Dili, 19 January 2015).

The official project was conducted between October 2013 and January 2015. From the US side, this trilateral project was a part of USAID's DAC project. With a contract value of $8.28 million, the whole DAC project (July 2010 – February 2015) aimed to assist Timorese farmers to move towards more diversified and income-generating farming, as well as to link with the market through technical training. Development Alternative Inc., a US-based private development company, was the US contractor for DAC—including this China–US–Timor-Leste trilateral project (USAID, 2015b). The Chinese contractor for the trilateral project was Long Ping High Tech Agriculture Corporation Ltd, which had been responsible for the hybrid rice demonstration project in Timor-Leste since 2008.

The main demonstration plot was located in Kotolau, Aileu district, 6 kilometres southeast of the capital of Dili. Chinese and US agricultural experts jointly hosted in-class training programs at this plot, with each side focusing on their own selected crops. The experts lectured in Chinese and English, respectively, with translation into Tetum, one of two official languages of Timor-Leste. Numerous topics were covered in the lectures, ranging from land preparation to planting and harvesting (Interview with Tobias dos Santos, Dili, 6 February 2015).[7] However, China and the US conducted their in-the-field technical assistance parts separately. USAID conducted some of their own activities in other demonstration plots, such as in Bobonaro district and Ainaro district (Interview with Lourenco Fontes, Dili, 19 January 2015).

This pilot technical assistance project had a small aid volume. China and the US were responsible for paying for their own agricultural experts. China's actual disbursement was approximately $210,000 (Timor-Leste MoF, 2015). The US disbursement is unknown, as the trilateral project is a part of the abovementioned DAC project of $8.28 million. More than 120 Timorese participated in China's five training sessions, each with a duration of two months (Interview, Dili, 3 February 2015).

A joint mission comprising officials and experts from China, the US and Timor-Leste conducted a final assessment of the trilateral project in April 2015 (USAID 2015f). Overall, the three partner countries expressed their satisfaction with the project's results. China and Timor-Leste wanted to

---

7   Tobias dos Santos, coordinator of extension workers from Timor-Leste MAF and four students from the National University of East Timor, who participated in the project training.

conduct a second phase (Interviews with Chinese aid experts and Timor-Leste MAF officials, Dili, 2, 3 and 6 February 2015). A senior official from Timor-Leste MFA said:

> This project is an experimental thing, looks good and the result is amazing …We hope to continue and expand trilateral cooperation. We are thinking of expanding trilateral cooperation in the future, maybe in agriculture, or other areas. (Interview, Dili, 29 January 2015)

Coordination was maintained during the project, though its extent was debated (Interviews with Lourenco Fontes, Chinese and US aid officials, Dili, 19 January and 4, 10 and 23 February 2015). Some Timor-Leste officials and student participants suggested that China's agricultural training should provide more detailed information rather than general theories and it should involve more participants in the whole cultivation process rather than just in the harvesting process (Interview with Tobias dos Santos, Dili, 6 February 2015). Relative to China and Timor-Leste, the US was more cautious about its assessment of the project. While acknowledging the achievements, it identified areas to be improved, including the selection of a demonstration site that was appropriate to the selected crops, clearly defining the responsibilities and strengthening the coordination (Interview with USAID officials and experts, Canberra, 14 January; Dili, 4 and 10 February 2015).

China's Motivations

The Chinese government has used this trilateral aid project as a diplomatic tool to build its cooperative image for managing bilateral relations with the US. The Chinese government and officials have emphasised the importance of promoting cooperation in China–US relations for the benefits of both countries. For example, China's then Deputy Foreign Minister Zhang Zhijun noted that 'if China and the US could not even cooperate in Asia-Pacific, how can they talk about cooperation globally' (Wang, 2011, para. 4). Chinese President Xi Jinping made this point clearer at the opening ceremony of the sixth round of the China–US S&ED in 2014: 'Both history and reality have shown that cooperation between China and the US will benefit both whereas confrontation will hurt both' (MFA, 2014a). In practice, the Chinese government has been working hard to persuade the US to build a new type of relation between two powers. Exploring cooperation with Washington DC in the development sector has been part of China's efforts in recent years, as was previously illustrated in their engagement since the late 1990s.

In this context, the Timor-Leste trilateral project has received substantial attention from China's leadership. It is the only project that is highlighted in the outcome list of President Xi Jinping's state visit to the US in September 2015 (MFA, 2015d). Together with the joint training program of Afghan diplomats, it is mentioned by Yang Jiechi, China's state councillor, as an example of cooperation in China–US bilateral relations (Yang, 2015).

In January 2014, Chinese Ambassador to Timor-Leste Tian Guangfeng visited the trilateral project and met with the Chinese agricultural experts from Long Ping High Tech, China's contractor for the project. His remarks provided clues regarding how the Chinese government has approached this project:

> The China–US–Timor-Leste trilateral agricultural project is the first agricultural project of cooperation between China and the US since the founding of the People's Republic of China. We need to fully commit ourselves to the project. This project carries a heavy political significance. It should show the image of China's foreign aid projects to the outside world … Ambassador Tian encouraged the Chinese agricultural mission to increase coordination with the US and Timor-Leste side and make this trilateral project 'a model of China's multilateral cooperation'. (Long Ping High Tech, 2014, para. 3; MOFCOM, 2014c, para. 1)

Aid officials from China, the US and Timor-Leste confirm that this project is the result of the strong commitment from senior politicians in the US and China. A senior official from the CAITEC (MOFCOM's think tank) revealed that the project was raised by China's MFA rather than MOFCOM. To this official, the project was designed to serve the China–US bilateral relations, as the two countries have been including development cooperation as a topic in their S&ED and they want to have something substantial (Interview, Beijing, 4 August 2015). This point received support from USAID official (Interview, Beijing, 5 August 2015), Gil Rangel da Cruz, executive secretary of food security and cooperation from Timor-Leste MAF, and his colleague, Octavio da Costa Monteiro de Almeida, director-general of planning (Interview, Dili, 2 and 3 February 2015).

China is also keen to promote its image as a responsible power among small states including Timor-Leste by delivering aid, including trilateral aid cooperation. On 20 May 2002, China became the first country to establish diplomatic relations with Timor-Leste, and Chinese aid flowed in. As China's Ambassador Tian Guangfeng said in 2012, the two countries have built the relationship 'into a perfect example of equality between large and small countries' (Tian, 2012, para. 2). Timor-Leste President Taur Matan Ruak said in September 2012 that 'Timor-Leste and China are allies for the purpose of alleviating poverty and promoting development' (Ruak, 2012, para. 11). To China, trilateral aid cooperation could serve as a new modality for combining China's strength in south–south cooperation, with the useful aid practices of traditional donors.

Agriculture is chosen due to its significance as a pillar industry in Timor-Leste. More than 70 per cent of families in the country rely on some sort of farming activity for their survival (Timor-Leste Government, 2011, p. 108). However, agricultural development in Timor-Leste faces tremendous challenges, including the shortage of knowledge. For example, though the agricultural GDP of Timor-Leste grew by just 2.9 per cent between 2000 and 2007, the production of major food crops—especially rice and maize—and cash crops was erratic and exhibited a very low productivity (Timor-Leste Ministry of Agriculture and Fisheries, 2012, p. 7). Agriculture has been listed as a focus for development by Timor-Leste in its strategic development plan 2011–2030 and the strategic plan 2014–2020 (Timor-Leste Government, 2011; Timor-Leste Ministry of Agriculture and Fisheries, 2012). The improvement and value addition of agricultural research and technology development are listed as two strategic objectives (Timor-Leste Ministry of Agriculture and Fisheries, 2012, p. xiii). Development targets have been set. For example, maize productivity is expected to increase from 1.25 metric tons/hectare (Mt/ha) to 1.54 Mt/ha by 2015 and to 2.5 Mt/ha in the period from 2016 to 2020 (Timor-Leste Ministry of Agriculture and Fisheries, 2012, p. 15). In April 2014, China signed an agreement with visiting Timor-Leste Prime Minister Kay Rala Xanana Gusmão. The two sides agreed to establish a comprehensive partnership and pledged to 'continue strengthening cooperation in food production and agricultural capacity building' (MOFCOM, 2014c). Therefore, Octavio da Costa Monteiro de Almeida, director-general of planning from Timor-Leste MAF, said that 'we decided to have cooperation in the area of food security and nutrition [in this trilateral project] because it is one of the important issues for Timor-Leste' (Interview, Dili, 3 February 2015).

Timor-Leste is a small nation and the low sensitivity of the agricultural sector is conducive to the initiation of this experimental project. This is also supported by the argument from Dr Helder da Costa: this project focused on agriculture in Timor-Leste because it had nothing to do with the strategic interests of China and the US, and 'the degree of friction is minus' (Interview, Dili, 10 February 2015).

Though the learning imperative was a less prominent factor compared to image building, China was also interested in learning from US practices in foreign aid and agriculture. As a Chinese senior official for this project noted:

> China agrees to conduct this trilateral project because China also wants to learn from the US agricultural technologies. For instance, China's previous technological breakthroughs in the sector of maize are closely linked to China's learning from the US. The US has mature experiences in areas including agricultural technologies and market promotion of agricultural products. China attaches importance to agricultural research, but there are gaps in areas such as market promotion. So, through this kind of trilateral project including even the US training materials, China wants to learn from US practices in these areas. (Interview, Dili, 3 February 2015)

China's desire to learn from US aid practice does not contradict the fact that experts from the two donor countries worked separately in some aspects of this trilateral project, such as on different selected crops and on harvesting separately. As trilateral cooperation is a new aspect in the China–US relations, working jointly on everything in a trilateral project is too ambitious at this stage. In addition to this learning desire, China is showing interest in testing trilateral cooperation as a new modality for promoting aid effectiveness. As early as 2010, China's Ambassador to Timor-Leste Fu Yuancong said:

> Under the framework of South–South cooperation, China will work with all parties concerned to conduct complementary and fruitful trilateral and regional cooperation on the basis of respecting the needs of recipient countries and jointly promote the process of global poverty alleviation. (Fu, 2010)

US's Motivations

The US has similar motivations. This trilateral project is mainly designed to serve its diplomatic relations with China—a rapidly growing power. As the detailed discussion in Section Two has demonstrated, the US government has dedicated growing efforts to engaging with China, a rapidly growing power, and to shaping it into a responsible stakeholder. It has regarded development cooperation as an important and less sensitive sector for enriching broader US–China bilateral relations. The US has expanded its conversations with China regarding aid cooperation and has even included the topic in the bilateral S&ED in recent years.

At the signing ceremony of the China–US–Timor-Leste trilateral project in 2013, Scott Ticknor, chargé d'affaires from the US Embassy in Dili, lauded the project: 'This trilateral endeavor is a testament to our [US–China] mutual commitment to peace and prosperity in Timor-Leste, and reflects new types of partnership in the Southeast Asia region' (US Embassy in Timor-Leste, 2013, para. 2). Katherine Duffy Dueholm, deputy chief of mission of the US Embassy in Dili, concurred with this view:[8]

> The goal of this trilateral project is to build confidence between China and [the] USA, and to bring the two countries together. It is a good thing to do a trilateral project. Cooperation in development and foreign aid is part of the broad China–US bilateral relations and bilateral cooperation. (Interview, Dili, 10 February 2015)

Promoting the understanding of China's foreign aid and integrating it into the international aid system is another motivation of the US. By engaging China in development cooperation, the US wants to 'encourage China to adopt internationally agreed standards on good donorship' (United States Agency for International Development, 2010). Richard L. Greene, deputy director of foreign assistance from the US Department of State, said at the 2008 high-level segment development cooperation forum of the UN Economic and Social Council that the US should work with other donors to sustain development progress (Greene, 2008, p. 2). A Chinese aid expert argued that this trilateral project also

---

8   Similar views have been expressed by Chinese aid officials and scholars during the author's interviews (Beijing, August–September 2015).

relates to the US's desire to learn from China's small-scale agricultural practices due to the similarities of small-scale agriculture in Timor-Leste (Interview, Dili, 3 February 2015).

In addition, the US has hoped to promote agricultural development in Timor-Leste through trilateral partnership. USAID has identified the inclusive development in agriculture in Timor-Leste as a central task in its five-year development strategy (2013–2018) (USAID, 2015b). It has pledged to 'place increased focus on improving agriculture productivity in terms of responding to the food crisis' (Greene, 2008, p. 5). While the Chinese side focused on the production of selected crops, the US focused on both production and marketing in their part of the project (Interview, Dili, 19 January 2015).

Timor-Leste's Motivations

Promoting cooperation among other powers on its soil is one major motivation of the Timorese government, and it serves its interest. Timor-Leste finds life easier and more comfortable with China and the US cooperating rather than competing in the country. Timor-Leste Foreign Minister Jose Luis Guterres noted in 2013 that he was interested in US Secretary of State Hillary Clinton's remark that 'the Pacific is big enough for all of us', as this means that there are opportunities for the US to cooperate with China in the Pacific (Everingham, 2013). The Timor-Leste government has been keen to hail this trilateral agricultural project as a diplomatic triumph. During his attendance at the World Food Day celebrations on 16 October 2013, Timor-Leste President Taur Matan Ruak was proud to announce that 'these two giant countries [China and the US] never work together. Only Timor-Leste can unite these countries under the trilateral cooperation in agriculture development' (Interview with Lourenco Fontes, Dili, 19 January 2015).

Another motivation of the Timorese government is to strengthen its ownership of foreign aid through various means, including trilateral partnership. As the former head for aid effectiveness at Timor-Leste MoF, Dr Helder da Costa highlighted the issue of donor fragmentation in Timor-Leste and emphasised that 'donors need to be on listening mode' and 'the country (Timor-Leste) must own their development agenda' (da Costa, 2015, pp. 5, 11). Much progress has been achieved. In 2012, the development partnership management unit was established within Timor-Leste's MoF to ensure the effective use of foreign aid and to promote aid coordination and harmonisation (Timor-Leste Ministry of Finance, 2014a, p. 6). An aid transparency portal has been established under the MoF as the online database to record all aid flows to Timor-Leste (Timor-Leste Ministry of Finance, 2014a, p. 6). Timor-Leste was also among the founding members of the G7+, an intergovernmental organisation that addresses post-conflict development challenges that fragile states face, including through the better use of foreign assistance and through promoting recipient-led strategies for development and south–south cooperation. This trilateral project is one such attempt to promote aid coordination. It is regarded as 'an attempt to reach out using each other's comparative advantages and helping' (Interview, Dili, 3 February 2015).

Conclusion

This chapter has examined the China–US engagement on development cooperation in recent years. In particular, it has traced the process of this engagement against the backdrop of China–US relations since 1990s and has explored the China–US–Timor-Leste trilateral aid project on food security in detail. One caveat is that, in light of the difficulty in accessing data in China and the US, some data from Wikileaks has been used, especially in the section on China–US high-level engagement in development cooperation. To maximise the data's reliability, I have made every effort to triangulate the data with the available and released official data—such as those by China MFA, Chinese official media and the US Department of State.

This chapter concludes that the learning imperative has played a minor role in China's conduct of trilateral aid cooperation with the US due to the short history of US aid to China. On the contrary, image building has been China's main driving force to pilot a trilateral partnership with the US. The purpose is to project China's image as a responsible stakeholder in development assistance to serve the broader China–US relationship. This point is similar to what I found in Chapters 4 and 5 regarding China's trilateral aid cooperation with the UNDP and Australia in Cambodia and PNG.

China and the US have agreed to build their trilateral development cooperation in Africa as 'a highlight and a new area of cooperation in the new model of China–US relations' (MFA, 2014b, para. 2). At the eighth China–US S&ED, the two donors pledged to expand their trilateral aid cooperation by continuing the joint training program for young Afghan diplomats, providing similar training for Afghan health and agricultural workers, exploring new areas of cooperation, exploring trilateral cooperation in Timor-Leste on aquaculture, exploring trilateral aid cooperation on food security in Africa and jointly supporting the goals and objectives of the comprehensive Africa agriculture development program (US Department of State, 2016).

However, trilateral cooperation between US and China is still in the early stage of experimentation, and progress should not be taken for granted. The pilot projects are small in scale and are technically based. Potential is there, but obstacles remain—including bureaucratic decentralisation, differences in development assistance goals, divergent methods of aid delivery, capacity gaps and other political considerations (Lu Boynton & Savoy, 2012, p. 9). Trust building takes time. For example, as a development expert mentioned, many MOFCOM officials were not receptive when USAID sent Jennifer Adams as the first development counsellor to China in September 2008. The longstanding mistrust between the two countries is deeply rooted and likely to remain (Lawrence, 2013, p. 2). More information and transparency from both sides are needed. The most challenging areas relate to democracy, good governance and human rights. Further dialogue on these difficult issues must also be promoted. The reactions from recipient countries are also mixed and demand further attention.

What deserves our special attention is the growing uncertainty in China–US relations since 2017 that has become a major obstacle for their trilateral aid cooperation. The Trump administration explicitly views China as a strategic rival and emphasises competition with the country. The Xi Jinping administration has seemingly behaved uncompromisingly in response. Affected by the heightened tensions in the bilateral relations, the two countries have suspended their trilateral aid cooperation, including cancelling the second phase of the planned trilateral aid project in Timor-Leste. In the future, if China–US bilateral relations improve, trilateral aid cooperation between the two countries is expected to grow steadily. If they do not improve, then the prospect of development cooperation would be bleak.

Tips from Professor Li Anshan, a senior expert on China–Africa relations at Peking University, are thought provoking. He cautions that China and the US should address a few questions before they can conduct genuine trilateral aid cooperation: 'Should we provide our help to African countries with aid conditions?', 'Can we decide the issue for Africans?' and 'Can we decide what Africa needs?' (Freeman III & Lu Boynton, 2011, pp. 44–45). To Professor Anshan, China and the US should reach an agreement on understanding 'condition' in Chinese terms and 'aid' in US terms; on choosing a proper project for cooperation; on choosing an African country as a partner and seeking their approval on the project; and on devising a clear division of responsibilities and ownership for the pilot project (Freeman III & Lu Boynton, 2011, pp. 45–46).

The following remarks provide some answers to the above questions. Following the advice here might be a way to ease the process of securing trilateral aid cooperation with China in the future. During a meeting with US Assistant Secretary for African Affairs Jendayi Frazer in October 2008, China Assistant Foreign Minister Zhai Jun said that further development cooperation with the US was possible, but that three principles had to be observed:

> First, respect the views of Africans and do not impose outside views on African countries. Second, seek to gradually increase cooperation, starting with countries with which the United States and China both enjoy good relations and focusing on concrete, small-scale projects in agriculture and health. Third, use existing mechanisms and framework rather than setting up new mechanisms for cooperation. (Wikileaks, 2008d)

7

Assessing China's Trilateral Aid Cooperation and Foreign Aid Reform

This chapter builds on the analysis in previous chapters and continues the discussion on China's trilateral aid cooperation. It will provide an overview of Chinese trilateral aid cooperation, including development partnerships, prominent features, China's official position and bureaucratic arrangement for trilateral aid cooperation. Trilateral aid cooperation, especially in China's cases, will then be assessed. The chapter will also examine China's foreign aid reform, of which trilateral aid cooperation is a manifestation, and the establishment of the CIDCA in 2018.

Overview of China's Trilateral Aid Cooperation

Development Partnerships

This research has revolved around China's motivations for trilateral aid cooperation. It concludes that China's adoption of trilateral aid cooperation is the result of its strong desire to build its global image as a responsible global power and for cognitive learning to improve its aid performance. This finding is based on the careful examination of China's three trilateral projects in Chapters 4, 5 and 6, as well as an understanding of China's other trilateral projects.

With regard to cognitive learning, we must emphasise once again that a large proportion of China's learning has been derived from the process of its acceptance of aid from traditional donors and multilateral development agencies. This process not only made Chinese actors believe that external aid could be beneficial to China's economic development, but also that the process increased their understanding of and trust in these partners, which contributed to the confidence of Chinese actors in undertaking trilateral aid cooperation.

Following the logic that Chinese actors are keen to improve China's global image and to promote cognitive learning, why have traditional donor states and multilateral agencies rather than China taken the lead in initiating the pilot projects? As demonstrated in previous chapters, traditional donor states and multilateral agencies have increased their interests in Chinese foreign aid in the last decade, especially after China pledged extensive amounts of aid to Africa at the 2006 summit of the forum on China–Africa cooperation in Beijing. In response to the anticipated significant expansion of China's aid, these players began to approach China and increase their engagement. In turn, the Chinese government agreed to become more involved in these kinds of engagements. Chinese officials believed that participating in trilateral proposals that were initiated by external partners could serve China's interests, including internationally projecting a cooperative image and facilitating China's practical learning from traditional donors. That is why China agreed to tentatively experiment with trilateral aid cooperation but refrained from being more proactive. China's reactive position is also related to its tradition of risk aversion when dealing with new approaches, such as trilateral aid cooperation. This is complicated by the Chinese government's doubts, as well as those of many of its agencies, regarding the motivations of external partners, especially traditional donor states, pursuing trilateral cooperation agreements with China, particularly in the early stage of engagement. That is also why China was more willing to test trilateral cooperation with UN agencies such as the UNDP, as it is considered by the Chinese government to be politically more neutral than Western donors.

China's strategic approach towards learning in the aid sector has demonstrated similar features to its practices in other fields of international affairs, such as arms control. As mentioned in Chapter 2, Ernst Haas (1990, pp. 3–4) explained two types of learning processes: adaptation and learning. Adaptation signifies the use of new means to achieve the same goal, while learning signifies the change of both goals and means on the basis of redefining actors' interests. Alastair Iain Johnston (1996) used these two concepts to analyse China's development of a more sophisticated and constructive arms control policy in the 1980s and 1990s. He argued that this was a process of adaptation—changing the means of engagement while avoiding a paradigm shift in China's realpolitik arms control policy—rather than a process of learning—a paradigm shift that would involve changes in China's basic assumptions regarding both the goals and means of arms control policy. My research has reached similar conclusions. China's growing enthusiasm for aid cooperation and engagement with traditional donors has been a process of adaptation. China's perception of cooperation with traditional donors *has* changed greatly since the 1970s—from allowing foreign aid to enter China, to piloting trilateral aid cooperation with traditional donors in Third World countries. China has mainly aimed to build its global image as a responsible global partner and to learn some useful aid practices from traditional donors to fill its own gap. This kind of learning has been selective and focuses on areas that are deemed suitable by the Chinese government. There is no change to China's aid paradigm, no shift in the goals and means of its aid program. China's basic perception of its aid as part of south–south cooperation has remained unchanged since the 1950s.

The extent to which international aid regimes independently influence China, including its adaptation of trilateral aid cooperation, also deserves attention. Again, Johnston has examined the influence of international institutions on China between 1980 and 2000, especially in the arms control sector. He argued that international institutions have played three roles in different settings: 1) mimicking—China as a novice in international affairs initially copied the behavioural norms of other states; 2) social influence—China's behaviour as a novice is judged by these states, as well as rewarded/punished; and 3) persuasion—China is encouraged to accept particular norms and values of the institutions (Johnston, 2007).

In the case of China's aid, as previous analysis has demonstrated, the traditional aid regime and its members—whether traditional donor states or international development agencies—have tried to integrate China into the international aid system and have encouraged China's adoption of their aid norms and practices. Their efforts have yielded some results, as China agreed to accept aid from these partners from the late 1970s and has expanded its development engagement and cooperation. Elements of mimicking, social influence and persuasion could be detected in the process of the engagement between China and traditional donor states and international development agencies. For example, a common goal of the US, Australia and the UNDP in the exemplary trilateral aid projects in Chapters 4–6 was to encourage China to learn from its aid practices, if not explicitly to shape China's aid practices. However, international engagement in itself would not have worked if China had not placed more emphasis on global image–building in its diplomacy, including aid delivery, because China could turn a blind eye to engagement efforts from traditional donors. Moreover, China's international engagement has been a reciprocal process. While traditional donor states and international organisations have tried to influence China, China has worked to consolidate some of its own rules in cooperation. For example, to reduce the risk of being regarded as getting closer to traditional donors and weakening its status as a south–south cooperation partner, China has insisted that trilateral aid cooperation be supported and preferably initiated by the developing countries. This 'condition' has been accepted by traditional donor states and international organisations in China's pilot trilateral projects.

There have also been finer distinctions for China's image building across diverse settings, whether in the development sector or beyond. China has placed increasing efforts on global image–building since the 2000s; however, its objectives vary with different development partners and different regions. To traditional donor states and international organisations who have taken the lead in engaging with China, China has aimed to project a benign image as a responsible stakeholder and a trustworthy development partner in response to their call for more coordination and cooperation. As the case of China–US trilateral cooperation has shown, China expects to build an image as a responsible stakeholder to serve the broader China–US relations. In contrast, as many developing countries face the growing challenge of aid coordination among donors, China has attempted to use trilateral aid cooperation to support the aid coordination between China and traditional donors in these recipient countries, which will improve China's image.

Further, China's motivations for global image–building in its broader diplomacy are not uniform. In Africa, China seeks to shrug off its negative neo-imperialist image—which is crucial, as China has kept emphasising its common identity with African countries as former colonies of Western powers. In Asia—China's immediate neighbourhood of intractable territorial disputes—image building in China's broad diplomacy is seemingly more about reassurance, especially in light of China's image as an assertive actor in the maritime realm and the perceptions of its neo-mercantilist approach towards commercial investment. For Pacific Island countries who are not a focus of China's diplomacy and economic outreach and who do not have territorial disputes with China, China's image building has focused on projecting the image of a good south–south cooperation partner. However, this distinction of global image–building in China's broad diplomacy is not that clear in relation to the specific concern of trilateral aid cooperation. This question deserves more investigation in the future, as China is currently still in the early stage of piloting trilateral aid cooperation in these regions. At this stage, it appears that China has aimed to use trilateral aid cooperation to improve aid coordination in recipient countries.

China's global image–building and cognitive learning vary in different settings. China has a nearly four-decade-long engagement with Australia and the UNDP regarding development cooperation, which has facilitated China's learning from the two partners. However, because China only began aid engagement with the US in 1999, China's learning of aid management from the US is limited. In this case, China's motive to build its image as a responsible stakeholder in the eyes of the US serves its broader bilateral relations.

Before concluding this subsection, it would be useful to briefly examine the case of Samoa. This would have been a most likely case for trilateral cooperation to occur, but it failed to eventuate, which confirms my findings. Among the Pacific Island countries, Samoa has performed well in managing aid effectively and promoting aid coordination among donors (Smith et al., 2014, pp. 18–19; Interview with Assistant Chief Executive of Samoa's Ministry of Finance Peseta Noumea, Apia, 26 February 2015). Due to this, Samoa has been running training sessions for aid officials from its Pacific neighbours, such as PNG, on how to promote aid coordination (Interview with Peseta Noumea, Apia, 26 February 2015). Samoa was also among the earliest Pacific Island countries to establish diplomatic relations with China.[1] This relationship has been recently lauded by China's Premier Li Keqiang, who in November 2015 referred to Samoa as 'a model of the relations between China and the Pacific island countries' (Chinese Embassy in Samoa, 2015, para. 8).

---

1   Fiji established diplomatic relations with China on 5 November 1975, and Samoa did so the following day.

Despite these favourable conditions, China is yet to initiate a trilateral aid project in Samoa. In this respect, Samoa lags behind the Cook Islands and PNG, who are already conducting trilateral aid cooperation with China on their own soil. Based on my research, the main reason for this is that it is currently the traditional donor states and multilateral development agencies, rather than the recipient countries or China, who have taken the lead in proposing trilateral projects. Although the Chinese government has agreed to pilot these new partnerships, its behaviour is mostly reactive rather than proactive. In the case of Samoa, there is little push from traditional donors for trilateral cooperation with China. Australia has historically focused its aid programs on the Melanesian countries, especially PNG, rather than on Samoa. Australia and China are also preoccupied with their trilateral project on malaria control in PNG and cannot expand this modality to other recipient countries (Interview with a senior Australian aid official, Port Moresby, 4 November 2014). Although Samoa is a top recipient of New Zealand's aid in the Pacific, New Zealand has made it clear that it will be concentrating on the pilot trilateral water supply project in the Cook Islands before extending trilateral partnerships to other recipient countries (Interview with David Nicholson, Wellington, 12 December 2014).[2]

Prominent Features

China has participated in a growing number of trilateral aid projects in recent years, as elaborated in Table 1. Close observation reveals some distinguishing features. First, these projects tend to be small in aid volume. Aside from the $53.2 million[3] China–New Zealand–Cook Islands trilateral project on water supply (Mabbitt, Hamilton, Raffe, Eggleton & Huttche, 2015, p. 23),[4] funding for Chinese trilateral projects is extremely modest. For example, the China–Australia–PNG trilateral project on malaria control has a budget of only AU$4 million. Second, the projects are technical in nature and focus on less sensitive areas, such

---

2   David Nicholson, director of Pacific development division, New Zealand Ministry of Foreign Affairs and Trade.

3   The estimated cost of the project is NZ$66.3 million, equivalent to US$53.2 million based on the exchange rate in August 2012, when the project agreement was signed. China Exim Bank agreed to provide US$18 million (RMB 117 million).

4   Although the governments of China and New Zealand highlight this project as trilateral, some analysts argued that this is not a trilateral project, but two bilateral projects in parallel. China built the main ring of the water supply while New Zealand is responsible for other issues, including connecting the main ring to the households.

as agriculture and food security, public health, disaster risk management and technical training. They do not cover politically sensitive issues like good governance, anti-corruption or human rights. The China–Australia–Cambodia trilateral irrigation dialogue (November 2013 – June 2014) is also categorised by China and Australia as a trilateral project.

China also has different policies for cooperating with traditional donor states and UN agencies on funding contributions. The Chinese government insists that traditional donor states provide funding in trilateral projects, while China contributes only technical expertise. China believes that this position is justified because it is still a developing country compared to traditional donors. Although China made financial contributions to its trilateral water supply project with New Zealand in the Cook Islands, this is an exceptional case because the China Exim Bank and the Chinese project contractor CCECC were eager to materialise a concessional loan agreement that was signed with the Cook Islands government before its expiry (Interview with Cook Islands Finance Minister Mark Brown, Apia, 27 February 2015). In contrast to its trilateral partnership with traditional donor states, China has funded some trilateral projects with UN agencies. To the Chinese government, China is a member of these organisations, and providing funding to UN agencies is not inconsistent with China's identity as a developing nation. Additionally, working with the UN could potentially lift China's global image as a responsible member state of the international community. Consequently, China financed the two phases of the China–UNDP–Cambodia trilateral aid project on cassava with $610,000 in total. Together with the UNDP, China has also approved an allocation of $500,000 for the trilateral project on disaster risk management in Malawi.

Building on the pilot projects, China is moving further towards testing different forms of trilateral cooperation. Similarly, it has started with the UNDP again due to their trust building over the past four decades. A UNDP official categorised the development of China–UNDP trilateral aid cooperation into three generations.[5] The first generation refers to projects that are conducted with pooled resources, especially joint funding from China and the UNDP in a Third World country. China and the UNDP identify a potential project for cooperation, which will combine China's expertise with international best practices from the UNDP.

5   Author's interview (Beijing, 30 July 2015). The rest of the paragraph is paraphrased, based on the remarks of this UNDP official.

The China–UNDP–Cambodia trilateral project on cassava,[6] the China–UNDP–Burundi trilateral project on renewable energy and the China–UNDP–Malawi trilateral project on disaster risk management fall into this category. The second-generation projects are entirely funded by a third developed country. China provides technical experts and know-how, while the UNDP manages the project. For example, the China–UNDP pilot projects on disaster risk management in Bangladesh and Nepal are fully funded by the UK's DFID. The government of Denmark funds the China–UNDP renewable energy trilateral projects in Ghana and Zambia, with approximately $5.3 million. The third-generation trilateral projects are still being developed. Ideally, the UNDP will implement one component of a large Chinese aid project. In particular, the UNDP will focus on the soft areas of this project, such as capacity building and system strengthening. This trilateral arrangement aims to complement existing Chinese aid practice, which usually focuses on physical infrastructure, and to assist China in improving its aid delivery system.

Official Position

The Chinese government is taking a cautious and incremental approach towards trilateral aid cooperation. This follows China's tradition of testing new decisions on a small scale before expansion. For example, in the early 1980s, China first tested the SEZs in the four cities of Shenzhen, Zhuhai, Shantou and Xiamen before expanding them to other cities in China and, eventually, beyond China's borders to parts of Africa (Bräutigam & Tang, 2011). China has handled trilateral aid cooperation in a similar manner. Presently, the Chinese government has shown interest in testing trilateral aid cooperation and has been open to proposals that traditional donor states and multilateral development agencies have offered. After several years' experimentation, China's MOFCOM is assessing the performance of this new modality.

Trilateral aid cooperation is still a supplementary pilot modality in China. China has not issued a clear policy or guiding document for trilateral aid cooperation. Each project is managed on a case-by-case basis. However, China's position on piloting this kind of aid project complies with the core of China's foreign aid policy since the 1950s: non-interference, respect

---

6   The UNDP has categorised the China–UNDP–Cambodia trilateral project on cassava into this first generation, though in reality, the project was mainly funded by China; the UNDP contributed expertise and management.

for sovereign equality and mutual benefit (State Council, 2011d, 2014).[7] The five principles identified by then Ambassador Liu Guijin in 2008 for China's participation in trilateral aid cooperation in Africa, the largest recipient of Chinese aid, remain instructive. This is the most detailed explanation available from China's official sources. Chinese officials and experts echoed these principles during my interviews.

> First, respect for Africa. No cooperation should be conducted at the cost of sovereignty, interest or dignity of any African country. In particular, we should heed the opinions of the African side on whether or not and how to conduct such cooperation, instead of imposing our opinions on the African side. Second, be pragmatic. Attention should be paid in such cooperation to combine good practices of other parts of the world with specific conditions of Africa to serve the actual needs of African countries and avoid 'one-size-for-all' practices that are neither practical nor effective. Third, step by step. We should start with small and easily operable projects and learn from experience and constantly improve our work. It is important to remember 'More haste, less speed'. Fourth, everyone doing his best. The key to success of the triangular cooperation is to let each party do what it is best at. When developed countries are involved in the triangular cooperation, their financial strength should be combined with developing countries' advantages in applicable technologies and cost. Fifth, efficiency. The triangular cooperation should make full use of existing authoritative cooperative mechanisms, such as the United Nations development assistance mechanism, to avoid overlapping institutions and waste of resources caused by setting up too many new mechanisms. (Liu, 2008, pp. 5–6)

Chinese officials have repeated these principles on other occasions, though briefly. For example, the China–US MOU on development cooperation, signed in September 2015, stated clearly that 'the principle of raised, agreed and led by recipient countries is a prerequisite for all

---

7   The three principles are also reflected in the eight principles for China's aid to other countries that were suggested by Premier Zhou Enlai during his visit to Africa in 1964. The eight principles include 1) China always bases itself on the principle of equality and mutual benefit in providing aid to other nations; 2) China never attaches any conditions or asks for any privileges; 3) China helps lighten the burden of recipient countries as much as possible; 4) China aims to help recipient countries gradually achieve self-reliance and independent development; 5) China strives to develop aid projects that require less investment but that yield quicker results; 6) China provides the best-quality equipment and materials of its own manufacture; 7) in providing technical assistance, China shall confirm that the personnel of the recipient country fully master such techniques; and 8) the Chinese experts are not allowed to make any special demands or to enjoy any special amenities.

cooperation' and that the areas of cooperation must be 'in accordance with the principle of recipient country ownership' (USAID, 2015c, pp. 1–2). The eighth China–US S&ED held in Beijing in June 2016 pledged that the two nations would promote trilateral aid cooperation under the principle that such cooperation is raised, agreed and led by recipient countries (US Department of State, 2016). The same principles were highlighted by China's Ambassador to South Africa Tian Xuejun on China–Western donors–Africa trilateral cooperation in November 2015, and by China's Assistant Foreign Minister Liu Haixing at the symposium on China–France–Africa trilateral cooperation held in Beijing in April 2016 (MFA, 2015e, 2016a).

The Administration of China's Trilateral Aid: Bureaucratic Arrangements

The Chinese government has committed high-level political support to existing trilateral projects. MOFCOM had dominated the approval process until the establishment of CIDCA in April 2018. Initiatives from traditional donor states and UN agencies for trilateral cooperation must go through MOFCOM for approval. MOFCOM had shown interest in conducting some selected trilateral projects without other agencies being involved, as is the case for the China–UNDP–Cambodia trilateral cassava project. Due to human and technical resource constraints, MOFCOM approved some trilateral initiatives, but invited line agencies in China to help progress them. One typical example is the China–Australia–PNG trilateral malaria control project. Although MOFCOM was involved in the negotiation and exploratory missions, China's National Health Commission is undertaking the technical work, including the selection and dispatch of Chinese medical experts.

Within MOFCOM, both the DITEA and the DFA had been involved in managing China's trilateral aid cooperation. In terms of human resources, the involvement of DITEA in China's trilateral cooperation is understandable, though its primary responsibility is to oversee foreign aid to China. This business of managing foreign aid to China has dwindled, as traditional donors have either phased out or reduced their aid programs in China. As such, DITEA has an incentive to take over some trilateral projects as a new area of business, as the reduction of incoming aid has left it with a surplus of staff and resources. In contrast, the DFA is severely understaffed and overwhelmed by the skyrocketing business of providing bilateral aid overseas. This greatly limits its appetite for initiating or managing trilateral cooperation. A MOFCOM aid official explained that DFA officials could hardly finish their daily work on China's aid projects overseas, let alone spare any energy to work on trilateral projects (Interview with Chinese aid official, Beijing, 4 August 2015). Under such circumstances, the DFA welcomes the involvement of DITEA in trilateral aid cooperation, while trilateral projects potentially give DITEA a new lease on life against a background of declining aid to China.

However, in terms of financial resources, the DFA still receives an annual allocation of foreign aid funding from China's MoF, while DITEA does not. For example, the China–UNDP–Cambodia trilateral cassava project was funded by the DFA. In this sense, the DFA 'has to' get involved in China's trilateral aid projects. Additionally, being the department tasked to oversee Chinese foreign aid, the DFA must be involved in the trilateral aid projects and ensure that they run well.

Consequently, both DITEA and DFA had been involved in Chinese trilateral aid cooperation. It is not surprising that DITEA officials sometimes attended the opening ceremony of a trilateral project, while DFA officials were involved in the inspection process. It is easier for DITEA and DFA to negotiate and divide the labour among themselves, as they answer to the same ministry (Interview with MOFCOM former senior aid official, Beijing, 1 September 2015). The China–UNDP–Cambodia trilateral project on cassava, as examined in Chapter 4, is a case in point. Both departments were involved in the project to some extent. The opening ceremony of the first phase in Hainan was addressed by Deputy Division Director Cai Fang from the DFA. The conclusion ceremony of the first phase was officiated by Deputy Director-General Zhu Hong from DITEA. Division Director Liang Hong from DITEA headed the joint monitoring and reviewing mission of the second phase.

Assessment of Trilateral Cooperation

The future of trilateral aid cooperation depends on whether positive experiences can be drawn from the pilot projects for all three parties involved. The existing literature expects trilateral aid cooperation to bring in added value—including facilitating cognitive learning and experience sharing among different types of donors and recipient countries and amplifying aid cooperation while facing challenges such as increased coordination and higher transaction costs relative to bilateral aid. A question remains: how far are these anticipated advantages and challenges borne out by the experience of trilateral projects on the ground? Based on my extensive interviews with aid officials and participants in Chinese trilateral aid projects, the following trends can be discerned.

Trilateral aid cooperation provides more learning opportunities than bilateral engagement for beneficiaries in recipient countries. These beneficiaries are exposed to technologies and practices from both traditional and emerging donors. They have the luxury of comparing and contrasting and choosing the more suitable ones for themselves. For example, China and Australia have completed a trilateral project on irrigation dialogue in Cambodia. Three official trips were organised to observe the different agricultural irrigation policies and practices in the three countries between 2013 and 2014. Dr Sokhem Pech, the main initiator of the project from Cambodia, explained their needs for implementing this trilateral project:

> We told them [partners from China and Australia] we want to know how you do water cooperatives, how you promote long-term sustainability [of irrigation], how you make sure you have water for farmers, and how you ensure you can collect fees for cost recovery and for long term sustainability financially and in terms of agricultural production. (Interview, Phnom Penh, 14 July 2015)

Dr Sokhem Pech seemed satisfied that these objectives appeared to have been achieved in this particular case. Sophak Seng, another main participant in the project from the Cambodia Irrigation Services Center, agreed with the evaluation (Interview, Phnom Penh, 10 July 2015).

Now, let us listen to the voices of four students from the National University of Timor-Leste. They participated in the China–US–Timor-Leste trilateral agricultural project and experienced technical training on the cultivation of maize from China and on the cultivation of onion, beans and garlic from the US. Although complaining that Chinese experts only taught general knowledge in the classroom by lecturing and that they only included farmers (not students) in the field practices relative to their US peers, these students were overall satisfied with what they learned (Interview with the four students, Phnom Penh, 6 February 2015). They also expressed a strong interest in learning how the Chinese experts could harvest maize on land that locals deemed unsuitable for growing corn (Interview with the four students, Phnom Penh, 6 February 2015).

In contrast to traditional donors, it must be asked: are the technologies from emerging donors more appropriate and acceptable to recipient countries than from traditional donors? Not necessarily. In addition to the potential advantage of combining the different strengths of traditional and emerging donors, the involvement of these different donors in a single aid project provides more options for recipient countries and exposes them to different practices. As China's trilateral aid cooperation is in its infancy, it will take some time for the beneficiaries in recipient countries to understand this new modality and then judge which technologies are more suitable for them (from China or traditional donors).

Some argue that linguistic and cultural similarities between emerging donors and recipient countries are advantageous for the involvement of emerging donors, but this is not inevitably the case. A study of German trilateral aid cooperation argued that linguistic and cultural similarities between emerging donors and recipient countries do not necessarily favour effectiveness (Lengfelder, 2015, pp. 7–9). One policy advisor from the German Ministry of Economic Cooperation and Development noted that some aid officials from emerging donors are drawn from the elite in their countries and have little firsthand experience with poverty and development (Lengfelder, 2015, p. 8). Further, it is natural for people to question the relevance of China's approaches in the context of Africa and the Pacific, where presumably cultural and linguistic similarities are lacking.

In terms of assessment, although Germany has been among the earliest pioneers in practising trilateral aid cooperation, German policymakers repeatedly suggest that it is still new and difficult to assess the effectiveness (Lengfelder, 2015, p. 8). Turning to China's trilateral cooperation, the differences between China and recipient countries such as PNG, Timor-Leste and Cambodia are substantial in terms of linguistics and cultures. Consequently, the workload of project preparation and management has increased.

Transaction cost is another contentious issue for trilateral projects. Trilateral aid cooperation involves additional donor engagement/input relative to bilateral aid. There are also considerable differences between traditional and emerging donors, ranging from guiding aid principles to practices on the ground. The complexity is reinforced by organisational culture and language differences in many occasions. These factors naturally lead to increased costs of coordination and negotiation for trilateral projects, as well as greater scrutiny in their home countries. Aid officials and researchers from both donor and recipient countries frequently mentioned the issue of additional costs.

Take the China–Australia–PNG trilateral malaria project as a typical example. The three countries began preparing and discussing the project shortly after the signing of the China–Australia MOU on development cooperation in April 2013. However, more than two years passed before the three sides finally signed the project agreement in October 2015. A senior Australian aid official commented on this, and his statement included the response from his counterpart in China's MOFCOM. These remarks are illustrative of Australian and Chinese perceptions regarding the issue of transaction costs:

> This malaria project is our first formal thing to have engagement [with China on development cooperation]. Even this project has taken a long time, much longer than it would take for such a small project. This project is 4 million Australia dollars in value. Compared with the Australia aid in PNG about half a billion per year, it is tiny. It has taken over a year, from October 2013 [the formal discussion between China and a visiting Australian and PNG delegation] to October 2014 [the project was agreed in principle]. This is a tiny project, but it takes a long time. But it is understandable. Mr Zhang, the division director from MOFCOM is quite open to this trilateral malaria project. He said, for China, this is a new thing. So, it takes a long time, and they are even very careful about wording. This is already quite quick [for China]. (Interview, Port Moresby, 4 November 2014)

Another senior Australian aid official expressed similar views:

> For the Australia–China–PNG trilateral malaria project, though the project volume is not big, the negotiation and coordination cost is huge. The project [was] supposed to start in early 2015, but it has not started yet. It is almost closer to the starting point. The three sides will finally sign the project agreement. The slow progress is not because either side intentionally delays the progress, but because trilateral cooperation is a new modality, and it takes time for the three countries to coordinate. (Interview, Beijing, 4 August 2015)

Some Chinese aid officials share these concerns. A Chinese aid official commented on the transaction cost of the China–UK (together with the UNDP) trilateral aid project on disaster relief management in Bangladesh and Nepal, linking it to the understaffing problem with China's ministries.

> For China's Ministry of Civil Affairs (MCA, main participant from China), they do not have much knowledge of the UK's Department for International Development (DFID). They hope to increase the understanding of DFID through the conduction of the trilateral project. But in practice, the challenge of coordination is daunting. For instance, The MCA's division that was involved in the project only has three staff including the division director. What makes the issue worse is that only the division director can speak English. He had to attend all the coordination meetings with DFID by himself. As he has a lot of other work to do every day, how can he spend that sort of time attending DFID's meetings? That's why MCA itself did not want to get involved, and designated the project to its affiliate, the China National Disaster Reduction Centre. (Interview, Beijing, 4 August 2015)

However, some aid practitioners have expressed different views regarding the transaction costs of trilateral cooperation. A major participant from Australia in the China–Australia–Cambodia triangular project on irrigation dialogue argued that triangular cooperation does not have to be more time consuming than any other multi-actor aid activity (Interview, Phnom Penh, 20 July 2015).

As China is emphasising its global image–building more and learning from traditional donors to improve its own aid practices, trilateral aid cooperation would be expected to grow slowly in China's foreign aid program. However, this should not be taken as given. Aid officials from both China and traditional donor nations repeatedly reminded me that they are closely following the progress of pilot projects. If these projects are perceived as—or reported to be—a success, this could lead to future cooperation. In the absence of positive results, it is likely that China and traditional donors would withhold and perhaps end the experiment. For example, Chinese officials told Australian aid officials that China would not consider anything else, whether in PNG or elsewhere, unless they observe how this malaria project proceeds (Interview with senior Australian aid official, Port Moresby, 4 November 2014). A senior New Zealand aid official said that:

> NZ is focusing on the current trilateral water project [in Cook
> Islands], to see how it progresses. NZ is open to other triangular
> cooperation opportunities with China, but will not push for them.
> (Interview, Wellington, 10 December 2014)

Merriden Varrall, a former UNDP senior representative in Beijing,
argued that China's Minister of Commerce, Gao Hucheng, who took
up his post in March 2013, has 'preferred a more cautious approach to
trilateral cooperation, and wanted to see evidence of success with the
existing projects before approving new initiatives' (Varrall, 2016, p. 28).
According to Varrall, Minister Gao's conservative and risk-averse manner
meant that MOFCOM's enthusiasm for trilateral aid cooperation
'distinctly waned', especially towards cooperation with traditional donor
states (Varrall, 2016, p. 28). However, some UNDP officials have argued
recently that MOFCOM, especially the DFA, has become more active
in exploring trilateral aid cooperation with the UNDP since late 2015 to
materialise the south–south cooperation fund that President Xi pledged
at the UN summit in September of the year (Interview, Canberra,
29 June 2016).

The Chinese government is still assessing the effectiveness of its pilot
trilateral aid projects. Its attitude towards future cooperation is not yet
fully formed and some confusion and uncertainty remains. A senior
Chinese aid official told me that China intended to learn more from the
traditional donors' aid practices, but that MOFCOM doubted whether
this can actually be achieved because its involvement in the process of
trilateral aid projects is so limited (Interview, Beijing, 4 August 2015).
Although China and traditional donors have started pilot trilateral
projects, substantial differences between their aid policies remain and
further engagement to boost understanding is expected from both sides.

Moreover, China and traditional donors are still confining their trilateral
cooperation to less sensitive areas, such as agriculture, public health, food
security and technical training. These areas are more acceptable to the
Chinese side and render cooperation more feasible. For example, health
appears to be a potential area for China–US trilateral aid cooperation,
including in Africa. Scholars from China and the US, such as Deborah
Bräutigam and vice president of the China Institute of International
Studies Liu Youfa proposed that the two superpowers could cooperate
in this area (Freeman III & Lu Boynton, 2011, pp. 11, 15). David H.
Shinn argued that cooperation in Africa's health sector is less likely to

cause political conditionalities from the US and therefore it will avoid potential objections from African countries (Shinn, 2011). Trilateral cooperation beyond these areas could be difficult to initiate at this stage. Equally important is how China has repeatedly conveyed the message to traditional donors that recipient countries' support is a precondition for its endorsement of trilateral cooperation. If recipient countries initiate and propose trilateral projects to China, then China will more likely approve them. Some officials from recipient countries have already complained that they were not consulted adequately in regard to, for example, the European Union's plan for trilateral cooperation in Africa (Wikileaks, 2010).

As China is familiarising itself with trilateral aid cooperation through the pilot projects, it is quite possible that China will continue to experiment with the current crop of 'familiar' traditional donor states and multilateral development agencies. It is likely that they will expand trilateral cooperation into more areas and with more donors. For example, building on their recent trilateral cooperation on agriculture in Timor-Leste and the joint training of Afghan diplomats, armies from China and the US conducted the disaster management exchange program in November 2015, which USAID said could 'advance coordination in humanitarian disasters taking place in a third country' (USAID, 2015e, p. 4).

Trilateral aid cooperation between China and the UNDP is expected to grow, as the two sides have shown interest in testing different types of trilateral cooperation and in expanding this modality. Similarly, China–UK trilateral cooperation is also expected to grow. As early as 2006, the UK's DFID launched a formal dialogue with China regarding development cooperation. The UK Parliament endorsed this engagement, believing that it was embedded within the UK's wider strategy for China: 'Getting the best for the UK from China's rise; fostering China's emergence as a responsible global player; and promoting sustainable development, modernisation and internal reform in China' (UK Parliament, 2009, p. 36). In October 2010, UK International Development Secretary Andrew Mitchell told the media that 'we are looking to work very closely with China' as a high priority for the UK government because this will enable the UK to 'do much more to speed up development in Africa' (Hawksley, 2010). A more recent development of China's trilateral cooperation relationships is that China and France are exploring opportunities for trilateral aid cooperation—and one such symposium was held in Beijing in April 2016. China's Assistant Foreign Minister Liu Haixing highlighted at the conference:

> To carry out trilateral cooperation between China, France and African countries conforms to the trend that nations promote cooperation of mutual benefits and strengthen interest integration to realise common development in the context of economic globalisation. (MFA, 2016a, para. 2)

It is likely that China will partner with more traditional donors in the future.

In terms of recipient countries, their initial request for such assistance will be a critical factor for China in determining whether it delivers aid bilaterally or trilaterally. It can be expected that China will do more trilateral aid cooperation in recipient countries who are struggling with aid coordination and who express a desire to boost aid coordination between China and traditional donors. Recipient countries that perceive more advantages in using Chinese aid to increase their leverage with traditional donors will prefer to receive bilateral aid from China rather than support trilateral cooperation. China is unlikely to undertake trilateral projects in these countries. This explains why a senior Chinese aid scholar commented that 'China will not conduct trilateral aid cooperation for the sake of cooperation itself if it comes at the expense of its relations with other developing countries' (Interview, Beijing, 30 August 2015). A possible method for identifying trilateral aid cooperation is by identifying recipient countries who have interests in this kind of cooperation. David H. Shinn suggested that the US and China will identify countries like Liberia, who seem to welcome trilateral cooperation, and focus on them (Shinn, 2011).

Chinese Aid Reform and the New Aid Agency

Trilateral aid cooperation is just one manifestation of Chinese foreign aid reform. To some extent, the future of Chinese trilateral cooperation also depends on the Chinese government's continued willingness to pursue aid reform. Therefore, it is worth elaborating on recent trends in Chinese aid reform.

In the short term, it is most likely that China will continue increasing foreign aid for the benefit of its economic, political and global-image interests. China is likely to align its aid program with recently announced initiatives, such as the AIIB, the BRI and the BRICS New Development Bank. It is also expected to link its foreign aid to the implementation of SDGs in developing countries.

China's poverty reduction at home and foreign aid provision are interrelated, despite being two seemingly different themes. China's own experience in eradicating poverty can be shared with other developing countries, though to what extent it can work in culturally diverse settings is debatable. Additionally, the international acknowledgement of China's efforts to reduce poverty at home and abroad is deemed conducive by the Chinese government to its global image–building, and it has strengthened its interests in development assistance. As a senior Chinese scholar who preferred to remain anonymous revealed:

> Chinese President Xi Jinping was credited for China's incredible contribution to achieving the Millennium Development Goals during the 2015 UN Summit [he was quite happy with this], which in turn reinforced China's commitment to poverty reduction at home and abroad. (Conversation with Chinese scholar, Canberra, February 2016)

This can be demonstrated by the convening of two of the highest-level conferences soon after President Xi's trip to the UN. On 23 November 2015, the political bureau of the CPC's central committee—the top decision-making organ in China—held a special conference on poverty reduction, a rare engagement with this issue at such a high level in China. The conference issued the 'Decision on Winning the Tough Battle on Poverty Reduction'[8] and also pledged to implement strict accountability for government officials (Xinhua, 2015c). In less than one week, the national conference on poverty reduction was held in Beijing and it was attended by all seven members of the standing committee of the CPC political bureau, as well as governors from all the provinces. President Xi instructed government officials at all levels to 'carry out more targeted and precise measures' to lift the remaining 70 million poor people out of poverty by 2020' (Xinhua, 2015a, para. 1).

---

8   President Xi's new approach to poverty alleviation—such as targeting the individual, employing the whole of government (not just the poverty alleviation bureau) and using many military metaphors—does mark a break with previous approaches, which targeted poverty counties and later villages.

On 15 December 2015, the China State Council held a news briefing on poverty reduction at China's 13th five-year plan. Liu Yongfu, director of the China State Council Leading Group Office of Poverty Alleviation and Development, responded to a question raised by Reuters regarding why China is providing foreign aid while it has more than 70 million people living in poverty. As a main decision-maker for China's poverty reduction[9] and international exchange on poverty reduction, his answer sheds some insight on understanding China's motivations behind aid:

> China is a developing country and also a responsible great power … While doing our own things well, we are supporting other [developing] countries by sharing our experiences even piloting poverty reduction within our capacity. We believe it is the right thing to do as we are a permanent member of the UN Security Council, the second largest economy in the world and a responsible great power. (State Council, 2015, para. 35)

It can also be said that China will not embrace all Western aid norms and abandon its own. The main reason why is that China will still hold tightly to its identity as a developing country, from which it has reaped and will continue to reap tremendous benefits. This identity will help China lobby for support from other developing countries, including at the UN, when disputes arise between China and the developed countries. Consequently, it is least likely that China will join the OECD in the short term, even though it is now the second-largest economy. Ye Jiang, director of the Institute for Global Governance Studies from Shanghai Institutes for International Studies, said that:

> China can play a role as a bridge between the South and the North, but will not become a member of OECD as the rich's club. China still sticks to the principle of 'common but differentiated responsibilities' in development cooperation. China will never commit to DAC's 0.7 per cent GNI target, as there is still a big poor population at home.[10]

---

9   Although China's poverty reduction at home and its foreign aid delivery are two separate issues, they are related to some extent. Many of China's foreign aid projects have roots in its poverty reduction at home. For example, China's emphasis on aiding infrastructure projects in recipient countries is derived from its experience of economic development at home.

10   Presentation at the 2016 Australasian aid conference at ANU, 10 February 2016.

In recent years, the OECD has strengthened efforts to engage with China, such as by establishing the China–DAC study group and providing training for Chinese officials, as discussed in Chapter 3. This engagement is paying off for the OECD, as China has demonstrated more readiness to cooperate with the OECD. In July 2015, China's Premier Li Keqiang became the first Chinese leader to visit OECD headquarters in Paris. During the visit, China agreed to join the OECD development centre, which represents itself as a platform for finding solutions to stimulate growth in developing countries, and pledged to 'share the development experience with other members of the OECD Development Centre and promote global economic growth' (B. Chen, 2015). OECD Secretary-General Angel Gurría credited this agreement as 'a historical and transformative opportunity for mutually beneficial knowledge-sharing [between China, OECD, and other developing countries]' (OECD, 2015b). China has also agreed to accept the OECD policy coherence for sustainable development, a policy tool used to integrate the various dimensions of sustainable development into policymaking and to ensure that they are mutually supportive (OECD, 2015a, p. 24). This can potentially improve the development coordination between China and OECD members in other developing countries.

Though encouraging, over-interpretation of China's membership must be avoided. In addition to 26 members of developed countries, another 22 developing countries (including India and Brazil) joined the OECD development centre prior to China. As a senior Chinese aid official reminded me, the OECD development centre is totally different from the OECD because the task of the former is centred on development research, much of which focuses on developing countries (Interview, Beijing, 4 August 2015). Moreover, as a senior Chinese scholar revealed, although the OECD sent an invitation to President Xi Jinping to visit its Paris headquarters during his visit to France in May 2015, China wanted to refrain from being too close to the OECD; therefore, it was Premier Li who visited OECD as a compromise. While significant, China sent its premier rather than its president, thereby signalling that this relationship did not yet merit a visit from the country's most senior leader (Conversation, Canberra, February 2016). A former senior Chinese aid official noted that China would not consider joining OECD DAC in the short term (Interview, Beijing, 1 September 2015).

The OECD case also indicated that neoliberalism theories, as mentioned in Chapter 2, are insufficient in explaining China's endorsement for trilateral aid cooperation. These theories tend to focus on the roles of international institutions in promoting cooperation among member states. However, China is still cautious about its engagement with the OECD. It has consciously kept its distance from this organisation. By staying out of OECD DAC, China is not bound by their regulations on aid delivery. Put another way, China's adoption of trilateral partnership in aid delivery is not a result of international institutions such as OECD DAC.

China International Development Cooperation Agency

It is useful to reflect on the establishment of CIDCA due to the move in many parts of the OECD—such as Australia, Canada and New Zealand—to discard separate aid agencies and integrate them with their foreign affairs' ministries. For example, the Abbott government integrated AusAID into DFAT in September 2013 and announced a new aid paradigm that is actually the old paradigm reincarnate with incremental changes, such as the alteration to the geographical aid focus (Corbett & Dinnen, 2015).

Chinese aid officials and analysts acknowledge the complexity and inadequacies of the Chinese aid management system. Xu Weizhong, director of the African Research Institute of China Institute of Contemporary International Relations and his colleague Wang Lei have argued that 'the fragmentation of aid funding and management has greatly compromised the efficiency of China's current inter-ministerial aid coordination system' (Xu & Wang, 2015). They strongly recommend that China establish a separate aid agency. A senior Chinese aid scholar revealed that MOFCOM's DFA also supported the creation of a 'China aid agency' because China's officials are overwhelmed by their current workload (Interview, Beijing, 30 August 2015). She also mentioned that some officials from the China Exim Bank also supported integrating the fragmented Chinese aid agencies into a 'China aid agency', as well as including the concessional loans under this new agency (Interview, Beijing, 30 August 2015). Professor He Wenping from CASS supported the idea of creating a 'China aid agency' because 'as Chinese foreign aid is growing fast, it means you are growing up, you are not able to put on the kid's clothes as you did before' (Interview, Beijing, 28 July 2015).

Amid these anticipations in March 2018, the China State Council announced the plan to establish an independent aid agency, CIDCA. In April, the vice ministerial–level CIDCA was officially launched in Beijing. Its main responsibilities are to strengthen Chinese aid planning, coordination and monitoring, and to fully support the BRI. Aid implementation is still the responsibility of existing aid agencies, including MOFCOM's three affiliates and the line ministries. After about six months' preparation, CIDCA started to function in late 2018.

The formation of CIDCA's senior management team provides a lens through which to understand the shift of power among China's ministries in aid management. Wang Xiaotao, a former deputy director of the China National Reform and Development Commission, became CIDCA's first director. This appointment, to the surprise of many analysts and even some officials from MOFCOM, can largely be interpreted as a compromise for MOFCOM and MFA, the two most important players in Chinese aid decision-making. As the China National Reform and Development Commission is the ministry that coordinates the BRI, Wang's appointment also reflects the Chinese government's desire to use aid to support the initiative—which is a signature project of President Xi Jinping. The first highest-ranking deputy director, Zhang Maoyu, worked in China's National Intellectual Property Administration for decades and had no experience with foreign aid, rendering his appointment surprising to many aid observers. The second highest-ranking deputy director, Zhou Liujun, was a former director-general of MOFCOM's Department of Trade in services and commercial services and of the Department of Outward Investment and Economic Cooperation. The third highest-ranking deputy director, Deng Qingbo, was previously China's ambassador in Dominica and Nigeria, as well as director-general of the MFA's Department of Party Related Affairs. The appointments of Zhou and Deng are telling signs that MOFCOM and MFA will continue playing significant roles in Chinese foreign aid.

In terms of reporting line, CIDCA will report directly to the State Council. To be more specific, it is under the supervision of State Councillor and MFA Minister Wang Yi. This is a strong signal that the MFA has power in the Chinese new aid system. Diplomacy will play a more prominent role in deciding Chinese aid spending. As the former custodian of Chinese aid, MOFCOM's role is weakened. However, it will continue to significantly influence, as the whole DFA has been relocated to CIDCA and now it forms most of the aid officials there.

Being a new organisation, CIDCA's influence on China's trilateral aid cooperation is yet to be observed. Its structural arrangement on trilateral cooperation is also unclear. However, as previously discussed, both MFA and MOFCOM (MOFCOM to a lesser extent) are supportive of piloting trilateral aid cooperation. It is expected that CIDCA will continue to test this modality with traditional donor states and UN agencies.

Some Thorny Issues

As China increases its foreign aid spending, it has paid more attention to the quality and effect of its aid. The Chinese government has become more conscious of the weaknesses in its aid delivery and has started to take remedial measures.

Infrastructure is a main area of concern. Li Xiaoyun and Wu Jin from the China Agricultural University argued in 2009 that 'the West's criticism on this issue [China's overemphasis on infrastructure projects] is reasonable to a great extent. China should pay attention to this issue in its aid to Africa' (Li & Wu, 2009, p. 53). However, despite the criticism, infrastructure is most likely to continue being the focus of Chinese aid. One reason is that China has a comparative advantage in this field in terms of cost and speed. Infrastructure projects are often large in scale and provide opportunities for China to export its equipment, building materials and workforce. Additionally, new initiatives such as the BRI, AIIB and the BRICS New Development Bank concentrate on supporting infrastructure construction in developing countries. A large proportion of Chinese foreign aid will be used to complement and support these new initiatives.

Another reason relates to the philosophy of the Chinese government, which originated in China's own development experience. The Chinese government regards infrastructure improvement as the first step for poverty reduction and economic development. It has formed an important component of China's own economic development plans. Even in the present day, building infrastructure remains a crucial tool for bolstering economic development in China's western regions. The proverb that 'to be rich you have to start by building a road' (*yao zhi fu, xian xiu lu*) has become embedded in the mindset of Chinese officials and civilians. This proverb is still daubed on the outside of many houses in rural China. As Wang Xiaoling, division director from the China International Poverty

Reduction Centre, emphasised, one of the important lessons that China gained from its past experience of lifting approximately 600 million Chinese citizens out of poverty is its reliance on development-oriented poverty reduction (Wang, 2014).

However, while continuing to highlight infrastructure, the proportion of Chinese aid in welfare-related projects is expected to grow (e.g. agriculture, health, education and technical training). The Chinese government is increasingly conscious of the criticism regarding its overemphasis on infrastructure projects, and it is becoming more economically capable of spending a greater proportion of its aid budget on welfare-related projects. China will also explore new types of aid partnerships. For example, during President Xi's visit to the US in September 2015, Zhang Xiangchen, China International Trade representative deputy (vice ministerial level at MOFCOM) and Bill Gates signed an MOU on development cooperation. Based on this, the Chinese government and the Bill and Melinda Gates Foundation pledged to promote development cooperation in the areas of agriculture and health in Africa (Y. Chen, 2015). This sends a positive signal that China is more open to working with leading global private foundations on aid cooperation.

Similarly, China will pay more attention to the environmental and corporate social responsibility issues that surround Chinese companies in delivering their aid. David Dollar argued that 'China, in general, does not subscribe to global standards of environmental and social safeguards' (Dollar, 2016, p. 4). To urge Chinese companies to honour their social responsibilities overseas, several guideline documents have been jointly issued by MOFCOM and the Ministry of Environmental Protection, including the 2013 guidelines for environmental protection for overseas investment and cooperation, as mentioned in Chapter 3. Though this guideline is not binding, companies breaching environmental protection laws in recipient countries will face penalties from their headquarters in China. More similar documents are likely to be issued. However, the 'principal–agent dilemma' will remain. While the Chinese government highlights its strategic and global image interest in providing foreign aid, the Chinese aid companies will continue prioritising their own economic benefits. Therefore, their short-term economic interests could have the upper hand in the competition against the long-term interests of the Chinese state in some occasions. Traditional donors face a similar issue in using private contractors to deliver their aid, in which 'boomerang aid' is common.[11] For example, the Australian government has insisted that its aid program must be in line with Australian national interests, and many aid projects are awarded to Australian private contractors (Aidwatch, 2012). One difference is that it is not mandated that a certain percentage of Australian aid has to be spent on Australian materials and equipment, while in China's concessional loan projects, no less than 50 per cent of materials and equipment are required to be purchased from China.

Will China Attend Donors' Roundtable?

China has frequently been criticised for not attending donors' roundtable meetings on development cooperation in recipient countries. Uidon Chung, deputy country representative of the Korean International Cooperation Agency in Dili, said that he has never seen Chinese aid officials at such meetings. He joked that traditional donors were often overjoyed when he attended the roundtable meetings because they mistook him for a Chinese aid official (Interview, Dili, 28 January 2015). Based on my field work in PNG, Timor-Leste and Cambodia, traditional donors and many aid officials from the recipient countries resent that China seldom attends the donors' roundtable meetings. A senior Chinese aid official gave the following reasons for this state of affairs:

> China does not often attend this sort of donors' coordination meeting because traditionally China has been cautious. Normally, China will respond by saying that these meetings are not led by recipient countries. If the meetings are indeed led by recipient countries, for instance many such meetings are hosted by the Ministry of Finance in African countries, in general China will turn up, no matter whether it will speak or not. If the meetings are not led by recipient countries, China will not attend in most circumstances. This is because China normally will 'draw the line' believing it and developed countries belong to different camps. In addition, Chinese Economic and Commercial Counsellor's offices in many countries are under-staffed. Individual officials from these offices often have varying attitudes towards this sort of donors' coordination meetings. This will also affect whether they will attend or not. (Interview, Beijing, 4 August 2015)

---

11 Many analysts have complained that much of traditional donors' aid that is pledged to their countries has returned to the donors through means such as awarding the contracts to companies from donor states and paying the salaries for consultants from these countries.

The capacity of recipient governments to manage aid coordination will influence China's attendance at such roundtable meetings. When they push hard, it is more likely that the economic and commercial counsellor's office in China's embassy will send staff to attend these meetings, though how active they will be at the meetings is another question. This concurs with the findings of Matthew Dornan and Philippa Brant, who examined Chinese aid to Vanuatu, Tonga, Samoa and the Cook Islands, arguing that Chinese aid is better managed in recipient countries with better aid coordination systems, such as Samoa and the Cook Islands (Dornan & Brant, 2014). However, the push from recipient countries is not a guarantee that China's representatives will attend aid roundtables. Based on my observations from 2006 to 2008, staff from the Chinese economic and commercial counsellor's office in Tonga did not actively participate in aid coordination meetings that were hosted by other donors, or even by the Tongan MoF. One main reason was that this office was understaffed and that the only two officials were preoccupied with other work, such as trade and investment promotion and hosting visiting Chinese delegations. China rarely showed up, even in Samoa, where the MoF led the aid coordination meetings, and if they did show up, they would often be late.

Conclusion

To summarise, this chapter extends from the analysis in the previous three chapters. An overview of China's trilateral partnership—including the main features, China's official policy and bureaucratic arrangement—is examined. It demonstrates that China regards trilateral aid cooperation as something new and that it is expanding the test with caution. China, together with traditional donors, is closely following the progress of the pilot projects.

As trilateral aid cooperation is a component of China's foreign aid reform, this chapter has also discussed some aspects of this reform process, particularly the newly established CIDCA. It argues that China would continue to pilot trilateral aid cooperation. There is also much room for China to increase its participation in the donors' roundtable meetings in recipient countries.

8

Conclusion

This concluding chapter presents my reflections on the research that was undertaken for this book. It steps back from the details of China's trilateral aid projects and focuses on two broad issues. The first relates to theories of international relations and how they may illuminate China's evolving pattern of trilateral aid cooperation. The second relates to the relationship between China's growing trilateral aid cooperation and its increasingly assertive diplomacy. The scope for future research on China's trilateral aid cooperation is also briefly discussed.

International Relations Theories and Aid

China's influence on global governance appears to be growing fast. New initiatives such as the AIIB and the BRI have gained significant attention, both globally and regionally. Being an integral part of China's imprint overseas, Chinese foreign aid has dramatically increased in the past decade, rendering the research on this topic timely and significant. The main research question of this project has been placed against this backdrop: what are the main factors that drive China to conduct an increasing number of trilateral aid projects? This remains a noticeably understudied topic. In my analysis of this central question, some other closely related questions have lingered and guided this research project: Should we bother to analyse China's trilateral aid cooperation? If so, how should we approach this phenomenon? Do some strands of international relations theories have more analytical power than others in this case? If so, why?

When this research project commenced in 2013, I was asked how important trilateral aid cooperation was in China's foreign aid program. Looking back, it is fair to say that trilateral aid cooperation merits academic and policy attention not because its aid volume is substantial, but because it signals broader changes in China's overall aid policy. China's trilateral projects are small in both project numbers and aid outlay relative to its bilateral aid projects. Bilateral aid projects still dominate China's aid delivery, and this trend seems likely to continue regardless of the growth in China's trilateral aid cooperation. However, as was asked in Chapter 1, why has China undertaken trilateral aid cooperation despite the obvious differences between its own aid policies and practices and those of the traditional donors? It is definitely not a trivial development because China's MOFCOM, then the main aid guardian, had been heavily involved in the selection and management of most of these trilateral aid projects. To me, this suggests that there is something more happening here that requires investigation and explanation.

Against this background, this book sets out to investigate a significant and seriously under-researched area of aid policy and practice. Its originality and contribution are primarily in the new empirical material that it brings to light, which is a main strength of this study. The analysis in this book indicates that China's trilateral aid cooperation is significant because it demonstrates that China can cooperate with traditional donors and that it is becoming more responsive to calls for cooperation from traditional donors. Meanwhile, the Chinese government, especially MOFCOM, is approaching this new aid modality cautiously and incrementally, and in a manner that is consistent with its larger—and evolving—aid and foreign policy priorities.

The second question follows from the first: if we accept that undertaking research on China's trilateral aid cooperation is worthwhile for the reasons provided, then what assistance can we obtain from the toolkit of international relations theories to help explain this phenomenon? As discussed in Chapters 1 and 2, different strands of international relations theory have been employed to explain foreign aid and China's bilateral aid. As China's trilateral aid cooperation is a new and evolving development, a comprehensive analysis that is based on the available empirical evidence has not been undertaken in the existing literature. This signified that I had to find the right theoretical tool.

Figure 23 is the roadmap of my analysis that leads to my adoption of a more eclectic approach. This roadmap explains that I performed a thorough desk review of China's trilateral aid projects. After careful consideration, constructivist theories and cognitive learning theories are employed and tested in this book, including in Chapters 3 to 6. These two strands of theory seemingly have more strength than some other international relations theories in addressing my research question and illuminated the subtle relationship between China's evolving identities, national interests and ideas for external cooperation amid social engagement. They appear to have more capacity than other theories in explaining China's adoption of trilateral aid cooperation with traditional donors. For example, neorealism argues that nations are preoccupied with boosting their security against other nations in the anarchic international structure. In this framework, donor states are expected to use foreign aid as a tool and to deliver it bilaterally to maximise their own strategic and economic gains. Therefore, it will be unlikely that two rivals such as China and the US would seek to promote trilateral aid cooperation and share the dividend of aid delivery. However, even as strategic rivalry between China and the US is becoming increasingly visible in Asia and the Pacific, the two nations have committed to trilateral aid cooperation in Timor-Leste and elsewhere.

Neoliberalism is also insufficient to explain this phenomenon. Neoliberals argue that although cooperation among nations is difficult, the growth of international/regional institutions promotes interstate cooperation. The problem is that China has insisted that its foreign aid is primarily about south–south cooperation, which is different from north–south cooperation. China is not a member of the OECD DAC, and it has refrained from subscribing to many regional arrangements on development cooperation, such as the Cairns Compact. Staying outside these institutions would logically make China's development cooperation with traditional donors difficult. Therefore, in accordance with neorealism, neoliberalism has difficulty explaining China's participation in trilateral aid cooperation. Conversely, constructivism and cognitive learning theories appear to have more explanatory power in illuminating China's willingness to explore trilateral aid partnership.

Step 1:	Step 2:	Step 3:
A comprehensive analysis of China's trilateral aid projects. **Conclusion:** Constructivism and cognitive learning theories of identity, interests, ideas and interaction seemingly have more strengths than other IR theories for analysing my research question.	Testing constructivism and cognitive learning theories. What are the changes in China's identity, interests and ideas? Why are these changes present? How does social interaction affect China's aid? Can constructivism and cognitive learning theories explain the findings?	Testing other IR theories, including neorealism and neoliberalism.

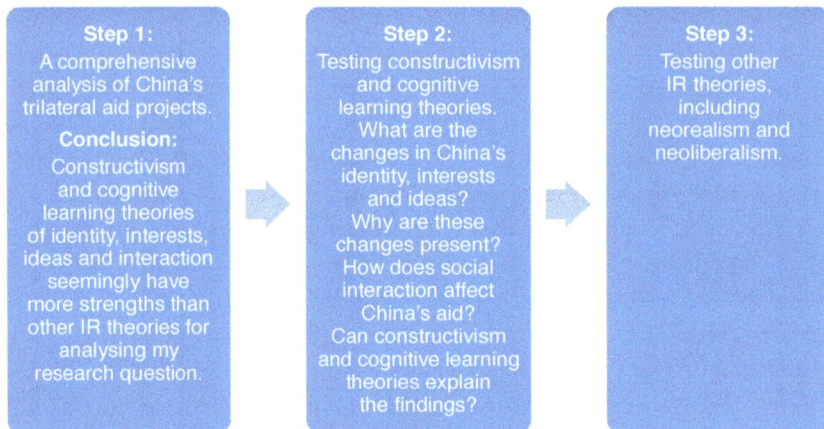

Figure 23. Analysis roadmap

Source. Compiled by the author from own analysis.

Constructivist and cognitive learning theories can also complement each other. As discussed in Chapter 2, constructivist theories and cognitive learning share much in common, as they both focus on identity, interests, ideas and interactions. While cognitive learning is derived from regime theory, a branch of international relations theory, many constructivist scholars have developed their theories through the empirical analysis of international regimes. The difference is that constructivism focuses more on the relations between identity, interests and ideas, while cognitive learning theories concentrate more on interactions involved in the learning process. Constructivist theories have consequently been used in this book to explain how and why China's identities, interests and ideas regarding development cooperation have changed, which led to China's adoption of trilateral aid cooperation in recent years. Cognitive learning theories are useful for analysing what and how China has learned from traditional donors and the UNDP during their interactions in development cooperation; they also provide an important rationale for China's preference for trilateral cooperation with these partners.

These theories have passed the test in the analysis of this book, which is also a contribution of this research to international relations theory. It lends further empirical support to constructivism and cognitive learning theories. From the perspective of identity, interests and ideas, this book has examined the evolution of China's calculation of national interests—both political and economic—as well as its global image–building. It argues that although China has three main identities (i.e. a socialist country, a developing country and a rising great power), the focus has shifted over time. China has given growing attention to its identity as a growing great power during the last decade. It is increasingly concentrating on building its global image as a responsible stakeholder—and the adoption and development of trilateral aid cooperation is understandable in this context, with its emphasis on cooperation between China, traditional donors and developing countries. An analysis of China's evolving identity focus, interest calculations and perceptions of cooperation will enrich our understanding of China's foreign policy.

From the cognitive learning perspective, the book has reviewed the nearly four-decade-long engagement between China and traditional donor states and UN agencies regarding development cooperation. China has had a dual experience as both an aid recipient and an aid donor during this period. China's attitude towards UN agencies and traditional donor states has undergone a gradual and ongoing shift away from outright distrust to cautious and qualified trust. During this engagement, China has realised that development cooperation with UN agencies and traditional donor states has brought both substantial financial resources and access to advanced technologies and new areas of learning for China's own domestic development. The cognitive learning process has also contributed to ideational change among Chinese aid officials, as China has learned and continues to learn from UN agencies and traditional donor states regarding how to reform and improve its own aid policies and practices.

In addition to the above two analytical perspectives, China's complicated bureaucratic system that administers foreign aid has also been examined as a critical domestic institutional context for policy decision-making regarding aid—one that comprises diverse agencies with different priorities and positions on trilateral aid cooperation. It has shown that although China's MFA actively promotes trilateral aid cooperation, the MOFCOM takes a more cautious approach. Other line ministries are broadly supportive of this new aid partnership. The China Exim Bank (the main provider of concessional loans) and Chinese SOEs (the main contractors for Chinese aid project) have ambiguous attitudes. The divergent priorities of China's different agencies have determined their subtly distinct attitudes towards trilateral aid cooperation. This book has also briefly analysed the CIDCA, which was created in April 2018. It argues that the MFA has had an upper hand in this round of aid management restructuring. Diplomatic interest will have more weight in the Chinese aid program. MOFCOM will continue to play a significant role in Chinese aid decision-making, though it is no longer the main custodian of aid. The influence of this new agency on Chinese foreign aid and trilateral cooperation is yet to be observed.

Building on the analysis from these three perspectives and the examination of three of China's recent trilateral aid projects (discussed in Chapters 4, 5 and 6), the research concludes that China's adoption of trilateral aid cooperation has been the result of its stronger desire to build its global image as a responsible global power and for cognitive learning to improve its aid performance.

It should be noted that the capability of constructivism and cognitive learning theories in explaining China's trilateral aid cooperation does not render other international relations theories irrelevant to helping explain China's overall approach to foreign aid. As mentioned earlier, it is most likely that bilateral aid will continue to dominate Chinese foreign aid. Bilateral aid has been used by the Chinese government as a diplomatic tool to serve its strategic and economic interest in many cases—as is the case with much OECD aid, which tends to flow to the former colonies of developed nations. Neorealism, which highlights nations' competition for power and security, clearly has a substantial ability to explain many cases of Chinese bilateral aid. For example, China increased its aid pledges to developing countries, such as in Africa, when it competed with Japan during Japan's bid for permanent UN Security Council membership in recent years. Another example is that China has provided much aid to woo ASEAN members (e.g. Cambodia and Laos) when its territorial disputes in the South China Sea have increased in recent years. These two cases are to be better explained by neorealism theories. As explained in Chapter 3, material interest also remains an important factor for Chinese stakeholders, such as state-owned construction contractors deciding whether they prefer to deliver aid bilaterally or trilaterally.

Does China's participation in trilateral cooperation arise from instrumentalism, a genuine, though gradual, acceptance of Western aid norms or a mixture of the two? The research argues that it is mostly a mixture of both. Strategically, China is intentionally placing more emphasis on its identity as a growing great power and on its national interest in global image–building. China is thus selectively piloting trilateral aid cooperation to improve its image as a responsible and cooperative stakeholder in global affairs. Technically, China also has a strong desire to improve its aid practices by learning from traditional donor states and multilateral development agencies who have demonstrated expertise in the areas that it lacks. This is a result of China's cognitive learning experience with these partners in development cooperation since the 1970s. China's ideas for development cooperation with these traditional donor partners have changed and have become more positive. Trilateral aid cooperation became an important way for China to continue the learning process—although 'what to learn' is filtered by the Chinese party-state, which defines what knowledge is deemed 'appropriate' and 'needed'.

Trilateral Cooperation and Foreign Policy

The categorisation of foreign aid as part of Chinese foreign policy is worth further discussion. On one side, China is conducting increasingly more trilateral aid cooperation projects with developed Western countries. This demonstrates China's willingness to engage in cooperative partnership and tackle many global issues rather than overthrow the traditional system. As Stuart Harris (2014, p. 183) argued, 'China shows little sign of wanting to move away from the existing international system or to change substantially the global order'. For example, in the development cooperation arena, China insists that south–south cooperation complements rather than replaces north–south cooperation.

However, a closer look at some of China's diplomatic decisions in recent years seems to indicate otherwise. The most notable examples relate to China's growing disputes with neighbouring countries in the East and South China Seas. China's foreign policy is becoming more assertive, as can be observed in the establishment of air defence identification zones, the building of artificial islands in the South China Sea and Foreign Minister Wang Yi's outburst in Canada in June 2016, declaring that questions pertaining to China's human rights record were 'arrogant' and 'unacceptable'. Neorealist theories that focus on a nation's pursuit of power and security appear to be in a better position for explaining this type of state behaviour.

In reviewing these seemingly opposing trends, is it inconsistent or contradictory that China seems to be supportive of cooperation on one hand while favouring confrontation on the other? Does China still care about its global image in conducting foreign relations? Does my finding that China partially participates in trilateral aid cooperation to build its global image still stand? Will Chinese trilateral aid cooperation be sustainable amid these growing strategic tensions with other countries?

China has been selective on the topic of cooperation in its foreign policy. As China's national capacity has rapidly increased due to the nearly four decades of spectacular economic growth, it naturally seeks to expand its national interest. This trend has become more notable since Xi Jinping took power in 2013. The current tensions focus on issues of territorial disputes, which are classified as China's 'core interests' (*hexin liyi*) (State Council, 2011a). These disputes revolve around historical issues that have become more pronounced in recent years. Additionally, growing nationalism in China and other countries who were involved in the disputes intensifies the strain.

Therefore, it is likely that the tension surrounding the issues of China's 'core interests' will continue and even escalate. It could negatively affect the prospect of Chinese trilateral aid cooperation with countries involved in the disputes. However, and on a more optimistic note, Chinese trilateral aid cooperation could also continue to grow because the tension between China and some other countries in sensitive areas requires more, rather than less, cooperation to enable the deepening of their broader bilateral relations. As Wang Jisi, dean of the school of International Studies at Peking University, argued: 'China will have to invest tremendous resources to promote a more benign image on the world stage' (Wang, 2011a, para. 33). Foreign aid is a relatively less sensitive area of foreign relations, and aid cooperation in areas such as agriculture and health is even less problematic. Trilateral aid cooperation in this case can potentially reduce the tension between China and partner countries in sensitive areas (e.g. the US). To some extent, trilateral aid is playing the role to ease the anxiety of traditional donors in regard to China's rise.

Unlike China's trilateral aid cooperation and its territorial disputes, Chinese initiatives like the BRICS New Development Bank, AIIB and the BRI could have two interpretations, based on my observations. Some analysts may regard these initiatives (especially those of BRICS New Development Bank and AIIB) as directly challenging the influence of existing providers of development finance (particularly the World Bank and the ADB). However, in addition to exporting China's oversupplied capacity in manufacturing, these initiatives could also be considered a part of China's efforts to demonstrate its growing global responsibility alongside its increasing economic power, which is linked to China's attempt to build a better global image.

A final point worth brief discussion is that even though foreign aid is an important component of China's foreign policy, economic activities and investment remain the central tasks in the minds of Chinese leaders.

This explains why the Chinese government has invested far more resources in promoting projects such as the BRI than in its foreign aid budget. China's adoption of trilateral aid cooperation in some cases demonstrates its growing attention to its global image and its stronger desire to use this modality for learning. However, this does not mean that China is willing to sacrifice its core economic interests. This is why bilateral aid still dominates China's aid delivery, and it is a trend that is likely to continue.

Scope for Future Research

Building on the innovative research of Chinese trilateral aid cooperation in this book, much more analysis can be conducted in the future. Although my conceptual framework has been focused on the relations between identity, interests and idea changes, the origin of China's identity change has been mentioned only briefly. This is a complicated issue that deserves a separate book in itself. The field work for this research is also focused on the Asia-Pacific region. My archival research and interviews with Chinese stakeholders have also covered some examples of Chinese trilateral cooperation in Africa. However, a more direct engagement with African stakeholders would enrich future research. Moreover, as mentioned earlier, most Chinese trilateral aid projects are either ongoing or they were finished recently. This research consequently does not include much longitudinal data, nor can it draw on project evaluations—though some tentative assessment was undertaken in Chapter 7.

As Chinese trilateral aid cooperation is still new and in the pilot stage, more data need to be collected in the future as existing projects evolve and new projects are launched. More in-depth case studies should be performed to enrich our understanding of the motivations behind China's aid program. More assessment of the effectiveness of trilateral aid cooperation will be needed to justify its continued existence and further expansion. It is not unthinkable that China may one day abandon this aid modality. Comparative studies between Chinese bilateral aid and trilateral aid, and between Chinese and non-Chinese trilateral cooperation, also deserve more academic attention. Another outstanding question is how China, traditional donors and recipient countries can play their respective roles well for the effectiveness of trilateral partnership. Empirically based research in the future to fill these gaps could facilitate a better understanding of China's trilateral aid cooperation.

Due to the complexity of donors' motivations, caution must be applied in generalising these research findings. As a Chinese aid official who has been deeply involved in trilateral aid cooperation reminded me:

> The motivations behind each trilateral aid project might vary. The motivation behind one particular project might not be able to apply to the other. For instance, trilateral aid cooperation between multilateral development agencies and China's Ministry of Science and Technology may have randomness. On some occasions, multilateral development agencies need to spend some money [before the end of the financial year] but do not know how to do that, so they approach China for cooperation [in order to spend the money]. (Interview, Beijing, 20 August 2015)

With the future in mind, what will China's foreign policy look like? Zheng Bijian, a long-time senior advisor to the Chinese leadership who coined the term 'Chinese peaceful rise', argued that China 'must gradually broaden different types of "convergence of interests" and build "communities of interests" with neighbouring countries and surrounding regions, as well as with all relevant countries and regions' (Zheng, 2013, p. 10). These ideas have been absorbed into China's foreign policymaking practices. For example, Chinese President Xi Jinping said at the 2014 central conference on work relating to foreign affairs—the highest-level arena for discussing China's diplomacy—that 'China needs to do well in its diplomacy with neighbouring countries to build "communities of common interests"' (Xinhua, 2014a, p. 12). Trilateral aid cooperation has evidently become part of China's diplomatic efforts to promote such 'convergence of interests' and 'communities of interests'. However, can China really achieve this ambitious objective? Is trilateral aid cooperation between China and traditional donor states or international organisations really a promising new trend? A Chinese agricultural aid official expressed his optimistic answer as follows:

> Developed countries have the enthusiasm to consolidate and extend their cooperation with China. China has the capacity to participate in trilateral aid cooperation. For recipient countries, they have the need to use foreign aid [whether in bilateral or trilateral form] to support national development. In this context, China's trilateral aid cooperation will have a bright future. (Interview, Beijing, 21 August 2015)

In the end, what will China's trilateral aid cooperation be like? We must wait and see!

References

Acharya, A. (1997). Ideas, identity, and institution-building: From the 'ASEAN way' to the 'Asia-Pacific way'? *The Pacific Review*, *10*(3), 319–346. doi.org/10.1080/09512749708719226.

Aidwatch. (2012). *Australia invented Pacific 'boomerang aid'*. Retrieved from www.aidwatch.org.au/stories/australia-invented-pacific-boomerang-aid/.

Akram, T. (2003). The international foreign aid regime: Who gets foreign aid and how much? *Applied Economics*, *35*(11), 1351–1356. doi.org/10.1080/00036 84032000100337.

Alden, C. (2012). China and Africa: The relationship matures. *Strategic Analysis*, *36*(5), 701–707. doi.org/10.1080/09700161.2012.712365.

Alesina, A. & Dollar, D. (2000). Who gives foreign aid to whom and why? *Journal of Economic Growth*, *5*(1), 33–63. doi.org/10.1023/A:1009874203400.

Alesina, A. & Weder, B. (2002). Do corrupt governments receive less foreign aid? *The American Economic Review*, *92*(4), 1126–1137. doi.org/10.1257/00028280260344669.

Asia Pacific Malaria Elimination Network. (2012). *Meeting summary: Malaria 2012: Saving lives in the Asia-Pacific and the 7th East Asia Summit*. Retrieved from static1.1.sqspcdn.com/static/f/471029/21330438/1356066142397/APMEN_Malaria+2012.pdf?token=vqaqytxKBbFnCF5yieuwZCughYs%3D.

Atkinson, J. (2010). China-Taiwan diplomatic competition and the Pacific Islands. *The Pacific Review*, *23*(4), 407–427. doi.org/10.1080/09512748.2010.495998.

Australian Agency for International Development (AusAID). (1999). *AusAID annual report 1998–1999*. Canberra, NSW: AusAID.

AusAID. (2001). *AusAID annual report 2000–2001*. Canberra, NSW: AusAID.

AusAID. (2004). *AusAID annual report 2003–2004*. Canberra, NSW: AusAID.

AusAID. (2005). *AusAID annual report 2004–2005*. Canberra, NSW: AusAID.

AusAID. (2006a). *AusAID annual report 2005–2006*. Canberra, NSW: AusAID.

AusAID. (2006b). *China Australia country program strategy: 2006–2010*. Canberra, NSW: AusAID.

AusAID. (2009). *AusAID annual report 2008–2009*. Canberra, NSW: AusAID.

AusAID. (2010a). *AusAID annual report 2009–2010*. Canberra, NSW: AusAID.

AusAID. (2010b). *China development cooperation report 2009*. Canberra, NSW: AusAID.

Australian Associated Press. (2013, 4 April). More Chinese influence in Pacific: Gillard. *Sydney Morning Herald*. Retrieved from www.smh.com.au/national/more-chinese-influence-in-pacific-gillard-20130404-2h8vr.html.

Australian High Commission. (2016). *Launch of the Australia-China-PNG trilateral malaria project*. Retrieved from png.embassy.gov.au/pmsb/587.html.

Australian Public Service Commission. (2013). *State of the service report: State of the service series 2012–2013*. Canberra, NSW: APSC.

Australian Senate. (2006). *China's emergence: Implications for Australia*. Canberra, NSW: Australian Senate's Foreign Affairs, Defence and Trade References Committee.

Batley, J. (2015). *Papua New Guinea's aid program in the region*. Retrieved from devpolicy.org/papua-new-guineas-aid-program-in-the-region-20150811/.

BBC. (2012, 13 July). *Asean nations fail to reach agreement on South China Sea*. Retrieved from www.bbc.com/news/world-asia-18825148.

Beijing Youth Daily. (2014a, 22 November). Xi Jinping jiang zai Feiji 'qingke' ba guo lingdaoren [Xi Jinping will 'treat' leaders from eight Pacific Islands countries in Fiji]. *Beijing Youth Daily*, p. A03.

Beijing Youth Daily. (2014b, 23 November). Xi Jinping: Ganxie Feiji xiezhu haiwai zhuitao [Xi Jinping expresses thanks to Fiji for helping chase corrupt Chinese officials overseas]. *Beijing Youth Daily*, p. A03.

Bennett, A. & Checkel, J.T. (2015). Process tracing: From philosophical roots to best practices. In A. Bennet & J.T. Checkel (Eds), *Process tracing: From metaphor to analytic tool* (pp. 1–37). Cambridge, UK: Cambridge University Press.

Bhattacharya, D. & Misha, F. (2015). China and the least developed countries: An enquiry into the trade relationship during the post-WTO accession period. In L. Wang (Ed.), *China's WTO accession reassessed* (pp. 474–498). Oxford, UK: Routledge.

Bishop, J. (2011, 13 April). Aid action in Oceania. *Sydney Morning Herald*. Retrieved from www.pina.com.fj/?p=pacnews&m=read&o=14501883304da 4f7a96365fc8eabc7.

Bishop, J. (2014). *Opening address—2014 Australasian aid and international development policy workshop*. Retrieved from www.foreignminister.gov.au/ speeches/Pages/2014/jb_sp_140213.aspx?ministerid=4 (site discontinued).

Bishop, J. (2015). Australia, China and PNG working together to tackle malaria. Retrieved from foreignminister.gov.au/releases/Pages/2015/jb_mr_151108. aspx (site discontinued).

Bland, B. & Dyer, G. (2011, 30 November). Clinton warning over aid from China. *Financial Times*. Retrieved from www.ft.com/content/33efc23c-1b35-11e1-85f8-00144feabdc0.

Boucher, R. (2005). *Joint press statement on the U.S.–China global issues forum*. Retrieved from 2001-2009.state.gov/r/pa/prs/ps/2005/44616.htm.

Brady, A. (2010). *Looking north, looking south: China, Taiwan and the South Pacific* (Vol. 26). Singapore, Malaysia: World Scientific Pub. Co. Inc.

Bräutigam, D. (2009). *The dragon's gift: The real story of China in Africa*. New York, US: Oxford University Press.

Bräutigam, D. (2011). Aid 'with Chinese characteristics': Chinese foreign aid and development finance meet the OECD-DAC aid regime. *Journal of International Development, 23*(5), 752–764. doi.org/10.1002/jid.1798.

Bräutigam, D. & Tang, X. (2011). African shenzhen: China's special economic zones in Africa. *The Journal of Modern African Studies, 49*(1), 27–54. doi.org/ 10.1017/S0022278X10000649.

Brenthurst Foundation, Chinese Academy of Social Sciences, Council on Foreign Relations and Leon H. Sullivan Foundation. (2007). *Africa–China–U.S. trilateral dialogue: Summary report*. New York, US: Brenthurst Foundation, Chinese Academy of Social Sciences, Council on Foreign Relations and Leon H. Sullivan Foundation.

Brookings Institute, China CASS and University of Ghana. (2013). *A trilateral dialogue on the United States, Africa and China—conference papers and responses*. Retrieved from www.brookings.edu/wp-content/uploads/2016/06/All-Trilateral-Compiliation.pdf.

Cable News Network. (2009). *U.S. slams deportation of Uyghur refugees from Cambodia to China*. Retrieved from edition.cnn.com/2009/WORLD/asiapcf/12/20/cambodia.uyghur.china/index.html.

Callahan, W.A. (2010). *China: The pessoptimist nation*. Oxford, UK: Oxford University Press.

Cambodia MAFF and UNDP Cambodia. (2013). *Project document: China–Cambodia–UNDP trilateral cooperation cassava project phase II*. Phnom Penh, Cambodia: UNDP.

Cambodia MAFF and UNDP Cambodia. (2015). *China–UNDP–Cambodia trilateral cassava project training manual for farmers*. Phnom Penh, Cambodia: Cambodia MAFF and UNDP Cambodia.

Cambodia MOP. (2014). *Cambodia national strategic development plan (2014–2018)*. Phnom Penh, Cambodia: Ministry of Planning.

Cambodian Government. (2004). *Address by Samdech HUN SEN, Prime Minister Royal Government of Cambodia—The rectangular strategy for growth, employment, equity and efficiency in Cambodia*. Retrieved from www.cdc-crdb.gov.kh/cdc/aid_management/RGC_Rectangular_Strategy_2004.pdf.

Cambodian Government. (2008). *Address by Samdech Akka Moha Sena Padei Techo Hun Sen Prime Minister of the Kingdom of Cambodia on 'rectangular strategy' for growth, employment, equity and efficiency Phase II*. Retrieved from www.ilo.org/wcmsp5/groups/public/---asia/---ro-bangkok/---sro-bangkok/documents/genericdocument/wcms_112939.pdf.

Cambodian Government. (2013). *Cambodia rectangular strategy—phase III*. Phnom Penh, Cambodia: Cambodian Government.

Cambodian Government. (2014). *Cambodia trade integration strategy 2014–2018*. Phnom Penh, Cambodia: Cambodian Government.

Carstensen, M.B. (2011). Ideas are not as stable as political scientists want them to be: A theory of incremental ideational change. *Political Studies, 59*(3), 596–615. doi.org/10.1111/j.1467-9248.2010.00868.x.

Carter, B. (2014, 16 December). Is China's economy really the largest in the world? *BBC News*. Retrieved from www.bbc.com/news/magazine-30483762.

Chandy, L. & Kharas, H. (2011). Why can't we all just get along? The practical limits to international development cooperation. *Journal of International Development, 23*(5), 739–751. doi.org/10.1002/jid.1797.

Checkel, J.T. (2001). Why comply? Social learning and European identity change. *International Organization, 55*(3), 553–588.

Checkel, J.T. & Katzenstein, P.J. (2009). Conclusion—European identity in context. In J.T. Checkel & P.J. Katzenstein (Eds), *European identity* (pp. 213–227). New York, US: Cambridge University Press.

Chen, B. (2015). *Zhongguo jiaru jinghe zuzhi fazhan zhongxin [China joins the OECD development centre].* Retrieved from politics.people.com.cn/n/2015/0702/c70731-27240497.html.

Chen, D. (2010). Nuli kaichuang yuanwai gongzuo xin jumian [Working hard to promote Chinese foreign aid]. *Qiu Shi,* (19), 42–44.

Chen, G. (2011, 20 October). Wei Zhongguo yuanjian de Tan Zan tielu zhao jiche [To produce locomotives for China-aided Tanzania–Zambia railway]. *Renmin Zhengxie Bao,* p. 5.

Chen, X. (2009). Xinshiqi zhongguo da waijiao de fangxiang [Direction for China's big diplomacy in a new era]. *Outlook Weekly,* (30), 41.

Chen, Y. (1987). Jixu zuohao duiwai yuanzhu gongzuo [Continue to do Chinese foreign aid well]. *International Economic Cooperation, 2,* 3–4, 16.

Chen, Y. (1980). Jingji xingshi yu jingji jiaoxun [Economic situation and economic lessons]. In Editorial Committee on Party Literature of the Central Committee of the Communist Party of China (Ed.), *Chen Yun wenxuan [Selected works of Chen Yun]* (pp. 276–282). Beijing, China: People's Publishing House.

Chen, Y. (2015). *Zhongguo shangwubu yu Gaici jijinhui qianshu fazhang hezuo liangjie beiwanglu [China's Ministry of Commerce and Gates Foundation signed the MOU on development cooperation].* Retrieved from world.people.com.cn/n/2015/0923/c157278-27624551.html.

Chin, G. & Thakur, R. (2010). Will China change the rules of global order? *The Washington Quarterly, 33*(4), 119–138. doi.org/10.1080/0163660X.2010.516145.

China Academy of Tropical Agricultural Sciences. (2012). Jianpuzhai mushu zhongzhi jishu peixunban zai zhongguo redai nongye kexueyuan haikou yuanqu kaiban [The training workshop on Cambodia cassava cultivation commenced at CATAS]. *World Tropical Agriculture Information,* (1), 13.

China Center for International Economic Exchange and United Nations Development Programme China. (2013). *Reconfiguring global governance— effectiveness, inclusiveness and China's global role.* Beijing, China: UNDP.

China Council for the Promotion of International Trade. (2007). *Woguo zouchuqu zhanlue de xingcheng ji tuidong zhengce tixi fenxi [The formation of China's go global strategy and analysis of the supporting policies].* Beijing, China: CCPIT.

China Embassy in Liberia. (2008). *Libiliya yuanzhuguo gaoji guanyuan daibiaotuan canguan wo yuanjian de li bi li ya daxue fen de er fenxiao xiangmu [Senior officials from donors in Liberia visited China-aided Fendell Campus of the University of Liberia].* Retrieved from lr.chineseembassy.org/chn/sghdhzxxx/t511859.htm.

China Embassy in the US. (2005). *'Zhongmei quanqiu shiwu luntan' shouci huiyi zai meiguo huashengdun zhaokai [The first meeting of the China–U.S. global issues forum was held in Washington].* Retrieved from www.china-embassy.org/chn/zmgx/t191690.htm.

China Embassy in Timor-Leste. (2011). *Chinese hybrid rice in Timor-Leste.* Retrieved from tl.china-embassy.org/eng/xwdt/t871209.htm.

China Exim Bank. (2014). *Zhongguo jinchukou yinhang liangyou daikuan yewu jieshao, youhui daikuangbu' [Introduction to the two loans of China Exim Bank, by department of concessional loans at China Exim Bank].* Retrieved from www.chinca.org/cms/html/files/2013-12/16/20131216102948872930302.pdf (site discontinued).

China Foundation for Poverty Alleviation. (2004). *Shoujie Zhongguo xiaochu pingkun jiang pingxuan jieguo jiexiao [The selection result for the First China Poverty Alleviation Award was announced].* Retrieved from www.china.com.cn/chinese/jingji/682981.htm.

China International Center for Economic and Technical Exchanges (CICETE). (2009). *Kechixu de xiao'e xindai fuping xiangmu [The sustainable microcredit poverty reduction projects].* Retrieved from www.cicete.org.cn/article/xmcgzs/fp/201510/20151001140810.shtml.

CICETE. (2014a). 1979–1981 Kaifashu yuanhua xiangmu [UNDP's aid to China in 1979–1981]. Retrieved from www.cicete.org.cn/article/lhgkfjh/article5.shtml.

CICETE. (2014b). *Kaifashu yuanhua di er ge guobie fang'an (1986–1990) [UNDP's second country plan for China (1986–1990)].* Retrieved from www.cicete.org.cn/article/lhgkfjh/article3.shtml.

CICETE. (2014c). *Kaifashu yuanhua di san ge guobie fang'an (1991–1995) [UNDP's third country plan for China (1991–1995)]*. Retrieved from www.cicete.org.cn/article/lhgkfjh/article2.shtml.

CICETE. (2014d). *Kaifashu yuanhua di si ge guobie fang'an (1996–2000) [UNDP's fourth country plan for China (1996–2000)]*. Retrieved from www.cicete.org.cn/article/lhgkfjh/article1.shtml.

CICETE. (2014e). *Kaifashu yuanhua di yi ge guobie fang'an (1981–1985) [UNDP's first country plan for China (1981–1985)]*. Retrieved from www.cicete.org.cn/article/lhgkfjh/article4.shtml.

CICETE. (2014f). *Zhongguo guoji jingji jishu jiaoliu zhongxin jianjie [a brief introduction to China International Center for Economic and Technical Exchanges]*. Retrieved from www.cicete.org.cn/article/aboutUs/zxjj.shtml.

CICETE and UNDP. (2008). *Project document: Strengthening the capacity of the international poverty reduction centre in China for south–south cooperation*. Beijing, China: UNDP.

China Overseas Fisheries Corporation. (2013, 6 November). Zhongguo nongfa xieshou nantai daoguo fazhan jinqiangyu yuye [China national agricultural group joins hands with South Pacific Island countries to develop the tuna industry]. *International Business Daily*, p. D4.

China's Permanent Mission to UN. (2015). *Changzhu lianheguo fudaibiao Wangmin dashi tan zhongguo de lianheguo huifei bili zengjia wenti [Deputy representative of China's permanent mission to the UN ambassador Wangmin talks about the increase of China's UN membership fee]*. Retrieved from www.china-un.org/chn/gdxw/t1327606.htm.

Chinese Embassy in Australia. (2012). *Shangwubu buzhang zhuli Yu Jianhua yixing fangwen aodaliya' [Assistant Commerce Minister Yu Jianhua and his delegation visited Australia]*. Retrieved from au.mofcom.gov.cn/article/zxhz/b/201211/20121108435505.shtml.

Chinese Embassy in Samoa. (2015). *State leaders of China and Samoa exchange congratulatory messages on 40th anniversary of establishment of diplomatic relations between two countries*. Retrieved from ws.chineseembassy.org/eng/xwdt/t1314123.htm.

Christensen, T.J. & Swan, J. (2008). *China in Africa: Implications for U.S. policy*. Retrieved from 2001-2009.state.gov/p/eap/rls/rm/2008/06/105556.htm.

Ciorciari, J.D. (2015). A Chinese model for patron–client relations? The Sino–Cambodian partnership. *International Relations of the Asia–Pacific, 15*(2), 245–278. doi.org/10.1093/irap/lcu021.

Clinton, H. (2011). Inaugural Richard C. Holbrooke Lecture on a Broad Vision of U.S.-China Relations in the 21st Century. Retrieved from 2009-2017. state.gov/secretary/20092013clinton/rm/2011/01/154653.htm.

Clinton, H. (2012). Remarks at the Pacific Islands forum post-forum dialogue. Retrieved from www.state.gov/secretary/20092013clinton/rm/2012/08/197266.htm?goMobile=0.

Cochrane, L. (2015, 31 July). Papua New Guinea to ban foreign advisers claiming they could be spying, make local staff lazy. *ABC News*. Retrieved from www.abc.net.au/news/2015-07-31/png-prime-minister-bans-foreign-advisors/6661946.

Copper, J.F. (1976). *China's foreign aid: An instrument of Peking's foreign policy.* Lexington, MA: Lexington Books.

Corbett, J. & Dinnen, S. (2015). Examining recent shifts in Australia's foreign aid policy: New paradigm or more incremental change? *Australian Journal of International Affairs, 70*(1), 87–103.

Corkin, L. (2011). Redefining foreign policy impulses toward Africa: The roles of the MFA, the MOFCOM and China Exim Bank. *Journal of Current Chinese Affairs, 40*(4), 61–90.

Council for the Development of Cambodia (CDC). (2008). *The Cambodia aid effectiveness report 2008.* Phnom Penh, Cambodia: CDC.

CDC. (2018). *Number of projects by last update (as of 20 December 2018).* Retrieved from odacambodia.com/index.asp.

Cui, P. (2010, 13 August). Yi wusi yuanzhu cu gongtong fazhan-xin zhongguo liushinian yuanwai gongzuo jishi [To promote common development by providing selfless foreign aid-a summary of Chinese foreign aid in the past six decades]. *People's Daily*, p. 6.

da Costa, H. (2015). *Key talking points for Helder da Costa, PhD secretary general.* Proceedings of the conference on Aid, Investment and Accelerated Development of Timor-Leste, 9 February, Dili. Retrieved from asiafoundation.org/resources/pdfs/OpeningRemarksDr.HelderdaCostaGeneralSecretaryg7Secretariat.pdf.

Dai, L. & Li, W. (2013, 3 September). Li Yuanchao huijian waiguo zhengyao [Li Yuanchao met with foreign leaders]. *People's Daily*, p. 2.

Davies, M., Edinger, H. Tay, N. & Naidu, S. (2008). *How China delivers Development assistance to Africa.* Stellenbosch, South Africa: Center for Chinese Studies, University of Stellenbosch.

de Haan, A. (2011). Will China change international development as we know it? *Journal of International Development, 23*(7), 881–908. doi.org/10.1002/jid.1732.

Department of Foreign Affairs and Trade (DFAT). (1998). *Australia DFAT annual report 1997–1998*. Canberra, Australia: Australian DFAT.

DFAT. (2013). *Memorandum of understanding (MOU) for a development cooperation partnership between AusAID and the Ministry of Commerce of the People's Republic of China (MOFCOM)*. Canberra, Australia: Australian DFAT.

DFAT. (2014). *A New direction for Australian aid in PNG: Refocusing Australian aid to help unlock PNG's economic potential*. Canberra, Australia: Australian DFAT.

DFAT. (2018). *Australian aid budget at a glance*. Retrieved from www.dfat.gov.au/about-us/corporate/portfolio-budget-statements/Pages/2018-19-australian-aid-budget-at-a-glance.aspx.

Department of National Planning and Monitoring (DNPM). (2010a). *Papua New Guinea development strategic plan 2010–2030*. Port Moresby, Papua New Guinea: PNG DNPM.

DNPM. (2010b). *Papua New Guinea medium term development plan 2011–2015*. Port Moresby, Papua New Guinea: PNG DNPM.

Devex Corporation. (2014). *Trilateral malaria project manager*. Retrieved from www.devex.com/jobs/trilateral-malaria-project-manager-386055.

Devi, S. (2014, 23 November). $50m more. *Fiji Times*. Retrieved from www.fijitimes.com/50m-more/.

Dollar, D. (2016). *China as a global investor* (Asia Working Group Paper No. 4). Washington, DC: Brookings Institution.

Donnelly, T. & Monaghan, C. (2007). *Legacy agenda, part III: The bush doctrine and the rise of China*. Washington, DC: American Enterprise Institute for Public Policy Research.

Dornan, M. & Brant, P. (2014). Chinese assistance in the Pacific: Agency, effectiveness and the role of Pacific Island governments. *Asia & the Pacific Policy Studies, 1*(2), 349–363. doi.org/10.1002/app5.35.

Du, S. & Yan, H. (2014, 23 November). Xi Jinping had a group meeting with leaders of Pacific Islands countries and delivered a keynote speech. *People's Daily*, p. 1.

Dyer, G., Anderlini, J. & Sender, H. (2011, 18 January). China's lending hits new heights. *Financial Times*. Retrieved from www.ft.com/content/488c60f4-2281-11e0-b6a2-00144feab49a.

Economic and Social Council. (2008). *Trends and progress in international development cooperation*. New York, US: UN ECOSCO.

Economy, E. & Levi, M. (2014). *By all means necessary: How China's resource quest is changing the world*. Oxford, UK: Oxford University Press.

Everingham, S. (2013). *Radio Current Affairs Documentary: East Timor Future*. Retrieved from www.abc.net.au/radionational/programs/archived/current affairsspecials/-east-timor-future/4437748#transcript.

Fejerskov, A.M. (2013). *European Union development cooperation in a changing global context*. Copenhagen, Denmark: Danish Institute for International Studies.

Field, M. (2011, 28 April). NZ shamed China over Fiji visit—WikiLeaks. *New Zealand Stuff*. Retrieved from www.stuff.co.nz/national/politics/4934713/NZ-shamed-China-over-Fiji-visit-WikiLeaks.

Fierke, K.M. (2010). Constructivism. In T. Dunne, M. Kurki & S. Smith (Eds), *International relations theories: Discipline and diversity* (pp. 177–194). New York, US: Oxford University Press.

Finance China Web. (2012). *Diqijie zhongguo jiankang chuanbo dahui [The seventh China health communication conference]*. Retrieved from finance.china.com. cn/industry/medicine/special/zgjk/.

Finnemore, M. (1996). *National interests in international society*. New York, US: Cornell University Press.

Firth, S. (2013). New developments in the international relations of the Pacific Islands. *Journal of Pacific History*, *48*(3), 286–293. doi.org/10.1080/002233 44.2013.812545.

Fish, I.S. (2013, 12 July). Aiding and abetting. *Foreign Policy*. Retrieved from foreignpolicy.com/2013/07/12/aiding-and-abetting/.

Fordelone, T.Y. (2013a). *Triangular cooperation: What can we learn from a survey of actors involved?* Paris, France: OECD.

Fordelone, T.Y. (2013b). *Triangular cooperation: What's the literature telling us?* Paris, France: OECD.

Forum Macao. (2015). East Timor gets US$50-mln loan from China EXIM Bank. Retrieved from www.forumchinaplp.org.mo/east-timor-gets-us50-mln-loan-from-china-exim-bank/.

Freeman III, C.W. & Boynton, X.L. (2011). *China's emerging global health and foreign aid engagement in Africa.* Washington, DC: Center for Strategic & International Studies.

Fu, Y. (2010). *China's foreign aid.* Retrieved from tl.china-embassy.org/eng/xwdt/t871206.htm.

Führer, H. (1994). *A history of the development assistance committee and the development co-operation directorate in dates, names and figures* (Vol. 2). Paris, France: Organisation for Economic Co-operation and Development.

Gabas, J. & Tang, X. (2014). *Chinese agricultural cooperation in sub-Saharan Africa: Challenging preconceptions.* Paris, France: Agricultural Research for Development (CIRAD).

George, A.L. & Bennett, A. (2005). *Case studies and theory development in the social sciences.* Cambridge, Massachusetts: MIT Press.

Gerring, J. (2007). *Case study research: Principles and practices.* New York, US: Cambridge University Press.

Ghosh, J. (2012, 7 August). Hillary Clinton's morally superior speech in Africa was deluded. *The Guardian.* Retrieved from www.theguardian.com/global-development/poverty-matters/2012/aug/07/hillary-clinton-speech-africa-deluded.

Gill, B. & Reilly, J. (2007). The tenuous hold of China Inc. in Africa. *The Washington Quarterly, 30*(3), 37–52. doi.org/10.1162/wash.2007.30.3.37.

Gilpin, R. (1981). *War and change in world politics.* Cambridge, UK: Cambridge University Press.

Global Partnership for Effective Development Cooperation. (2014). *Mexico high level meeting communiqué: First high-level meeting of the global partnership for effective development co-operation: Building towards an inclusive post-2015 development agenda.* Mexico City, Mexico: Global Partnership for Effective Development Cooperation.

Glosny, M.A. (2006). *Meeting the development challenge in the 21st Century: American and Chinese perspectives on foreign aid* (Policy Brief No. 21). New York, US: National Committee on United States–China Relations.

Godement, F. (2017). *Expanded ambition, shrinking achievements: How China sees the global order* (Policy Brief March 2017). London, UK: European Council on Foreign Relations.

Goh, E. (2016). *Rising China's influence in developing Asia.* Oxford, UK: Oxford University Press.

Gong, W. (2004, 3 September). Quanguo dui fazhanzhong guojia jingji waijiao gongzuo huiyi zaijing zhaokai [The national conference on China's economic diplomacy with developing countries was held in Beijing]. *People's Daily*, p. 2.

Greene, R.L. (2008). *Identifying gaps and obstacles—'Allocating more aid: Where should it go?'* New York. UN Economic and Social Council 2008 High-level Segment Development Cooperation Forum, New York, 30 June.

Greenhill, R., Prizzon, A. & Rogerson, A. (2013). *The age of choice: Developing countries in the new aid landscape.* London, UK: Overseas Development Institute.

Gries, P.H. (2004). *China's new nationalism: Pride, politics, and diplomacy.* Berkeley, US: University of California Press.

Grimm, S., Rank, R., McDonald, M. & Schickerling, E. (2011). *Transparency of Chinese aid—An analysis of the published information on Chinese external financial flows.* Stellenbosch, South Africa: Center for Chinese Studies, University of Stellenbosch.

Guo, S. & Blanchard, J.F. (2008). *'Harmonious world' and China's new foreign policy.* Lanham, US: Lexington Books.

Haas, E.B. (1990). *When knowledge is power: Three models of change in international organizations.* Berkeley, US: University of California Press.

Haggard, S. & Simmons, B.A. (1987). Theories of international regimes. *International Organization, 41*(3), 491–517. doi.org/10.1017/S00208183 00027569.

Hamanaka, S. (2016). Insights to great powers' desire to establish institutions: Comparison of ADB, AMF, AMRO and AIIB. *Global Policy, 7*(2), 288–292. doi.org/10.1111/1758-5899.12304.

Han, X. & Ren, C. (2008). Gaoduan renshi yanzhong de lianheguo [UN in the eyes of high-level officials]. *International Communications, 1*, 24–27.

Hanson, F. (2008a, 22 August). China's support of Fiji does little for Fijians. *Sydney Morning Herald.* Retrieved from www.smh.com.au/politics/federal/chinas-support-of-fiji-does-little-for-fijians-20080821-3zk8.html.

Hanson, F. (2008b). *The dragon looks south*. Sydney, Australia: Lowy Institute for International Policy.

Harris, S. (2014). *China's foreign policy* (Vol. 1). Cambridge, UK: Polity Press.

Hart, A.F. & Jones, B.D. (2010). How do rising powers rise? *Survival*, *52*(6), 63–88. doi.org/10.1080/00396338.2010.540783.

Hasenclever, A., Mayer, P. & Rittberger, V. (1997). *Theories of international regimes* (Vol. 55). Cambridge, UK: Cambridge University Press.

Hasenclever, A., Mayer, P. & Rittberger, V. (2000). Integrating theories of international regimes. *Review of International Studies*, *26*(1), 3–33. doi.org/10.1017/S0260210500000036.

Hawksley, H. (2010, 5 October). UK seeks China aid partnership in Africa. *BBC News*. Retrieved from www.bbc.com/news/world-africa-11444441.

Hayward-Jones, J. (2013). *Big enough for all of us: Geo-strategic competition in the Pacific Islands*. Sydney, Australia: Lowy Institute for International Policy.

He, K. & Feng, H. (2012). Debating China's assertiveness: Taking China's power and interests seriously. *International Politics*, *49*(5), 633–644. doi.org/10.1057/ip.2012.18.

He, W. (2010). Zhongguo yuanzhu feizhou: fazhan tedian, zuoyong ji mianlin de tiaozhan [China's aid to Africa: Development feature, functions and challenges]. *West Asia and Africa*, *7*, 12–19.

He, W. (2011). Cong yuanzhu youxiaoxing dao fazhang youxiaoxing: yuanzhu linian de yanbian ji zhongguo jingyan de zongyong [From aid effectiveness to development effectiveness: The aid discourse evolution and the role of China's experience]. *West Asia and Africa*, *9*, 120–134.

He, X. (2015). 2014 nian 1–12 yue Zhongguo-jianpuzhai zhongdian chanpin jinchukou fenxi [An analysis of the major export and import commodities between China and Cambodia from January to December 2014]. Retrieved from customs.caexpo.com/data/country/2015/03/26/3642206.html (site discontinued).

Heiligendamm Process. (2009). *Workshop on triangular cooperation: Opportunity for shared responsibility in Africa*. Tunis, Tunisia: Heiligendamm Process.

Henderson, J. & Reilly, B. (2003). Dragon in paradise: China's rising star in Oceania. *The National Interest*, *72*, 94–104.

Hook, S.W. (1995). *National interest and foreign aid*. Boulder, US: L. Rienner Publishers.

Horta, L. (2014, 8 February). The dragon and the sleeping crocodile—China and Timor-Leste. *Macau Hub*. Retrieved from www.macauhub.com.mo/en/2014/02/08/the-dragon-and-the-sleeping-crocodile-china-and-timor-leste/.

Hou, M. (2006). Aodaliya duihua yuanzhu ji qi yingxiang [The role of Australian aid in China's economic growth]. *Journal of East China Normal University [Philosophy and Social Science]*, 38(6), 83–88.

Hu, J. (2005, 15 September). Cujin pubian fazhan, shixian gongtong fanrong [Promote common development and achieve shared prosperity]. *People's Daily*, p. 3.

Hu, J. (2007, 16 October). Zai Zhongguo gongchandang di shiqici quanguo daibiao dahui shang de baogao [Report to the 17th national congress of CPC]. *People's Daily*, p. 2.

Huang, Y. & Ding, S. (2006). Dragon's underbelly: An analysis of China's soft power. *East Asia*, 23(4), 22–44. doi.org/10.1007/BF03179658.

Hutchison, A. (1975). *China's African revolution*. London, UK: Ebenezer Baylis & Son Ltd.

Ifeng. (2015, 6 September). Zhongguo neng bu neng jieshou nanmin [Can China accept refugees?]. *Ifeng News*. Retrieved from news.ifeng.com/a/20150906/44592259_0.shtml.

Ikenberry, J & Lim, D. (2017). *China's emerging institutional statecraft— The Asian infrastructure investment bank and the prospects for counter-hegemony* (Policy Report April 2017). Washington, DC: Brookings Institute.

International Economic Cooperation. (1998). Quanguo duiwai jingjin maoyi gongzuo huiyi zai jing zhaokai [The national conference on foreign trade and economic cooperation was held in Beijing]. *International Economic Cooperation*, 2, 1.

International Poverty Reduction Center in China. (2007). *Zhongguo guoji fupin zhongxin zhanlue dingwei he fazhan guihua (2006–2010) [The strategic positioning and development plan of the International Poverty Reduction Center in China (2006–2010)]*. Retrieved from www.iprcc.org.cn/Home/Index/skip/cid/1396.html.

Jackson, R. & Sørensen, G. (2007). *Introduction to international relations: Theories and approaches* (3rd ed.). New York, US: Oxford University Press.

Jia, Q. (2010). Exception to the rule: The Obama administration and China– U.S. relations. *Korean Journal of Defense Analysis*, 22(2), 249–264.

Jin, X. (2014). *Renmin Ribao: Zhongguo Jinchukou yinhang chengli ershi nian lai chengjiu feiran, zhuli guoji jingji hezuo yu guojia fazhan [People's Daily: China export–import Bank has made great achievements in promoting China's international economic cooperation and supporting China's economic development since it was established twenty years ago].* Retrieved from m.eximbank.gov.cn/info/circus/201806/t20180610_3434.html.

Johnston, A.I. (1996). Learning versus adaptation: Explaining change in Chinese arms control policy in the 1980s and 1990s. *China Journal*, (35), 27–61.

Johnston, A.I. (2007). *Social states: China in international institutions (1980–2000).* Princeton, US: Princeton University.

Kahler, M. (2013). Rising powers and global governance: Negotiating change in a resilient status quo. *International Affairs, 89*(3), 711–729. doi.org/10.1111/1468-2346.12041.

Kapiszewski, D., Maclean, L. & Read, B. (2015). *Field research in political science— Practices and principles.* Cambridge, UK: Cambridge University Press.

Kaunda, K. (1966). *African development and foreign aid.* Retrieved from legacy.fordham.edu/halsall/mod/1966Kaunda-africadev1.html.

Kelly, D. (2006). Politics of identity in post-reform China. In D. Kelly, R.S. Rajan & G.H.L. Goh (Eds), *Managing globalization: Lessons from China and India* (pp. 413–438). New Jersey, US: World Scientific Publishing Company.

Kennedy, S. (2010). The myth of the Beijing consensus. *Journal of Contemporary China, 19*(65), 461–477.

Keohane, R.O. (1984). *After hegemony: Cooperation and discord in the world political economy.* Princeton, US: Princeton University Press.

Kharas, H. (2007). *The new reality of aid.* Washington, DC: Brookings Institute.

Kitano, N. (2016). *Estimating China's foreign aid II: 2014 update* (Working Paper No. 131). Tokyo, Japan: JICA Research Institute.

Kragelund, P. (2011). Back to BASICs? The rejuvenation of non-traditional donors development cooperation with Africa. *Development and Change, 42*(2), 585–607. doi.org/10.1111/j.1467-7660.2011.01695.x.

Krasner, S.D. (Ed.). (1983). *International regimes.* Ithaca, NY: Cornell University Press.

Kurlantzick, J. (2007). *Charm offensive: How China's soft power is transforming the world.* New Haven, US: Yale University Press.

Kuziemko, I. & Werker, E. (2006). How much is a seat on the Security Council worth? Foreign aid and bribery at the United Nations. *Journal of Political Economy*, *114*(5), 905–930. doi.org/10.1086/507155.

Lai, H. & Lu, Y. (2012). *China's soft power and international relations*. New York, US: Routledge.

Lakshmanan, I.A.R. (2012, 6 September). Clinton visits East Timor for first trip since independence. *Bloomberg News*, Retrieved from www.bloomberg.com/news/2012-09-06/clinton-visits-east-timor-for-first-trip-since-independence-1-.html.

Lampton, D.M. (2007). The faces of Chinese power. *Foreign Affairs*, *86*(1), 115–127.

Lampton, D.M. (2008). *The three faces of Chinese power: Might, money, and minds*. Berkeley, US: University of California Press.

Lampton, D.M. (2014). *Following the leader: Ruling China, from Deng Xiaoping to Xi Jinping*. Berkeley, US: University of California Press.

Lancaster, C. (2007a). *The Chinese aid system*. Washington, DC: Center for Global Development.

Lancaster, C. (2007b). *Foreign aid: Diplomacy, development, domestic politics*. Chicago: University of Chicago Press.

Lancaster, C. (2009). Sixty years of foreign aid: What have we learned? *International Journal*, *64*(3), 799–810.

Lardy, N.R. (2014). *Markets over Mao: The rise of private business in China*. Washington, DC: Peterson Institute for International Economics.

Larsen, E. (2012). *Making waves in Rarotonga: Clinton's three messages about U.S. Pacific strategy*. Retrieved from csis.org/publication/making-waves-rarotonga-clintons-three-messages-about-us-pacific-strategy.

Lawrence, S.V. (2013). *U.S.–China relations: An overview of policy issues*. Washington, DC: Congressional Research Service.

Leach, M. (2016). Timor-Leste. *The Contemporary Pacific*, *28*(2), 466–473. doi.org/10.1353/cp.2016.0051.

Lemos, A. & Ribeiro, D. (2007). Taking ownership or just changing owners? In F. Manji & S. Marks (Eds), *African perspectives on China in Africa* (pp. 63–70). Oxford, UK: Pambazuka Press.

Lengfelder, C.S. (2015). Why triangular development cooperation? Germany and the emerging powers. *German Politics*, *25*(1), 1–24. doi.org/10.1080/09644008.2015.1024239.

Li, A. (2014). Guoji yuanzhu de lishi yu xianshi: lilun pipan yu xiaoxi pingxi (shang) [History and presence of international assistance: Theoretical critiques and effectiveness analysis (first half)]. *International Aid*, 1, 52–59.

Li, A. (2015). Guoji yuanzhu de lishi yu xianshi: lilun pipan yu xiaoxi pingxi (xia) ([History and presence of international assistance: Theoretical critiques and effectiveness analysis (second half)]. *International Aid*, 1, 40–45.

Li, B. (2014). *Remarks by H.E. Li Baodong vice foreign minister of the People's Republic of China at the post-2015 development agenda workshop*. Retrieved from www.fmprc.gov.cn/mfa_eng/wjdt_665385/zyjh_665391/t1162124.shtml.

Li, N., Ye, Z. & Mi, L. (2002). *Zhu Rongji Zongli yu Jianpuzai shouxiang Hun Sen juxing huitan [Premier Zhu Rongji held talks with Cambodia Prime Minister Hun Sen]*. Retrieved from people.com.cn/GB/shizheng/16/20021103/857000.html.

Li, X. & Wu, J. (2009). Zhongguo duifei yuanzhu de shiji jingyan yu mianlin de tiaozhan [A study of China's ODA to Africa]. *China Agriculture University Journal of Social Sciences*, *26*(4), 45–54.

Lieberthal, K. & Wang, J. (2012). *Addressing U.S.–China strategic distrust*. Washington, DC: Brookings Institute.

Lin, L. (2015, 26 September). Zhongmei qianshu fazhan hezuo liangjie beiwanglu [China and the U.S. signed the MOU on development cooperation]. *People's Daily*, p. 2.

Lin, M. (1987). Fazhan yuanzhu yu hezuo [Development, foreign aid and cooperation]. *International Economic Cooperation*, 11, 20–21.

Liu, G. (2008). Speech by Ambassador Liu Guijin on south–south cooperation and triangular cooperation at the first development cooperation forum. New York: The First Development Cooperation Forum of UN Economic and Social Council, 30 June.

Liu, G. (2010). Dangdai meiguo 'minzhu yuanzhu' jiexi [An analysis of contemporary American democracy assistance]. *American Studies Quarterly*, 3, 24–38.

Liu, J. & Huang, X. (2012). *Zhongguo dui taipingyang diqu tigong fazhang yuanzhu shuyu nannan hezuo fanchou [China's aid to the Pacific belongs to the south–south cooperation]*. Retrieved from news.xinhuanet.com/world/2012-08/31/c_112916154.htm.

Liu, S. (1956). *Zai zhongguo gongchandang dibaci quanguo daibiao dahui shang de zhengzhi baogao [The political report at the eighth national congress of Communist Party of China]*. Retrieved from news.xinhuanet.com/ziliao/2004-12/29/content_2392066.htm.

Long Ping High Tech. (2014). *Tian Guangfeng dashi shicha zhong mei dong sanfang hezuo xiangmu [Ambassador Tian Guangfeng visited the China–U.S. –Timor-Leste trilateral agricultural project]*. Retrieved from www.lpht.com.cn/Info.aspx?ModelId=1&Id=2169 (site discontinued).

Long, Y. (2015). Zhongguo yu lianheguo hezuo de zhanlue jueze [The strategic choice of China's cooperation with the UN]. *Management Observer, 568,* 46–47.

Lowy Institute. (2011). *The future state of the world as it relates to the Australian aid program*. Sydney, Australia: Lowy Institute for International Policy.

Lowy Institute. (2018). *Pacific aid Map*. Retrieved from pacificaidmap. lowyinstitute.org.

Lu Boynton, X. & Savoy, C.M. (2012). *U.S.–China Parallel Development Assistance Goals—Building on common interests*. Washington, DC: Center for Strategic & International Studies.

Lum, T. (2013). *U.S. assistance programs in China*. Washington, DC: Congressional Research Service.

Lum, T., Fischer, H., Gomez-Granger, J. & Leland, A. (2009). *China's foreign aid activities in Africa, Latin America, and Southeast Asia*. Washington, DC: Congressional Research Service.

Lum, T. & Vaughn, B. (2007). *CRS report for Congress—The Southwest Pacific: U.S. interests and China's growing influence*. Washington, DC: Congressional Research Service.

Mabbitt, R., Hamilton, D., Raffe, B., Eggleton, D. & Huttche, C. (2015). *Cook Islands national infrastructure investment plan*. Rarotonga, Cook Islands: Cook Islands Government.

Macao Hub. (2009). *East Timor to negotiate loan from China for infrastructures*. Retrieved from www.macauhub.com.mo/en/2009/10/15/7938/.

Maddison, A. (2006). *The world economy: Volume 1: A millennial perspective and Volume 2: Historical statistics*. Paris, France: OECD Publishing.

Manning, R. (2006). Will 'emerging donors' change the face of international cooperation? *Development Policy Review, 24*(4), 371–385.

Mao, X. (2010). Guoji yuanzhu geju yanbian qushi yu zhongguo duiwai yuanzhu de dingwei [The changing landscape of international assistance and the position of Chinese foreign aid]. *International Economic Cooperation*, 9, 58–60.

Mao, X. (2011, 11 July). Zhongguo dui wai yuanzhu jinru xin de fazhan jieduan [Chinese foreign aid has entered into a new stage of development]. *International Business Daily*, p. 1.

Mao, X. (2012). Zhongguo duiwai yuanzhu fangshi huigu yu chuangxin [Review and innovation on ways of Chinese foreign aid delivery]. *International Economic Cooperation*, 3, 89–91.

Mao, Z. (1956, 12 November). Jinian Sun Zhongshan xiansheng [Commemorate Dr Sun Yetsat]. *People's Daily*, p. 1.

Marshall Foundation. (2015). *History of the Marshall plan*. Retrieved from marshallfoundation.org/marshall/the-marshall-plan/history-marshall-plan/.

McEwan, C. & Mawdsley, E. (2012). Trilateral development cooperation: Power and politics in emerging aid relationships. *Development and Change*, 43(6), 1185–1209. doi.org/10.1111/j.1467-7660.2012.01805.x.

Mearsheimer, J.J. (2010). Structural realism. In T. Dunne, M. Kurki and S. Smith (Eds), *International relations theories: Discipline and diversity* (pp. 77–94). New York, US: Oxford University Press.

Mehta, P.S. & Nanda, N. (2005). *Trilateral development cooperation: An emerging trend* (Briefing Paper No. 1). Jaipur, India: CUTS Centre for International Trade, Economics & Environment.

Miller, L.H. & Su, X. (2011). Artemisinin: Discovery from the Chinese herbal garden. *Cell*, 146(6), 855–858.

Ministry of Agriculture (China). (2015). *Zhong Mei liangguo nongyebu xuqian nongye ji xiangguan lingyu hezuo liangjie beiwanglu [China and the U.S. renewed their MOU on cooperation in agriculture and other areas]*. Retrieved from www.moa.gov.cn/zwllm/gjjl/201509/t20150927_4843831.htm.

Ministry of Commerce (China) (MOFCOM). (2006). *Cong zhong ao fanzhan hezuo xin zhanlue kan duo/shuangbian fanzhan yuanzhu zhengce de fazhan qushi [To view the development of bilateral/multilateral development assistance policies from the perspective of the new China-Australia development cooperation policy]*. Retrieved from zys.mofcom.gov.cn/article/d/200609/20060903191338.shtml.

MOFCOM. (2007a). *Wang Shichun sizhang huijian Aodaliya guoji kaifashu fu shuzhang [Director General Wang Shichun met with the deputy director general of AusAID].* Retrieved from search.mofcom.gov.cn/swb/recordShow.jsp?flag= 0&lang=0&base=iflow_4&id=yws200703044993111&value=(%E6%BE% B3%E5%A4%A7%E5%88%A9%E4%BA%9A) (site discontinued).

MOFCOM. (2007b). *Yuanwaisi lingdao huijian Aodaliya guoji kaifashu fu shuzhang [Leaders from the Department of Foreign Aid met with the deputy director general of AusAID].* Retrieved from search.mofcom.gov.cn/swb/ recordShow.jsp?flag=0&lang=0&base=iflow_4&id=yws2007100516552 01&value=(%E6%BE%B3%E5%A4%A7%E5%88%A9%E4%BA%9A) (site discontinued).

MOFCOM. (2009a). *Fu Ziying fubuzhang huijian meiguo guowuyuan zhengce guihua bangongshi zhuren si luo te [Vice Minister Fu Ziying met with Slaughter, director of policy planning of the U.S. Department of State].* Retrieved from yws.mofcom.gov.cn/article/u/200907/20090706402903.shtml.

MOFCOM. (2009b). *Guanyu fazhan de duihua: G8+5 hai li gen da mu jincheng fazhan gongzuozu duihua qingkuang [A dialogue on development: Working group discussion on development in the G8+5 Heiligendamm process].* Retrieved from yws.mofcom.gov.cn/article/u/200907/20090706405679.shtml.

MOFCOM. (2009c). *Yuanwaisi lingdao huijian Aodaliya guoji fazhanshu fu shuzhang [Leaders from the Department of Foreign Aid met with the deputy director general of AusAID].* Retrieved from yws.mofcom.gov.cn/article/ gzdongtai/200904/20090406192036.shtml.

MOFCOM. (2009d). *Yuanwaisi pai zhu fu aodaliya jinxing yuanwai kaocha jiaoliu [The Department of Foreign Aid sent a delegation to visit Australia on foreign aid exchanges].* Retrieved from yws.mofcom.gov.cn/ article/u/200903/20090306105421.shtml.

MOFCOM. (2009e). *Yuanwaisi paiyuan canjia ao guoji fazhan yuanzhu xiangmu pinggu peixunban [Officials from the Department of Foreign Aid attended AusAID training on aid evaluation].* Retrieved from yws.mofcom.gov.cn/ article/u/200903/20090306105406.shtml.

MOFCOM. (2010). *Yuanwai shiye jieshao [Introduction to Chinese foreign aid].* Retrieved from yuanwaizhan.mofcom.gov.cn/syjsarticle/syjs/201007/342_1. html (site discontinued).

MOFCOM. (2011a). *Guojisi fu sizhang Zhu Hong chuxi di si jie yuanzhu youxiaoxing gao jibie luntan [Deputy Director General Zhu Hong of the Department of International Trade and Economic Affairs attended the 4th high-level aid effectiveness forum meeting]*. Retrieved from gjs.mofcom.gov.cn/article/al/an/201112/20111207876088.shtml.

MOFCOM. (2011b). *Yu shangwubu guoji jingji hezuo shiwu ju Li Wenmin juzhang wangshang jiaoliu [Online interview with Li Wenmin, director-general of MOFCOM's Agency for International Economic Cooperation]*. Retrieved from interview.mofcom.gov.cn/detail/201605/1610.html.

MOFCOM. (2011c). *Yu zhongguo guoji jingji jishu jiaoliu zhongxin Yao Shenhong zhuren wangshang jiaoliu [Online interview with Wao Shenhong, director-general of China International Center for Economic and Technical Exchanges]*. Retrieved from interview.mofcom.gov.cn/detail/201605/1614.html.

MOFCOM. (2011d). *Yu shangwubu guoji shangwu guanyuan yanxiu xueyuan Jin Xu yuanzhang wangshang jiaoliu [Online interview with Jin Xu, director-general of MOFCOM's Academy for International Business Officials]*. Retrieved from interview.mofcom.gov.cn/detail/201605/1618.html.

MOFCOM. (2012). *Zhong Jian liangguo qianshu er ling yi er nian jingji jishu hezuo xieding he goumai xinzhou liushi feiji de lixiang huanwen [China and Cambodia signed the agreement of economic and technical cooperation and the exchange of note on purchasing the MA 60 aircrafts from China]*. Retrieved from cb.mofcom.gov.cn/article/zxhz/tzdongtai/201202/20120207980073.shtml.

MOFCOM. (2013a). *Aodaliya duihua fazhan yuanzhu jiankuan [An overview of Australian aid to China]*. Retrieved from gjs.mofcom.gov.cn/article/ar/as/201006/20100606985153.shtml.

MOFCOM. (2013b). *Li Jinzao: Zhongguo jiang benzhe jinlierwei de yuanze, zhubu jiada cumao yuanzhu lidu [Li Jinzao: China will gradually increase its support for aid for trade within its capacity]*. Retrieved from www.mofcom.gov.cn/article/ae/ai/201307/20130700194789.shtml.

MOFCOM. (2013c). *Shangwubu zhaokai zhongguo qiye zouchuqu luxing shehui zeren zhuanti xinwen fabuhui [MOFCOM hosts press conference specialized on the honouring of social responsibilities by China's companies going overseas]*. Retrieved from www.mofcom.gov.cn/article/fbhfn/fbh2013/201302/20130200040491.shtml.

MOFCOM. (2014a). *Duiwai yuanzhu guanli banfai (shixing) [Measures for the Administration of Foreign Aid (trial)]*. Retrieved from yws.mofcom.gov.cn/article/gzdongtai/201411/20141100803904.shtml.

MOFCOM. (2014b). *Shangwubu zhaokai duiwai yuanzhu guanli banfa jiedu meiti chuifenghui [MOFCOM held the media debriefing on the measures on the Administration on Foreign Aid].* Retrieved from yws.mofcom.gov.cn/article/gzdongtai/201412/20141200825416.shtml.

MOFCOM. (2014c). *Zhu dongdiwen dashi Tian Guanfeng shicha zhongmeidong sanfang hezuo nongye xiangmu [Chinese ambassador to Timor-Leste Tian Guanfeng visited the China–U.S.–Timor-Leste trilateral agricultural project].* Retrieved from yws.mofcom.gov.cn/article/b/201407/20140700648580.shtml.

MOFCOM. (2015a). *2014 nian shangwu gongzuo nianzhong zongshu zhiliu: Shenghua gaige, duiwai yuanzhu gongzuo shixian xinfazhang [Part six of the review on MOFCOM's work in 2014: Deepening the reforming and China's foreign aid achieved new development].* Retrieved from www.mofcom.gov.cn/article/ae/ai/201501/20150100868073.shtml.

MOFCOM. (2015b). *Gao Hucheng chuxi zhongfei hezuo luntan di liu jie buzhao ji huiyi [Gao Hucheng attended the sixth ministerial meeting of the forum on China–Africa cooperation].* Retrieved from www.mofcom.gov.cn/article/ae/ai/201512/20151201200686.shtml.

MOFCOM. (2015c). *Shangwubu zhaokai lixing xinwen fabuhui (2015 nian shi yue ba ri) [MOFCOM held the regular press release (October 8 2015)].* Retrieved from www.mofcom.gov.cn/article/fbhfn/fbh2015/201510/20151001128093.shtml.

MOFCOM. (2015d). *Zhong Ao Baxin qianshu nueji kongzhi sanfang fazhan hezuo shidian xiangmu xieyi [China, Australia and Papua New Guinea signed the pilot trilateral project agreement on malaria control].* Retrieved from gjs.mofcom.gov.cn/article/zhongyts/201510/20151001147813.shtml.

MOFCOM. (2016). *Jigou jianjie [A brief introduction to the organisation].* Retrieved from jjhzj.mofcom.gov.cn/article/guanywm/201608/20160801375907.shtml.

MOFCOM. (2017). *Minister Zhong Shan and Minister of Trade of Australia Steve Ciobo sign MOU on strengthening development coperation.* Retrieved from english.mofcom.gov.cn/article/newsrelease/significantnews/201703/20170302540884.shtml.

MOFCOM and UNDP. (2010). *Memorandum of understanding for strengthened cooperation between the government of the People's Republic of China and the United Nations Development Programme.* New York, NY: MOFCOM, UNDP.

Ministry of Finance (China). (2016). *Guoji caijin hezuo si [The Department of International Economic and Financial Cooperation].* Retrieved from gjs.mof.gov.cn/pindaoliebiao/dhjz/.

Ministry of Foreign Affairs (China) (MFA). (1993). *Zhou Enlai waijiao huodong dashiji (1949–1975) [Chronicles of Diplomatic events of Zhou Enlai (1949–1975)]*. Beijing, China: World Affairs Press.

MFA. (2006). *Cui Tiankai buzhang zhuli zai zhongmei quanqiu shiwu luntan di er ci huiyi kaimushi shang de zhici [Remarks by China's Assistant Foreign Minister Cui Tiankai at the opening of the second meeting of China–U.S. global issues forum]*. Retrieved from www.fmprc.gov.cn/123/wjdt/zyjh/t266815.htm.

MFA. (2007). *Dai Bingguo fu waizhang yu meiguo changwu fu guowuqing nei ge luo peng te juxing huitan [Deputy Foreign Minister Dai Bingguo held talks with U.S. Deputy Secretary of State Negroponte]*. Retrieved from www.fmprc.gov.cn/web/wjb_673085/zzjg_673183/xws_674681/xgxw_674683/t300902.shtml.

MFA. (2008a). *Li Jinzhang fubuzhang huijian meiguo zhuli guowuqing Xiangnong [Li Jinzhang met with U.S. Assistant Secretary of State Shannon]*. Retrieved from www.mfa.gov.cn/chn//pds/wjb/zzjg/xws/xgxw/t518537.htm (site discontinued).

MFA. (2008b). *Zhongmei juxing di san ci feizhou shiwu chuoshang [China and the US held their third African affairs consultation]*. Retrieved from www.fmprc.gov.cn/web/wjb_673085/zzjg_673183/fzs_673445/xwlb_673447/t517823.shtml.

MFA. (2013). *Zhongfei hezuo luntan jieshao [An introduction to the forum on China–Africa cooperation]*. Retrieved from www.focac.org/chn/ltda/ltjj/t933521.htm (site discontinued).

MFA. (2014a). *The sixth round of China–US strategic and economic dialogue and the fifth round of China–US high-level consultation on people-to-people exchange open in Beijing Xi Jinping attends and addresses the joint opening ceremony*. Retrieved from www.fmprc.gov.cn/mfa_eng/zxxx_662805/t1173485.shtml.

MFA. (2014b). *Waijiaobu fu buzhang Zhang Ming zhuchi zhongmei di liu lun feizhou shiwu cuoshang [China's vice Foreign Minister Zhang Ming co-hosted the sixth round of China–U.S. African affairs consultation]*. Retrieved from www.fmprc.gov.cn/web/wjb_673085/zygy_673101/zm_673151/xgxwz_673153/t1219231.shtml.

MFA. (2014c). *Zhongguo yu bayuyaxinjineiya de guanxi [China's relations with Papua New Guinea]*. Retrieved from www.fmprc.gov.cn/mfa_chn/gjhdq_603914/gj_603916/dyz_608952/1206_608978/sbgx_608982/ (site discontinued).

MFA. (2015a). *Xi Jinping delivers important speech at UN sustainable development summit, stressing to realize common development of all countries from new starting point of post-2015 development agenda*. Retrieved from www.fmprc.gov.cn/mfa_eng/zxxx_662805/t1302359.shtml.

MFA. (2015b). *Xi Jinping yu meiguo zongtong Ao Ba Ma juxing huitan [Xi Jinping held talks with U.S. President Obama]*. Retrieved from www.fmprc.gov.cn/web/zyxw/t1300766.shtml.

MFA. (2015c). *Xi Jinping zai meiguo zongtong Ao Ba Ma juxing de huaying yishi shang de zhici [President Xi Jinping's remarks at the welcome ceremony hosted by U.S. President Obama]*. Retrieved from www.fmprc.gov.cn/web/zyxw/t1300765.shtml.

MFA. (2015d). *Xi Jinping zhuxi dui meiguo jinxing guoshi fangwen zhongfang chengguo qingdan [Outcome list of President Xi Jinping's state visit to the US]*. Retrieved from www.fmprc.gov.cn/web/zyxw/t1300767.shtml.

MFA. (2015e). *Zhu nanfei dashi Tian Xuejun jiu zhongfei hezuo luntan fenghui jieshou nanfei duli chuanmei zhuanfang [Chinese ambassador to South Africa Tian Xuejun received interviews from Independent Media on FOCAC summit]*. Retrieved from www.fmprc.gov.cn/web/dszlsjt_673036/ds_673038/t1318890.shtml.

MFA. (2015f). *Zhu Zha De shiguan linshi daiban Nie Bo huijian Meiguo zhu Zha De shiguan daiban [Chargé d'affaires of the Chinese embassy in Chad Nei Bo met with chargé d'affaires from the US embassy]*. Retrieved from www.fmprc.gov.cn/web/wjdt_674879/zwbd_674895/t1328552.shtml.

MFA. (2016a). *Waijiaobu buzhang zhuli Liu Haixing chuxi zhong fa fei sanfang hezuo yantaohui kaimushi [Assistant Foreign Minister Liu Haixing attended the opening ceremony of the symposium on China–France–Africa trilateral cooperation]*. Retrieved from www.mfa.gov.cn/web/wjbxw_673019/t1355118.shtml.

MFA. (2016b). *Wang Yi talks about China's four-point consensus on South China Sea issue with Brunei, Cambodia and Laos*. Retrieved from www.fmprc.gov.cn/mfa_eng/zxxx_662805/t1358478.shtml.

Mo, J. & Liu, S. (2009). Kaizhan yu nan taipingyang daoguo hezuo tancha kaifa shenhai kuangchan ziyuan [To conduct cooperation with South Pacific Island countries for the exploration of deep sea minerals and resources]. *Sci-Tech Stars*, Feb, 120–122.

Mo, N. (2013). Jian Zhong lianheguo qianshu mushu kaifa xiangmu beiwanglu, tigao mushu zhongzhi zaipei jiagong chukou nengli [China, Cambodia and UNDP signed the MOU on cassava to increase the cultivating, processing and exporting capacity of cassava in Cambodia]. Retrieved from hi-in.facebook.com/124023714419000/posts/188436974644340/.

Moisés, N. (2007). Rogue aid. *Foreign Policy*, (159), 95–96.

Morgenthau, H. (1962). A political theory of foreign aid. *The American Political Science Review, 56*(2), 301–309.

Morton, K. (2012). *Learning by doing: China's role in the global governance of food security* (Working Paper No. 30). Bloomington, US: Research Center for Chinese Politics and Business, Indiana University.

National Department of Health (PNG). (2014). *National malaria strategic plan 2014–2018*. Port Moresby, Papua New Guinea: PNG NDH.

Naughton, B. (2011). China's economic policy today: The new state activism. *Eurasian Geography and Economics, 52*(3), 313–329. doi.org/10.2747/1539-7216.52.3.313.

Nye, J.S. (1990). Soft power. *Foreign Policy*, 80, 153–171.

Nzikou-Massala, M. (2014, June–July). Know-how from China. *SPORE*, pp. 18–19.

Organisation for Economic Co-operation and Development (OECD). (2011). *The China–DAC study group*. Retrieved from www.oecd.org/dac/dac-global-relations/china-dac-study-group.htm.

OECD. (2012a). *Conclusions: Brainstorming meeting on triangular cooperation*. Paris, France: OECD.

OECD. (2012b). *Trade-related south–south co-operation: China*. OECD.

OECD. (2012c). *Triangular cooperation: Emerging policy messages and interim findings from analytical work*. Paris, France: OECD.

OECD. (2014). *Active with the People's Republic of China*. Paris, France: OECD.

OECD. (2015a). *Better policies for development 2015: Policy coherence and green growth*. Paris, France: OECD Publishing.

OECD. (2015b). People's Republic of China joins the OECD development centre. Retrieved from www.oecd.org/dev/press-release-china-joins-oecd-development-centre.htm.

OECD. (2016a). *Dispelling the myths of triangular co-operation—Evidence from the 2015 OECD survey on triangular co-operation*. Paris, France: OECD.

OECD. (2016b). *ODA 1960—15 trends*. Retrieved from www2.compareyourcountry.org/oda?cr=20001&cr1=oecd&lg=en&page=1.

OECD. (2017). *Development finance of countries beyond the DAC*. Retrieved from www.oecd.org/development/stats/non-dac-reporting.htm.

OECD. (2018). *Table 1: Net official development assistance from DAC and other countries in 2017.* Retrieved from www.oecd.org/development/financing-sustainable-development/development-finance-data/ODA-2017-complete-data-tables.pdf.

Pankaj, A.K. (2005). Revisiting foreign aid theories. *International Studies, 42*(2), 103–121. doi.org/10.1177/002088170404200201.

Pantoja, E. (2009). *Triangular cooperation: New paths to development—Summary report of the discussions and experiences presented in the 1st international symposium on triangular cooperation.* Paris, France: OECD.

Pei, Y. (2004, 3 December). Zhiyou yihan bubi danyou-zhuanjia dui riben ni quxiao duihua zhengfu kaifa yuanzhu de jiedu [Regrets but no concern—Interpretation from experts on Japan's plan to stop aid to China]. *International Business Daily*, p. 1.

Peng, H. (2013). *Zhongding guoji zhongbiao yuan jianbuzhai nongye shiyanlou xiangmu [Zhongding International Engineering Co, Ltd. won the bid for the China-financed Cambodia agricultural laboratory building project].* Retrieved from www.ziec-e.com/news/677.html.

Pennington, M. (2011, 2 March). Clinton says US in direct competition with China. *The Washington Post.* Retrieved from www.washingtonpost.com/wp-dyn/content/article/2011/03/02/AR2011030202888.html.

People's Daily. (1956, 23 June). Zhong Jian jingji yuanzhu xieding [The economic aid agreement between China and Cambodia]. *People's Daily*, p. 1.

People's Daily. (1992, 16 December). Lianheguo kaifa jihua shu wuchang yuanzhu 165 wai meiyuan, zhongguo changqi guihua yu hongguan jingji guanli yanjiu zuo qi shishi [UNDP provides 1.65 million US dollar grants to China and the research on China's long-term planning and macroeconomic management started yesterday]. *People's Daily*, p. 2.

People's Daily. (2006, 28 September). Dierjie Zhongguo xiaochu pingku jiang ruwei houxuan danwei ji geren jieshao [An introduction to the nominated institutions and individuals for the Second China Poverty Alleviation Award]. *People's Daily*, p. 16.

People's Daily. (2009, 23 December). Waijiaobu juxing lixing jizhehui [The Ministry of Foreign Affairs held the routine press conference]. *People's Daily*, p. 14.

People's Daily. (2010, 15 August). Quanguo yuanwai gongzuo huiyi zaijing zhaokai [The national conference on foreign aid is held in Beijing]. *People's Daily*, p. 1.

PNG Department of National Planning and Monitoring. (2008). *PNG commitment on aid effectiveness: A joint commitment of principles and actions between the Government of Papua New Guinea and development partners.* Port Moresby, Papua New Guinea: PNG DNPM.

PNG Department of Treasury. (2014). *2014 national budget volume 1—Economic and development policies* (Vol. 1). Port Moresby, Papua New Guinea: PNG Department of Treasury.

PNG Government. (2011). *Papua New Guinea vision 2050.* Port Moresby, Papua New Guinea: PNG Department of Treasury.

Pompeo, M.R. (2018). *Remarks on 'America's Indo-Pacific economic vision'.* Retrieved from china.usembassy-china.org.cn/remarks-on-americas-indo-pacific-economic-vision/.

Portugese MFA. (2013). *Policy dialogue on triangular cooperation: Summary of discussion.* Lisbon, Portugal: Portugese Ministry of Foreign Affairs.

Powles, M. (2007). China looks to the Pacific (Occasional Paper No. 1). CSCSD, pp. 43–55.

Pu, P. (2009). Zhongguo lianheguo waijiao de tedian ji juxian [Characteristics and limitations of China's UN diplomacy]. *Teaching and Research, 6,* 82–87.

Qi, G. (1995). Zai xin xingshi xia jinyibu gaige yuanwai gongzuo-quanguo yuanwai gaige gongzuo huiyi zai jing zhaokai [To further foreign aid reform under the new circumstance—The national conference on foreign aid reform was held in Beijing]. *International Economic Cooperation, 11,* 4–5.

Qian, H. & Tang, L. (2000). Zhongguo wushi nian nueji fangzhi gongzuo de chengjiu yu zhanwang [Achievements and prospect for malaria prevention and control in China in the past five decades]. *Chinese Journal of Epidemiology, 21*(3), 225–227.

Ramo, J.C. (2004). *The Beijing consensus.* London, UK: Foreign Policy Centre.

Reus-Smit, C. (2013). Constructivism. In A. Linklater (Ed.), *Theories of international relations* (pp. 217–240). Houndmills, Basingstoke: Palgrave Macmillan.

Richardson, S. (2010). *China, Cambodia, and the five principles of peaceful coexistence.* New York, US: Columbia University Press.

Riddell, R. (1987). *Foreign aid reconsidered.* Baltimore, US: Johns Hopkins University Press.

Riddell, R. (2007). *Does foreign aid really work?* New York, US: Oxford University Press.

Rittberger, V. & Mayer, P. (1993). *Regime theory and international relations.* Oxford, UK: Clarendon Press.

Rozman, G. (2012). *East Asian national identities: Common roots and Chinese exceptionalism.* Stanford, US: Stanford University.

Ruak, T.M. (2012). *Dong di wen zongtong Luwake zai zhongguo zhu dong shiguan guoqing liu shi san zhounian zhaodaihui shang de jianghua [Speech by Timor-Leste President Ruak at the reception of Chinese embassy in Timor-Leste to commemorate the 63rd anniversary of the founding of the People's Republic of China].* Retrieved from tl.chineseembassy.org/chn/3/t975618.htm.Rudd, K. (2008). *Australia, the United States and the Asia Pacific region.* Washington, DC: Brookings Institute.

Rudd, K. (2011). *Government's response to the independent review of aid effectiveness.* Retrieved from parlinfo.aph.gov.au/parlInfo/genpdf/chamber/hansardr/1874cb21-d37a-4c79-b92a-33a8298c9cbe/0199/hansard_frag.pdf;fileType=application%2Fpdf.

Samy, Y. (2010). China's aid policies in Africa: Opportunities and challenges. *The Round Table, 99*(406), 75–90. doi.org/10.1080/00358530903513756.

Sato, J., Shiga, H., Kobayashi, T. & Kondoh, H. (2010). *How do 'emerging' donors differ from 'traditional' donors—An institutional analysis of foreign aid in Cambodia.* Tokyo, Japan: JICA Research Institute.

Sato, J, Shiga, H., Kobayashi, T. & Kondoh, H. (2011). 'Emerging donors' from a recipient perspective: An institutional analysis of foreign aid in Cambodia. *World Development, 39*(12), 2091–2104. doi.org/10.1016/j.worlddev.2011.04.014.

Savage, L. & Eyben, R. (2013). Emerging and submerging powers: Imagined geographies in the new development partnership at the Busan fourth high level forum. *Journal of Development Studies, 49*(4), 457–469.

Schimmelfennig, F. (2015). Efficient process tracing—Analyzing the causal mechanisms of European integration. In A. Bennet & J.T. Checkel (Eds), *Process tracing: From metaphor to analytic tool* (pp. 98–125). Cambridge, UK: Cambridge University Press.

Schulz, N. (2010). *Workshop report and concept note: Triangular cooperation in the context of aid effectiveness—Experiences and views of EU donors.* Madrid, Spain: Spanish Agency for International Development Cooperation.

Shambaugh, D. (2013). *China as a global power: Understanding Beijing's competing identities*. Washington, DC: George Washington University.

Shen, D. (2005). Guanfang fazhan yuanzhu: Zuoyong, yiyi yu mubiao [ODA: Functions, significance and objectives]. *International Economic Cooperation, 9*, 30–32.

Shen, Z. (2001). Xin zhongguo jianli chuqi sulian duihua jingji yuanzhu de jiben qingkuang (shang)—Laizi zhongguo he eguo de dang'an cailiao [Basic information on the Soviet Union's aid to PRC in the early days (part one)—Based on archival data from China and Russia]. *Russian Studies, 1*, 53–66.

Shi, L. (1989). *Dangdai zhongguo de duiwai Jingji hezuo* [China today: Economic cooperation with foreign countries]. Beijing, China: China Social Sciences Press.

Shi, Y. (2006). Zhongguo de bianqian yu zhongguo waijiao zhanlue fenxi [An analysis of China's evolution and its diplomatic strategy]. *The Journal of International Studies, 1*, 31–44.

Shi, Z. (2004, 8 December). Zhongguo li biye shuiping hai henyuan [China is still far from graduation]. *International Business Daily*, p. 1.

Shie, T.R. (2007). Rising Chinese influence in the South Pacific: Beijing's 'Island Fever'. *Asian Survey, 47*(2), 307–326. doi.org/10.1525/as.2007.47.2.307.

Shinn, D.H. (2009). China's engagement in Africa. In J.S. Morrison & J. Cooke (Eds), *African Policy after President Bush* (pp. 142–161). Washington, DC: Center for Strategic and International Studies.

Shinn, D.H. (2011). *United States–China collaboration on health and agriculture in Africa*. Retrieved from www.scribd.com/doc/56154100/United-States-China-Collaboration-on-Health-and-Agriculture-in-Africa.

Shinn, D.H. (2012a). China, Africa and implications for the United States. Retrieved from www.chinausfocus.com/foreign-policy/china-africa-and-implications-for-the-united-states/.

Shinn, D.H. (2012b, 18 January). The U.S. reassesses the China–Africa relationship. *International Policy Digest*. Retrieved from www.international policydigest.org/2012/01/18/the-u-s-reassesses-the-china-africa-relationship/ (site discontinued).

Shinn, D.H. (2015). *China and the United States in Africa: Cooperation or competition?* Retrieved from www.academia.edu/10874660/China_and_the_United_States_in_Africa_Cooperation_or_Competition.

Shirk, S.L. (2007). *China, fragile superpower.* New York, NY: Oxford University Press.

Shu. (1989). Jingmaobu fubuzhang Li Lanqing qiangdiao: duiwai yuanzhu shi xiang you shenyuan yiyi de gongzuo [Deputy Minister Li Lanqing of the Ministry of Foreign Trade and Economic Cooperation emphasized: Providing foreign aid is a job of far-reaching significance]. *International Economic Cooperation, 4,* 3–4.

Six, C. (2009). The rise of postcolonial states as donors: A challenge to the development paradigm? *Third World Quarterly, 30*(6), 1103–1121. doi.org/10.1080/01436590903037366.

Smith, G. (2013). Nupela Masta? Local and expatriate labour in a Chinese-run nickel mine in Papua New Guinea. *Asian Studies Review,* 37(2), 178–195. doi.org/10.1080/10357823.2013.768598.

Smith, G., Carter, G., Mao, X., Tararia, A., Tupou, E. & Xu, W. (2014). *The development needs of Pacific Island countries.* Beijing, China: UNDP China.

Smith, G. & D'Arcy, P. (2013). Introduction: Global perspectives on Chinese investment. *Pacific Affairs, 86*(2), 217–232. doi.org/10.5509/2012862217.

Song, L. & Wu, Y. (2013). Zhongguo dui jianpuzhai de yuanzhu: Pingjia ji jianyi [China's aid to Cambodia: Evaluation and suggestions]. *International Economic Cooperation, 6,* 54–58.

Song, W. (2015). Zhongguo duiwai yuanzhu yiyi de zaisikao [Rethinking on the significance of Chinese foreign aid]. *International Economic Cooperation, 1,* 81–84.

Sørensen, C.T.N. (2015). The significance of Xi Jinping's 'Chinese dream' for Chinese foreign policy: From 'Tao Guang Yang Hui' to 'Fen Fa You Wei'. *Journal of China and International Relations, 3*(1): 53–73. doi.org/10.5278/ojs.jcir.v3i1.1146.

State Council. (2010). *White paper of China–Africa economic and trade cooperation (2010).* Retrieved from english.cri.cn/6909/2010/12/23/2741s611673.htm.

State Council. (2011a). *China's peaceful development.* Beijing, China: China State Council.

State Council. (2011b). *Guoxinban juxing zhongguo de duiwai yuanzhu baipishu xinwen fabuhui ([Press conference hosted by China's State Council Information Office on the release of China's white paper on foreign aid].* Retrieved from www.scio.gov.cn/xwfbh/xwbfbh/wqfbh/2011/0426/.

State Council. (2011c). *Guwuyuan xinwenban fabiao zhongguo de heping fazhang baipishu [The State Council Information Office released the white paper on peaceful development]*. Beijing, China: China State Council.

State Council. (2011d, 22 April). Zhongguo de duiwai yuanzhu [China's foreign aid]. *People's Daily*, p. 22.

State Council. (2013, 29 August). White paper of China–Africa economic and trade cooperation (2013). *Xinhua*. Retrieved from news.xinhuanet.com/english/china/2013-08/29/c_132673093.htm.

State Council. (2014, 11 July). Zhongguo de duiwai yuanzhu (2014) [China's foreign aid (2014)]. *People's Daily*, p. 22.

State Council. (2015). *Guoxinban jiu 'shisanwu' tuopin gongjian gongzuo youguan qingkuang juxing fabuhui [The State Council Information Office held the news conference on the poverty reduction work in the 13th five-year plan]*. Retrieved from www.scio.gov.cn/xwfbh/xwbfbh/wqfbh/2015/33909/index.htm.

Stringer, K.D. (2006). Pacific Island microstates: Pawns or players in Pacific rim diplomacy? *Diplomacy & Statecraft, 17*(3), 547–577. doi.org/10.1080/09592290600867636.

Styllis, G. & Sony, O. (2015, 5 January). First Cassava shipment of major deal leaves port. *Cambodia Daily*. Retrieved from english.cambodiadaily.com/news/first-cassava-shipment-of-major-deal-leaves-port-75322/.

Su, C. (2005). Faxian zhongguo xinwaijiao: Duobian guoji zhidu yu zhongguo waijiao xinsiwei [Rediscovering Chinese foreign relations: Multilateral international institutions and China's new thinking on diplomacy]. *World Economics and Politics, 4*, 11–16.

Sun, G. (1993). Sun Guangxiang tan yuanwai tizhi gaige [Sun Guangxiang talks about foreign aid reform]. *International Economic Cooperation, 5*, 10–11.

Sun, T. & Zhou, T. (2015). *Duiwai yuanzhu guizhi tixi bijiao yanjiu [A comparative study on regulatory systems of foreign aid]*. Beijing, China: Social Sciences Academic Press (China).

Tarzi, S.M. (2003). International regimes and international relations theory: Search for synthesis. *International Studies, 40*(1), 23–39. doi.org/10.1177/002088170304000102.

Task Team on South–South Cooperation. (2011). *Towards effective south–south and triangular coopereration* (Good Practice Paper). Paris, France: TT–SSC.

Taylor, I. (2006). China's oil diplomacy in Africa. *International Affairs, 82*(5), 937–959. doi.org/10.1111/j.1468-2346.2006.00579.x.

Teiwes, F. & Sun, W. (2010). Xiandaihua gongshi de xingcheng: dadao 'Sirenbang' zhi shiyijie sanzhong quanhui qijian Zhongguo de jingji zhengce 1976–1978 [An evolving consensus on modernization: PRC economic policy from the purge of the 'Gang of Four' to the Third Plenum 1976–1978]. In Z. Jiamu (Ed.), *Dangdai Zhongguo yu tade Fazhan Daolu [Contemporary China and its development road]* (pp. 404–422). Beijing, China: Contemporary China Publishing House.

Terhalle, M. (2011). Reciprocal socialization: Rising powers and the West. *International Studies Perspectives, 12*(4), 341–361. doi.org/10.1111/j.1528-3585.2011.00442.x.

The Economist. (2009, 26 June). Taiwan's president and China—Sorry, the offer's closed. *The Economist.* Retrieved from www.economist.com/asia/2009/06/25/sorry-the-offers-closed.

The Economist. (2014, 21 August). What China wants. *The Economist.* Retrieved from www.economist.com/leaders/2014/08/21/what-china-wants.

Thier, A. (2014, 23 May). Engaging China on global development [blog post]. Retrieved from blog.usaid.gov/2014/05/engaging-china-on-global-development/.

Tian, G. (2012). *A perfect example of good-neighborly and amicable relationship: A new chapter for the friendship between China and Timor-Leste.* Retrieved from tl.chineseembassy.org/eng/is/t931857.htm.

Timor-Leste Government. (2011). *Timor-Leste strategic development plan 2011–2030.* Dili, Timor-Leste: Timor-Leste Government.

Timor-Leste Ministry of Agriculture and Fisheries. (2012). *Strategic plan 2014–2020.* Dili, Timor-Leste: Timor-Leste MAF.

Timor-Leste Ministry of Finance (MoF). (2014a). *State budget 2015 development partners—Book 5.* Dili, Timor-Leste: Timor-Leste MoF.

Timor-Leste MoF. (2014b). *State budget 2015 special funds—Book 6.* Dili, Timor-Leste: Timor-Leste MoF.

Timor-Leste MoF. (2015). *Projects by funding source: China.* Retrieved from www.aidtransparency.gov.tl/reportsPublicView.do.

Timor-Leste MoF. (2018). *State budget 2018 development partners—Book 5.* Dili, Timor-Leste: Timor-Leste MoF.

Tongan Ministry of Information and Communications. (2010). *CCECC subcontracts Fletcher Construction Ltd. to build a new Vuna international passenger wharf in Nuku'alofa'*. Retrieved from www.mic.gov.to/ministry department/14-govt-ministries/internal-affairs/1545-ccecc-subcontracts-fletcher-construction-ltd-to-build-a-new-vuna-international-passenger-wharf-in-nukualofa (site discontinued).

Trevett, C. (2011, 10 September). China's aid its own to spend, says Key. *New Zealand Herald*. Retrieved from www.nzherald.co.nz/nz/news/article.cfm?c_id=1&objectid=10750699.

Tulloch, J., Christophel, E.M., Ear, S., Meek, S., Ringwald, P., Ortega, L. & Wongsrichanalai, C. (2012). *Joint assessment of the response to Artemisinin resistance in the greater Mekong sub-region*. Retrieved from apps.who.int/iris/bitstream/handle/10665/251841/artemisinin-resistance.pdf?sequence=1&isAllowed=y.

UK Parliament. (2009). *DFID and China—Third report of session 2008–2009*. London, UK: UK's House of Commons International Development Committee.

UN Cambodia and Cambodian Government. (2010). *United Nations development assistance framework (2011–2015)*. Phnom Penh, Cambodia: UN Population Fund.

United Nations. (1979). *Agreement between the government of the People's Republic of China and the United Nations Development Programme*. Retrieved from www.ilo.org/dyn/legprot/fr/f?p=2200:52:0::NO:52:P52_CONTENT_REPOSITORY_ID,P52_FORMAT:103416,BINARY:NO.

United Nations Development Programme (UNDP). (2001). *Second country cooperation framework for China (2001–2005)*. New York, NY: UNDP.

UNDP. (2009a). *Enhancing south–south and triangular cooperation: Study of the current situation and existing good practices in policy, institutions, and operation of south–south and triangular cooperation*. New York, NY: UNDP.

UNDP. (2009b). *UNDP zhiding yu zhongguo jianli nan nan hezuo quanxin zhanlue huoban guanxi jihua [UNDP formulated a plan to establish a new strategic partnership with China for south–south cooperation]*. Retrieved from www.ecdc.net.cn/news/detail.aspx?ClassID=8&ContentID=15.

UNDP. (2010). *United nations development assistance framework (2011–2015)*. Beijing, China: UNDP.

UNDP. (2013). *UNDP strategic plan: 2014–17*. New York, NY: UNDP.

UNDP. (2015a). *Annual project report 2014—United Nations Development Programme Cambodia: China–Cambodia–UNDP trilateral cooperation cassava project phase II (01 Jan 2014 – 31 Dec 2014)*. Phnom Penh, Cambodia: UNDP Cambodia.

UNDP. (2015b). *Human development report 2015*. New York, NY: UNDP.

UNDP. (2015c). *In-depth*. Retrieved from www.cn.undp.org/content/china/en/home/ourwork/south-south-cooperation/in-depth/.

UNDP. (2015d). *A world of development experience*. Retrieved from www.undp.org/content/undp/en/home/operations/about_us.html.

UNDP Cambodia. (2012). *Cambodian officials complete training in cassava cultivation techniques in China*. Retrieved from www.kh.undp.org/content/cambodia/en/home/stories/cambodian-officials-complete-training-in-cassava-cultivation-tec0.html.

UNDP China. (2005). *United Nations development assistance framework for the People's Republic of China (2006–2010)*. Beijing, China: UNDP.

UNDP China. (2012). *UNDP China trilateral and south–south cooperation: Highlights from 2011*. Beijing, China: UNDP.

UNDP China. (2013a). *The New UNDP–China partnership for south–south and global issues: 2012 Highlights*. Beijing, China: UNDP.

UNDP China. (2013b). *UNDP administrator Helen Clark completes official visit to China*. Retrieved from www.undp.org/content/china/en/home/presscenter/pressreleases/2013/09/round-up-of-administrator-s-bilateral-meetings-in-china/.

UNDP China. (2014a). *Trilateral cooperation success for China–Cambodia–UNDP cassava project*. Retrieved from www.cn.undp.org/content/china/en/home/presscenter/articles/2014/12/trilateral-cooperation-success-for-china-cambodia-undp-cassava-p/.

UNDP China. (2014b). *UNDP–China partnership for south–south and global issues: 2013 highlights*. Beijing, China: UNDP.

UNDP China. (2014c). *Workshop for south–south cooperation providers: Preparing for the Mexico high level meeting on the global partnership for effective development cooperation*. Beijing, China: UNDP.

UNDP China. (2015a). *2015 report on the sustainable development of Chinese companies overseas*. Beijing, China: UNDP.

UNDP China. (2015b). *China–Cambodia–UNDP trilateral cooperation on cassava*. Retrieved from www.cn.undp.org/content/china/en/home/operations/projects/south-south-cooperation/overview-trilateral-cooperation-projects/china-cambodia-undp-trilateral-cooperation-on-cassava.html.

UNDP China. (2015c). *China–Ghana–UNDP trilateral cooperation on renewable energy*. Retrieved from www.cn.undp.org/content/china/en/home/operations/projects/south-south-cooperation/overview-trilateral-cooperation-projects/china--ghana-undp-trilateral-cooperation-on-renewable-energy.html.

UNDP China. (2015d). *Enhancing China's south–south policy dialogue on poverty reduction*. Retrieved from www.cn.undp.org/content/china/en/home/ourwork/povertyreduction/successstories/enhancing-china_s-south-south-policy-dialogue-on-poverty-reducti/.

UNDP China. (2015e). *South–south & global cooperation*. Retrieved from www.cn.undp.org/content/china/en/home/ourwork/south-south-cooperation/south-south-cooperation.html.

UNDP China. (2015f). *UNDP–China partnership on south–south and global cooperation: 2014 highlights*. Beijing, China: UNDP.

United States Agency for International Development (USAID). (2010). Cooperation with China on international development. Retrieved from photos.state.gov/libraries/china/240500/pdf/USAID-China%20Cooperation%20on%20International%20Development%2009%2002%2010.pdf.

USAID. (2013). *USAID/U.S. Embassy Beijing newsletter March 2013*. Retrieved from pdf.usaid.gov/pdf_docs/pnaeb765.pdf.

USAID. (2014). *USAID/U.S. Embassy Beijing newsletter May 2014*. Retrieved from photos.state.gov/libraries/china/705061/usaid/USAID%20Beijing%20Newsletter%202014-may-english.pdf.

USAID. (2015a). *Agency financial report: Fiscal year 2015*. Washington, DC: USAID.

USAID. (2015b). *Developing agricultural communities*. Retrieved from www.usaid.gov/timor-leste/project-descriptions/developing-agricultural-communities.

USAID. (2015c). *Memorandum of understanding on U.S.–China development cooperation and the establishment of an exchange and communication mechanism between the United States Agency for International Development and the Ministry of Commerce of the People's Republic of China*. Retrieved from www.usaid.gov/sites/default/files/documents/1870/9-24-15-Final%20MoU%20on%20Development%20Cooperation%20-%20USAID-MoFCOM-%20Clean.pdf.

USAID. (2015d). *USAID: China*. Retrieved from www.usaid.gov/china.

USAID. (2015e). *USAID/U.S. Embassy Beijing newsletter December 2015*. Retrieved from photos.state.gov/libraries/china/705061/usaid/usaid-2015-dec.pdf.

USAID. (2015f). *USAID/U.S. Embassy Beijing newsletter July 2015*. Retrieved from photos.state.gov/libraries/china/705061/usaid/usaid-2015-july-english.pdf.

USAID China. (2013). *USAID mission*. Retrieved from www.usaid.gov/who-we-are/mission-vision-values.

US Department of State. (2005a). *Rice, Chinese leaders stress constructive, growing relationship*. Retrieved from iipdigital.usembassy.gov/st/english/texttrans/2005/03/20050320125853uhyggep2.012271e-02.html-axzz3tlbVoxQo.

US Department of State. (2005b). *Whither China: From membership to responsibility?* Retrieved from 2001-2009.state.gov/s/d/former/zoellick/rem/53682.htm.

US Department of State. (2009). *Report to Congress on assistance by the People's Republic of China to governments and entities in Latin America and Africa*. Retrieved from www.usaid.gov/sites/default/files/cr_china_7071f3.pdf.

US Department of State. (2011). *U.S.–China cooperation in Asia–Pacific*. Retrieved from iipdigital.usembassy.gov/st/english/texttrans/2011/07/20110722102020su0.5174633.html-axzz3udFMIxxo.

US Department of State. (2012). *Joint statement on the U.S.–China strategic and economic dialogue outcomes of the strategic track May 3–4, 2012*. Retrieved from www.state.gov/r/pa/prs/ps/2012/05/189287.htm.

US Department of State. (2013). *U.S.–China strategic and economic dialogue outcomes of the strategic track*. Retrieved from www.state.gov/r/pa/prs/ps/2013/07/211861.htm.

US Department of State. (2014a). *List of U.S.–China cooperative projects*. Retrieved from www.state.gov/r/pa/prs/ps/2014/01/220530.htm.

US Department of State. (2014b). *U.S.–China strategic and economic dialogue outcomes of the strategic track*. Retrieved from www.state.gov/r/pa/prs/ps/2014/07/229239.htm.

US Department of State. (2015). *U.S.–China Strategic and Economic Dialogue VII Strategic Track Select Outcomes*. Retrieved from 2009-2017.state.gov/r/pa/prs/ps/2015/06/244203.htm.

US Department of State. (2016). *U.S.–China strategic & economic dialogue outcomes of the strategic track.* Retrieved from www.state.gov/r/pa/prs/ps/2016/06/258146.htm.

US Embassy in Timor-Leste. (2013). *Timor-Leste, United States, and China sign first Asian trilateral.* Retrieved from www.facebook.com/USEmbassyDili/.

US General Accounting Office. (2004). *Subject: Foreign assistance: U.S. funding for democracy-related programs (China).* Retrieved from www.gao.gov/assets/100/92476.html.

US Government. (2011). *Feeding the dragon: Reevaluating U.S. development assistance to China.* Retrieved from www.gpo.gov/fdsys/pkg/CHRG-112hhrg71262/html/CHRG-112hhrg71262.htm.

US House of Representatives. (2005). China's influence in Africa—Hearing before the subcommittee on Africa, global human rights and international operations. Retrieved from commdocs.house.gov/committees/intlrel/hfa22658.000/hfa22658_0.HTM.

van der Veen, M. (2011). *Ideas, interests and foreign aid.* New York, NY: Cambridge University Press.

Var, V. (2011). *Cambodia's strategic situation: Current and future threats* (Master's dissertation). Centre for Defence and Strategic Studies, Australian Defence College, Canberra, ACT.

Var, V. (2014). *Holding the balance between the superpowers: Cambodia's strategy for development* (Master's dissertation). Strategic Studies Institute, United States Army War College, Carlisle, PA.

Varghese, P. (2014). *Address to Centre for Defence and Strategic Studies course.* Retrieved from www.dfat.gov.au/news/speeches/Pages/140212-defence.aspx.

Varrall, M. (2013). Chinese views on China's role in international development assistance. *Pacific Affairs, 86*(2), 233–255.

Varrall, M. (2016). Domestic actors and agendas in Chinese aid policy. *The Pacific Review, 29*(1), 21–44. doi.org/10.1080/09512748.2015.1066414.

VOA. (2009). *Chinese president signs cooperation agreements with Liberia.* Retrieved from www.voanews.com/archive/chinese-president-signs-cooperation-agreements-liberia.

Waley-Cohen, J. (1999). *The sextants of Beijing: Global currents in Chinese history.* New York, NY: W.W. Norton.

Waltz, K.N. (1979). *Theory of international politics*. New York, NY: Random House.

Walz, J. & Ramachandran, V. (2011). *Brave new world: A literature review of emerging donors and the changing nature of foreign assistance* (Working Paper No. 273). Washington, DC: Center for Global Development.

Wang, C. (1994). Zhongguo duiwai yuanzhu gongzuo zai gaige zhong qianjin [Chinese foreign aid moves forward in the process of reform]. *International Economic Cooperation*, 2, 6–8.

Wang, C. (1996). Tuixing duiwai yuanzhu de xin fangshi, cujin yu fazhanzhong guojia de youhao hezuo [To promote new forms of foreign aid and enhance friendly cooperation with developing countries]. *International Economic Cooperation*, 2, 7–9.

Wang, C. (2001). *Zhongguo gaoceng moulue-waijiao juan [Wisdom of Chinese leadership: Volume of foreign policy]*. Xi'an, China: Shaanxi Normal University Publishing Press.

Wang, C. (2009). Jiejian guoji jingyan kexue tuijin duiwai yuanzhu [Learn from international experience to promote foreign aid in a scientific way]. *International Economic Cooperation*, 6, 42–44.

Wang, C. (2011, 12 May). Zhongmei cuoshang yatai shiwu zheshe le shenme [Reflections of the China–U.S. consultation on Asia–Pacific affairs]. *People's Daily*. Retrieved from world.people.com.cn/GB/14621397.html.

Wang, D. (2005, 25 October). Lianheguo duihua wuchang yuanzhu de huigu he zhanwang [Retrospect and prospect of UN grants to China]. *International Business Daily*, p. 3.

Wang, H. & Rosenau, J.N. (2009). China and global governance. *Asian Perspective*, 33(3), 5–39.

Wang, J. (2011a). *China's search for a grand strategy: A rising great power finds its way*. Retrieved from www.foreignaffairs.com/articles/67470/wang-jisi/chinas-search-for-a-grand-strategy.

Wang, J. (2011b). Zhongguo de guoji dingwei wenti yu 'taoguang yanghui, yousuo zuowei' de zhanlue sixiang [The international positioning of China and the strategic principle of 'keeping a low profile' while getting something accomplished]. *International Studies*, 2, 4–9.

Wang, K., Li, J. & Li, Y. (2015). *Zhongguo mianchu waizhai shi qiongdafang? Wu shishi ni dei zhidao [Is China's exemption of debts owned by foreign countries over-generous as China itself is poor? Five facts you must know]*. Retrieved from politics.people.com.cn/n/2015/0928/c1001-27640009.html.

Wang, M. (2013). *Statement by Ambassador Wang Min at the launch event of the UNDP report 'leveraging change for better lives: UNDP in Asia and the Pacific'.* Retrieved from www.china-un.org/eng/gdxw/t1076738.htm.

Wang, M. (2015). *Changzhu lianheguo fu daibiao Wang Min dashi zai lianheguo nan nan hezuo gaojibie weiyuanhui bihui qijian tebie huiyi shang de fayan [Statement by Ambassador Wang Min, China's deputy representative to the UN at the high-level committee of UN south–south cooperation closing segment].* Retrieved from www.fmprc.gov.cn/web/dszlsjt_673036/ds_673038/t1295029.shtml.

Wang, X. (1988). Guanyu woguo yuanwai zhanlue wenti [Strategic issues relating to Chinese foreign aid]. *International Economic Cooperation, 2,* 5–7.

Wang, X. (2014). *Zhongguo de duiwai yuanzhu 2014 baipishu jiedu [Interpretation of China's white paper on foreign aid (2014)].* Retrieved from fangtan.china.com.cn/2014-07/14/content_32941793.htm.

Wang, X. & Yu, F. (2017). China health aid to the Pacific Island countries. In Y. Changsen (Ed.), *Annual report on development of Oceania (2016–2017)* (pp. 229–249). Beijing, China: Social Sciences Academic Press (China).

Wang, Y. (2001). Xin shiji de zhongguo yu duobian waijiao [China and its multilateral diplomacy in the new era]. *Pacific Journal, 4,* 3–12.

Wang, Y. (2013). *Wang yang zai di er jie zhongguo taipingyang daoguo jingji fazhan hezuo luntan ji 2013 zhongguo guoji lvse chuangxin jishu chanpinzhan kaimushi shang de yanjiang [Speech by Wang Yang at the opening ceremony of the 2nd China–Pacific Islands countries economic development and cooperation forum & China international green innovation products and technology show].* Retrieved from www.fmprc.gov.cn/mfa_chn/zyxw_602251/t1097478.shtml.

Wei, H. (1999). Woguo duiwai yuanzhu fangshi gaige de jingyan yu wenti [Experience and problems on the reform of Chinese foreign aid delivery]. *International Economic Cooperation, 5,* 4–8.

Wei, S. (1992, 17 August). Jianchi duli zizhu de heping waijiao zhengce [Adhere to the independent foreign policy of peace]. *People's Daily,* p. 5.

Wei, X. (2011). Zhongguo yuanzhu feizhou yu tisheng zhongguo ruan shili [Chinese aid to Africa and promotion of Chinese soft power]. *Journal of the University of International Relations [Central Party School of the Communist Party of China], 1,* 31–36.

Wei, Z. (2014). Zhongguo duobian waijiao liushi nian: chengjiu yu tiaozhan [The six decades of China's multilateral diplomacy: Achievements and challenges]. *Contemporary World, 10,* 20–23.

Wen, J. (2006). Jiaqiang huli hezuo, shixian gongtong fazhan [To promote cooperation of mutual benefits and achieve common development]. *State Council Bulletin, 15*, 10–11.

Wendt, A. (1992). Anarchy is what states make of it: The social construction of power politics. *International Organization, 46*(2), 391–425.

Wendt, A. (1999). *Social theory of international politics* (Vol. 67). Cambridge, UK: Cambridge University Press.

Wesley-Smith, T. (2007). *China in Oceania: New forces in Pacific politics.* Honolulu, Hawai'i: East-West Center.

Wesley-Smith, T. (2010). China's Pacific engagement. In T. Wesley-Smith & E.A. Porter (Eds), *China in Oceania: Reshaping the Pacific?* (pp. 27–48). New York, NY: Berghahn Books.

Wikileaks. (2006). *Prospects for coordination with China on foreign aid limited.* Retrieved from www.wikileaks.org/plusd/cables/06BEIJING17108_a.html.

Wikileaks. (2007). *GOE/PRC: China signals willingness to cooperate with the United States in Ethiopia.* Retrieved from www.wikileaks.org/plusd/cables/07ADDISABABA3068_a.html.

Wikileaks. (2008a). *Aid administrator Fore's meeting with Chinese VM Yi.* Retrieved from www.wikileaks.org/plusd/cables/08TOKYO1166_a.html.

Wikileaks. (2008b). *Development assistance dialogue proposal delivered to China.* Retrieved from www.wikileaks.org/plusd/cables/08BEIJING179_a.html.

Wikileaks. (2008c). *A/S Shannon leads U.S.–China Latin America subdialogue.* Retrieved from www.wikileaks.org/plusd/cables/08BEIJING4152_a.html.

Wikileaks. (2008d). *U.S.–China Africa Sub-dialogue: A/S Frazer and AFM Zhai Jun discuss assistance, conflicts and cooperation.* Retrieved from www.wikileaks.org/plusd/cables/08BEIJING3996_a.html.

Wikileaks. (2008e). *U.S.–China dialogue on foreign assistance: Your meeting with Vice Minister Yi.* Retrieved from wikileaks.org/plusd/cables/08BEIJING1225_a.html.

Wikileaks. (2010). *African embassies suspicious of US–China development cooperation in Africa.* Retrieved from www.wikileaks.org/plusd/cables/10BEIJING367_a.html.

Windybank, S. (2005, 7 July). The China syndrome. *Policy Magazine*, pp. 1–6.

World Health Organization (WHO). (2013). *East Asia summit endorses new malaria leaders alliance.* Retrieved from www.who.int/malaria/news/2013/aplma/en/.

WHO. (2014). *WHO China celebrates World Health Day—Lessons from China on combating vector-borne diseases.* Retrieved from www.wpro.who.int/china/mediacentre/releases/2014/20140404/en/.

Wu, L. (2010). *Zhongguo dui qita guojia de jingji yuanzhu [China's economic assistance to other countries].* Retrieved from www.hprc.org.cn/wxzl/wxxgwd/201001/t20100126_42743.html.

Wu, Q. (2009a, 21 July). Dishiyici zhuwai shijie huiyi zaijing zhaokai [The 11th Ambassadors' conference was held in Beijing]. *People's Daily*, p. 1.

Wu, Q. (2009b). *Hu Jintao: Woguo gaige fazhan wending mianlin xin de jiyu he tianzhan [Hu Jintao: Our reform, development and stability face new opportunities and challenges].* Retrieved from politics.people.com.cn/GB/1024/9687405.html (site discontinued).

Wu, S. (2004, 10 May). Lianheguo kaifa jihua shu tigong jishu zhichi, woguo baohu chouyangceng chengji shou biaozhang [Our country's achievements in ozone protection with UNDP technical support was accredited]. *International Business Daily*, p. 8.

Wye, R. (2011). China's leadership transition. In D.L. Shambaugh (Ed.), *Charting China's future: Domestic and international challenges* (pp. 22–32). New York, NY: Routledge.

Xi, J. (2015a). President Xi Jinping delivers speech at FOCAC summit: Full text. Retrieved from english.cri.cn/12394/2015/12/05/4083s906994.htm.

Xi, J. (2015b, 29 September). Xi Jinping zai di qishi jie lianheguo dahui yibanxing bianlun shi de jianghua (quanwen) [Address by President Xi Jinping at the 70th UN General Assembly (full text)]. *Xinhua.* Retrieved from news.xinhuanet.com/world/2015-09/29/c_1116703645.htm.

Xinhua. (1963, 9 August). Mao Zhuxi jiejian feizhou pengyou fabiao zhichi feizhou heiren douzheng de shengming [Chairman met with African friends and released the statement to support the struggle of American blacks]. *People's Daily*, p. 1.

Xinhua (1964, 31 December). Zai di san jie quanguo renmin daibiao dahui di yi ci huiyi shang Zhou Enlai zongli zuo zhengfu gongzuo baogao [Premier Zhou Enlai delivered the government report at the first session of the Third National People's Congress]. *People's Daily*, p. 1.

Xinhua. (2002). Jiang Zemin zai dang de shiliuda shang suozuo de baogao [Jiang Zemin delivered the report at the 16th CPC national congress]. Retrieved from news.xinhuanet.com/newscenter/2002-11/17/content_632296.htm.

Xinhua. (2005). *Zhonggong zhongyang pizhun Chen Yi Li Fuchun 'guanyu jiaqiang duiwai jingji jishu yuanzhu gongzuo lingdao de qingshi baogao' [Comments of the Chinese government on the report produced by Chen Yi and Li Fuchun 'request for instructions on strengthening foreign economic and technical assistance'].* Retrieved from news.xinhuanet.com/ziliao/2005-01/05/content_2419146.htm.

Xinhua. (2006). *Zhongmei guanxi: 'Liyi youguanfang de beihou' [China–U.S. relations: What are behind the 'stakeholders'].* Retrieved from news.xinhuanet. com/world/2006-06/04/content_4644008.htm.

Xinhua. (2008). *Wen Jiabao huijian meiguo changwu fu guowuqing nei ge luo peng te [Wen Jiabao met with U.S. Deputy Secretary of State Negroponte].* Retrieved from www.gov.cn/jrzg/2008-01/17/content_860739.htm.

Xinhua. (2012). *Zhuanjia tan Hu Jintao Zhuxi fangwen Jianpuzhai chengguo [Experts talked about the achievements of President Hu Jintao's visit to Cambodia].* Retrieved from news.xinhuanet.com/world/2012-04/02/c_111732730_2.htm.

Xinhua. (2014a, 30 November). Zhongyang waishi gongzuo huiyi zai jing juxing [Central conference on work relating to foreign affairs was held in Beijing]. *People's Daily.* Retrieved from politics.people.com.cn/n/2014/1130/c1024-26118788.html.

Xinhua. (2014b). *Xi Jinping chuxi zhongyang waishi gongzuo huiyi bing fabiao zhongyao jianghua [Xi Jinping attended the central conference on work relating to foreign affairs and delivered important speech].* Retrieved from news.xinhuanet. com/2014-11/29/c_1113457723.htm.

Xinhua. (2014c). *Xi Jinping zai Fei Ji meiti fabiao shuming wenzhang [Xi Jinping published signed article in Fiji media].* Retrieved from news.xinhuanet.com/ world/2014-11/21/c_1113342112.htm.

Xinhua. (2015a). *China pledges resolute measures to root out poverty by 2020.* Retrieved from www.chinadaily.com.cn/china/2015-11/29/content_22527642.htm.

Xinhua. (2015b). *Shouquan fabu: Zhonggong zhongyang guanyu zhiding guomin jingji he shehui fazhan di shisan ge wunian guihua de jianyi [Authorised to release: Recommendations from the Central Committee of the Chinese Communist Party for the 13th five-year plan for economic and social development].* Retrieved from news.xinhuanet.com/fortune/2015-11/03/c_1117027676.htm.

Xinhua. (2015c). *Zhonggong zhongyang zhengzhiju zhaokai huiyi [The political bureau of the Central Committee of Chinese Communist Party held the conference].* Retrieved from news.xinhuanet.com/politics/2015-11/23/c_1117234411.htm.

Xinhua. (2015d). *Zhuwai shilingguan jingshang jigou gongzuo huiyi zai jing zhaokai [The conference on the work of economic offices in China's diplomatic missions overseas was held in Beijing].* Retrieved from news.xinhuanet.com/politics/2015-03/02/c_1114492937.htm.

Xinhua. (2016). *Di ba lun zhongmei zhanlue yu jingji duihua kuangjia xia zhanlue duihua juti chengguo qingdan [China–US strategic and economic dialogue outcomes of the strategic track].* Retrieved from news.xinhuanet.com/world/2016-06/08/c_1119007842_2.htm.

Xu, W. & Wang, L. (2015). *Guanyu jiaqiang he gaishan zhongguo duiwai yuanzhu de jianyi [Advice on the strengthening and improvement of Chinese foreign aid].* Retrieved from rcid.cau.edu.cn/module/download/downfile.jsp?classid=0&filename=1502091336532045613.pdf.

Xu, X. & Zhu, D. (2018). *Wang Yi yingyue huijian ao da li ya waizhang pei en [Wang Yi met with Australian Minister for Foreign Affairs Payne].* Retrieved from www.xinhuanet.com/world/2018-09/25/c_1123478931.htm.

Xue, L. & Xiao, H. (2011). Zhongguo duiwai yuanzhu zai jianpuzhai [China's foreign aid to Cambodia]. *Around SouthEast Asia, 12,* 24–30.

Xue, L. (2013). Zhou Enlai duiwai yuanzhu sixiang yanjiu [Research on Zhou Enlai's thinking on foreign aid]. *Party History Research & Teaching, 3,* 68–77.

Yahuda, M. (2013). China's new assertiveness in the South China Sea. *Journal of Contemporary China, 22*(81), 446–459. doi.org/10.1080/10670564.2012.748964.

Yamashiro Fordelone, T. (2011). Triangular co-operation and aid effectiveness. *OECD Journal, 2010*(1), 47–67. doi.org/10.1787/gen_papers-2010-5kgc6 cl31rnx.

Yan, X. (1996). *Zhongguo guojia liyi fenxi [Analysis of China's national interests].* Tianjin, China: Tianjin People's Publishing House.

Yan, X. (2006). Hexie shehui yu hexie shijie de zhengce guanxi [The policy relationship between a harmonious society and a harmonious world]. *International Politics Quarterly, 1,* 14–15.

Yang, J. (2009). China in the South Pacific: Hegemon on the horizon? *The Pacific Review, 22*(2), 139–158. doi.org/10.1080/09512740902815292.

Yang, J. (2011). *The Pacific Islands in China's grand strategy: Small states, big games.* New York, NY: Palgrave Macmillan.

Yang, J. (2015, 21 September). Building a better China–U.S. relationship with President Xi's visit. *Seattle Times.* Retrieved from www.seattletimes.com/opinion/building-a-better-china-us-relationship-with-president-xis-visit/.

Ye, Q. (2016). *Zhongguo zhengshi shenqing jiaru guoji yimin zhuzhi [China has formally applied to join the International Organization for Migration].* Retrieved from www.chinanews.com/gn/2016/06-13/7902909.shtml.

Yi, X. (2010). *Keynote speech by Mr. Yi Xiaozhun, vice minister of commerce, P. R. China at 2010 High-Level Segment Development Cooperation Forum.* New York, NY: UN Economic and Social Council 2010 High-Level Segment Development Cooperation Forum.

Yu, C. (2016). The Pacific Islands in China's geo-strategic thinking. In M. Powles (Ed.), *China and the Pacific: The view from Oceania* (pp. 89–97). Wellington, New Zealand: Victoria University Press.

Zhang, D. (2015). *China–United States–Timor-Leste trilateral aid cooperation project on agriculture.* Retrieved from ips.cap.anu.edu.au/sites/default/files/IB-2015-10-Zhang-ONLINE.pdf.

Zhang, D. (2017a). *China's south–south cooperation with Pacific Island countries in the context of the 2030 agenda for sustainable development.* Beijing, China: UNDP China.

Zhang, D. (2017b). Why cooperate with others? Demystifying China's trilateral aid cooperation. *Pacific Review, 30*(5), 750–768. doi.org/10.1080/09512748.2017.1296886.

Zhang, D. (2018). A tango by two superpowers: China–US cooperation in trilateral aid and implications for their bilateral relations. *Asian Journal of Political Science, 26*(2), 181–200. doi.org/10.1080/02185377.2018.1462218.

Zhang, D. & Smith, G. (2017). China's foreign aid system: Structure, agencies, and identities. *Third World Quarterly, 38*(10), 2330–2346. doi.org/10.1080/01436597.2017.1333419.

Zhang, G. & Feng, Y. (2011). China's UN diplomacy: 1971–2011. *Strategic Analysis, 35*(6), 973–981. doi.org/10.1080/09700161.2011.608860.

Zhang, J. (2010). Bufujia tiaojian de yuanzhu: Zhongguo duifei yuanzhu zhengce de xingcheng [Aid with no strings: The formation of China's foreign aid policy toward Africa]. *Foreign Affairs Review, 5,* 20–34.

Zhang, Q. (2006). Lengzhan hou zhongguo canyu duobian waijiao de tedian fenxi [Analysis of the major characteristics of China's multilateral diplomacy in the post-Cold War era]. *International Forum, 8*(2), 55–61.

Zhang, R. & Ye, L. (2015). *Meizhong peixun A Fu Han waijiaguan, sinian tuozhan hezuo lingyu [The U.S. and China jointly train Afghan diplomats and have expanded the scope of cooperation in four years].* Retrieved from www.voachinese. com/content/voa-news-us-china-afghan-diplomat-training-program-2015 0909/2954972.html.

Zhang, Y. (1989, 4 January). Jieshou yuanzhu duoyu dui wai yuanzhu, woguo yi chengwei jing shouyuanguo [China receives more external aid than its aid overseas and becomes a net recipient]. *People's Daily*, p. 1.

Zhang, Y. (2007). China and the emerging regional order in the South Pacific. *Australian Journal of International Affairs, 61*(3), 367–381. doi.org/10.1080/ 10357710701531537.

Zhang, Y. (2012). *Checkbook diplomacy aimed at reining China.* Retrieved from www.chinadailyasia.com/news/2012-05/28/content_114099.html.

Zhang, Y., Gu, J. & Chen, Y. (2015). *China's engagement in international development cooperation: The state of the debate.* Brighton, UK: Institute of Development Studies.

Zhang, Y. & Huang, Y. (2012). Zhongguo he xifang zai duiwai yuanzhu linian shang de chaiyixing bianxi [Analysis of different aid conceptions between China and the West]. *Contemporary International Relations, 2*, 41–47.

Zhao, C. & Wang, X. (2014). *Shangwubu jiu zhongguo de duiwai yuanzhu 2014 baipishu da jizhe wen [MOFCOM officials answering questions from journalists regarding China's white paper on foreign aid (2014)].* Retrieved from yws.mof com.gov.cn/article/u/201510/20151001145192.shtml.

Zhao, X. & Jin, C. (1991). Zhong Ao hezuo xiangmu huode chenggong [The cooperation project between China and Australia achieved success]. *International Talent, 8*, 33.

Zhao, Z. (1983). Zhao Ziyang zongli zai zhongguo shehui kexuyuan he di san shijie jijinghui lianhe juban de Beijing nan nan huiyi shang de jianghua [Remarks by premier Zhao Ziyang at the south–south conference co-hosted by China Academy of Social Science and the third world foundation in Beijing]. *The Bulletin of State Council PRC, 8*, 259–262.

Zheng, B. (2013). China's path of peaceful development in the second decade of the 21st century. *China International Studies, 3*, 5–18.

Zheng, Y. (1998, 30 October). Chenggong hezuo de fanli—Oumeng duihua yuanzhu shuping [An example of successful cooperation—An analysis of EU's foreign aid to China]. *People's Daily*, p. 6.

Zhou, C. (1991, 24 April). Zhongguo zhengfu yu lianheguo kaifa jihua shu qianshu yuanzhu xieyi [Chinese government signed an aid agreement with UNDP]. *People's Daily*, p. 4.

Zhou, H. (2002). Meiguo de duiwai yuanzhu zhengce [Foreign aid policy of the U.S.]. *International Trade, 1*, 26–30.

Zhou, H. (2008). Zhongguo duiwai yuanzhu yu gaige kaifang sanshinian [China's foreign aid and 30 years of reform]. *World Economics and Politics, 11*, 33–43.

Zhou, H. (2010). Zhongguo yuanwai liushinian de huigu yu zhanwang [Look back and look forward: Sixty years of China's foreign aid]. *Foreign Affair Review, 5*, 3–11.

Zhou, H. (2015). *Foreign aid in China*. New York. NY: Springer, Social Sciences Academic Press (China).

Zhou, H. & Xiong, H. (2013). *Zhongguo yuanwai liushi nian [China's foreign aid: 60 years in retrospect]*. Beijing, China: Social Sciences Academic Press (China).

Zhou, Q. (2010). Zhongguo dui lianheguo weihe xingdong taidu de bianhua jiqi yuanyin [China's changing attitudes and reasons for UN peacekeeping operation]. *Human Rights, 2*, 54–59.

Zhou, Q. (2013). Xinshiji yilai de meiguo duiwai yuanzhu [U.S. foreign assistance since the new millennium]. *World Economics and Politics, 9*, 23–51.

Zhou, T. & Mao, X. (2013). Aodaliya duiwai yuanzhu toumingdu zhidu he shijian [Policy and practice of Australian aid transparency]. *International Economic Cooperation, 9*, 60–63.

Zhu, F. (2008). Zai 'Taoguang Yanghui' yu 'Yousuo Zuowei' zhijian qiu pingheng [Seek a balance between 'Taoguang Yanghui' and 'Yousuo Zuowei']. *Contemporary International Relations, 9*, 27–28.

Zhu, L. (2010a). *China's foreign policy debates: Chaillot Papers, September*. Paris, France: European Union Institute for Security Studies.

Zhu, Z. (2010b). *China's new diplomacy: Rationale, strategies, and significance*. Burlington, VT: Ashgate.

Zimmermann, F. & Smith, K. (2011). More actors, more money, more ideas for international development cooperation. *Journal of International Development, 23*(5), 722–738. doi.org/10.1002/jid.1796.